# EVALUATING FAMILY SUPPORT

Thinking Internationally, Thinking Critically

# WILEY SERIES
## in
# CHILD PROTECTION AND POLICY

*Series Editor:*  Christopher Cloke,
NSPCC, 42 Curtain Road,
London EC2A 3NX

This NSPCC/Wiley series explores current issues relating to the prevention of child abuse and the protection of children. The series aims to publish titles that focus on professional practice and policy, and the practical application of research. The books are leading edge and innovative and reflect a multi-disciplinary and inter-agency approach to the prevention of child abuse and the protection of children.

This series is essential reading for all professionals and researchers concerned with the prevention of child abuse and the protection of children. The accessible style will appeal to parents and carers. All books have a policy or practice orientation with referenced information from theory and research.

# EVALUATING FAMILY SUPPORT

## Thinking Internationally, Thinking Critically

*Edited by*

## Ilan Katz
*Children and Young People's Unit, London, UK*

## John Pinkerton
*Queen's University of Belfast, UK*

**WILEY**

*Other Wiley Editorial Offices*

John Wiley & Sons Inc., 111 River Street, Hoboken, NJ 07030, USA

Jossey-Bass, 989 Market Street, San Francisco, CA 94103-1741, USA

Wiley-VCH Verlag GmbH, Boschstr. 12, D-69469 Weinheim, Germany

John Wiley & Sons Australia Ltd, 33 Park Road, Milton, Queensland 4064, Australia

John Wiley & Sons (Asia) Pte Ltd, 2 Clementi Loop #02-01, Jin Xing Distripark, Singapore 129809

John Wiley & Sons Canada Ltd, 22 Worcester Road, Etobicoke, Ontario, Canada M9W 1L1

Wiley also publishes its books in a variety of electronic formats. Some content that appears in
print may not be available in electronic books.

*Library of Congress Cataloging-in-Publication Data*

Evaluating family support : thinking internationally, thinking critically /
    edited by Ilan Katz and John Pinkerton.
         p.     cm.—(Wiley series in child protection and policy)
    Includes bibliographical references and index.
    ISBN 0-471-49723-1 (Paper : alk. paper)
        1. Family services—Evaluation.   2. Family services—Evaluation—Case studies.
3. Family policy—Evaluation.   4. Family policy—Evaluation—Case studies.
I. Katz, Ilan.   II. Pinkerton, John, 1953–   III. Series.
HV697.E93   2002
362.7—dc21                                                              2002151901

*British Library Cataloguing in Publication Data*

A catalogue record for this book is available from the British Library

ISBN 0-471-49723-1

Typeset in 10/12pt Palatino by TechBooks, New Delhi, India
Printed and bound in Great Britain by TJ International Ltd, Padstow, Cornwall
This book is printed on acid-free paper responsibly manufactured from sustainable forestry
in which at least two trees are planted for each one used for paper production.

# CONTENTS

**Part IV:   Towards an International Agenda**

# LIST OF ILLUSTRATIONS

## FIGURES

## TABLES

# ABOUT THE EDITORS

**Dr Ilan Katz** is Team Leader of the Children's Fund prevention team in the Children and Young People's Unit, England, a cross-cutting government department which addresses children at risk of social exclusion. He was previously Head of the Practice Development Unit and Acting Head of Research at the NSPCC. He has researched extensively in the areas of child protection, family support and child welfare, with a particular interest in comparative studies, race and ethnicity and parents with mental health problems. He is an honorary Senior Research Fellow at the Centre for the Evaluation of Public Policy at Brunel University and a Fellow of the Institute for the Study of Children, Families and Social Issues at Birkbeck, University of London. He authored *The Construction of Racial Identity in Children of Mixed Parentage: Mixed Metaphors* (Jessica Kingsley, 1996) and co-edited (with Amal Treacher) *The Dynamics of Adoption* (Jessica Kingsley, 2001).

**Dr John Pinkerton** is Senior Lecturer and Head of the School of Social Work at the Queen's University Belfast, Northern Ireland, where he is involved with post-professional qualification training. Previously he was Senior Research Fellow in the Centre for Child Care Research attached to the School. In addition to regional government-funded research in the areas of family support, young people leaving State care and young people home-in-care, he has carried out a range of project evaluations and policy appraisals. He has as particular interests the process of relating research to policy and practice development and was seconded to the Minister for Children in the Republic of Ireland to work on the development of the National Children's Strategy. His publications include, as co-editor, *Family Support: Direction from Diversity* (Jessica Kingsley, 1999) and, as co-author, *Family Support: Linking Project Evaluation to Policy Analysis* (Ashgate, 2000).

# LIST OF CONTRIBUTORS

**Gunvor Andersson** is Professor of Social Work, University of Lund, Sweden.

**Stephen Budde** is Senior Research Associate at Chapin Hall Center for Children and Lecturer at the School of Social Service Administration, University of Chicago, USA.

**John Canavan** is Research and Evaluation Officer with the Western Health Board, Ireland, and Joint Research Manager of the Child and Family Research and Policy Unit, a partnership between the Health Board and the National University of Ireland, Galway.

**Monit Cheung** is Professor of Social Work, University of Houston, Texas, USA, Chair of the Children and Families Concentration and Associate Director of the Child Welfare Education Project. She is a licensed advanced clinical practitioner and Director of Clinical Service at the Asian American Family Counseling Center in Houston.

**Lorraine Cooper** is a Lecturer in Social Work at the University of Central Lancashire, England.

**Pat Dolan** is Regional Coordinator for Family Support Services with the Western Health Board, Ireland, and Joint Research Manager of the Child and Family Research and Policy Unit, Ireland.

**Ruth Gardner** is NSPCC Senior Research Fellow at Royal Holloway, University of London, England.

**Robbie Gilligan** is Professor of Social Work and Social Policy and Director of the Children's Research Centre, Trinity College Dublin, Ireland.

**David Ham** is Research Assistant, Department of Psychology, Griffith University, Queensland, Australia.

**Catherine Hazlett** is Principal Officer in the Family Affairs Unit, Department of Social, Community and Family Affairs, Ireland.

**Rachael Hetherington** has recently retired as Director of the Centre for Comparative Social Work Studies, Brunel University, England.

**Chi-Kwong Law** is Associate Professor, Department of Social Work and Social Administration, University of Hong Kong.

**Corinne May-Chahal** is Professor of Child Care at the University of Central Lancashire, England.

**Sandra McElhinney** is currently Research Consultant with the Drug Information and Research Unit, Department of Health, Social Services and Public Safety, Northern Ireland.

**Robyn Munford** is a Professor at the School of Social Policy and Social Work, Massey University, New Zealand.

**Peter Pecora** is Senior Director of Research Services, Casey Family Programs, and Professor at the School of Social Work, University of Washington, Seattle, USA.

**Nuala Quiery** is currently working as a counsellor with the Nexus Institute in Northern Ireland, previously having worked as a research psychologist with the Greater Shankill Early Years Project.

**Harry Rafferty** is a Senior Educational Psychologist and Director of Developmental and Educational Psychology in the School of Psychology, Queen's University Belfast, Northern Ireland.

**Jackie Sanders** is a Social Service Manager and Policy Analyst and works as Director of the Barnardos Child and Family Research Centre, New Zealand.

**Ian Shochet** is Director, Clinical Training, Department of Psychology, Griffith University, Queensland, Australia.

**Noel Sheehy** is a Professor and Developmental and Social Psychologist in the School of Psychology, Queen's University Belfast, Northern Ireland.

**Karen Trew** is a Senior Lecturer in the School of Psychology, Queen's University Belfast, Northern Ireland.

**Jane Tunstill** is Professor of Social Work at Royal Holloway, University of London, England.

# FOREWORD

Around the world, parents are experiencing greater stress as they try to make a living and raise their children. By initiating a cross-national conversation that broadens and deepens discussion about the definition, provision and evaluation of family support services, this book's editors and other authors have made an important contribution to efforts to assist these families and their children. The emphasis on evaluation is also especially timely because more countries are facing tough choices on how to allocate limited resources for social and educational programmes. As a result, demands for research-based programmes and for evidence about the effectiveness and comparative benefits of such programmes are increasing.

Family support as a policy area, a field of service, and as an arena for evaluation is relatively new. Soliciting contributions from multiple countries, the editors have stimulated the field's development by putting together a provocatively rich and diverse set of evaluation case examples and views about the roles, value and challenges inherent in family support provision and evaluation. The papers invite cross-cultural comparison and thereby prompt the reader to examine and critique existing or develop new approaches to family support provision and evaluation. The editors' introductory and concluding chapters also advance the international conversation by laying out a provisional cross-national descriptive framework for family support and by posing an open systems evaluation model for consideration and development.

This book represents a significant cross-national step towards a broader global discussion about family support and its evaluation. The next step is to go global, by including representatives from Africa, Asia and elsewhere in the developing world in the discussion about how to support families in their parenting roles and to assess the results. A more global focus is critical at this point for several reasons. First, neither the more nor the less developed countries are making all the adaptations necessary to support childrearing families. Both have much to learn from each other about family support programmes and policies. Further, as major economic transitions and urbanization occur in developing countries, parents there have less access to their extended families and other supports, more work-related constraints, and more need for education and child care. This is likely to increase the demand for information about family support and its adaptation in different national and cultural contexts. More inclusive global discussion of experiences with family support and exchange of information about how the public, civil and private sectors do and could support parenting families in different countries therefore could be very productive for everyone now. This volume suggests several key challenges that transcend national boundaries and it thereby offers an excellent departure point for further international and global conversation about family support and its evaluation.

Situating evaluation in its inescapably political context, the editors point out the first basic challenge of getting programmes to evaluate at all given the risks of damage they face from negative or insubstantial findings. They note that the risks of not evaluating are growing more serious for family support because there is not enough evaluation evidence to make a compelling case for these programmes in a policy world that increasingly requires it. It is also risky for a field of practice not to have nuanced information about the elements and processes that lead to positive outcomes to help in designing or improving services.

The implication of this assessment is that the current somewhat scattershot approach to evaluation is now less viable for family support if it is to grow as an area of service and policy. The new basic challenge, therefore, is to examine and share if and how different countries and non-governmental organizations work with programmes to create an overarching evaluation strategy for family support (for an example of this for the field of home visitation, see The Home Visit Forum at www.gse.harvard.edu/hfrp). Such a strategy should include an evolving research agenda, an investment plan that makes good use of scarce evaluation resources, and include an emphasis on and the means to share the ongoing results widely to support and improve family support policy and programmes.

As the editors note, there are multiple views about what family support is and should do within and across countries. They are often predicated on different ideological positions and judgements about relationships between the family and the State. This makes it a major challenge to unify the field through a single definition, theory of change or a common core set of outcomes. At least in these early stages of family support, however, this diversity may be a benefit. This will be so if it encourages an initially broad, field-wide set of evaluation questions and theories of change to test the likely possibility that there are multiple effective pathways to supporting families. This also would help address another major challenge facing family support, that of systematically carrying out evaluation research that recognizes diversity in order to accumulate actionable knowledge about what works for whom, how, where and why.

The service delivery values and principles behind family support are challenging evaluators in many countries to experiment with different evaluation approaches and measures (for a description of current innovative practices in the United States, see The Evaluation Exchange, vol. VIII, no. 1, Spring 2002, at www.gse.harvard.edu/hfrp). Family support principles emphasize strength-based, non-deficit partnerships between participants and providers, flexible and culturally sensitive services, and participant empowerment through involvement in planning, governance and, increasingly, evaluation. As a result, as this book attests, there is a growing body of literature and experience in different countries with both experimental and more participatory and action research-oriented evaluation designs, including some that involve families in getting and using data for community and social change (Weiss and Greene, 1992).

Similarly, family support advocates are pushing evaluators to reduce their reliance on only measures that track the prevention or reduction of problems and to develop more strength-based measures to assess improvements in child, family and community well being. The challenge now is to continue the international discussion that has begun with this volume, probing particularly to understand and debate how these alternative evaluation approaches and measures actually work, their costs and benefits, and their place in a country's overall strategy to assess and improve family support initiatives.

The three previously noted challenges are subsumed by a fourth that the editors frame in their concluding chapter for further international discussion: What is the appropriate role and vision for family support evaluation in the future? Reviewing the experiences described by the volume's contributors and drawing on systems theory to critique and expand the ecological theory now predominant in family support evaluation, they propose an open systems model. Systems thinking highlights the influences of factors in the political and social context that lead to constant change, conflict and unanticipated consequences, thereby underscoring how much is outside the control of both programmes and evaluation. At best, family support programmes form only one of the services necessary to support parents in their childrearing. Similarly, evaluation is only one of the many factors that influence programmes and policies. It, too, is situated in power relationships and sometimes causes conflict and unanticipated consequences. At a minimum, then, programmers and evaluators need to proceed with humility, mindful of the limits of what they can provide and resolve. Given this, what is the vision for the future?

At least three features are vital for an evolving and productive future for family support and its evaluation. First, as this volume's editors conclude, it is critical to set the inviolable standard that the primary function of evaluation is to provide credible data and results about what is evaluated. This ensures the value of evaluation and its contribution to determining what to do to support parenting families. Second, given the reality of constant change in families, programmes, policies and resources, evaluators should help to create a culture of enquiry, experimentation and continuous learning in the family support arena. This involves building the capacity to get and use evaluation data and performance-tracking information for ongoing self-assessments and programme redesign or even elimination. While this transition to using information in an ongoing way is difficult to achieve, it is rapidly emerging as a hallmark or performance standard for quality programmes. Finally, the demand for evaluation to inform family policy and programme development is likely to increase everywhere in the next ten years. Developing an accessible array of electronic as well as print-based means to share evaluation experiences, methods and results, and to debate how to address key evaluation challenges, is the third key feature in this vision. This volume illustrates how valuable such a global exchange could be.

Heather B. Weiss
*Harvard Family Research Project*

## REFERENCE

Weiss, H.B. and Greene, J. (1992) An empowerment partnership for family support and education programs and evaluations. *Family Science Review*, **5**, 131–149.

# ACKNOWLEDGEMENTS

We would like to thank all those involved in the production of this book. In particular we are grateful to Chris Cloke, NSPCC, who, as series editor for this NSPCC/Wiley collaboration, judged it a worthwhile enterprise at the start and provided detailed editing comments on the text that emerged at the end. We also appreciated the willingness of the contributors to become involved in the project and their patience as it turned into a much more protracted process that any of us had anticipated. As has rightly come to be expected, we also wish to acknowledge the contribution of the families whose lived experience of family support services has defined so much of what is in the pages that follow.

# Part I

## THE NEED FOR INTERNATIONAL COMPARISON

# 1

# PERSPECTIVE THROUGH INTERNATIONAL COMPARISON IN THE EVALUATION OF FAMILY SUPPORT

*John Pinkerton and Ilan Katz*

The aim of this book is to contribute to cross-national exploration of family support in search of a better understanding of what it entails and how it is best evaluated. The varied content in the chapters that follow, and the tone of serious engagement apparent in them all, are ample evidence of continuing enthusiasm for family support—'probably the primary policy matter facing child welfare' (Frost, 1997, p. 201). At the same time, the material presented here is a register of the difficulties and complexities, both conceptual and operational, that still surround the term. This chapter considers why this double message exists. It also considers the place of evaluation in developing policy and practice in this context and why it is helpful to use international comparisons in developing both an understanding of family support and the appropriate means for evaluating it. In that way the chapter opens out an agenda against which the range of contributions which follow in the subsequent chapters can be considered. It also provides a means for considering, in the light of those contributions, whether it is desirable and feasible to work towards a unified, global view and what evaluation has to offer the future development of family support.

## CLARIFICATION THROUGH COMPARISON

Family support is a perspective on child welfare that is born of a dilemma. The special place of the family in meeting social care needs is widely accepted, but so too is it recognised that the contemporary forms and functions of family life

*Evaluating Family Support: Thinking Internationally, Thinking Critically.*
Edited by I. Katz and J. Pinkerton. © 2003 John Wiley & Sons, Ltd.

are under immense pressure. This dilemma impacts on all family members, but is particularly pertinent to those who have a high degree of dependence—not only children, the primary focus of this book, but also elderly people and people with disabilities. The capacity of families to cope with social care needs also has major implications for the form and function of state services. Given the widespread experience of high-cost, low-quality care where the state has attempted a solution by directly substituting its own services for family life, the best way forward for both the state and families would seem to be to prevent the necessity for such invasive interventions through the development of family support.

It would be wrong, however, to regard the promotion of family support as just a pragmatic response to managing necessary change in the relationship between the state and family life. In regard to children, family support is also a principled position in line with the global aspirations of the United Nations' Convention on the Rights of the Child (UNCRC). Although the historic importance of the UNCRC is primarily the recognition it gives to children in their own right, it also places special emphasis on supporting the family in carrying out its caring and protective functions.

> The family, as the fundamental group of society and the natural environment for the growth and well being of all its members and particularly children, should be afforded the necessary protection and assistance so that it can fully assume its responsibilities within the community. (Hill and Tisdall, 1997, Appendix)

Family support appears to be a necessary and appropriate means of achieving a new and effective way to deliver services. It is based on the use of the power and authority of the state to promote welfare through enhancing parental capacity and responsibility within the context of the family as a key institution of civil society.

Yet, as most people working in the area will attest, family support as public policy and its expression in service provision is no simple matter. Reviewing the literature shows that, despite its deep roots in the history of child welfare, family support as a coherent policy and practice perspective is still at a relatively early stage in its development (Pinkerton et al., 2000). Although there is widespread commitment to family support, including legislative mandates, there exists considerable confusion and debate over what exactly it means in policy terms and whether it is a policy that can be made to work in practice through the development of projects and programmes. What constitutes family support is open to both narrow and broad definitions. These difficulties revolve around clarifying value-based welfare assumptions as much as they reflect the limitations of existing empirical data about what constitute the necessary ingredients for a successful family support project or programme. Lurking in the shadows of the debate there is also an uncomfortable recognition that it is only through extensive political, social and economic changes that the systemic shift can be achieved that is necessary to place family support at the centre of any childcare system.

One means of helping to clarify and grapple with the various dimensions to family support, and test its effectiveness, is to explore these issues through comparing and contrasting existing evaluations of policy and practice in the area. There is a general view, not necessarily substantiated, that family support has benefited from the increased use of evaluation as a means of understanding and judging both the process and outcomes of service delivery in order to improve planning, resourcing and practice in all areas of child welfare. Evaluation is recognised as having an important part to play in advancing the policy and practice goals of citizenship, consumerism, quality control, value for money, performance measurement, and public accountability. This, in part, reflects 'the context of the changing political economy of social welfare in which evaluation has become a significant managerialist strategy for efficiency and control' (Everitt and Hardiker, 1996, p. 19). It also represents a concern for critical reflection and the resulting empowerment of both practitioners and service users.

Comparison has the potential to take understanding of family support beyond the present situation of a rich but disparate pool of descriptive case studies which can only be loosely cross-referenced by the prescriptive generalities that make up so much of the family support literature. Comparison allows for patterns of convergence and divergence to emerge and, through attempts to answer what lies behind these patterns, sharpens the focus on what constitutes the essential features of effective family support—or indeed whether or not such core features exist. Comparing the results of evaluation also helps to assess the strengths and weaknesses of evaluation. In particular, comparison can help in the necessary exploration of the limits and possibilities of evaluation as a means of highlighting and suggesting responses to difficulties within family support that reflect issues of social and political power. These find expression in the micro politics of family support within the relationships between disciplines, professions, organisations and sectors and across the divides between commissioners, providers and service users. The politics of family support also beg questions about much broader societal processes and structures.

To benefit from maximum diversity in making comparisons it seems sensible to draw material from as wide a range of contexts as possible. Accordingly, making use of existing contacts and the ease of international communication enabled by the widespread use of English and e-mail, material has been gathered for this book from a range of countries across the globe. It is, nevertheless, important to stress that no claim is being made to the representative nature of the contributions. It is clear from even the most cursory glance at the contents page that the coverage is restricted, as well as enabled, by the common language and access to information technology. It is also important to recognise that such opportunistic sampling cannot easily provide either integrated data or theory. At some point the priority for advancing understanding of family support may well be international meta-analyses and cross-national multi-site studies which can confidently identify global pressures and trends and benchmark policy and practice. But a working assumption behind the production of this book is that the development of family support has not yet reached that point.

> It is increasingly acknowledged that developments in any single country cannot be explained without setting them in the context of wider—global—changes. Yet there is a danger that the new orthodoxy may make it rather easy to espouse a comparative approach without being quite clear why or what questions can be most helpfully illuminated through comparison. (Cochrane, 1993, p. 1)

The pertinent questions at this time are more descriptive than prescriptive. Concern needs to be with clarifying how family support in varied national contexts is being understood:

- What does the term mean to its advocates and practitioners and to those intended to benefit from it?
- How is it expressed in policy terms?
- In what organisational settings is it regarded as being practised?
- Are there particular intervention programmes associated with it?
- What aspects of a programme or setting have to be described if the substance of the support is to be grasped?

Thus the aim of this book is to give the contributors an open platform to share how, in their particular circumstances and from their various perspectives, they are making sense of family support and the appropriate method of evaluating it. Through the experiences, concepts, and methodologies shared, the intended result is to provide a set of international reference points. These reference points can then be used to provide fresh ideas and new perspectives that can help in surfacing the dimensions that tend to lie hidden behind the overarching concept of family support. In this way it is hoped that more insightful and radical thinking will be encouraged and a sense of direction become apparent.

Given that family support is a field characterised by a disorientating degree of variety, the very open approach to comparison being adopted for this book makes it difficult to identify the detail and the substance of the differences and similarities within the material presented. A clear, albeit provisional, conceptual framework or model is required to help to engage with the variety of ideas and experiences being shared. As Titmus, a major figure in the development of post-war British social policy, observed: 'the purpose of model building is not to admire the architecture, but to help us to see some order in all the disorder and confusion of facts, systems and choices' (quoted by Hardiker et al., 1991b, p. 18). The model required here to help with establishing some order needs to give equal attention to the substantive issues of family support and to methods of evaluation (see Figure 1.1). A basic assumption behind the production of this book is that family support is at a stage in its development where questions about how best to evaluate it are as important as questions about the nature of the provision itself. If significant advances are to be made, not only does more attention need to be given to describing and analysing the forms and functions of family support, but there is also a need to give priority to understanding how best to undertake that description and analysis. Evaluations need to reflect the traditional research process of problem definition, research design, execution and report, but must do so in a way that is fitted to the present state of knowledge about the policy and practice of family support and in a way that extends the existing methodologies used to research this area.

## THINKING ABOUT FAMILY SUPPORT

In thinking about family support, the central message given by the combined framework in Figure 1.1 is that, as with any child welfare issue, the focus must be on the relationship between *needs, services, processes* and *outcomes*. For family support this means giving attention to needs generated within the family as a key institution of civil society and services provided through projects and programmes delivered directly or indirectly by the state. The state, as used here, can be defined as 'a set of agencies claiming supreme authority for the co-ordination and continuity of a population within a particular territory, backed by a virtual monopoly of force' (McLennan et al., 1984, p. 3). Civil society is 'all those social institutions and relationships which arise, through voluntary association, outside the sphere of direct state control' (McIntosh, 1984, p. 20). These definitions usefully draw attention to the interdependence of state and civil society, in that each is defined by contrast to the other. They also draw attention to the relationships between power and authority, which constitute both types of social institution.

Figure 1.1 presents the relationship between family need in civil society and family support as services provided in the main by the state. That relationship unfolds as a process down a time line that results in outcomes for those involved. From this perspective it is clear that while it is essential to focus on the dynamic between the four-core components (needs, services, process and outcomes), there are key issues for clarification in relation to each of them. As regards need, this requires attention to what exactly are the needs in question and why do they require support services? An initial response to those questions is to say that the needs are for social care that was met

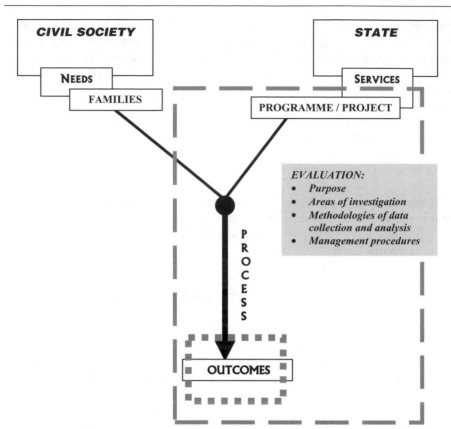

**Figure 1.1**  Family support evaluation: A combined framework

in the past by the family but which that core institution of civil society is
no longer capable of meeting. Social care is defined here as: 'the sum of the
helping (and when needs be controlling) resources available . . . informally by
community networks or formally by the public services' (NISW, 1982). Today
in regard to social care, just as with education and health at earlier points in
history, state intervention is required to supplement the capacity of the family
as a social institution. That, however, is to beg questions about the special role
of the family in relation to social care.

Despite a general recognition of the central place of the family as an institution providing social care within civil society, defining what a family
is today and was in the past proves difficult (Crow and Allen, 2000). Close
consideration shows that the term 'is both ambiguous and emotive' (Hill
and Tisdall, 1997, p. 65). It encompasses a fluid mix of ideas and empirical
material covering biological relatedness, parent/child role sets, shared living
arrangements within a single household, and long-term bonds of affection

and mutual obligation. The contradictory nature of family life has also been commented on. 'While it is true that many of our happiest moments and closest relationships are within families... there are also a whole range of negative experiences in families ranging from plain unhappiness to abuse, neglect and exploitation' (Frost and Stein, 1989, p. 5). The family not only provides the context for its members to provide each other with mutually rewarding continuity and stability, but is also the site of gender inequality, domestic violence, child abuse and all kinds of power struggles between and among children and adults.

It is also generally accepted that while the focus can differ in degree, any satisfactory understanding of the family must take into account both relationships within the family and relationships between the family and its immediate neighbourhood and wider societal context. The complexity, pressures and change which characterise contemporary family life reflect not only shifting cultural expectations about personal relationships but also changing patterns of work, housing, transport and leisure within the context of national and global socio-economic structures of inequality. Changes in the structure and context of family life have coincided and contributed to a moral uncertainty surrounding the institution. Although it is not sustainable to make an exclusive claim for any particular family arrangement, there are, within the UK, certain periodic attempts to reassert a link between the positive outcomes of family life and what traditionally has been regarded as the morally accepted family form, based on two-parent heterosexual marriage (Home Office, 1998; Morgan, 1998). These attempts to shore up past certainties are expressed in a number of ways: blaming individual family members for the perceived failures in family functioning; couples lack commitment to one another and their children; mothers and fathers lack the skills and motivation to provide satisfactory parenting; children lack self-discipline and respect for authority. More positively there has also been a growing interest in parenting, which, along with education and employment, is seen as one of the major routes to social inclusion. There is increasing research aimed at understanding parents' own perceptions of their role, which shows that they feel a need for information, advice and counselling. Linked with that there is a growing body of research demonstrating the effectiveness of interventions aimed at improving parenting skills and addressing problems associated with bringing up children (Moorman et al., 2001).

An alternative response to the uncertainty and diversity of present-day family life is to shift from a structural functionalism to a concern for the quality of the experience of family members as they negotiate their lives together, whether it is within a nuclear, extended, reconstituted, lone-parent or substitute family. This open, interactive perspective seems more accurately and helpfully to address the difficulties in identifying the contemporary functions and features of family. Using this perspective Porter (quoted in Pithouse and Lindsell, 1995) has identified the role of the 'good' family as being to:

- instil cultural, social, spiritual, and moral values
- support the social, emotional and material needs of family members
- nurture and provide socially necessary care
- aim for the well-being of all family members
- provide security, belonging, connectedness and companionship
- foster a sense of moral obligation to others.

Given the prolonged and regular interaction required to negotiate, in a sustained fashion, the diversity and detail involved in such outcomes, it is reasonable to assume that they will be achieved in the main within the informal social care networks of kinship, friendship and neighbourhood. However, it is necessary to be mindful of how oppressive relations of inequality based on class, race, gender and age can also be expressed and sustained within these networks (Crow and Allen, 2000). Despite the limitations of these networks, especially when they struggle with conditions of adversity, it is within them that the necessary affection, sense of mutual obligation, energy, creativity, continuity and stability are to be found.

The intermeshing of state and civil society has already been noted. Even those informal social care networks that are best able to optimise the quality of life experienced by family members will still draw on more formal services as required. From the perspective on need being suggested here, the challenge for formal services in understanding and responding to family need is no longer a question of making good the deficits within family functioning, linked or not to particular family structures. The issue for formal state services becomes how to ensure the relationships and resources required within the informal networks to achieve positive, subjectively experienced, quality of life outcomes. This opens wide the possibilities of stating those services that might be classified as support. As one senior social services manager interviewed in a Northern Ireland study of family support observed: 'Family support is whatever supports families' (Pinkerton et al., 2000, p. 11). Similarly, the Audit Commission in England and Wales, when searching for an operational definition, ended up with: 'any activity or facility provided either by statutory agencies or by community groups or individuals, aimed at providing advice and support to parents to help them in bringing up their children' (Audit Commission, 1994, p. 39).

Family support services draw on a continuum of interventions from the specialist therapeutic through to community and self-help. It includes pre-natal classes, early childhood education, parent education, day care, family centres, after school clubs, home and school liaison, child abuse and neglect prevention programmes, neighbourhood-based resource centres and mutual help support groups. The danger of such an inclusive view is that family support as a term loses any useful meaning. One solution to this is not to try to find a neatly bounded definition that includes or excludes particular activities, programmes or projects. Instead it is accepted that what, at any time and in any place, should be regarded as family support is contingent on a mixture of factors: the definition, level and assessment of existing need; the existing and potential capacity of informal social care networks within particular families and neighbourhoods; the services that are being provided or could be developed; and the general social policy goals being pursued.

If this contingent perspective is taken, as with the approach to the family suggested above, it is not so much the form but the quality of the relationships associated with family support that become its distinctive characteristic. This is in line with the view that family support is best seen as a set of prescriptive values.

> Chief among these values is a deep respect for the complex tasks involved in family care giving, particularly parenting. The relationship between parent and professional is defined as essentially collegial... active partners in search of formal and informal supports necessary to carry out the difficult tasks of parenting. (Whittaker, 1993, p. 6)

From that value base, and drawing on what is known from evaluations of a range of family support and preventative projects and programmes within the UK, seven key characteristics can be identified:

- partnership with users
- creative and responsive services
- attention to outreach and engagement
- siting in the home or neighbourhood
- understanding and respect for issues of race and culture
- interagency and interdisciplinary co-operation
- clarity about the relationship to child protection.

Partnership with both children and adult service users provides the foundation for creative and responsive services (Pinkerton, 2001). Without it there cannot be effective outreach and engagement, which is where some of the most difficult and critical practice challenges to family support lie. If contact is not made and engagement is not successfully negotiated, there cannot be the unfolding process through which family support is expressed. Siting family support services in the home or neighbourhood of those using them is not only an effective means of outreach but also introduces resources into local social care networks. Building capacity in this way helps with the linking of isolated individuals and families to existing informal support systems. It also sensitises services to the cultural context within which they need to work. Within the UK, despite general recognition of the promise and challenge of ethnic diversity, there has been limited progress in this area: 'there appears to be little or no recognition that some change in the way we organise the protection of children or the support of families may be necessary because of the failure to protect black children or to support black families.' (Butt and Box, 1998, p. 8). Interagency and interdisciplinary cooperation is another area which, despite long-standing recognition of its importance, seems extraordinarily difficult to achieve.

A particularly important dimension in defining family support is the relationship between it and child protection. The interface between child protection and family support is dealt with differently in different parts of the world (Gilbert, 1997; Hetherington, Chapter 6 in this volume). In some countries the issue is dealt with in a much more holistic way than is possible in the English-speaking world. Nevertheless these dilemmas are part of family support work throughout the world. Opinions range from regarding child protection and family support as opposite ends of the child welfare spectrum to the view that family support is child protection or that family support is a way of preventing child abuse. Within the UK, since the publication of an influential summary and commentary on a set of 20 government-funded research studies into child protection (Department of Health, 1995a, 1995b), the debate has been about how to integrate family support and child protection in a way that neither stigmatises support services nor lowers safety thresholds to a level that endangers children (Department of Health, 1994; Harper, 1996; Parton, 1997).

Achieving the desired integration in practice is extremely challenging. On one level child protection can be regarded as an important but not dominant aspect of family support. From this perspective the need for protection can be seen as one of many needs which children can have. Child protection work can therefore be integrated into a more holistic approach to family work. Even in emergencies, when the child has to be removed, the basic attitude is one of trust. However, that is not how it tends to be in practice. Child protection looms much larger. It is subject to different guidance and different laws and, most fundamentally, a completely different mind frame—while family support is voluntary and consensual, child protection involves risk assessment, surveillance and suspicion. Integrating child protection with family support requires practitioners to be open to working simultaneously in a 'supportive' and a 'suspicious' frame of mind. Practitioners have to behave in an authoritative way while avoiding being authoritarian and exercising power arbitrarily. They also have to try to keep in mind the different and competing needs of family members. The fundamental dilemma for practitioners is not that they have to negotiate the positioning of a case on a continuum from 'care' to 'control' but rather that they have to keep in mind two potentially incompatible ways of thinking about their work.

Policy makers and practitioners have struggled with this problem in the UK for over a decade and it will be posed sharply once again by the Victoria

Climbié inquiry—a public inquiry set up to review the death of an 8-year-old girl from West Africa who was killed by her great aunt and her aunt's boyfriend (www-victoria-climbie-inquiry.org.uk). This case was dealt with as a low risk family support problem and practitioners ignored warning signs because the case was not labelled 'child abuse'. It remains to be seen whether that inquiry will find a way to go beyond what has been the general approach of developing increasingly detailed guidance. The latest version of the *Working Together* government guidance on child protection (Department of Health, 1999) attempts to address the issue through giving complex guidance as to how to manage the different processes involved. This procedural approach has affected family support in various ways. For example, even small voluntary agencies providing informal support to families or working with children are now required to have detailed child protection policies, and to carry out police checks on their staff and volunteers. The administrative and accountability issues are becoming an increasing burden for the management of these services. Even where family support has been seen as a way of preventing abuse, procedures are in evidence. Sure Start, one of the UK government's major investments in preventive family services, has the lowering of re-registrations on the child protection register as one of its four core targets. It also has detailed guidance on child protection issues and a clear requirement for all funded services to have child protection policies and to train practitioners in child protection issues.

## THINKING ABOUT EVALUATION

A basic premise of this book is that the complexity and confusion that is apparent within the field of family support can be helpfully addressed through evaluation. This is because evaluation allows for 'both the generation of evidence about an activity, a policy, a programme or a project, and the process of making judgements about its value' (Everitt and Hardiker, 1996, p. 4). That, however, is not to suggest that evaluation, as an approach to understanding and as a means to effectively develop family support, is without its own difficulties. Evaluation is represented in Figure 1.1 as potentially encompassing each of which encompasses the different aspects of family support to different degrees. The broken lines indicate that it is possible (a) to focus an evaluation solely on outcomes, (b) to widen it out to the programme/project, the process that unfolds in its work and its outcomes, or (c) to take the widest focus possible considering every aspect of family support from the nature of civil society and the state down to the specific outcomes being achieved by a particular programme/project.

Figure 1.1 draws attention to four key aspects of evaluation: purpose; areas of investigation; methodologies of data collection and analysis; and management procedures. As regards purpose there is the tension between evaluation as a tool of managerialist control and as a method of empowerment for front-line staff and service users. In addition to that central and often unacknowledged issue, there are other questions that require to be considered:

- What should be the areas of investigation for an evaluation?
- What attention should be given to understanding need and what balance should be struck between need as expressed in the lives of particular families and its context within civil society?
- To understand services, how much attention should be given to the nature of the state and the policy framework in which a project is working?
- What weight should be given to the various aspects of the organisational context?
- Should evaluation be primarily concerned to understand process or to measure outcome?
- What techniques for data collection and analysis are available, appropriate and effective?
- What procedures should be followed in managing the various stages of an evaluation?

One reaction to the fact that, at present, these are difficult and, at times, contentious questions for family support evaluators, is to regard them as evidence of the underdeveloped state of evaluation in the area. The implicit assumption is that as evaluators become more skilled consensus will emerge as to how best these questions should be answered. Such a view is consistent with what has been called the 'engineering model' of applied research. In this model the development of a policy or practice solution is seen as a direct output of evaluation. The purpose is clear: to solve the commissioner's problem. If this is not being achieved, attention needs to be given to improving technical competence in the areas of design, execution and reporting. An alternative view regards such privileging of evaluation and technical competence as naive. Based on a 'limestone model' of applied research, it anticipates that the impact of an evaluation will take time and will be indirect and quite possibly unintended like water entering and gradually percolating through limestone without it being clear where or when it will emerge, and probably only then as a trickle (McWhirter, 1993). Such effect as there is will largely be mediated by other more influential social, technical, economic and political factors (Kelly, 1998).

A third perspective is possible which allows for the realities that prompt the other two but does not require choosing between them. Evaluation can be seen to be about developing a technically rigorous understanding of a practice or policy issue in order to contribute to the effective management of the issue, and at the same time it can be acknowledged that the contribution of evaluation is only one part of a complex interplay between a range of influences. This 'social system model' of applied research (Pinkerton, 1998) focuses on change as a function of systemic interaction expressing social structural and interpersonal power relations. From this perspective evaluation is accepted as inevitably being a continuous, recursive, highly divergent and emergent process that is likely to have a range of both predictable and unpredictable outcomes. Evaluation is itself part of the negotiated social construction of what it is that is being evaluated and, in turn, what is being evaluated can significantly determine what constitutes evaluation.

Whatever the limitations on its influence, basic to maximising the impact of an evaluation is ensuring the technical competence and scientific rigour that informs it. This does not necessarily mean solely pursuing quasi-experimental hypothesis testing, designed to come as close to randomised controlled trials as can be achieved. There is a growing recognition that sterile debate between this or that type of evaluation, and in particular about the status of randomised controlled trials, has to be replaced with a more graded and interlocking view of different methods (Hill, 1998; Gilligan, 2000). What is required is to ensure that methods are chosen which are appropriate for the purpose of the particular evaluation. Rather than think in terms of a hierarchy of methods it is more helpful to think of a repertoire, covering experimental, quasi-experimental, descriptive and action research techniques, which can be selected according to their fitness for purpose.

Choices made about methods will go some way to determining the techniques available for both data collection and analysis. That said, whatever method is chosen or developed, it will be important to ensure that the associated techniques combine methodological rigour and objectivity with the capacity to judge the real world substance, function and worth of the setting or practice being considered. One means of increasing methodological rigour is the use of standardised measures, particularly where these can provide a baseline of existing or deficient psychosocial functioning within families. Such baselines are essential for later measurement and assessment of the impact of family support interventions. Capacity to demonstrate effectiveness in this, or any other, way is likely to grow in importance for research on family support. There is a wide variety of measurements of individual health and well-being, family functioning and social support available. Attempts have been made to identify and test how useful such instruments are for evaluating family support (Pithouse et al., 1998; McAuley, 1999; Statham, 2000), but, as yet, within the UK there is no definitive guide to their relationship to one another, their appropriateness for particular tasks, or their ethical implications.

Managing the evaluation process is as important as choice of method and instruments. This starts with the negotiating of acceptance by those delivering the services and those using them. This brings with it important ethical issues about informed consent which need serious consideration, not least in relation to children (McAuley, 1998). The fuller the active involvement of service users and staff, the better the research is likely to be. Although it is resource intensive, work on ensuring involvement pays dividends in increased participation, clearer and better understood instruction, improved accuracy and standardisation, and effective checks against a whole range of errors to which the researcher is prone as an outsider. One family support study in England directly involved users and providers in determining the indicators for evaluating a programme (Frost, 1996). Engagement and participation by stakeholders should start as early as possible in the research process and continue throughout (Pinkerton, 1998). A participatory approach to managing family support evaluation needs to include discussion about likely time frames, expected levels of involvement and continuing feedback. It is important to recognise that there are real concerns to be addressed for the evaluator when taking this approach, about loss of objectivity and restricting the range of research tools available for use.

In any evaluation of family support a balance must be struck between the demands of technically achievable, objective measurement and the need to adequately represent and address the fundamental purpose of the policy or practice. 'Evaluation is not a search for cause and effect, an inventory of present status, or a prediction of future success. It is something of all of these, but only as they contribute to understanding substance, function and worth' (Stake and Denny, quoted in Everitt and Hardiker, 1996, p. 52).

The particular balance struck between these two aspects of evaluation determines the extent to which any particular piece of work is formative or summative in character.

- Formative evaluation is concerned with providing information for policy or practice improvement, modification and management and its focus is on process, but can include measures of effectiveness in achieving desired outcomes.
- Summative, or impact, evaluation is concerned primarily with determining how effective a particular policy or practice has been in achieving its stated outcomes.

These two types of evaluation are not exclusive alternatives but rather ends of a continuum. In the immediate to mid-term future, variations on formative evaluation are likely to offer most to family support: not least because the policy context is likely to remain fluid. The challenge facing evaluators is how best to develop the scientific sophistication of the methods they use while more firmly embedding the process, from commission through design and execution to impact, in the lived realities of policy and practice.

## ADDRESSING AN OPEN AGENDA

As stated at the start of this chapter the aim of this book is to provide an open platform for contributors to share how, in their particular circumstances and from their various perspectives, they are making sense of family support and the appropriate means to evaluate it—in other words, how they are dealing with the issues discussed in the previous two sections. The result is a rich mix, ranging across all aspects of the combined framework of Figure 1.1. The five chapters in Part II highlight a range of underpinning issues of relevance for any evaluation of family support. Jane Tunstill (Chapter 2) draws out a challenging set of political, conceptual and technical issues. What she has to say about such issues as social policy shifts, competing approaches among evaluators, the 'slippery concept' of need, the 'thorny issue' of outcome, reaching the user and the absence of satisfactory baseline and contextual data makes it very clear that all the aspects of Figure 1.1 are in dynamic interplay with one another.

Having a secure conceptual base is a major asset in grappling with the challenges identified by Tunstill, and the next two chapters each detail a key concept of particular relevance to family support. May-Chahal, Katz and Cooper (Chapter 3) discuss 'social inclusion' within the context of an ecological approach as a means of drawing issues of poverty, employment, community, and inequality of opportunity into the family support frame. They not only deal with the theoretical aspects of the term but also with how it can be operationalised. Although this is not a new perspective, there is growing attention to resilience as a key research and practice concept within child welfare and Gilligan (Chapter 4) argues for its place in family support and its evaluation. He too combines discussion of the constituent elements of the concept, and of family support, with consideration of how it might be operationalised in practice by those providing services and those evaluating them. In the other two chapters in this part of the book, Pecora (Chapter 5) and Hetherington (Chapter 6) demonstrate the case for taking a comparative view. Pecora shares a typology of family-centred services which he uses to review and draw out general messages from a large number of separate projects and evaluations carried out across America in varied circumstances. Hetherington discusses a number of inter-country comparative projects in Europe, in one example extended to Australia, to show how it is possible to uncover the characteristics of social welfare structures and the values and unspoken assumptions that help to determine how they function.

In Part III a set of nine evaluation 'case studies' are presented from around the world: America, Australia, Hong Kong, Ireland, New Zealand, Sweden and the United Kingdom. In the first of these Hazlett (Chapter 7), from the vantage point of a senior civil servant, discusses the place of family support and its evaluation within the Republic of Ireland. She describes the development of a family policy that not only recognises the traditional valuing of family but also sees family support as necessary to sustain the recent growth of the 'Celtic Tiger' economy. She highlights the role of government-commissioned evaluation in the development of the policy and in its application. Two academics, Cheung and Law (Chapter 8), focus on the experience of one of the original Asian Tiger economies, Hong Kong, to describe the historical development of family services in 'a multi-cultural environment connecting the East and the West'. They identify the place of evaluation within this development and discuss contemporary issues such as service quality standards, process audits, culturally relevant outcome measures and information technology. They advocate the future use of an evaluation framework based on credibility, creativity, cultural sensitivity, feasibility and result utility.

Cultural sensitivity is also a major theme in the description and discussion of an evaluation involving a large national family support agency in New Zealand by Sanders and Munford, a social work academic and an agency-based researcher and policy analyst (Chapter 9). They use the experience of this three-stage programme, which has been underway since 1994, to tease out key features in the design and execution of inclusive evaluation, not least the ethical concerns. They also present findings from their national context on the factors that contribute to effective family support. The varied family support services of another voluntary organisation, the National Society for the Prevention of Cruelty to Children, covering England, Scotland and Northern Ireland, are the subject of Gardner's review of the process and findings of a two-stage evaluation (Chapter 10). While measuring change in the lives of children and parents was the major aim, the evaluators were also interested in 'aggregated scores for networks and views of the neighbourhood to produce a community climate score'.

Community has an important place in the three chapters that follow. In the case of Quiery and her colleagues (Chapter 11), the Early Years Project in Northern Ireland, which this team of university-based social psychologists evaluated, was explicitly part of a local urban community regeneration initiative. They set out the theoretical foundations of their work as a transactional model of early child development and an ecological model of the individual in the community, describe their set of questionnaires instruments and present findings suggesting some gains for both mothers and children. Budde's account (Chapter 12) is of a four-site evaluation of a major American foundation's Community Partnership for Protecting Children Initiative. The goal of this initiative is to enhance the ability of entire communities to keep children safe from abuse and neglect, drawing on both the strengths of informal social networks within neighbourhoods and the services of public and private agencies. Attention is given in the chapter to cross-site issues that are particularly apparent in an evaluation of this scale, such as uniform application of a theory of change and the collection of comparable information in diverse circumstances. The evaluation of two local community-based projects for children and young people in the west of Ireland, one at the start of the 1990s and the other at the end, are the subject of the contribution in Chapter 13 from Canavan, a career researcher and Dolan, primarily an operational manager. They show how wider social policy change facilitated and directed developments in both family support services and their evaluation. They also suggest that greater sophistication in evaluation techniques does not of itself ensure that evaluators develop the necessary critical perspective on the needs and services involved in family support.

The last two case studies of Part III come from Sweden and Australia and both concern national programmes. Shochet and Ham (Chapter 14), university-based psychologists, describe a universal family and school-based programme developed as part of the Australian Mental Health Strategy to reduce the incidence of depression in adolescents. The theoretical underpinnings and the content of the Resourceful Adolescent Programme for young people and its parallel programme for parents are described, along with the controlled trial of their effectiveness. The contact person/family service is the most frequently used statutory child welfare service in Sweden. Yet as Andersson (Chapter 15) points out, this form of family support, positioned between universal child welfare services and services to children at risk, has been subject to very little evaluation. From her position as an academic researcher and teacher, she describes the work that has been undertaken, including her own, which gave particular attention to evaluating the scheme from the perspectives of the four key types of actor involved—the social workers, the volunteer contact families, the children and young people, and their families.

The chapters that make up Parts II and III of the book draw on a limited but varied range of national experiences. They highlight and detail the aspects of family support and its evaluation that are suggested by the combined framework of Figure 1.1 and discussed in the ealier sections of this chapter. The book ends (Chapter 16) by revisiting both those issues and, in the light of the experiences, concepts, and methodologies shared in the preceding chapters, asks three questions:

- What is emerging as the key themes of convergence and divergence internationally?
- Is it desirable and feasible to work towards a unified global view of family support?
- What has evaluation to offer the future development of family support world wide?

## REFERENCES

Audit Commission (1994) *Seen But Not Heard: Co-ordinating Community Child Health and Social Services for Children in Need*. London: HMSO.

Butt, J. and Box, L. (1998) *Family Centred: A Study of the Use of Family Centres by Black Families*. London: REU.

Clarke, J., Cochrane, A. and McLaughlin, E. (Eds) (1994) *Managing Social Policy*. London: Sage.

Cochrane, A. (1993) Comparative approaches and social policy. In A. Cochrane and J. Clarke (Eds), *Comparing Welfare States: Britain in International Context*. London: Sage.

Crow, G. and Allen, G. (2000) Communities, family support and social change. In J. Canavan, P. Dolan and J. Pinkerton (Eds), *Family Support: Direction from Diversity*. London: Jessica Kingsley.

Department of Health (1994) *Children Act Report, 1993*. London: HMSO.

Department of Health (1995a) *Child Protection: Messages from Research*. London: HMSO.

Department of Health (1995b) *Children Act Report, 1994*. London: HMSO.

Department of Health (1999) *Working Together to Safeguard Children*. London: The Stationery Office.

Everitt, A. and Hardiker, P. (1996) *Evaluating for Good Practice*. Basingstoke: Macmillan.

Frost, N. (1996) *Negotiated Friendship—Home Start and the Delivery of Family Support*. Leicester: Home-Start.

Frost, N. (1997) Delivering family support: Issues and theories in service development. In N. Parton (Ed.), *Child Protection and Family Support*. London: Routledge.

Frost, N. and Stein, M. (1989) *The Politics of Social Welfare*. Hertfordshire: Harvestor Wheatsheaf.

Gilbert, N. (1997) *Combatting Child Abuse: International Perspectives and Trends*. New York: Oxford University Press.

Gilligan, R. (2000) Family support: Issues and prospects. In J. Canavan, P. Dolan and J. Pinkerton (Eds), *Family Support: Direction from Diversity*. London: Jessica Kingsley.

Hardiker, P., Exton, K. and Barker, M. (1991a) The social policy contexts of prevention in child care. *British Journal of Social Work*, **21**(4).

Hardiker, P., Exton, K. and Barker, M. (1991b) *Policies and Practices in Preventative Child Care*. Aldershot: Avebury.

Harper, N. (1996) *Children Still in Need—Refocusing Child Protection in the Context of Children in Need*. London: Association of Directors of Social Services/NCH Action for Children.

Hill, M. (1998) Effective professional intervention in children's lives. In M. Hill (Ed.), *Effective Ways of Working with Children and Their Families*. London: Jessica Kingsley.

Hill, M. and Tisdall, K. (1997) *Children and Society*. London: Longman.

Home Office (1998) *Supporting Families—A Consultation Document*. London: The Home Office.

Kelly, G. (1998) The influence of research on child care policy and practice: The case of 'Children Who Wait' and the development of the permanence movement in the United Kingdom. In D. Iwaniec and J. Pinkerton (Eds), *Making Research Work: Promoting Child Care Policy and Practice*. Chichester: John Wiley & Sons.

McAuley, C. (1998) Child participatory research: Ethical and methodological considerations. In D. Iwaniec and J. Pinkerton (Eds), *Making Research Work: Promoting Child Care Policy and Practice*. Chichester: John Wiley & Sons.

McAuley, C. (1999) *The Family Support Outcome Study*. Ballymena: Northern Ireland Health and Social Services Board.

McIntosh, M. (1984) The family, regulations and the public sphere. In G. McLennan, S. Held and S. Hall (Eds), *State and Society in Contemporary Britain*. Cambridge: Polity Press.

McLennan, G., Held, S. and Hall, S. (1984) Editors' Introduction. In G. McLennan, S. Held and S. Hall (Eds), *State and Society in Contemporary Britain*. Cambridge: Polity Press.

McWhirter, L. (1993) *Social science research and policy processes: Relationships, tensions and skills*. Conference Paper, Belfast: Department of Social Work, Queens University.

Moorman, A., Ball, M. and Henricson, C. (Eds) (2001) *Understanding Parents' Needs: A Review of Parents' Surveys*. London: National Family and Parenting Institute.

Morgan, P. (1998) An endangered species? In M.E. David (Ed.), *The Fragmenting Family: Does It Matter?* London: IEA Health and Welfare Unit.

NISW (1982) *Social Workers—Their Role and Tasks.* National Institute of Social Work. London: Bedford Square Press.

Parton, N. (ed.) (1997) *Child Protection and Family Support. Tensions, Contradictions and Possibilities.* London: Routledge.

Pinkerton, J. (1998) The impact of research on policy and practice: A systemic perspective. In D. Iwaniec and J. Pinkerton (Eds), *Making Research Work: Promoting Child Care Policy and Practice.* Chichester: John Wiley & Sons.

Pinkerton, J. (2001) Developing partnership practice. In P. Foley, J. Roche and S. Tucker (Eds), *Children in Society: Contemporary Theory, Policy and Practice.*

Pinkerton, J., Higgins, K. and Devine, P. (2000) *Family Support—From Policy Analysis to Project Evaluation.* Aldershot: Ashgate.

Pithouse, A. and Lindsell, S. (1995) Family care in the community: A case study of a family centre and its effectiveness in reducing child abuse. *Social Services Research*, No. 4.

Pithouse, A., Lindsell, S. and Chueng, M. (1998) *Family Support and Family Centre Services.* Aldershot: Ashgate.

Statham, J. (2000) *Outcomes and Effectiveness of Family Support Services. A research review.* London: Institute of Education.

Whittaker, J. (1993) *Change Paradigms in Child and Family Services: Challenges for Practice, Policy and Research.* Dublin: Social Studies Press.

# Part II

## UNDERPINNING ISSUES

# 2

# POLITICAL AND TECHNICAL ISSUES FACING EVALUATORS OF FAMILY SUPPORT

*Jane Tunstill*

It is an obvious temptation for any researcher whose work involves the evaluation of government policy to claim that, in her or his specific area of study, the relevant theoretical concepts are especially complex, and that the subject matter of their research is most vulnerable to policy change and political whim. Of course, a strong case could be made along these lines for most of the evaluation areas that fall within the broad remit of social policy, including, for example, social security, crime, and family policy. Certainly, within the raft of child-welfare initiatives, the topic area of family support would qualify for a place in this league. It straddles the boundaries of all three areas, as well as the contested territory of social care and social work. The purpose of this chapter is to provide an overview of the key policy and research questions that have traditionally made—and continue to make—the task of studying it so challenging, and to identify some of the more recent factors that underline the importance of accomplishing this task successfully.

Central among these more recent issues is the new emphasis on monitoring outcomes and the move towards evidence-based practice and policy which is now a key tenet of most government initiatives within the UK. Even 10 years ago, the political, theoretical and technical dimensions of social care evaluation may have been consigned to the realm of interesting academic debate. Such issues might have preoccupied researchers, and indeed enthused a generation of social research students. However, at the level of the commissioner of research, or indeed the individual citizen-recipient of its application, such questions might still have seemed marginal by comparison with the availability of funds—or indeed of information about services. However,

*Evaluating Family Support: Thinking Internationally, Thinking Critically.*
Edited by I. Katz and J. Pinkerton. © 2003 John Wiley & Sons, Ltd.

such marginality has no place in the new evidence-based world which is exemplified by the emerging domination of the performance indicator. The commissioning, execution and dissemination of research into family support play a key role in the rationalization or evolution of policies towards children and families.

There is a perennial topicality in definitions of family support: definitions rarely remain static. The boundaries of those areas of provision which can be seen to fall within such a definition are in flux all the time. They will change depending on the nature of the overall social policy approach of successive governments and they reflect prevailing policy ratios such as those between universal and selective services, between family and non-family policy, and between more and less intervention. At the present time *Sure Start* provides a very clear example of the potential breadth of services, multi-agency delivery and community-based access to a range of services, all of which are intended to benefit children within their own families (Glass, 1999).

However, the subject matter of this chapter is evaluative issues rather than the nature of services as such, and the chapter starts by discussing key de-velopments in the social-policy arena, followed by a brief outline of current tensions between schools of methodological thought, before going on to iden-tify some key conceptual and technical issues which confront family support evaluators. It is not intended to provide an exhaustive list of these issues. The main purpose of the chapter is to flag up the complex relationship between politics and research, and draw attention to the significance of this overlap in respect of family support evaluation. The illustrations chosen all relate to policy in the UK, but they have a resonance with other European and North American countries who have experienced similar sorts of social policy evo-lution and so, it is hoped, have a wider relevance. Prominence will be given to one particular, and indeed crucial, aspect of family support provision as a vehicle for exploring the research territory in question. This service area, the subject of research by the author, is that wherein local government social services departments are likely to commission or provide support to families who are disadvantaged or are experiencing particular difficulties in their lives (Statham, 2000, p. 1).

## POLITICAL ISSUES

### Developments in Social Policy

It is, of course, the characteristics of social policy that exert the most pervasive influence on the work of social researchers—an influence far more powerful than the outcomes of academic debate about research techniques. This tru-ism would apply in any era but is especially relevant in the last part of the twentieth century and beginning of the twenty-first. Size and visibility are clearly part of the explanation:

> In the past few years social policy has risen to the top of the political agenda in Britain. The nature of the welfare state, having once seemed uncontroversial and even dull, is now deeply contested and its institutions subject to a seemingly permanent revolution. With the total bill for social provision topping £200 billion, there is little wonder that both cost-conscious politicians and tax-weary citizens should focus so single-mindedly on welfare.
>
> (Ellison and Pierson, 1998, p. 1)

However, there are other more subtle factors in the relationship between policy and research and these can be found in the specific characteristics of policy. The social policy of both the previous Conservative and the current Labour government reflects a set of common and enduring themes, although of course there are many differences in their underlying ideologies and the way in which policy is designed and implemented. Wilding (1992) identified the main characteristics of 1980s policy:

- a disenchantment with collectivism
- centralization
- managerialism
- a reduced role for the local authority
- an emphasis on enabling as opposed to service-delivery role
- increased concern with the true cost of services
- cutting expenditure.

To these, on the basis of 1990s policy evolution, one might add:

- the explicit introduction of market principles into public policy
- rights accruing to individuals as customers rather than citizens
- an assault on professional status
- the rediscovery of family
- the existence or not of an *underclass*
- the concept of social exclusion.

Taken together these respective policy characteristics constitute three overarching policy themes which are already influencing the work of family support researchers, and whose impact is likely to increase further. Firstly, there is the emergence of 'the audit society', to use Power's term (1997). He argues that:

> the explosion of auditable management control systems has occurred at a time when there is a heightened awareness of risk and a diminution of trust in experts. The solution has been to lessen reliance upon experts and instead to transfer trust into audit systems. An apparently greater sense of safety and control is thus generated as the emphasis shifts, from trust in individuals, towards an audit of the quality of expert services.
>
> (Powers, quoted in Trinder and Reynolds, 2000, p. 9)

Secondly, there is the new heightened focus on human need (Doyal and Gough 1991). As Hewitt (1993, p. 62) argues, 'the major implication of the new politics of welfare is to revisit the relationship between universal and particular needs'. This is nowhere more clearly exemplified than by the current UK legal framework for delivering family support services via the implementation of services for children in need, as defined for England and Wales by Part 3 of the 1989 Children Act and its equivalent in the other UK jurisdictions (Tisdall et al., 1998).

Thirdly, there is the high profile for issues of family life and social control. This debate includes the view that 'the growth of the welfare state has undermined the purpose and role of families in modern societies whilst ostensibly seeking to help them...and [has] manifested itself in a number of public debates about family obligations in the context of divorce, community care, child abuse and neglect and the emergence of an "underclass family type"' (Rodger, 1996, p. 5).

## The Politics of Research

The politics of social research in this period manifest similarly dramatic tensions. Perhaps researchers have rarely been characterized by their generosity or lack of competitiveness towards each other. The competitive nature of research funding, whose negative impact is now amplified by the formal research assessment exercise undertaken by government within the university system, has probably aggravated these tensions (Fisher, 1999). A more recent development is the way in which these rivalries are now played out explicitly on the basis of theoretical and methodological debates, which thrive on the lack of current consensus around a range of core questions: the concept of evaluation; the notion of effectiveness; the nature of evidence; the scientific status of competing models of social research. While there has, in the past, been some rivalry between researchers using quantitative methods and those using qualitative methods, the starkest disagreements are now between those evaluators who espouse a positivist/experimental approach and those who favour a non-positivist/non-experimental approach.

> Within social work research, these debates have been manifest in assertions, on the one hand, about the pre-eminence of experimental studies rooted in the traditions of positivism, and on the other, about the primacy of interpretive approaches which challenge the overriding salience of any single intervention or outcome. (Cheetham et al., 1992, p. 139)

Trinder has analysed these tensions in detail and provides an engrossing account of a struggle for supremacy between diverse approaches.

> Research and evaluation has had a long but uncontested history in social work and probation . . . the nature and role of research has continued to generate intense and often acrimonious exchanges. Debate in the US and UK, has frequently been polarised between experimental/empirical and non-experimental camps.
>
> (Trinder and Reynolds, 2000, p. 141)

Trinder had previously (1996) developed a typology of research traditions in social work based on a distinction between 'empirical practice' and 'pragmatism'. The former places emphasis on experimental designs—randomized controlled trials (RCTs), meta-analysis and single-case designs. Its focus is on identifying the relative effectiveness of different interventions. Characteristically, this type of research:

- draws on health/medical research styles;
- is founded on the positivist notion that the world and its phenomena are essentially knowable and measurable;
- assumes that sufficient rigour in design will produce the truth which, once discovered, can be used to determine evidence-based practice;
- emphasizes the random-controlled trial with experimental design and randomly assigned control groups as the only way to test and re-test whether or not an intervention works;
- regards quasi-experimental designs with a non-randomized control group, pre-experimental designs, client-opinion studies, and surveys as simply not rigorous enough to evaluate effectiveness.

Pragmatism, by contrast, primarily uses non-experimental quantitative designs supplemented by qualitative research. Its focus tends to be on identifying how systems work, and their outcomes. It characteristically:

- steers a course between the scientific empiricism of the positivists and the 'messier' politicized approach of the participative/critical researchers;
- abandons the search for irrefutable scientific proof;
- designs research on the basis of technical rather than epistemological or ontological grounds;
- has a strong preference for non-experimental quantitative methods of data collection using non-experimental methods;
- freely incorporates qualitative methods in a secondary or supplementary role.

In addition, Trinder identifies a third school: the empowerment/critical approach, which is characterized by an emphasis on primarily qualitative design and a focus on using research to highlight and challenge inequality. She argues that this approach has so far been much less influential than the other two. Indeed, exponents of this approach tend to view the concept of effectiveness with some suspicion.

What has elevated these methodological debates to their present position of importance is the context in which they are now held. These competing traditions now have as their battleground the terrain of evidence-based policy and practice. While the concept of evidence-based practice has the highest profile in medicine, it has had a pervasive influence beyond this and has 'to differing degrees influenced research activity and challenged professional identities in professions as diverse as medicine, social work, clinical psychology, nursing and education' (Trinder and Reynolds, 2000, p. 17). This new world seems to be here to stay. It has been given a high profile by government through public statements such as:

> We need to be able to rely on social science and social scientists to tell us what works and why, and what types of policy initiatives are likely to be most effective. And we need better ways of ensuring that those who want this information can get it easily and quickly. (Blunkett, 2000)

The new context is also reinforced by government at the level of organizational change:

> We are now proposing the creation of a new institution to accelerate the drive for quality—the Social Care Institute for Excellence (SCIE)—whose work will inform management, practice, regulation, training, inspection and review. SCIE will draw together and disseminate what works best in social care, in order to ensure that social services are no longer a postcode lottery, lessen the present lottery of care in social services and to promote greater consistency across the country. (DoH, 2000, p. 9)

But just because current government social policy puts a stress on outcomes, including their cost-effectiveness, it cannot be assumed that there is, could be or should be a political or research consensus around the status of methodologies, any more than one can be assumed around the desirability of various outcomes. Trinder (1996) has made the point that 'research is highly political and that methodologies are therefore not neutral sets of techniques to be picked out of textbooks'. The absence of a seamless transition from research into practice means that there is a very large overlap between issues that can be defined as political and those that can be defined as technical.

> Like any other data, empirical evidence about the effectiveness of social policies and programmes is a product of data collection procedures and the assumptions on which they are based. The concept of effectiveness derives from particular ways of thinking and makes sense only in relation to its context.
> (Cheetham et al., 1992)

If the measurement of outcomes is itself a contested notion, then no wonder the choice of desired outcomes triggers such robust debate between policy makers and practitioners. Little surprise, then, that it is difficult to draw a clear line between the technical and political issues facing evaluators. However, the remainder of this chapter attempts to do exactly that and to highlight two sets of challenges—conceptual and technical—which will inevitably have a bearing on the work of family support evaluators. These will be discussed in the context of family support provision as laid down in Part 3 of the Children Act 1989.

## SPECIFIC CHALLENGES FOR RESEARCHERS

### Conceptual Challenges and Policy Driven Considerations

As was indicated above, the parameters of activity which, at any point in time, will be conceptualized as family support depend on changing political and professional conceptions. These will not only be explicit ones about services but also implicit ones about the role of the family and the nature of childhood. Over time there have been some profound changes in the way in which law handles these issues and in the related evolution of professional practice. In the context of those services within the UK which come within the focus of this book, the main conceptual, theoretical and legal shifts have been from protection to prevention to family support to children in need and, arguably since 1997, to parenting.

The way in which services and their underlying assumptions are conceptualized carries clear messages for the way in which they are to be evaluated. For example, in the 1960s the dominant legal and professional concept, as enshrined in the 1963 Children and Young Persons Act, was the prevention of the reception of children into care. The research world responded with an emphasis on measuring rates of reception into care, to the unhelpful exclusion of other things. The transition to a subsequent set of professional aspirations in part resulted from research and in part from the impact of political ideology. Packman's work (1993) was of special significance in this period, in that she identified the tendency of social workers to reduce prevention to a strict gate-keeping role by providing or refusing to provide care for children without offering alternative support. Her work pointed to the need for a wider perspective, including the provision of alternative solutions for family problems. The political values of the period were receptive to these messages and combined to refocus social policy on the positive value of the family, as seen within the various documents that led to the Children Act 1989, to suggest the value of a wider concept of family support.

Even within the wording of the 1989 Act, however, the promisingly gener-ous and universal concept of family support had already been diluted on the basis of concerns about the likely demand on resources. Such dilution was provided by the invention of the concept of 'the child in need'. It could, of course, have been predicted that the highly selective nature of most of the then Conservative government's social policy would provide unlikely soil for the seeds of a broader approach within childcare legislation to flourish. All too soon it became evident that the emphasis on children in need had led to undue attention being given to ascertaining need, primarily in order to prioritize access to services (Aldgate and Tunstill, 1995).

The point to note here is that conceptions of the family support task rarely stand still. Although the official legal framework for family support remains the 1989 Children Act, since the election of the current government there have been other developments outside of primary legislation which have begun to change the focus, and indeed the language, away from children in need towards the concept of 'parenting'. This can be seen very clearly in current policy statements from government, in the establishment of a National Family and Parenting Institute and in the introduction of Parenting Orders in the 1998 Crime and Disorder Act. Such shifts in the conceptual frameworks carry very obvious implications for any research activity that will be subsequently commissioned. If the emphasis is to be on parenting, then clearly a central research task is likely to be ascertaining the calibre of parenting, as opposed to the measurement of need.

However, it is within the law that the clearest expression of the dominant childcare discourse can be found. Accordingly, the value base and the specific requirements of the current legislative framework need to be considered. The law is now underpinned by a clear set of principles, foremost among which are:

- the need to safeguard and promote the welfare of children within their own homes;
- the wide definition of child need;
- the value of involving the full range of statutory, voluntary and community agencies and professional disciplines;
- the importance of working in partnership with parents;
- the supportive role of providing care through accommodation of children and young people.

The following discussion is limited to selecting some, rather than trying to identify all, of the challenges that arise from this framework. First, there is the complexity of definition of the term 'family support'. As was argued at the outset, there is still no consensus on this. The definitions quoted below each suggest a rather different emphasis which could be taken up by evaluators or service providers:

> Any activity or facility provided either by statutory agencies or by community groups or individuals, aimed to provide advice and support to parents to help them in bringing up their children. (Audit Commission, 1994, p. 82)

> Family support is about the creation and enhancement, with and for families in need, of locally based (or accessible) activities, facilities and networks, the use of which have outcomes such as alleviated stress, increased self esteem, promoted parental/carer/family competence and behaviour and increased parental carer capacity to nurture and protect children. (Hearn, 1995, p. 3)

> The type of services which local authorities have a duty to provide or purchase for the purpose of promoting the welfare of children in need, wherever possible within their own homes. (Gibbons et al., 1995, p. 151)

The range of activities and facilities potentially covered under family support means that, as a minimum, the task of evaluation must address: multidisciplinary service provision; longitudinal outcomes; outcomes for both children, parents and family groups; outcomes for the community; the impact of family support provision on other elements of the childcare system.

The joint tasks of safeguarding and promoting welfare underline the complexity of categorizing services intended, in the broadest sense, to enhance parental behaviour. For example, can boundaries be located, and if so where, between services which may involve the assessment of parental competence, services which remedy the deficits so identified, and services which build on existing levels of parental competence where no specific deficit has been identified? The current raft of new initiatives, for example *Sure Start*, will fall uneasily across these categories. Indeed, it is likely that the mark of 'New' Labour policies towards children and families will be more initiatives that span the universal/selective divide. The research challenge which derives from this categorization issue is the need to collect the baseline data to underpin subsequent evaluations. These will need to be sufficiently sound and extensive to permit the evaluation of specific services.

It is perhaps worth sounding an optimistic note here by referring to the British Economic and Social Research Council Millennium Cohort Study (MCS) which began in May 2001 as a possible source of help to researchers in the future. On the other hand, an alternate pessimistic reading might be to confirm the current political emphasis on parent and family culpability in subsequent childhood problems. Early publicity about the MCS places particular emphasis on:

> understanding the social conditions surrounding birth and early childhood as being fundamental to the study of the whole of the life course. This applies across the range, from the analysis of social exclusion through investigation of the influence of early circumstances on health over the life course to the evidence base for major policy initiatives such as 'Sure Start'.... major questions about the prospects for children born in 2000–1 concern poverty

and wealth, the quality of family life, and its support by public policy and the broader community.... Issues to emerge from future sweeps of the cohort will include advantage and disadvantage in education, health, employment and the *parenting of the next generation* ...

(Smith and Joshi, 2000, p. 31; author's italics)

The emphasis on partnership and early access to services complicates the definition of what constitutes a referral, and indeed what is a case. In comparison with being a child on a register, or being looked after, a child whose family are using a family centre may not even be recorded. Indeed, good practice around stigma reduction and facilitating access to services may positively require such invisibility. It is not too fanciful to argue that the *best* provision, i.e. that easily accessed at the time of crisis, where no formal (recorded) point of entry exists, may be therefore impossible to evaluate! In particular it is important to know more about the relationship between professional referral and self-referral. Research commissioned by the Department of Health (Smith, 1996; Tunstill and Aldgate, 2000) has pointed to the fact that the two populations are very similar.

In many ways by far the most substantial challenge posed to the whole task of evaluating family support is the breadth of the legal definition of 'need'. Indeed, Weale has called it a 'slippery concept' (1983) and there are at least four major variations on the theme of need, which include both psychologically and sociologically derived definitions. Three are well known, one more recent. They represent examples of the overlap between conceptual and technical challenges. The first of these is Maslow's hierarchy of need (1970) with its six types of need: physiological; safety needs; social needs; esteem; knowledge and understanding; self-actualization. These are set within a framework built on a hierarchy from necessity up to aspiration, and underline the relevance of taking a life course approach to need. Kellmer Pringle's four aspects of need, as a basis for child development, are also well known: love and security; new experiences; praise and recognition; responsibility (1975).

Bradshaw (1972) developed a very well known four-part taxonomy of need: expressed; felt; normative; comparative. This incorporates an operational element which is central to the concerns of social policy researchers and especially family support evaluators. His discussion of expressed need, for example, underlines the requirement for evaluators to integrate the question of access into their work. His concern with normative need highlights the significance of stigma. His words of caution about the concept are also worth noting:

> The concept of need has always been too imprecise, too complex, too contentious to be a target for policy (and therefore) leaves a lot to be desired both as an epidemiological identifier and also as basis for evaluating the performance of policies. (Bradshaw, 1972)

The Looked After Records developed by the Department of Health (DoH, 1995) have had a high profile over the last decade and provide an example of how it may be marginally easier to list children's needs in the context of a specific service for children. This is the relatively small group of children whose unmet needs are probably greatest and who therefore experience the most extensive level of service, i.e. looked after children. Their needs are considered along seven dimensions:

- health
- education
- identity
- family and social relationships
- social presentation
- emotional and behavioural development
- self-care skills.

Schedules based on this framework are now being developed, to extend its use beyond application to looked after children, for use in the community with children living with their families. It is intended that this framework will 'provide a valuable foundation for policy and practice for all professionals and agencies who manage and provide services to children in need and their families' (DoH, 2000). The assessment will take account of three interrelated systems or domains: the child's developmental needs; parenting capacity; and family and environmental factors. 'The interaction or the influence of these dimensions on each other requires careful exploration during assessment, with the ultimate aim being to understand how they affect the child or the children in the family' (DoH, 2000).

## Prioritization

Not only is the definition of need difficult conceptually, but in the world of policy and practice the 'duty to meet need' conflicts with the requirement to prioritize access for some children and their families over others. This introduces both implicit and explicit thresholds into the family support system. Awareness that need—when defined in a way that exceeds available resources—leads to thresholds has very largely come from the data produced by the Department of Health commissioned studies of the operation of the child protection system in England—as reviewed in the highly influential *Messages from Research* (DoH, 1995).

Thresholds not only establish who is to receive which service; they also mark the point beyond which one set of actions relevant to one stage of the process is superseded by those applicable to a successive stage.

The influences on thresholds are diverse, and include financial considerations and professional judgements. The siting of the threshold will differ not only from local authority to local authority but also between personal social services and other statutory services, such as health and education, where disparities will be aggravated by both the intentions of other legislation (such as the Education Reform Act) and by different professional constructions of need and priority.

## TECHNICAL CHALLENGES/RESEARCH-DRIVEN CONSIDERATIONS

The chapter now turns to identifying some examples of the specific, more obviously technical research issues that must be taken into account in planning national or local evaluation studies of family support.

### Information Availability Issues

It may appear, given the centrality of planning and information in the new social policy world, that the least difficult problem a family support evaluator will encounter is the absence of information to provide baseline or contextual data for her or his work. Aldgate and Tunstill (1995) undertook a national study for the Department of Health which was intended to be a broad sweep of the national scene in respect of provision for children in need under Section 17 of the Children Act 1989. Its purpose was to present a broad picture of the range of approaches to implementing this aspect of the new legislation adopted by the majority of local authorities during the first 18 months of implementation. Information was obtained on the following areas:

- identifying the key challenges for implementation
- working across the organizational divide
- deciding priorities for service provision
- provision of services.

However, the study revealed the lack of a systematic data-collection system for children in need. The data-collection system was dependent on whether a team had collated figures or not; whether local audits had been conducted in recent years by the social services department or an outside agency, and so forth. The data collected was often scattered, of varying sample size, and unconnected such that it could not serve to provide a comprehensive picture of children in need in a local authority. There were also problems arising from the absence of adequate computer hardware and software; variability in the scale and scope of research units; and inadequate staffing for data analysis. Reflecting these difficulties the study attributed the shortcomings of service development in this area in part to the lack of social services research staff and to the technical problems of information management.

Deficits in data collection have remained a common theme in reviews of family support. A Social Services Inspectorate report, published in December 1997—which was overall very critical of the failure of social services departments to meet the aims and objectives of Section 17, and in particular to refocus services away from child protection to family support—raised continuing questions about the quality of monitoring undertaken and information produced by the departments.

> Overall management information was poor in most SSDs. Managers had little information about throughput of work or the demand being experienced at the front line. Resource shortfalls were consistently not recorded, so that the information was not available for future planning. Information systems relating to *Looking after Children Good Outcomes* were better, but it was not clear how they informed the wider picture of need in family support services. (SSI, 1997)

> There was a consistent picture of poor work on measuring outcomes. This was associated with a lack of quality monitoring and evaluation of complaints, or user surveys. It would have helped the SSDs to identify the extent of demand for their services, and what they had done well, in order to develop effective family support services. (SSI, 1997)

## Mapping/Auditing Services

The conviction that children's welfare depends on the satisfaction of a range of regularly and infrequently acknowledged needs, including physical, intellectual, emotional, social and behavioural, and that health has physical and mental aspects, maximizes the number of agencies that can and should play a role in providing family support services. There is little evidence that the departments with a statutory responsibility for such provision always have a very accurate knowledge of the various agencies operational in their area. This has been a common and recurring theme in the literature since the early 1990s (Gibbons, 1990). A national mapping exercise, commissioned by the National Family and Parenting Institute (Henricson et al., 2001) was undertaken in order to identify parent support projects. Both replies to the questionnaire survey and interviews with local authority respondents underlined the difficulty of keeping this information up to date.

In addition to the task of identification, some of the other questions to be raised in this context include:

- Is there a shared perception about which services are to be categorized as child support, which as parent support and which as family support?
- Is there a common language to discuss *need, threshold* and *outcome*?
- Do agencies other than social services, for example health and education, acknowledge and share information about their role in providing family support?

The first of these is a particularly thorny issue. One of the assumptions underpinning the provision of family support is that children's development is normally best enhanced by remaining, if possible, within their own families. In order for this to happen, support either can or should be provided to the parents, their children or both. In the case of parents there are then several routes through which this support might be provided. It might be specifically within their role as parents; but could alternatively be provided to them as adults, or indeed as partners in a relationship. Parent craft classes, alcohol dependency services and marriage relationship counselling, which provide examples of the three respective categories, may all, *de facto*, support a family. The question that has to be asked is: Would such a variety of services be identified as falling within the category of family support services in a services audit?

## SPECIFIC MIXED ECONOMY ISSUES

### Potential Commercial Value of Data

There is clear encouragement in current childcare, as in other, legislation to develop a mixed economy of welfare by maximizing the partnerships between statutory, voluntary and private sectors. This has conferred a potential commercial value on data which, in the past, would not have been seen to carry such significant financial implications. It is likely to be an issue for both statutory agencies as well as voluntary and private ones. This may complicate a range of research tasks, including the negotiation of access, the selection of appropriate research sites, and the presentation and dissemination of findings. If independent sector agencies are in a competitive tendering situation then they may, for example, feel less than enthusiastic about opening up evaluation opportunities to researchers; or indeed of permitting the publication of negative findings. Even the more recent conceptual framework of Best Value (DoH, 1999), which has replaced the earlier Compulsive Competitive Tendering Process, will not necessarily have reduced this tension. Indeed, the emphasis on Best Value may well constitute a new set of extra research challenges, given the relatively small numbers of welfare economists who have either an interest or expertise in cost-effectiveness research.

### Reaching the User

While, in theory, aimed at bringing the advantage of private sector consumer status to public service users, the incorporation of the market and the quasi-market mechanisms may hinder the process of exploring the views of the user of services. For example, where services are contracted out, there will inevitably be a further layer of administrative processes, which may impede, or indeed facilitate, the commissioning or execution of research. In addition, it is possible that there will be a temptation for subcontractors to want to pass on only positive feedback and so only those users judged to be satisfied will be contacted by the agency to take part in evaluation. There is always a tension around the eliciting of user views, in the independent sector or elsewhere, given that service users may well be understandably apprehensive about expressing critical opinions, lest this be taken into account by service providers and result in negative consequences for the individual or family concerned.

## Organizational Characteristics

The diverse organizational characteristics of the independent sector agencies which deliver family support can exert their own pressures. Their size and income base vary enormously. This will have considerable implications for the agency resources, such as staffing and computer hardware and software, which can have a major bearing on the internal or external research process. Perhaps even more importantly, there is a brisk rate of change within the independent sector. There is a considerable possibility that projects will change or terminate in the course of a study. Agencies within the independent sector are probably more vulnerable to both changes in commissioning priorities and to cuts in public spending over a shorter period of time than are the statutory services.

## Choosing/Assessing/Interpreting Outcomes

A final technical challenge to be identified relates to the issue of outcomes. This is where some of the thorniest policy-driven pressures meet the most difficult of the technical ones. There is obviously a close connection between outcome and evaluation. All interventions are outcome oriented because in essence the only justification for any sort of intervention into the privacy of the family is the expectation that positive change will ensue. So, for example, childcare social work success or failure has traditionally been measured in such terms as a child at risk ceasing to be so, or a child in an out-of-home placement being reunited with her or his family or found permanent substitute family care.

In the sphere of personal social services, the definition of an outcome is by no means as straightforward as it may sound. One of the basic challenges is to distinguish between an output and an outcome. One well-known approach for doing this involves making a distinction between service-based and client-based outcomes. Cheetham and her colleagues (1992), for example, make a distinction between the nature, extent and quality of what is provided (service outcome) and the effects of a provision on its recipients (client outcome). A similar approach is adopted by Hardiker and her colleagues (1991), who talk about service and client levels of output. Knapp (1984) and others highlight the distinction between intermediate and final outcomes. By the former they mean 'indicators of performance, service or activity rather than indicators of effect, influence or impact' and, by the latter, 'changes in individual well-being compared with levels of well-being in the absence of a caring intervention'.

While these distinctions are clearly important and helpful they are potentially problematic within the field of family support, where the distinction between what constitutes an input and what is an outcome is less clear than may be the case with other social care services. There is a particularly ambiguous line at the lower end of the intervention tariff involving universal services such as day care, and services on the boundary between universal and low-level selectivity, such as a drop-in group or a family centre. In both cases there is likely to be a close relationship between the form and style of the services, as seen by those delivering them, and what the service users see themselves getting from the service. In that sense the service input is the client outcome.

Pinkerton and his colleagues (2000) have reviewed the prevention and family support research literature and suggest that the following agency characteristics are likely to be associated with successful family support programmes:

- partnership with users;
- sited in the home or neighbourhood;
- understanding and respect for issues of race and culture;
- interagency/interdisciplinary co-operation;
- creative and responsive services with attention to outreach and engagement;
- clarity about the relationship to child protection.

It can be seen how all of these project characteristics reside on the boundary between input and output, and thereby pose a challenge to the evaluative task.

The complexity of determining what constitutes an outcome is further illustrated by the five different types identified by Parker and his colleagues. They distinguished between: public outcomes; service outcomes; professional outcomes; family outcomes; and child outcomes (Parker, 1998; Parker et al., 1991). Public outcomes highlight the fact that childcare interventions are largely publicly financed, organized and made within a framework determined by public statute.

Public bodies are held accountable for what happens so there is a range of public expectations about what should be achieved or forestalled and these may conflict and also change over time. Service outcomes are another way of asking: Outcomes for whom? They may differ according to, for example, the perspectives taken by social services managers as opposed to elected members or to voluntary sector management boards. Professional outcomes reflect professional activity, both successful and unsuccessful, with the focus on the means and manner of the change coming about as well as on the child's changed situation.

Family outcomes are also complex. It cannot be assumed that there are common interests on the part of all family members. For example, keeping a family intact may be at the cost of the ill treatment of a victimized child; conversely, keeping a behaviourally challenging child at home may be at the cost of all the other members of the family. Outcomes for children are no less complex. Which kinds of outcome can be agreed as most important for the well-being of children? How are emotional needs to be balanced against identity needs? There is a constant danger that children's perceptions of their needs will be overshadowed by adult or professional interpretations of the outcomes that are of special importance. Obviously it is also essential to take account of children's own wishes and desires; not only is a child's present sense of well-being an intermediate outcome of value in itself, but will have an influence on future development. A happy child is more likely to have the confidence to succeed at school and to develop close relationships with adults and peers than a child who is miserable or resentful.

Parker and his colleagues also discuss the implications of the timing of outcome and assessment. This is a key question in the area of family support. It is not only a matter of giving sufficient time for an intervention to impact but also there may be a temporary improvement or deterioration in whatever outcome is being assessed. The evaluation of the *Headstart* programme in the USA revealed significant gains in IQ scores in the disadvantaged children by the time they entered mainstream schooling, but these gains were subsequently lost. However, in their late teens the children in the experimental group were found to have fewer difficulties than the controls, although these benefits had occurred in spheres other than their measured intelligence alone. The two lessons for the family support evaluator are that the timing of an outcome assessment must be chosen carefully and that the commissioning of longitudinal studies is essential if the full extent of relevant outcomes is to be understood.

## CONCLUSION

This chapter has attempted to draw attention to the complexity of the task of family support evaluation by identifying some of the political and technical issues which bedevil it. However, while all these concerns merit consideration in their own right, the real challenge derives from the way in which they interact. It needs to be recognized that the overlap between the political and the technical exerts a profound effect at every stage of the research process, from the selection of desired outcomes, through the funding and timing of studies, to the aggregation and attribution of outcomes. In many ways the outcome dilemma represents a microcosm of the whole issue. To embark on a study of family support provision without taking account of the political context in which it is delivered is as much a research hazard as failing to take account of the timing of an outcome measurement. If those who undertake or use evaluations do not give due regard to all these issues and their inter-action, there is a real risk that rather than being part of the answer, they will become part of the problem fuelling the difficulties surrounding the optimum development of policies for family support.

## REFERENCES

Aldgate, J. and Tunstill, J. (1995) *Making Sense of Section 17: Implementing Services for Children in Need within the 1989 Children Act*. London: HMSO.

Audit Commission (1994) *Seen But Not Heard: Co-ordinating Community Child Health and Social Services for Children in Need*. London: HMSO.

Blunkett, D. (2000) *Influence or irrelevance: Can social science improve government?* Secretary of State's ESRC Lecture. London: ESRC/DFEE.

Bradshaw, J. (1972) The concept of social need. *New Society*, **19**, 640–643.

Cheetham, J., Fuller, R., McIvor, G. and Petch, A. (1992) *Evaluating Social Work Effectiveness*. Buckingham: Open University Press.

DoH (1995) *Child Protection: Messages from Research*. London: Department of Health.

DoH (1999) *A New Approach to Social Services Performance: Consultation Document*. London: Department of Health.

DoH (2000) *A Quality Strategy for Social Care*. London: Department of Health.

Doyal, L. and Gough, I. (1991) *A Theory of Human Need*. Basingstoke: Macmillan.

Ellison, N. and Pierson, C. (Eds) (1998) *Developments in British Social Policy*. Basingstoke: Macmillan.

Fisher, M. (1999) Social work research, social work knowledge and the research assessment exercise. In B. Broad (Ed.), *The Politics of Social Work Research and Evaluation*. Birmingham: Venture Press.

Gibbons, J. (1990) *Family Support and Prevention: Studies in Local Areas*. London: HMSO.

Gibbons, J., Conroy, S. and Bell, C. (1995) *Operating the Child Protection System: A Study of Child Protection Practices in English Local Authorities*. London: HMSO.

Glass, N. (1999) Sure Start: the development of an early intervention programme for young people in the United Kingdom. *Children and Society*, **13**(4), 257–264.

Hardiker, P., Exton, K. and Barker, M. (1991) The social policy contexts of prevention in childcare. *British Journal of Social Work*, **21**, 341–359.

Hearn, B. (1995) *Child and Family Support and Protection: A Practical Approach*. London: National Children's Bureau.

Henricson, C., Katz, I., Mesie, J., Sandison, M. and Tunstill, J. (2001) *National Mapping of Family Services in England and Wales*. London: National Family and Parenting Institute.

Hewitt, M. (1993) Social movements and social need. *Critical Social Policy*, **37**, 52–74.

Kellmer Pringle, M. (1975) *The Needs of Children*. London: Hutchinson.

Knapp, M.R.J. (1984) *The Economics of Social Care*. Basingstoke: Macmillan.

Maslow, A. (1970) *Motivation and Personality*. London: Harper & Row.

Packman, J. (1993) From prevention to partnership: Child welfare services across three decades. *Children and Society*, **7**(2), 183–195.

Parker, R. (1998) Reflections on the assessment of outcomes in child care. *Children and Society*, **12**(3), 192–201.

Parker, R.A., Ward, H., Jackson, S., Aldgate, J. and Wedge, P. (Eds) (1991) *Looking After Children: Assessing Outcomes in Child Care*. London: HMSO.

Pinkerton, J., Higgins, K. and Devine, P. (2000) *Family Support: From Project Evaluation to Policy Analysis*. Aldershot: Ashgate.

Power, M. (1997) *The Audit Society: Rituals of Verification*. Oxford: Oxford University Press.

Rodger, J.R. (1996) *Family Life and Social Control: A Sociological Perspective*. Basingstoke: Macmillan.

Smith, K. and Joshi, H. (2002) The Millennium Cohort Study. *Population Trends, Spring* (107), 30–35: Office for National Statistics.

Smith, T. (1996) *Family Centres and Bringing up Young Children*. London: HMSO.

SSI (1997) *Informing Care. Inspection of Social Services Department Information Strategies and Systems*. Great Britain: Social Services Inspectorate.

Statham, J. (2000) *Outcomes and Effectiveness of Family Support Services: A Research Review*. London: Institute of Education, University of London.

Tisdall, K., Lavery, R. and McCrystal, P. (1998) *The Children (NI) Order 1995 and the Children Scotland Act 1995*. Belfast: CCCR.

Trinder, L. (1996) Social work research: The state of the art (or science). *Child and Family Social Work*, **1**, 233–242.

Trinder, L. and Reynolds, S. (2000) *Evidence Based Practice: A Critical Appraisal*. Oxford. Blackwell.

Tunstill, J. and Aldgate, J. (2000) *Services for Children in Need: from Policy to Practice*. London: TSO.

Ward, H. (ed.) (1995) *Looking after Children: Research into Practice*. London: HMSO.

Weale, A. (1983) *Political Theory and Social Policy*. London: Macmillan.

Wilding, P. (1992) The public sector in the 1990s. *Social Policy Review*, **4**. Canterbury, University of Kent: Social Policy Association.

## Further Reading

Logan, S. and Spencer, N. (1996) Smoking and other health related behaviour in the social and environmental context. *Archives of Disease in Childhood*, **74**, 176–179.

Sinclair, R., Hearn, B. and Pugh, G. (1997) *Preventive Work with Families*. London: National Children's Bureau.

Tunstill, J. (1997) Implementing the family support clauses of the 1989 Children Act: Legislative, professional and organisational obstacles. In N. Parton (Ed.), *Child Protection and Family Support*. London: Routledge.

# 3

# SOCIAL EXCLUSION, FAMILY SUPPORT AND EVALUATION

*Corinne May-Chahal, Ilan Katz and Lorraine Cooper*

Since the groundbreaking work of Bronfenbrenner (1979), the ecological approach has been increasingly important to the understanding of how children develop and the types of interventions which are most likely to benefit their development. There has been a growing awareness that the context in which families live is all-important in developmental outcomes. It is now seen as axiomatic that in order to facilitate changes in the lives of children it is necessary to intervene not only with individual children and families, but to alter their neighbourhoods and the broader society in which they live (Buchanan, 1999). For parents and carers to function effectively they need access to networks of support from friends, neighbours and the extended family. Where the family is vulnerable, it needs support from services provided by professionals and volunteers. There is also an acknowledgement that different sections of the population differ in their access to resources and are excluded from some of the resources available to those living in 'mainstream' society.

Vogelvang (1997) describes the ecological approach as one of the major theoretical underpinnings of family support, but he acknowledges that practitioners struggle with the implications of this theory in the planning and delivery of services. Baldwin and Carruthers (1998) offer examples of research, indicating that 'childcare problems', including high rates of child protection referrals, are common in areas where there are high crime rates, poor school attendance, underachievement, drug use and teenage pregnancies (Brown and Madge, 1982; Essen and Wedge, 1982; Blackburn, 1991; Baldwin and Spencer, 1993; Spencer, 1996; Reading, 1997). These problems in themselves lead to family stress, breakdown and an inability to raise children effectively. 'Considerable evidence exists in research studies that the vast majority of children and households subject to child protection interventions are living

*Evaluating Family Support: Thinking Internationally, Thinking Critically.*
Edited by I. Katz and J. Pinkerton. © 2003 John Wiley & Sons, Ltd.

in poverty and come from the most marginalised and deprived sections of society' (Parton, 1997). Parton is talking about child protection services in the UK, but there is some evidence that these patterns are repeated to a greater or lesser extent across Europe (Pringle, 1998; CAPCAE, 1998). However, the terms 'social exclusion' and 'family support' are not easy to define, and there is little consensus as to their exact nature. This chapter[1] examines the definitions of both 'social exclusion' and 'family support' and reviews what previous research has indicated about the means by which family support can facilitate social inclusion. It then goes on to indicate how this perspective may be relevant to the evaluation of family support.

## FAMILY SUPPORT

Family support can mean anything from financial and/or social protection measures to intensive material and/or practical support with home workers living with a family on a 24-hour basis. A USA perspective is provided by Whittaker (1997), who believes that family support often applies to families with dependent children who are at risk of breakdown through violence and neglect and is generally defined in those terms (see also Pecora, Chapter 5, and Budde, Chapter 12, in this volume). Such definitions place an emphasis on parenting and reflect the legitimisation of family support as being founded in the needs of children. The basic *raison d'être* of family support is seen as the prevention of future difficulties for children. Indeed, as Tunstill (Chapter 2) points out, the term 'family support' is relatively recent, and 'prevention' is one of its more recent predecessors. In the context of demographic changes and social protection policy, therefore, current definitions of family support can unnecessarily restrict what could be a crucial and more comprehensive form of service.

The range of family support services across Europe is vast. Such services can be broadly seen in terms of the 'support' that families require for ensuring the health and well-being of children. This includes financial security, the provision of health, education and welfare services, and the assurance of safe streets, good environments and strong communities. On the other hand, family support may be thought of in terms of specific services which explicitly identify 'support' of families as part of their provision. The term can refer to a specific approach, 'a way of dealing with life crisis and problems, including abuse within families, which takes account of any strengths and positive relationships within these families' (Gardner, 1998). In this approach individuals, families, groups and communities are seen to have inherent strengths and resources that are sometimes negatively affected by internal and environmental forces (Leon, 1999). In the USA, Comer and Fraser suggest that family support is 'rooted more in prevention than in remediation' (1998, p. 134). Some services focus their work on the children, others on the entire family, or indeed the community. Baartman (1997) points out that the term 'family support' suggests a certain homogeneity of methodology, which could not be further from the truth. In distinguishing between different family support programmes he notes that the focus of family support can be broad or narrow, can vary in terms of intensiveness and can be further differentiated according to the professional status of the helper. Currently family support varies both between European member states and within them, with regard to all of these aspects.

Family support narrowly focused on parenting can individualise problems and have a tendency to divert attention towards skill rather than the wider social context. A wider interpretation, however, could play an important role in the development of social inclusion strategies. For example, family support offers a point of access to the most marginalised members of society. Yet by and large the focus of family support has not been on social inclusion as either an aim or a methodology. Holman (1998a) identified reducing inequality and social deprivation as a precondition of effective family support. Gardner (1998) suggests that family support initiatives should recognise that they themselves control resources and have the power to reduce inequality through working in an alliance with wider anti-poverty strategies. Such strategies facilitate social inclusion and are strengthened by models of family support that seek to empower service users, providing a climate or setting in which individuals or groups can take positive action on their own behalf.

Empowering models of family support, which seek to challenge social exclusion, have great potential if these aims are made overt and measurable in programme implementation. This would mean that, in addition to methods aimed at improving parenting, life skills and relationships between family members, a fourth component would be added: methods that promote social inclusion.

## SOCIAL EXCLUSION AND POVERTY

Many have welcomed the use of the term 'social exclusion', as an improvement on the concept of 'poverty'. Many of the characteristics explicitly included in definitions of social exclusion can also be seen to be part of the experience of poverty. However, it can be argued that poverty is an inadequate description of the conditions of the lives of some in society. Some writers have suggested that social exclusion is an extreme form of poverty, stating that the socially excluded are the worst off and the poorest among the poor (Abrahamson, 1996). It has also been argued, however, that there is no clear definition of how social exclusion is distinct from poverty (Levitas, 1999). According to Howarth et al. (1999): 'Poverty and social exclusion are concerned with a lack of possessions, or an inability to do things, that are in some sense considered normal by society as a whole.' Some writers have attempted to identify differences between research into poverty and social exclusion. Room (1998) differentiates between studies of poverty and social exclusion along five dimensions:

- the move from the study of financial indicators to multidimensional disadvantage;
- the move from a static to a dynamic analysis;
- the move from the individual household to the local neighbourhood;
- the move from a distributional to a relational focus;
- the connotation of separation and permanence, and a discontinuity in relationships with the rest of society.

Room argues that the first three aspects have to some extent been explored in more recent studies of poverty and they do not represent a significant departure from the past. However, a significant new emphasis has been the move from a distributional to a relational focus. This interpretation of social exclusion focuses on relational issues—inadequate social participation, lack of social integration and lack of power—rather than concentrating solely on the distribution of wealth. The discontinuity in relationships with the rest of society is also seen as a distinct feature of social exclusion, and he has made a significant contribution to the discussion in a number of areas worth exploring in greater depth. Room (2001) looks in detail at what triggers entry, duration and exit, those events or attributes that exacerbate exclusion or conversely facilitate inclusion. This analysis also creates space for discrimination as a crucial dynamic in the understanding of exclusion.

Perhaps the most fundamental difference between poverty and social exclusion lies in the policies and practices that are developed to combat them. Poverty suggests an extreme lack of economic and material resources and the implied solution is redistribution of financial resources; that is, to raise benefit levels as a means of alleviating financial deprivation (Levitas, 1999). Such a response may not enable people to develop economic or social 'investments' to prepare them to take advantage of opportunities in the future. Social exclusion is distinguishable from poverty in that it is 'dynamic, processual, multidimensional and relational, and it allows space for the understanding that discriminatory and exclusionary practices may be the causes of poverty' (Room, 2001). The implication is that any solution has to take into account such complexities. In line with the ecological approach, solutions can be identified at four levels of intervention: individual, family, community and government. There is a need for action at all levels and from differing sources. Room's analysis adds a dynamic and relational aspect between each of these levels which leads to consideration of the role of family support in facilitating social inclusion.

## CHILDREN, POVERTY AND SOCIAL EXCLUSION

Research indicates that the wider social context is very significant in terms of the safety and well-being of children. Poverty is identified across several studies in the USA as a factor that placed children at risk from neglect (Brassard et al., 1993; Brown et al., 1998; Drake and Pandey, 1996; Coulton et al., 1999; Gable, 1998).[2] There has also been a large body of research in the USA on the adverse outcomes of poverty for children (Brooks-Gunn et al., 1997a, 1997b). In the UK, Brown and Madge (1982) concluded: 'evidence showed that various aspects of harm and social and educational disadvantage were closely connected with the limitations imposed by adverse economic circumstances' (cited in Baldwin and Carruthers, 1998).

Parents living in deprived circumstances find it difficult to meet the needs of their children, and poverty and social exclusion prevent their being able to discharge their parenting role effectively. Poverty, deprivation and social exclusion can be seen to be catapulting children into the 'in need' category (Baldwin and Spencer, 1993; Melton and Barry, 1994).

· Childhood poverty is of particular importance in terms of social policy, not only because children suffer disproportionately to other groups, but also because their experiences of poverty in childhood will have implications for their adult lives: 'Childhood lays the foundations for adult abilities, interests, and motivations and, hence, is the keystone for assuring equal opportunities for adults' (Ashworth et al., 1994, p. 659).

It is evident that to support families effectively one must consider the context in which they are living. Environmental and political processes create and reinforce problems that families encounter (Leon, 1999). The relationships between poverty, self-confidence, parenting skills and the ability to develop and sustain networks of support form complex interactive processes rather than simple causal ones (Dore, 1993). Dore argues that parents who are poor are constantly confronted with their powerlessness in relation to the world. They internalise feelings of inadequacy, which lead to overwhelming anxiety and depression, which in turn affect their ability to fulfil the parenting role. Adverse environment, unabating stressful events and limited internal and external resources undoubtedly are not unconnected and are likely to result in difficulties with parenting.

## CHILD POVERTY IN EUROPE

There are many studies throughout Europe identifying poverty as a feature of childhood for a significant number of children (Leon, 1999; Ashworth et al., 1994). Data on the prevalence of child poverty in EU countries can be found in the Luxembourg Income Survey (LIS) and the European Community

Table 3.1   Percentage of people in poverty in selected
            European countries

| Country | Household | Individuals | Children |
|---|---|---|---|
| Belgium | 13% | 13% | 15% |
| Germany | 13% | 11% | 13% |
| France | 16% | 14% | 12% |
| Ireland | 21% | 21% | 28% |
| Netherlands | 14% | 13% | 16% |
| United Kingdom | 23% | 22% | 32% |

Source: Eurostat (1997) (cited in Bradshaw, 1999).

Household Panel (ECHP); however, the percentage varies significantly between countries (Table 3.1).

Bradshaw (1999) notes that when indicators of non-financial poverty are assessed, there are again differences between the countries, but it is interesting that the average rank is rather different from the indicator of financial poverty derived from the same survey. In particular Luxembourg, The Netherlands and the UK move up the league table, and Denmark and France move down the league table, when a wider range of non-monetary poverty indicators is employed.

The Luxembourg Income Survey looks at the percentage of children in families with incomes below fractions of median income, circa 1990.

Bradshaw (1999) notes that while data sets—such as the Luxembourg Income Survey—which study comparative child poverty may be very useful, they take time to become available. The European Community Household Panel survey is even less up to date.

The UK has suffered more than other countries in relation to the increase in the number of impoverished children as a proportion of the child population (Gregg et al., 1999). There is considerable evidence that, since the late 1970s, children have been the biggest casualties as a result of changes in the economic conditions, demographic structure and social policies of the UK. The overall poverty rate increased from 9% to 25% between 1979 and 1996/7 compared with 10% to 35% for children (Bradshaw, 1999).

Table 3.2   Poverty threshold in selected European countries

| | 40% (ranking) | 50% (ranking) | 60% (ranking) |
|---|---|---|---|
| Belgium | 1.7 (4) | 4.1 (6) | 11.0 (7) |
| France | 4.4 (11) | 8.7 (11) | 15.5 (13) |
| Germany | 2.1 (8) | 4.3 (7) | 11.0 (7) |
| Netherlands | 4.5 (12) | 6.9 (10) | 11.7 (9) |
| United Kingdom | 6.9 (17) | 16.1 (18) | 26.0 (19) |

Source: Eurostat (1997) (cited in Bradshaw, 1999).

## FAMILY SUPPORT AND SOCIAL EXCLUSION

Poverty and problems of social exclusion are thus part of the difficulties faced by a significant number of families in terms of ensuring the health and well-being of their children. What evidence is there that family support services are addressing this? Holman (1988, 1998) identified reducing inequality and social deprivation as a precondition of effective family support. Almost a decade later, Colton and Williams (1997) suggest that the daily agenda for social welfare practitioners in the UK is dominated by the consequences of increasing social polarisation and note that, more than any other factor, poverty threatens the practical achievement of proactive family support services. Those who access family support, irrespective of whether child maltreatment is involved, are more likely to be experiencing poverty (Lloyd, 1996; Comer and Fraser, 1998).

It is suggested that family support initiatives recognise that they themselves control resources and have the power, working in alliance with wider anti-poverty strategies, to reduce inequality. Such strategies go some way towards promoting social inclusion and are strengthened by models of family support that seek to empower service users, providing a climate or setting in which individuals or groups can take positive action on their own behalf (Gardner, 1998). While not all family support services see this as an explicit aim, a number of projects in the USA and in the UK have attempted to take account of environmental stress and disadvantage in developing preventative programmes.

Long (cited in Lloyd, 1996) defined Save the Children centres by their explicit aim to ameliorate poverty. Save the Children centres are not to be viewed within the crisis-oriented model of interventions that offer therapeutic help to families and children in need, but are firmly based within the community development framework. They provide practical responses to locally defined need. The principles of open access, self-referral and user participation are fundamental to this approach. Emphasis is placed on inclusionary strategies in the process of service delivery; how services are provided is as important as what is provided. The anti-poverty strategy that underpins this work has two themes. The services seek to provide better beginnings for children and new opportunities for adults. In this approach social inequality is perceived to lie at the root of social problems, including child abuse. Indeed the challenge to the provision of services by Save the Children has been as a result of the rise in unemployment and child and family poverty (Bradshaw, 1992; Oppenheim, 1994; Lloyd, 1996).

The Springboard Initiative in Ireland is another example of family support (pilot projects) that explicitly identifies problems that families encounter in their wider context. The findings of the current evaluation will be of interest to those concerned with the links between families with difficulties ensuring the health and well-being of their children, the wider context of poverty and social exclusion, and the provision of family support (see Canavan and Dolan, Chapter 13, in this volume).

In 1990 Gibbons et al. found that multiple sources of support, including family, friends, volunteers and, most significantly, day care, helped parents under stress to overcome their problems more easily. This echoes earlier findings of Garbarino (1979) that the existence of accessible support networks provided a protective influence against child abuse in severely disadvantaged neighbourhoods. The research suggested that service users and trained volunteers, backed by welfare rights and legal specialists, offered more appropriate services than social workers.

Schorr (1989) looked at the common elements of successful family support programmes; they included:

- comprehensiveness;
- offering a broad spectrum of services;
- social, emotional, health care, and practical help;
- intensiveness;
- family and community orientation;
- staff with time and skills to develop relationships of trust, respect, collaboration;
- continuity of small committed team;
- support from their organisations to be flexible and cross bureaucratic boundaries;
- the shape of the programme being developed from the needs being served rather than the precepts and the service orientation of professional agencies and their bureaucratic boundaries.

Despite the paucity of research on family support, and despite the differences of definition and scope both within and between countries in Europe, it is becoming increasingly clear that successful family support projects address family problems at a minimum of three levels:

- direct support for children/carers in individual or group sessions that address issues of parenting and family difficulties;
- support for parents which relates to their functioning outside the family— i.e. helping them to develop skills which will enable them to function in the community and the work environment;
- services and activities aimed not at individual families but at changing the context in which socially excluded families have to live.

Programmes which offer only some of these components need to do so in a context in which families have access to the other elements of the overall package.

## PARTICIPATION

In France social exclusion is concerned with a lack of social solidarity in the Durkheimian sense—a break in the bonds between an individual and society. In the 1980s, the term was used to refer to social disintegration, which, if reflected in the rupture in the relationship between the individual and society, might threaten social cohesion (Cousins, 1999).

Elsewhere in Europe social exclusion has been seen as a situation in which people are denied their 'full effective rights of citizenship in the civil political and social spheres' (Lister, 1999). The European Observatory on National Policies for Combating Social Exclusion defines it in relation to 'the social rights of citizenship . . . to a basic standard of living and to participation in the major social and occupational opportunities of the society' (Room, 1993, p. 14). Social exclusion has also been called an 'incomplete citizenship' due to deficiencies in the possession of citizenship rights and inequalities in the status of citizenship. Similarly the European Foundation for the Improvement of Living and Working Conditions (EFILWC) defines social exclusion as 'the denial or restriction of effective participation in economic, social, political and cultural life' (Walker and Walker, 1997; Barry and Hallett, 1998; Stevens et al., 1999). Scherr (1999) notes that 'Anyone who is forced to secure his or her own material and mental survival on a day-to-day basis may not be formally, but is *de facto* prevented to a great extent from actively participating in politics, education, and culture.'

What constitutes social exclusion is dependent on judgements both within and about society in assessing what comprises adequate participation (Gordon, 1998). Moreover Barry (in Barry and Hallett, 1998) has argued that 'participation' itself is an equally elusive and ill-defined concept. Participation can be seen as an end in itself, or as a means to an end, in that it can be used as a vehicle with which to address the problems that lead to social exclusion. One characteristic of socially excluded people is that they are largely excluded from mainstream discussions on exclusion and possible solutions (Croft and Beresford, 1992). If those who are excluded are not represented in the discussion, this mirrors and compounds the problem. People should be 'enabled to develop their own analyses and be part of the broader process of constructing knowledge and developing analysis and critiques' (Barry and Hallett, 1998).

## EMPLOYMENT

The social integrationist discourse argues that integration into the labour market is crucial to combat social exclusion and that paid work is central to this (Levitas, 1999). In the UK it has been argued that the 'New' Labour government has identified integration in the labour market as the primary solution to social exclusion. This reflects a global trend towards labour market inclusion. Some have argued that exclusion from paid work is considered a problem not so much because of the consequences for individuals, but because it threatens social cohesion. Its opposite is not participation but integration—integration through paid work. The political implications of this are that social policies should focus on employment as opposed to welfare initiatives aimed directly at increasing forms of social participation (Gordon, 1998).

Paid work, though important, does not in itself necessarily guarantee an escape from social exclusion. It fails to recognise the experiences of those in poorly paid jobs with poor conditions of work. The very nature of work itself and the conditions can contribute to social exclusion. Moreover, Levitas (1999) argues that inclusion through work policies may in itself be exclusionary, e.g. the economic pressure put on lone mothers to undertake paid work will exclude them from the possibility of full-time parenting. It undervalues other forms of work such as unpaid work in the home, including caring for the dependants, and community and voluntary work (Lister, 1999). Moreover, work may not be the most appropriate answer to the problems encountered by many marginalised groups who cannot work, such as people with disabilities or those who have left the labour market (Barry and Hallett, 1998; Levitas, 1998; Silver, 1994).

Factors related to employability are crucial in determining who escapes from poverty (Room, 2001). Levitas, in her description of the moral underclass discourse, emphasises the moral and cultural causes of poverty, which have been included in the rhetoric from the Social Exclusion Unit in the UK. This identifies individuals as contributors to their own exclusion.

## COMMUNITY

The centrality of the community and/or neighbourhood to the debate has been noted by many authors (Gibbons et al., 1990; Holman, 1994; Forest and Kearns, 1999). The extent to which particular territories or areas are the object of social exclusion, as well as the individuals and groups who live within them, has been documented. In the USA there is now a well-established raft of research that attempts to relate outcomes for children to the characteristics of the community in which they live. The research is largely a response to the writings of Wilson (1987), who claimed that black inner-city children in the USA are increasingly becoming part of an 'underclass' and that this is caused by larger demographic changes such as jobs moving out of the inner cities, black middle-class people leaving for the suburbs and the increasing racial divisions of neighbourhoods. It also shows that although it is beneficial for white teenagers to live in a neighbourhood where there are children from different social strata, the same is not true for black children. Research has studied the use of neighbourhood groups as a preventative resource for exclusion (Holman, 1988; Gibbons et al., 1990). In the UK the government's Social Exclusion Unit has acknowledged the importance of neighbourhoods (SEU, 2001a). Community development is a trend seen throughout Europe (Henderson, 1997). In the UK an increasing amount of research is being conducted into the potential of self-help schemes to combat social exclusion, and research such as that completed by Williams and Winderbank (1999) has found that while there is a considerable amount of unmet need in communities, people are unable to get work done or mutually to support each other because of a lack of money, equipment, time, skills, confidence, physical abilities and social networks, together with a perceived lack of a local sense of community and a mistaken fear of losing benefit entitlement. The researchers concluded that policies were required to help people do more for themselves through 'bottom-up' initiatives, such as Local Exchange Trading Schemes and new 'top-down' initiatives, including reform of the voluntary and community sectors of the New Deal for Communities and the introduction of an Active Citizen Credit scheme, to tackle issues related to benefit entitlement and social exclusion at a local level.

Levitas (1998) suggests that an understanding of 'social' in social exclusion is underdeveloped. She notes that Demos addresses this in terms of networks and social capital. Social capital refers to 'the quality of contacts people have and networks they plug into, the norms of trust, reciprocity and goodwill, the sense of shared life across the classes, and the capacities to organise that these ties afford, or more simply to 'those relationships which provide people with a sense of trust and community'.

Social capital has been described as 'the features of social life networks, norms and trust that enable participants to act together more effectively to pursue shared objectives' (Putnam, 1995). Campbell (1998) identified five aspects of social capital:

- the existence of community networks, which together constitute the civic community in the voluntary state and personal spheres, and the density of networking between these spheres;
- civic identity—people's sense of belonging to the civic community;
- norms governing the functioning of networks, in particular, norms of confidence that others will help and trust others;
- attitudes to networks, positive attitudes to institutions, etc.;
- civic engagement—a contribution to network functioning.

Social capital helps us to understand why people are excluded and to focus on ways in which we can develop community-based responses. Some have argued that those societies with high levels of social policy should be more able to facilitate the development of social capital (Corrigan and King, 1999).

## COMMUNITY AND FAMILY SUPPORT

The model used by Save the Children clearly reflects a community development approach. Community development methods are evidence of a commitment to '...enable people living in poor communities to participate in
projects, and to increase the strengths of such communities by enhancing the
capabilities of individuals to enter into reciprocal exchanges, the basis of a
social network' (Cannan et al., 1992). Save the Children's open access policy
is, according to Lloyd, 'Based on the key principles to offer a variety of provision, flexibility and responsiveness, lack of stigma, participation of users...'
(1996, p. 149). Such family support also offers services to children in need
under the UK Children Act 1989. Nevertheless, their broad range of users
are 'predominantly united by poverty'. The use of family support by parents
who have maltreated their children alongside parents who are merely looking for a means of support is not without problems, and tensions between
these different types of users is illustrated by Lloyd (1996).

In a recent study of Home Start family support services in the UK, it
was found that many of the families availing themselves of support experienced isolation, poverty and housing difficulties. Often families faced multiple stresses (McAuley, 1999). Home Start explicitly encourages families to
widen their network of relationships and to use effectively other support and
services within the community.

It is clear that while facilitating social inclusion as a political activity is
not always an explicit aim of family support initiatives, it is well recognised
that many of the factors that constitute social exclusion also impinge on child
welfare and parenting, and activities to ameliorate such circumstances are
often adopted in service aims.

Recently in the UK, family support has been more explicitly linked with
the reduction of poverty and social exclusion. A number of area-based government initiatives have been started which aim at providing high levels of
service to children and families in poor neighbourhoods. The most developed of these is Sure Start, which is aimed at children under 4 years of age.
Over £1 billion will be spent in 500 neighbourhoods on developing services
for families of children in their early years, reaching a third of all children in
poverty by the year 2005:

> Sure Start is a cornerstone of the Government's drive to tackle child poverty and
> social exclusion. It is based on firm evidence of what works.... They will be con-
> centrated in neighbourhoods where a high proportion of children are living in
> poverty and where Sure Start can help them to succeed by pioneering new ways
> of working to improve services.... Local programmes will work with parents
> and parents-to-be to improve children's life chances through better access to:
>
> • Family support
> • Advice on nurturing
> • Health services
> • Early learning. (Sure Start Unit, 2001)

The theory of change on which the programme is based goes beyond providing extra resources for increased early years services. It is focused on small neighbourhoods, and part of its remit is to impact on the neighbourhood itself. It is also intended to change the way services interact with each other. The programme is managed locally by a partnership of agencies, including the voluntary sector, and partnerships are also required to have representation from users and the local community. The community is also required to be consulted about services. Improved outcomes for children are expected from this combination of more intense service provision, high levels of user involvement and control, improved inter-agency working and impact on the neighbourhood.

Sure Start is being introduced nationally by a large-scale evaluation which includes a longitudinal follow up of a cohort of 10 000 children, an implementation study, and a local context analysis as well as an economic evaluation. Each local programme is also given a budget for local evaluation, which is controlled by the programme itself.

## INEQUALITY OF OPPORTUNITY

It has been noted above that social exclusion is not randomly distributed in societies, and certain groups within society are more likely to be socially excluded than others. It is now well established that people from minority ethnic communities, including migrants and asylum seekers, are more likely than established indigenous populations to be subject to poverty and social exclusion. Research (Butt and Box, 1998) has shown that people from these communities suffer not only from *overt* racism, which marginalises them in their neighbourhoods, but also from *institutional* racism. In comparison with the indigenous population they:

- lack access to the labour market;
- have lower educational attainment and are more likely to be excluded from school;
- live in poorer housing;
- have more health problems but less access to health services;
- are more likely to be involved in the criminal justice system;
- are disproportionately involved in the 'control' aspects of social services (such as being in children's homes or being investigated for child abuse) and less involved with the 'caring' services (such as family support).

The status of immigrants in some European countries may preclude take-up of health or social services.

There is an important gender dimension to the understanding of social inclusion. In the UK lone mothers represent a significantly high proportion of the population who are living in poverty. The barriers to many of these women and their children participating in employment include poor or expensive childcare facilities for young and school-age children, low wages and rigid working conditions that do not allow mothers to exercise their parenting responsibilities at times when children are unwell or when childcare arrangements fall through.

Women are much more likely to be users of family support (and other social services) than men, and more than one author has commented on the difficulty of engaging men in child welfare services (Lazar et al., 1991). This implies that if family support services are successfully to target the social exclusion of their users, then they must refer to the exclusion of women as a specific issue.

## INDICATORS OF SOCIAL EXCLUSION

The selection of indicators to measure social exclusion is an inherently political activity. The indicators that are chosen and are seen as most important depend on views of the nature of social exclusion and its causal links to poverty (Levitas, 1998). This is clearly demonstrated in the indicators identified by the 'New' Labour government in the UK to monitor the progress made in tackling social exclusion. The indicators identified by the UK government (SEU, 2001b) are grouped into four areas for monitoring progress: children and young people, working age, older people, and communities.

Two research studies illustrate the use of indicators to measure social exclusion. The first is the research on Non-Monetary Indicators of Poverty and Social exclusion (NMIPS), where poverty was identified as 'deprivation due to lack of resources' and social exclusion as 'exclusion from basic social systems' (CESIS, 1999). Social systems in the NMIPS research included: social system (family, neighbourhood, society and labour market); economic system; institutional system; territorial system; and symbolic reference system. This research adopts a wider remit of the study of social exclusion which includes relational issues. While it looks at the participation of people in the economic system and the consequential access to monetary resources, it goes beyond this, considering social ties evident within the different social systems of family, neighbourhood and the wider society. It looks at the relationship between institutions and individuals, including political and welfare systems as a source of possible inclusion/exclusion. It considers the territorial system in which an entire area can be the object of social exclusion. Madanipour et al. (1998) refer to acute forms of social exclusion that find a spatial manifestation in neighbourhoods proposing that spatial exclusion is the most visible and evident form of exclusion: 'spatial segregation defines immediate everyday living conditions and determines, at least in part, subsequent life course trajectories. Such determination is a consequence of differential access to spatially defined collective services and in particular schools' (Byrne, 1999, p. 10).

Finally the symbolic reference system is also included. This is concerned with an individual's sense of self, sense of self-esteem and identity, interests, motivations and future prospects. These elements of social exclusion are not mutually exclusive; for some they can be 'joined-up problems'. Nor are they comprehensive, as people who experience social exclusion do not necessarily do so in all spheres.

The second relevant research is by Burchardt et al. (1999), who found five dimensions for older people to be able to participate in society. The research notes that this list is not definitive but that other authors come to similar conclusions (Muffels and Berghman, 1992; Oppenheim, 1994; Paugam, 1995; Walker and Walker, 1997). The dimensions include:

- a reasonable standard of living;
- a degree of security;
- to be engaged in an activity valued by others;
- to have some decision-making power;
- to be able to draw support from immediate family, friends and wider community.

The measures used for these dimensions were based on:

- consumption of minimum level of goods and services considered normal to society;
- possession of accumulated savings, pension entitlements, owning property, participation in growing prosperity;
- engaging in economically or socially valued activity, paid work, education or training, retirement or looking after family;
- political activity, engaging in some collective effort to improve or protect the immediate or wider social and physical environment including voting, membership of political parties, membership of local or national campaigning groups;
- social activity, engaging in significant interaction with family or friends, identifying with a cultural group or community and availability of emotional support.

The research notes that the ability of individuals to participate on each of these dimensions is affected by a wide range of factors, operating at different levels and interacting with one another: individuals' own characteristics (such as health, educational qualifications); events in individuals' lives (such as partnership breakdown, job loss); characteristics of the local neighbourhood (for example, concentration of unemployment, transport links); social/civil/political institutions of society (such as welfare resources, racism).

The extent to which a person is involved in a socially valued activity is very subjective. In the list of valued activities, the research includes being in retirement and looking after a family. Neither of these situations involves economic activity, which is highly valued in western society. The authors differentiate between an individual and societal perspective on this issue. For the individual, self-respect may be generated through being engaged in a culturally valued activity such as looking after a family. But for society as a whole, individuals who are not engaged in productive economic activity can be perceived as a drain on resources. It is difficult for individuals to divorce themselves from the culture to which they belong and thus the value society places on activities inevitably leads to feelings of exclusion or inclusion. While resources are narrowly defined as having the potential to generate money, as opposed to human resources which improve the quality of life for people and cannot be costed in monetary terms, exclusion will result.

## RESPONSIBILITY FOR SOCIAL EXCLUSION

Any methods for promoting social inclusion must address the issue of where responsibility for change lies. In some conceptions of social exclusion it is thought to be individuals not systems that require change. It has also been argued within the UK that the drive to tackle social exclusion is not adequately funded or resourced and is more concerned with building the capacity and resilience of excluded people and their families, thus enabling them to take on more responsibility. One could argue that the term clearly puts the responsibility on to individuals and releases the government from its obligations.

Veit-Wilson (1998) distinguishes between 'weak' and 'strong' versions of social exclusion. In the 'weak' version the solutions lie in altering excluded people's disabling characteristics and enhancing their integration into dominant society. This does not take account of discrimination. The 'strong' version considers who is doing the excluding and therefore aims for solutions that reduce the powers of exclusion. In the 'weak' version, inclusion is accomplished through changing individuals, whereas the 'strong' version is about change at societal level. An ecological approach to promoting inclusion would have to work at both individual and societal levels, and family support can have an important role here. At an individual level it can raise confidence and self-esteem, promoting inclusion by signposting users to other services, including employment and childcare, and at a local community level by promoting community involvement and building up networks.

Since social exclusion is recognised as being the effect of a combination of linked problems, any means of facilitating inclusion will have to reflect this complexity. Family support services may be best placed to facilitate inclusion at a number of levels. Leon (1999) prefers a biopsychosocial approach, which asserts that client problems are complex, usually involve more than one aspect of client functioning and require multidimensional interventions that address the whole client system.

The cycle of disadvantage studies (Brown and Madge, 1982) challenged ideas that personal factors should be the main focus of intervention in improving social behaviour. Problems in behaviour were shown to be linked to continuities of a harmful environment more than personal characteristics.

What professionals, academics and policy makers define as social exclusion determines the solutions that are thought to be required to resolve the problem. This is also true in relation to poverty. The preferred definition of social exclusion will be mirrored in how it is measured (Levitas, 1999). This is illustrated by looking at the indicators currently identified by the 'New' Labour government in the UK. Levitas uses three models to illustrate how social exclusion is construed. Silver (1994) has distinguished a three-fold typology of social exclusion based on different theoretical perspectives, political ideologies and national discourses. Levitas refers to the:

- Redistributive Discourse (RED)
- Social Integrationist Discourse (SID)
- Moral Underclass Discourse (MUD).

These are models which, as she points out, in reality, often combine to some extent. The redistributive discourse (RED) sees social exclusion as a consequence of poverty. Lack of resources prevents individuals from carrying out social obligations such as parenting. This model assumes that it is essential to raise benefit levels to combat social exclusion. However, one could argue that while welfare systems to a greater or lesser degree (many would suggest the latter) protect against 'interrupted consumption', they largely ignore enabling people to develop 'investments' to prepare them to take advantage of opportunities in the future.

The social integrationist discourse (SID) asserts that the aim of policy is not merely wealth redistribution, but that social exclusion can only be combated by taking active steps to integrate marginalised individuals and communities into society. Community cohesion, antidiscriminatory legislation, improved transport and wider access to services are seen as essential components of the overall strategy. Mainstream institutions such as work practices, police attitudes and lack of access to culture are seen as barriers for these individuals and communities to participate in society and improve their financial situation.

The moral underclass discourse (MUD) places some of the blame for social exclusion on the individuals and groups who are excluded. Single parents, for example, are seen as having chosen a lifestyle which commits their children to low socio-economic status. This view also places responsibility on immigrants to learn the language of their host country. Failure to do so is seen as their responsibility and therefore they are partly blamed for economic failure and racism. A more benign form of this discourse asserts that social exclusion is always a two-way process, and that while it is the primary responsibility of mainstream society to ensure that social institutions are as inclusive as possible, it is also the responsibility of members of marginalised communities to engage with society as much as possible.

## COMPARATIVE STUDIES

Comparative studies in the area of social welfare systems have tended to be descriptive 'holistic' overviews of the welfare systems of different countries or collections of countries (Sale and Davies, 1990; Esping-Anderson, 1990; Fox-Harding, 1996; Pringle, 1998), or statistical comparisons that relate the numbers of children in care, court proceedings, etc. (Ruxton, 1996). In the 1990s a number of studies attempted in various ways to compare the actual practice of professionals in different countries and to relate their practice to the systems and structures of the countries in which they work (Cooper et al., 1995, 1997; Hetherington et al., 1997; Wattam, 1999). These studies have tended to focus on 'child protection' rather than 'family support'—i.e. on the 'control' rather than the 'care' elements of child welfare. The findings of these studies are fairly consistent—that child welfare systems in continental Europe are based on solidarity and subsidiarity, as opposed to the rights-based systems characteristic of Anglo-Saxon countries. The implications are that the continental systems tend, paradoxically, to be more interventionist but less confrontational than the Anglo-Saxon systems, and that, consequently, welfare systems are viewed more positively by their users and potential users despite more children spending time in care on the continent. Another difference was that in continental Europe, the divide between 'child protection' on the one hand, and 'family support' on the other, is not as rigid as that in Anglo-Saxon countries. In the UK there is a distinct child protection system, whereas, for example, in Belgium children are referred to social services because of a problematic upbringing (see Cooper et al., 1997). However, in recent years there seems to be a convergence in most of Europe, with concern being expressed in several countries that resources are being cut, and that more and more attention is being paid to investigating child protection as opposed to providing long-term support for high-risk families. An added shared European dimension, which has been little studied, is that there could be a widening gap between services available to citizens and those for migrants and asylum seekers.

## IMPLICATIONS FOR EVALUATION

Although the ecological approach is now the orthodox theoretical underpinning for much of the thinking about family support, it is not clear that these theories have fully taken into account the implications of this approach to research and evaluation in this area. Similarly, poverty and social exclusion are seldom addressed as specific foci for evaluations of family support, although they are part of the hidden backdrop to the research.

It is therefore important for evaluators to develop ways of measuring the extent to which family support actually addresses the issues of poverty and social exclusion at the individual level. One way of doing this is through cost-effectiveness evaluations, where part of the effectiveness of the intervention is the job status and remuneration of the child when he or she reaches employment. However, this is a very narrow focus on economic benefit and is also expensive and long term. More realistically for most evaluations, short-term changes in the employment/income of parents can be studied, along with the usual measures of user satisfaction and child functioning. Measuring social capital and social exclusion would be more complex. Burke et al. (2001) identified several dimensions which could potentially be used by evaluators to measure social inclusion at the individual level. These factors include:

- number, intensity and duration of social networks
- access to informal and formal support
- control over own lives
- feeling safe in the community
- involvement in community organisations
- experiences of racism or other forms of discrimination.

Research mirrors practice in tending to see poverty, social exclusion and neighbourhood deprivation as the context or environment (or in research terms, the independent variable or input) in which the programme is operating, rather than the object of the work or the evaluation (the dependent variable or outcome).

Outcome research tends to focus on the impact of the service on individual children and their parents (usually mothers). Sometimes the wider family is also studied, but evaluation seldom focuses on the impact of the programme on the neighbourhood as a whole. The research question would have to be widened from asking the extent to which the programme reduced the amount of social exclusion for children who were service users. The question would have to become: To what extent did the programme reduce social exclusion of children and families in the local neighbourhood?

Such evaluations would try to establish a baseline and follow-up data about such issues as:

- the amount of graffiti on walls in the area
- crime statistics for the neighbourhood
- children excluded from school
- racist attacks on children in the neighbourhood
- access for disabled children to leisure activities
- access for all children in the neighbourhood to social facilities
- evidence of feeling safe.

Some evaluations, such as the Sure Start national evaluation, are beginning to tackle these issues (see www.bbk.ac.uk/ness), but this analysis still presents major problems for evaluation of neighbourhood-based programmes which largely depend on measured impacts on users of family support services as their major source of data. Consider the following example:

> D, a 3-year-old child with disruptive behaviour, attends a family support pro-
> gramme with his mother. His behaviour improves, but not significantly as mea-
> sured by the Strengths and Difficulties Scale. At his kindergarten his teacher is
> able to give him less attention and devotes more attention to G and H, two other
> children who have not attended the programme. Their behaviour improves con-
> siderably owing to the teacher's attention. They are part of the control group.

This research would show that (at least some of) the control group benefited more than the experimental group and might therefore conclude that the intervention was not effective. However, this would be a wrong interpretation of the effects of the intervention. If the programme explicitly adopts a social exclusion/inclusion focus, this type of indirect effect on non-users will be increased, and it may not be valid to contrast 'users' and 'non-users' of the programme.

Another facet of this community orientation relates to evaluations of the implementation or processes of the programme. It is important in any such evaluation to focus on the process by which the project has been set up, and the degree to which this process is congruent with the promotion of social inclusion in the local community. It is also crucial to place the particular family support project in the context of other local programmes to combat social exclusion.

The list of community level measures could include measures about agency function such as:

- the degree of 'joined upness' in the working of local statutory agencies and NGOs;
- the degree to which community members are able to influence the development of local services;
- the degree to which services are based on an assessment of local needs;
- the level of knowledge of local residents about the range of services available to them.

Of course there are some issues that are known to be associated with social exclusion which family support cannot address directly, although service organisations can press for change. For example, access to transport is known to be associated with social exclusion, but it is unlikely that family support projects will directly address the provision of public transport to a local neighbourhood.

A third area relevant to evaluation is the need to situate family support within the larger policy context in relation to social exclusion. Measures to combat social exclusion of children and families include such factors as changes to the benefit and employment systems, urban regeneration programmes, health and education initiatives, crime reduction programmes, etc. Family support projects will interact with these other initiatives and programmes at the local level, but there is much potential for involving family support in policy evaluations of social exclusion and vice versa.

Finally there is the question of ethics and involvement. It is not good enough for evaluations to measure social inclusion, as evaluation itself can either increase or decrease social exclusion. Guba and Lincoln (1989) place user empowerment at the centre of evaluation, and while this is not always possible, evaluations of family support should at the very least not increase the exclusion of users.

## CONCLUSION

The study of social exclusion and family support have different historic roots, and come from different academic traditions. While family support is mostly targeted at the most deprived families and neighbourhoods, family support programmes seldom identify combating social exclusion as a specific aim. Evaluations of family support, while paying lip service to the ecological model, tend to focus on individual outcomes for children and families. They do not tend to address the issues of the reduction of poverty and social exclusion, nor do they focus on neighbourhood or community variables as core outcomes for family support. Yet many of the activities that constitute family support can lead to the reduction of poverty and social exclusion, and family support projects often engage with communities and neighbourhoods.

We suggest here that these issues should be made more explicit in the aims of family support programmes, and that evaluative methodologies should be developed which are able to address the complexities of measuring social exclusion at both the individual and the community level. This will require rethinking some of the assumptions behind the practice and evaluation of these programmes.

## NOTES

1. This chapter is based on a research project which looked at the relationship between family support and social exclusion in four European countries: England, Belgium, France, and the Netherlands (Burke et al., 2001).
2. See Hooper (2002) for a review of the literature on poverty and child abuse.

## REFERENCES

Abrahamson, P. (1996) *Social Exclusion in Europe: Old Wine in New Bottles*. Paper presented at ESF Conference 26–30 March 1996, Blarney, Ireland.
Ashworth, K., Hill, M. and Walker, R. (1994) Patterns of childhood poverty: New challenges for policy. *Journal of Policy Analysis and Management*, **13**(4), 658–680.

Baartman, H.E.M. (1997) Home-based services: To each his own? In W. Hellinckx, M. Colton and M. Williams (Eds), *International Perspectives on Family Support*. Aldershot: Arena.

Baldwin, N. and Carruthers, L. (1998) *Developing Neighbourhood Support and Child Protection Strategies. The Henley Safe Project*. Aldershot: Ashgate.

Baldwin, N. and Spencer, N.J. (1993) Deprivation and child abuse: Implications for strategic planning in children's services. *Children in Society*, **7**(4).

Barry, M. and Hallett, C. (eds) (1998) *Social Exclusion and Social Work Issues of Theory, Policy and Practice*. Lyme Regis: Russell House Publishing Limited.

Blackburn, C. (1991) Family poverty: What can health visitors do? *Health Visitor*, **64**, 11.

Bradshaw, J. (1992) *Child Poverty and Deprivation in the UK*. London: National Children's Bureau for UNICEF.

Bradshaw, J. (1999) Child poverty in comparative perspective. A conference paper given at *Developing Poverty Measures: Research in Europe Defining and Measuring Poverty*. University of Bristol, 1 and 2 July 1999.

Brassard, M., Hart, S. and Hardy, D. (1993) The psychological maltreatment rating scale. *Child Abuse and Neglect*, **17**, 715–729.

Bronfenbrenner, U. (1979) *The Ecology of Human Development: Experiments by Nature and Design*. Cambridge, Mass.: Harvard University Press.

Brooks-Gunn, J., Aber, L. and Duncan, G. (1997a) *Neighborhood Poverty Volume 1: Context and Consequences for Children*. New York: Russell Sage Foundation.

Brooks-Gunn, J., Aber, L. and Duncan, G. (1997b) *Neighborhood Poverty Volume 2: Policy Implications in Studying Neighborhoods*. New York: Russell Sage Foundation.

Brown, J., Cohen, P., Johnson, J. and Salzinger, S. (1998) A longitudinal analysis of risk factors for child maltreatment: Findings of a 17 year prospective study of officially reported and self reported child abuse and neglect. *Child Abuse and Neglect*, **22**(11), 1065–1078.

Brown, M. and Madge, N. (1982) *Despite the Welfare State*. London: Heinemann Educational Books.

Buchanan, A. (1999) *What Works for Troubled Children?* Family support for children with emotional and behavioural problems. Essex: Barnardos.

Burchardt, T., LeGrand, J. and Piachaud, D. (1999) Social exclusion in Britain 1991–1995. *Social Policy & Administration*, **33**(3), 227–244.

Burke, J., Cooper, L. Katz, I. and Wattam, C. (2001) *Social Inclusion and Family Support: A Survey of Six Countries*. London: NSPCC; University of Central Lancashire (UCLAN).

Butt, J. and Box, L. (1998) *Family Centred: A Study of the Use of Family Centres by Black Families*. London: Race Equality Unit.

Byrne, D. (1999) *Social Exclusion*. Buckingham: OUP.

Campbell, C. (1998) *Social Capital and Health*. London: HDA.

Cannan, C., Berry, L. and Lyons, K. (1992) *Social Work in Europe*. Basingstoke: Macmillan.

CAPCAE (1998) *Moving Towards Effective Prevention Strategies for Child Abuse in Europe*. http://www.uclan.ac.uk/facs/health/socwork/research/units/child/index.htm

CESIS (1999) *Non-Monetary Indicators of Poverty and Social Exclusion*. Report commissioned by Eurostat. Centro de Estudos para a Intervencao Social.

Colton, M. and Williams, M. (1997) Supporting children in need and their families through a change in legislation: A case study based on the impact of the Children Act in England and Wales. In W. Hellinckx, M. Colton and M. Williams (Eds), *International Perspectives on Family Support*. Aldershot: Arena.

Comer, E.W. and Fraser, M.W. (1998) Evaluation of six family support programs: Are they Effective? *Families in Society; The Journal of Contemporary Human Services*, **79**(2), 134–147.

Cooper, A., Hetherington, R. and Katz, I. (1997) *A Third Way? A European Perspective on the Child Protection/Family Support Debate*. NSPCC; Brunel University. Department of Social Work. London: NSPCC.

Cooper, A., Hetherington, R., Baistow, K., Pitts, J. and Spriggs, A. (1995) *Positive Child Protection: A View from Abroad*. Lyme Regis: Russell House Publishing.

Corrigan, P. and King, E. (1999) Cash in on social capital. *Local Government Chronicle*, 13/8/1999.

Coulton, C., Korbin, J. and Su, M. (1999) Neighborhoods and child maltreatment: A multi-level study. *Child Abuse and Neglect*, **23**(11), 1019–1040.

Cousins, C. (1999) Social exclusion in Europe: Paradigms of social disadvantage in Germany, Spain, Sweden, and the United Kingdom. *Social Policy and Politics*, **26**(2), 127–146.

Croft, S. and Beresford, P. (1992) The politics of participation. *Critical Social Policy*, **35**, 20–44.

Dore, M. (1993) Family preservation and poor families: When 'Homebuilding' is not enough. *Families in Society*, **74**, 545–556.

Drake, B. and Pandey, S. (1996) Understanding the relationship between neighbourhood and specific types of child maltreatment? *Child Abuse and Neglect*, **20**(11), 1003–1018.

Esping-Anderson, G. (1990) *The Three Worlds of Welfare Capitalism*. Princeton, NJ: Princeton University Press.

Essen, J. and Wedge, P. (1982) *Continuities in Childhood Disadvantage*. London: Heinemann Educational Books.

Forrest, R. and Kearns, A. (1999) *Joined-up Places? Social Cohesion and Neighbourhood Regeneration*. York: Joseph Rowntree Foundation.

Fox-Harding, L.M. (1996) *Family, State and Social Policy*. Basingstoke: Macmillan.

Gable, S. (1998) School age and adolescent children's perceptions of family functioning in neglectful and non-neglectful families. *Child Abuse and Neglect*, **22**(9), 859–867.

Garbarino, J. (1979) Assessing the neighbourhood context of child maltreatment. *Child Abuse and Neglect*, **3**, 1059–1069.

Gardner, R. (1998) *Family Support Practitioners Guide*. Birmingham: Venture Press.

Gibbons, J., Thorpe, S. and Wilkinson, P. (1990) *Family Support and Prevention: Studies in Local Areas*. NISW Crown Publications.

Gordon, D. (1998) Definitions of concepts for the perceptions of poverty and social exclusion. In J. Bradshaw, D. Gordon, R. Levitas, S. Middleton, C. Pantazis, S. Payne and P. Townsend (Eds), *Perceptions of Poverty and Social Exclusion 1998. Report on Prepaparatory Research*. Bristol: Townsend Centre for International Poverty Research.

Gregg, P., Harkness, S. and Machin, S. (1999) Poor kids: Child poverty in the United Kingdom. *Children's Rights*, **161**, 4–6.

Guba, E.G. and Lincoln, Y.S. (1989) *Fourth Generation Evaluation*. Newbury Park, CA: Sage.

Henderson, P. (1997) Community involvement in Europe: Pushing at an open door? *Social Work in Europe*, **4**(2).

Hetherington, R., Cooper, A., Smith, P. and Wilford, G. (1997) *Protecting Children: Messages from Europe*. Lyme Regis: Russell House.

Holman, B. (1994) Research review: Children and poverty. *Children and Society*, **8**(1), 69–72.

Holman, B. (1988) *Putting Families First: Prevention and Child Care*. London: Macmillan.
Holman, B. (1998) From children's departments to family departments. *Child and Family Social Work*, **3**, 205–211.
Hooper, C.-A. (2002) Maltreatment of children. In Bradshaw, J. (Ed.) *The Well-being of Children in the UK*. London: Save the Children.
Howarth, C., Kenway, P., Palmer, G. and Miorelli, R. (1999) *Monitoring Poverty and Social Exclusion*. York: Joseph Rowntree.
Lazar, A., Sagi, A. and Fraser, M. (1991) Involving fathers in social services. *Children and Youth Services Review*, **13**(4) 287–300.
Leon, A.M. (1999) Family support model: Integrating service delivery in the twenty-first century. *Families in Society; The Journal of Contemporary Human Services*, **80**(1), 14–24.
Levitas, R. (1998) *The Inclusive Society? Social Exclusion and New Labour*. Basingstoke: Macmillan.
Levitas, R. (1999) *What is Social Exclusion?* International Conference Series on Developing Poverty Measures: Research in Europe.
Lister, R. (1999) First steps to a fairer society. *The Guardian*, 9 June 1999.
Lloyd, E. (1996) The role of the centre in family support. In C. Cannan and C. Warren (eds), *Social Action with Children and Families*. London: Routledge.
Madanipour, A., Cars, G. and Allen, J. (Eds) (1998) *Social Exclusion in European Cities. Processes, Experiences and Responses*. London: Jessica Kingsley Publishers.
McAuley, C. (1999) *The Family Support Outcomes Study: Home Start*, UK.
Melton, G.B. and Barry, F.D. (1994) *Protecting Children from Child Abuse and Neglect: Foundations for a New National Strategy*. New York: Guilford Press.
Muffels, R. and Berghman, J. (1992) *The incidence and evolution of poverty in the '80s*. Working papers of the European Scientific Network on Household Panel Studies, 24. Walferdange, Colchester: European Science Foundation, Scientific Network on Household Panel Studies.
Oppenheim, C. (1994) *The Welfare State: Putting the Record Straight*. London: Child Poverty Action Group.
Parton, N. (ed.) (1997) *Child Protection and Family Support. Tensions, Contradictions and Possibilities*. London: Routledge.
Paugam, S. (1995) The spiral of precariousness: A multidimensional approach to the process of social disqualification in France. In G. Room (Ed.), *Beyond the Threshold: The Measurement and Analysis of Social Exclusion*. Bristol: Policy Press.
Pringle, K. (1998) *Children and Social Welfare in Europe*. Buckingham: Open University.
Putnam, D. (1995) *Making Democracy Work. Civic Traditions in Modern Italy*. New Jersey: University Press.
Reading, R. (1997) Poverty and the health of children and adolescents. *Archive of Disease in Childhood*, **76**(5), 463–467.
Room, G. (1993) *Agencies, Institutions, and Programmes: Their Interrelationships and Co-ordination in Efforts to Combat Social Exclusion*. Luxembourg: European Observatory on National Policies to Combat Social Exclusion, Office for Official Publications of European Communities.
Room, G. (1998) *Social Exclusion, Solidarity and the Challenge of Globalisation*. University of Bath: Bath Social Policy Papers No. 27.
Room, G. (2001) Trajectories of social exclusion: The wider context. In D. Gordon and P. Townsend (Eds), *Breadline Europe*. Bristol: Policy Press.
Ruxton, S. (1996) *Children in Europe*. London: NCH Action for Children.
Sale, A. and Davies, M. (Eds) (1990) *Child Protection Policies and Practice in Europe*. London: NSPCC.

Scherr, A. (1999) Transformations in social work: From help towards social inclusion to the management of exclusion. *European Journal of Social Work*, **2**(1), 15–25.

Schorr, L. (1989) *Within our Reach: Breaking the Cycle of Disadvantage*. Almeda: RAND.

SEU (2001a) *National Strategy for Neighbourhood Renewal*. Social Exclusion Unit http://www.cabinet-office.gov.uk/seu/index/national_strategy.htm

SEU (2001b) *Preventing Social Exclusion*. Report by the Social Exclusion Unit. London: Cabinet Office.

Silver, H. (1994) Social exclusion and social solidarity: Three paradigms. *International Labour Review*, **133**(5–6), 531–578.

Spencer, N. (1996) *Poverty and Child Health*. Oxford: Radcliffe Medical Press.

Stevens, A., Bur, A.M. and Young, L. (1999) Partial, unequal and conflictual: Problems in using participation for social inclusion in Europe. *Social Work in Europe*, **6**(2).

Sure Start Unit (2001) *What is Sure Start?* http://www.surestart.gov.uk/aboutWhatis.cfm?section=2

Veit-Wilson, J. (1998) *Setting Adequacy Standards*. Bristol: Policy Press.

Vogelvang, B. (1997) In W. Hellinckx, M. Colton and M. Williams (Eds), *International perspectives on Family Support*. Aldershot: Arena.

Walker, A. and Walker, C. (Eds) (1997) *Britain Divided: The Growth of Social Exclusion in the 1980's and 1990's*. London: Child Poverty Action Group.

Wattam, C. (1999) *Family support, prevention and child abuse*. Unpublished paper presented to the SIFS project workshop, March 1999.

Whittaker, J.K. (1997) Intensive family preservation work with high risk families: Critical challenges for research, clinical intervention and policy. In W. Hellinckx, M. Colton and M. Williams (Eds), *International Perspectives on Family Support*. Aldershot: Arena.

Williams, C. and Winderbank, J. (1999) *Informal Employment in the Advanced Economies: Implications for Work and Welfare*. London: Routledge.

Wilson, W.J. (1987) *The Truly Disadvantaged: The Inner City, the Underclass, and Public Policy*. Chicago: University of Chicago Press.

## Further Reading

Abrahamson, P. and Hansen, F.K. (1996) *Poverty in the European Union*. European Parliament, Brussels.

Anderson, B. (1998) Mobilising local communities. *Young Minds Magazine*, May/June **34**, 16–18.

Batchelor, J., Gould, N. and Wright, J. (1999) Family centres: A focus for the children in need debate. *Child and Family Social Work*, **4**, 197–208.

Butler, I. and Roberts, G. (1997) *Social Work with Children and Families*. London: Jessica Kingsley.

Cheetham, J. and Fuller, R. (1998) Social exclusion and social work: Policy, practice and research. In M. Barry and C. Hallett (Eds), *Social Exclusion and Social Work Issues of Theory, Policy and Practice*. Lyme Regis: Russell House Publishing Limited.

Coohey, C. (1995) Neglectful mothers, their mothers, and partners: The significance of mutual aid. *Child Abuse and Neglect*, **19**(8), 885–895.

DoH (1989) *The Children Act*. London: Department of Health.

Dominelli, L. (1999) Neo-liberalism, social exclusion and welfare clients in a global economy. *International Journal of Social Work*, **8**, 14–22.

DSS: *Opportunity For All—Tackling Poverty and Social Exclusion*. Government Report. http://www.dss.gov.uk/hq/pubs/poverty/main/chapt2b.htm

Golding, P. (1986) *Excluding the Poor*. London: Child Poverty Action Group.

Gore, C. (1995) Introduction: Markets, citizenship and social exclusion. In G. Rodgers, C. Gore and J.B. Figueiredo (Eds), *Social Exclusion: Rhetoric, Reality, Responses*. Geneva: International Institute for Labour Studies, International Labour Organisation.

Hall, P.A. (1997) *Social Capital: A Fragile Asset in the Wealth and Poverty of Networks. Tackling Social Exclusion*. London: Demos Collection Issue 12.

Hargreaves, R.G. and Hadlow, J. (1995) Preventative intervention as a working concept in child-care practice. *British Journal of Social Work*, **25**, 349–365.

Heron, E. and Dwyer, P. (1999) Doing the right thing: Labour's attempt to forge a new welfare deal between the individual and the state. *Social Policy and Administration*, **33**(1), 91–104.

Home Office (1998) *Supporting Families: A Consultation Document*. Home Office. http://www.homeoffice.gov.uk/acu/suppfam.htm

Housden, P. (1997) Involve society in solutions. *Local Government Chronicle*, 31/10/1997.

Howze Browne, D. (1986) The role of stress in the commission of subsequent acts of child abuse and neglect. *Journal of Family Violence*, **1**(4).

Johnson, D. (1999) Centred on the family. *Community Care*, 28 January–3 February.

Lister, R. (1998) Citizenship on the margins: Citizenship, social work and social action. *European Journal of Social Work*, **1**(1), 5–18.

Little, M. and Mount, K. (1999) *Prevention and Early Intervention with Children in Need*. Aldershot: Ashgate Publishing Limited.

National Evaluation of Sure Start (2001) Methodology Reports. www.bbk.ac.uk/ness/reports.htm

Peri 6 (1997a) *Escaping Poverty from Safety Nets and Networks of Opportunity*. London: Demos.

Peri 6 (1997b) Social exclusion: Time to be optimistic. In *The Wealth and Poverty of Networks: Tackling Social Exclusion*. London: Demos Collection Issue 12.

Robbins, D. (1998) Social exclusion explained. *Family Policy Bulletin*, Autumn 1997/1998.

Room, G. (1993) *Anti-Poverty Action Research*. Bristol: SAUS Publications.

Room, G. (ed.) (1995) *Beyond the Threshold. The Measurement and Analysis of Social Exclusion*. Bristol: Policy Press.

RTC (1999) *Towards a Europe For All: How Should the Community Support Member States to Promote Social Inclusion*. Report on Round Table Conference. Brussels, 6–7 May, 1999.

Scholte, E.M., Colton, M., Casas, F., Drakeford, M., Roberts, S. and Williams, M. (1999) Perceptions of stigma and user involvement in child welfare services. *British Journal of Social Work*, **29**, 373–391.

Schneider, J.A. (1997) Welfare-to-network. In *The Wealth and Poverty of Networks: Tackling Social Exclusion*. London: Demos Collection Issue 12.

Sinclair, R., Hearn, B. and Pugh, G. (1997) *Preventative Work with Families*. London: National Children's Bureau.

Stepney, P., Lynch, R. and Jordan, B. (1999) Poverty, exclusion and New Labour. *Critical Social Policy*, **19**(1), 109–127.

Street, C. (1999) Monitoring poverty and social exclusion among children and young adults. *Young Minds Magazine*, January/February, **38**, 20.

Sutton, C. (1999) *Helping Families with Troubled Children*. Chichester: John Wiley & Sons.

Tracy, E.M. and Whittaker, J.K. (1990) The social network map: Assessing social support in clinical practice. *Families in Society; The Journal of Contemporary Human Services*, **41**(8), 461–470.

Van den Bogaart, P. (1997) The application of intensive programs: Hometraining in the Netherlands. Evaluation and its impact on practice. In W. Hellinckx, M. Colton and M. Williams (Eds), *International Perspectives on Family Support*. Aldershot: Arena

Wainwright, S. (1999) Anti-poverty strategies: Work with children and families. *British Journal of Social Work*, **29**, 477–483.

Young, J. (1999) *The Exclusive Society*. London: Sage.

# 4

# THE VALUE OF RESILIENCE AS A KEY CONCEPT IN EVALUATING FAMILY SUPPORT

*Robbie Gilligan*

Resilience as a concept has attracted increasing attention from researchers and practitioners in the child and family field in recent years. In this chapter, it will be argued that resilience provides a useful perspective from which to engage with the issues in evaluating family support intervention. With such global concepts as resilience and family support, it is clearly necessary to look at their constituent elements when addressing their relevance to the design and conduct of evaluation. The chapter will set out key aspects of resilience and family support and then suggest how evaluation might be applied to family support with the aid of a resilience lens. The chapter marshals insights from a range of sources with the aim of sharpening understanding of how a resilience-led perspective can enhance practice and evaluation in family support.

## WHAT IS RESILIENCE?

Resilience refers to a dynamic process encompassing positive adaptation within the context of significant adversity. It has been suggested that there are implicit within this notion two critical conditions (Luthar, Cicchetti and Becker, 2000, p. 543):

- exposure to significant threat or severe adversity;
- achievement of positive adaptation despite major assaults on the developmental process.

*Evaluating Family Support: Thinking Internationally, Thinking Critically.*
Edited by I. Katz and J. Pinkerton. © 2003 John Wiley & Sons, Ltd.

From that perspective, it can be seen that three elements are essential to understanding resilience. Resilience arises from a 'process' and results in 'positive adaptation' in the face of 'adversity'. A person may display resilience in the face of adversity in three different ways: by 'overcoming the odds . . . [or] sustaining competence under pressure . . . [or] recovering from trauma' (Fraser, Richman and Galinsky, 1999, p. 136). One issue not easily resolved because of differing views among scholars is the extent of positive adaptation implied in the use of the term resilience. Is it to be judged by a high degree of success, or reasonable functioning, or survival or even a moderation of the degree of adverse developmental trajectory in the face of stressors?

In considering the concept of resilience it is important to appreciate that it is not to be seen as a personality characteristic. Resilience should not be seen as residing in an individual as a fixed quality. Rather it may be considered as deriving from a process of repeated interactions between the person and facets of the surrounding context in that individual's life. It may be more helpful and accurate to think of a person's, and particularly a child's, trajectory of development displaying resilience at certain points or over certain periods. In other words, the trajectory of development in a given phase is more favourable than might be expected given the adverse circumstances. It may also be the case that an individual may display resilience in one domain of functioning, for example a child in school, and yet not in another, for example the same child at home. The cases described below (from Gilligan, 2001) serve to illustrate this point.

*Case Illustration 4.1*
'Charlie' is a successful boxer whose sporting prowess features regularly in the regional media in the area in which he lives. He is the eldest in his family and has effectively reared the other six children on his own from his mid-20s because of family circumstances and is generally regarded as doing a very good job of it.

When 'Charlie' was 11 years old home life was difficult and he was on the fringe of a lot of trouble with the law. His father had a serious heroin problem and a history of crime. But at that time 'Charlie' also had an interest and a talent for boxing and received the advice and strong encouragement of a boxing coach.

It is 'Charlie's' own view that the relationship he had with his boxing coach changed the course of his life—and indirectly it seems the lives of his younger siblings (Example shared by a workshop participant)

*Case Illustration 4.2*
A teenager living on a very deprived public housing estate in a largish town had a father who was frequently in prison and a mother who was chemically dependent. She was doing poorly in school and seemed a likely candidate for early drop out. Out of the blue she made a positive connection with a new young English teacher. With her encouragement and support, the girl caught up and is now talking seriously, and realistically, about studying law at university.
                              (Personal communication from a workshop participant)

*Case Illustration 4.3*
From the start S (foster mother) would bring me up to the tennis courts, sometimes with a school friend, and we would play simple tennis games until I

got the hang of the skills. For many years the local tennis club provided a social as well as a sporting environment for me—I befriended many people, some my own age, some a good deal older—whom I still keep in touch with. I also went on to coach in the local Tennis League for a few years as well as coaching in a camp in the US for the summer.

(Personal communication from a contented graduate of foster care)

## WHAT IS FAMILY SUPPORT?

For the purpose of our discussion we may take family support to mean social support delivered in, through, or for the family—either collectively, or for one or more of its individual members. Such support may come from different sources: from household members, from extended family, or from other social network members such as neighbours or friends, each acting on their own initiative out of a sense of social obligation or social solidarity. It may come from lay people or social-network members mobilized by professionals. It may also come directly from services delivered personally by professionals. In the case of children, family support may come from parents, siblings, grandparents, other relatives, neighbours, parents' friends and so on.

Family support seeks to influence positively the morale and functioning of the family and/or the surrounding social context as it impinges on the family's life. Family support may involve combinations of relationships and activities, which, crucially for their positive impact, are perceived as both supportive and available. For some people the perception or expectation that support will be available may prove as helpful as actually *calling up* such support. Family support may involve practical help, advice, information, education, supportive listening, or participation in group or community activities.

## WHY IS RESILIENCE RELEVANT TO FAMILY SUPPORT?

It has been suggested that 'the risk and resilience perspective has the potential to be an organising force for the theoretical bases and practice principles informing social work intervention' (Fraser, Richman and Galinsky, 1999, p. 141). It offers helpful insights as to the timing, levels and direction of intervention required in the lives of families needing support. The fruit of family support efforts may be greater resilience in the face of adversity on the part of a child, a parent or the whole set of family members. Enhancing resilience in even one part of the family system may strengthen the functioning of other family members or the unit as a whole. Progress in one area may have a positive ripple effect in others, as systems-thinking suggests. Progress in even one domain of one family member's life may have a transforming effect on the family's view of itself and its possibilities.

Family support activities can take many forms, many of which may seem removed from narrow conceptions of child protection or child welfare interventions. Yet an isolated, poor, lone mother encouraged and facilitated to participate in adult education classes may uncover or reawaken interests and talents that will sustain her deeper involvement in education and possibly lead on to better quality job opportunities. The ensuing boost to her self-esteem and social confidence, not to mention financial circumstances, may impact favourably on how she plays her parenting role, and on her child's developmental progress. The person who prompted her to take the risk of trying out the adult education class has set in train a sequence of positive developments, the fruits of which may include greater resilience not only for the mother but also for the child.

## WHY IS RESILIENCE RELEVANT TO EVALUATING FAMILY SUPPORT?

The purpose of evaluation is closely linked to conceptualizing, describing and measuring processes and outcomes. In the diverse and often fuzzy field of family support, the paradigm of resilience may offer a helpful organizing frame for thinking about and unpacking the outcomes sought. It may help to avoid excessive preoccupation with inputs, rather than desired outcomes for service users. What becomes more important is whether a quantum of inputs can be shown to have protective impact in terms of the functioning or development of an individual family member or whole family. Has the child a stronger engagement with supportive adults? Has the parent more self-confidence or more social skills? These are some of the questions likely to be prompted by a resilience-led family support evaluation.

Resilience-informed evaluation may thus influence the nature of data to be gathered by practitioners and researchers, and in particular may ensure a focus on strengths and competencies as well as on risks and deficits. It may help to lend more focus to efforts at family support intervention and evaluation to think in terms of enhanced resilience being the underlying purpose of intervention, or the ultimate outcome sought. Within a risk and resilience perspective, an aim of family support work might be to reduce risk factors or at least to augment protective factors in a family's social functioning and social context.

## WHAT CAN BE LEARNT ABOUT RESILIENCE FROM THE LIFE OF CHILDREN AND FAMILIES LIVING IN ADVERSITY?

In the following section we will consider evidence from two major naturalistic research studies which both shed light on protective factors in the lives of developing children.

## Philadelphia Study

Drawing on perspectives from psychology and sociology, Furstenberg and his colleagues (1999) undertook a study of family and neighbourhood influences on early adolescent development. The study involved 482 parent-and-teen pairs in five inner-city neighbourhoods of Philadelphia in the early 1990s. Data was gathered by way of in-person interviews and self-administered questionnaires. The sample was reasonably representative of the population of the city, although the researchers concede that the requirement that participants had a phone (for screening purposes) probably led to an under-representation of the very poorest households, and an over-representation of stable households. Additional data was gathered later from a sample of 35 parent-and-teen pairs using qualitative interviews and observation.

How should successful development in conditions of adversity be measured? The aim of the study was to explore how families managed their adolescent transitions, often in unpromising conditions. A key concept in the study is 'family management'—how parents manage not only the internal world of the family but also how they manage the family's, and more critically the young person's, interaction with the outside world as represented in peer group, school, neighbourhood and so on.

> Family management is a process by which parents build, invest, and deploy social capital—drawing upon social knowledge, information and resources—in the interest of protecting and providing for their children and fostering their long-term prospects. (Furstenberg et al., 1999, p. 13)

Furstenberg and colleagues identify two broad management strategies used by parents: 'promotive strategies that foster children's talents and opportunities and preventive strategies that reduce children's exposure to various types of dangerous circumstances' (p. 71).

In their study, Furstenberg and colleagues employed four measures of adolescent success—academic competence, activity involvement, problem behaviour, and self-competence and psychological adjustment—deriving these from their research experience and knowledge of the relevant literature and evidence (1999, pp. 46–52). Four measures were involved:

- *academic competence*—based on 'reports of parents and youth regarding grades, school problem behaviour (such as expulsion and suspension) and retention [holding back a year]';
- *activity involvement*—based on responses by parents and young people as to whether the young person participated in listed 'after-school activities including athletics, extracurricular activities at school, organised sports in the community, church activities and summer recreational programs';
- *problem behaviour*—based on five categories: youth reports of 'delinquent behaviour' (for example, theft, prostitution, drug dealing, vandalism);

'risky behaviour' (for example, going to court, running away, engaging in sex); 'substance abuse' (for example, drinking alcohol, smoking cigarettes, using street drugs); 'school truancy'; and parent and youth reports of 'aggressive behaviour' (for example, physically hitting or pushing someone);

- *self-competence and psychological adjustment*—based on youth self-reports of self-esteem and self-efficacy and parent and youth reports of resourcefulness and experiences of depressive emotional states.

The researchers also explored the dimensions of parenting practices that seemed to emerge as salient in terms of adolescent outcomes (p. 110). These included support for autonomy, positive family climate, discipline effectiveness, parental investment (in managing and supporting the young person's spare-time activities), restrictiveness, adjustments to cope with the family's financial realities, links to community institutions and links to positive social networks.

Furstenberg and colleagues argue that efforts to help parents and youngsters in difficult social conditions must focus both on the inside world of the family (in terms of how it manages family life and family interactions with the outside world) and on the outside world which impinges on the family. Approaches neglecting one of these dimensions will be flawed in their view. These researchers found that children living in a high-risk environment were almost five times as likely to succeed if their families 'engage in highly effective in-home practices and are also highly successful at managing the external world'. For children in moderate-risk environments with similar families, they were 'almost eight times as successful as in the worst case scenario'. Children with favourable family conditions and favourable life circumstances were 'almost fourteen times more likely to succeed than the youth living in the worst conditions' (1999, pp. 181–182).

Furstenberg and colleagues observe that 'the implications of these findings are that youth require both effective parents and benign environments to do well' (1999, p. 182). They also go on to say that:

> effective parenting does not occur in isolation; it is linked to the resources available to parents in the form of money, institutional support, social connections and the like. We also know that psychologically resourceful parents can make do with less. At the same time, we have learned along with other researchers that making do with less ultimately reduces the parents' reservoir of psychological resources. (1999, pp. 182–183)

## Kauai Longitudinal Study

The Kauai Longitudinal Study is a birth cohort study of 505 individuals born in 1955 on the island of Kauai in Hawaii involving a follow-up from the prenatal period to the age of 32 (Werner and Smith, 1992). A significant focus of the overall study has been the progress of 72 individuals (42 girls and 30 boys) identified as vulnerable because they had encountered four or more risk factors before age 2, but whose development had nevertheless overcome the odds. These resilient individuals had developed 'into competent, confident and caring persons who expressed a great desire to make use of whatever opportunities came along to improve themselves' (p. 55).

What distinguished the experience of the individuals who displayed resilience? Werner and Smith outline a number of factors evident in their own study (and, they say, echoed in many others). These include:

> Temperamental characteristics that elicit positive social responses from parents, peers and teachers; efficacy, playfulness and self-esteem; competent caregivers and supportive adults (other than parents) who foster trust and a sense of coherence or faith; and 'second chance' opportunities in society at large (at school, at work, in church, in the military) which enable high risk youths to acquire competence and confidence. (p. 187)

The precise configuration may vary—there is no single template for resilient development, but the evidence here suggests a happy combination of personal qualities and supportive relationships and contexts surrounding the vulnerable young people as they grow up.

> [Where a child's] parent is incapacitated or unavailable, other persons in a youngster's life can play such an enabling role, whether they are grandparents, older siblings, caring neighbours, family day-care providers, teachers, ministers, youth workers... Big Brothers and Big sisters, or elder mentors. Such informal and personal ties to kith, kin and community are preferred by most children and families to impersonal contacts with formal bureaucracies. These ties need to be encouraged and strengthened. (Werner and Smith, 1992, pp. 208–209)

What shines through Werner and Smith's work, and the evidence from the Philadelphia Study is the sheer ordinariness of the influences and supports which cumulatively may make the critical difference.

In early thinking about resilience, it was considered as if it were an intrinsic quality of the person. In current understanding there is more emphasis on developmental processes and domains. Resilience is not seen as a final state, which, if fortunate, one attains on some permanent basis. A person may almost be said to move in and out of the state of resilience: it is a fluid state. There is a second sense in which the pervasive state of resilience does not apply: one may show resilience in one domain of one's life but not in another. But achieving resilience in one domain may have a spill-over effect into the youngster's wider life. The factors and qualities which support resilience may be found in the child, but they may also reside in contexts surrounding the child in which the child's development is nested.

## RESILIENCE AND FAMILY SUPPORT

Development may be seen as occurring along a pathway influenced by the person's genetic blueprint and the interactions with succeeding social experiences. While what goes before influences what happens next, outcomes are not cast in stone. Things happen and, in retrospect, these may prove to have been key turning points, for good or ill, on the pathway of development. Certain experiences and qualities, born at least in part from social experience, seem to be protective in the face of adversity and more associated with favourable outcomes. These appear to include:

- a strong sense of stability, reliability, supportiveness and connectedness in key social relationships, i.e. the sense of a secure base;
- a positive appraisal of the self, i.e. self-esteem;
- multiple social roles;
- connections into supportive relationships and institutions whose support and backing can be drawn down as necessary, i.e. social capital.

In addition to these key concepts, there are a number of central messages which resilience research offers the field of practice in family support.

- Prevention and change efforts can be effective at other points beyond the more widely recognized critical stage of early childhood, for example support in adolescence.
- Points-of-life transitions seem particularly fruitful opportunities for intervention.
- Children and parents live their lives in a series of domains. Interventions may need to be designed with a view to influencing experiences in a number of different domains.
- Favourable progress in even one domain may spill over into other domains.
- One-off or short-term interventions are unlikely to have the enduring impact which may be sought to tackle more embedded problems in the lives of children or families.
- It may be more productive to focus on assets, strengths and protective factors rather than on problems, deficits and risk factors, especially where these latter features seem well embedded or intractable.
- The protective factors which underlie resilience may be most potent in cases of high and established risk.

Resilience may also offer useful reminders about the range of possible sources of helpful intervention. Resilience may be promoted by well-designed formal interventions delivered by professionals or formally recruited and supported lay people. Resilience may also be enhanced by the spontaneous expression of solidarity and social obligation by family, neighbours or friends, whose efforts remain free of professional influence. But serendipity may also play its part in the release of resilience, if it is allowed.

However, the use of the resilience perspective also requires a certain caution. People may move in and out of a state of resilience. A display of resilience in one or more domains of functioning at one point of development is not a guarantee of its continuing presence in that or other domains over time. Resilience should not be seen as a necessarily enduring quality. It remains a conditional quality of the ongoing mutual interaction between the person and the salient contexts in their lives. Intervention needs to be well informed by a sensitive and realistic appreciation of the evidence on positive outcomes. Where there are complex problems cultivated over many years in mutually reinforcing processes, it is unrealistic to expect to find 'magic bullets'—whether resilience or anything else—which will easily transform the situation. As Thompson and Ontai (2000, p. 673) have observed in relation to social support, it may not only be unrealistic but actively unhelpful to have excessive expectations of any such helping approach. If adopted too naively there is a corresponding likelihood that an approach will ultimately be discarded naively also. Evaluators will find a sound basis for resisting pressures to demand too much of family support if they ground their work in an understanding of resilience. It provides a framework that challenges overly simplistic assumptions about the possibilities of positive change in unpromising conditions.

*Case Illustration 4.4*
'John' joined a foster family consumed with football. Initially he joined in as a player but soon gave up, unable to deal with the rules and the sanctions of the game. This was accepted, without fuss, by his foster carers. Later in the placement he wanted to take up playing football again. This time he coped well with the demands of the rules and of team play. Stable and positive foster care had nurtured his growing maturity. (Example shared by a workshop participant)

*Case Illustration 4.5*
A young woman in care had been an extremely good diver and had been tipped to go far competitively. However the problems associated with entering and living in care (including drug use) led her away from diving. At a later point, partly due to pressure from people she loved, she resumed training with her old coach, but it didn't work out. She had moved on and was a different person—she no longer had the ambition or motivation to pursue her previous commitment to the sport. (Personal communication from a social worker)

## DESIGNING FAMILY SUPPORT TO ENHANCE RESILIENCE

Consideration will now be given to examples of two possible sources of resilience enhancing family support—programmes delivered by professionals and those delivered by lay people. The focus will be on highlighting features of these programmes which might be considered resilience enhancing. Before considering the relevant evidence, it is important to reiterate that resilient outcomes may emerge in the absence of dedicated intervention. The natural capacity for solidarity and support in families and communities may combine with serendipity to produce spontaneous resilient outcomes for children in adverse conditions.

## Formally Designed Programmes Delivered by Professionals

A useful example of formally designed programmes delivered by professionals are those targeted at early childhood. Karoly and colleagues (1998) offer a major independent review of the impact of targeted early intervention programmes for children and families, with special reference to 10 US programmes with detailed evaluative data. They draw favourable conclusions about the impact on life trajectories for children and parents from their review of research on the 10 early-childhood intervention programmes which had been evaluated with the use of multiple indicators of progress, follow-up design and matched controls.[1] They note that many gains were found for programme participants when compared to control groups. Variously short and longer term, these included:

- gains in emotional or cognitive development for the child, typically in the short run, or improved parent–child relationships;
- improvements in educational process and outcomes for the child;
- increased economic self-sufficiency, initially for the parent and later for the child, through greater labour-force participation, higher income, and lower welfare usage;
- reduced levels of criminal activity;
- improvements in health-related indicators, such as child abuse, maternal reproductive health and maternal substance.

The differences found between programme participants and control group members were often impressive:

> ... the Early Training Project, Perry Preschool, and the Infant Health and Development (IHDP) found IQ differences between treatment participants and controls at the end of program implementation that approached or exceeded 10 points, a large effect by most standards. The difference in rates of special education and grade retention at age 15 in the Abecedarian project participants exceeded 20 percentage points. In the Elmira, New York, Prenatal/Early Infancy Project (PEIP), participating children experienced 33 percent fewer emergency room visits through age 4 than the controls and their mothers were on welfare 33 percent less of the time. In the Perry Preschool program, children's earnings when they reached 27 were 60 percent higher among program participants.
> (Karoly, et al., 1998, pp. xv–xvi)

Karoly et al. (1998, pp. 109–10) counsel caution in terms of identifying the critical elements of intervention design, on the basis that there is still insufficient research of the right type. Nevertheless, they acknowledge that existing evidence suggests that certain features seem likely to be important: duration of time spent on pre-school and school-age interventions; more intensive participation in intervention services; combining pre-school and after-school interventions; combining home visits and centre-based day care; targeting both child and parent; and more training for care providers.

Many of the points listed by Karoly and colleagues are echoed in the research review of features of early childhood programmes associated with the prevention of later delinquency by Yoshikawa (1994). He proposes that the evidence supports a programme design with the following features:

- an intervention of at least two years' duration,
- high quality educational infant day care/pre-school,
- informational and emotional support on development and child-rearing for parents,
- pre-natal/post-natal care for the mother, and educational and vocational counselling/training if not otherwise available.

## Formally Designed Programmes Delivered by Lay People

The resilience-enhancing potential of home-based volunteer support schemes for vulnerable parents is illustrated in the words of an Australian mother who had been told by her GP and paediatrician that the sibling rivalry between her young children was to be expected:

> I had to live with it, not being able to leave the baby for a second in case the toddler would harm him and it was worse not having any family here to be a support. The volunteer recommended the social worker at the health centre, who recommended pre-school, the toddler got into day care and it got better from there. Now she loves the baby. It was practical help I needed not platitudes from the professionals. (Mother quoted in Taggart et al., 2000, p. 5)

The mother's comment clearly illustrates how the trajectory of that parenting relationship and the children's development was favourably altered by the impact of the volunteer. Her support led to positive outcomes where otherwise the picture might have been much bleaker. The common ground the mothers shared with the volunteers seemed very important. The main themes emerging from the research interviews with the mothers in this scheme seemed to be their experience of friendship with the visitor and their common experience of motherhood which was shared with the volunteer visitor.

An Irish evaluation of a lay home-visiting support scheme for new mothers used a randomized controlled trial design (Johnson, Howell and Molloy 1993) and represents part of a growing research and practice interest in this type of intervention. Considerable gains were found for those children and parents in the intervention group. The children in the intervention group were more likely than the control group children to have received all of their primary immunizations, to be read to, to be read to daily, to have played more cognitive games, to be more exposed to nursery rhymes; they were also less likely to have begun cows' milk before 26 weeks and to have inappropriate intake or amounts in their diet. Similarly, the mothers in the intervention group, when compared to the control group mothers, had better diet, had more positive feelings, were less likely to be tired, were less likely to feel miserable, were less likely to want to stay indoors, and were less likely to display negative feelings.

A follow-up study at seven years has found sustained beneficial effects of the programme on facets of child outcomes, parenting skills and maternal self-esteem, and positive effects on subsequent children (Johnson et al., 2000). The trajectory of child development, mother–child relations and maternal morale seem to have been favourably affected by an intervention based on structured monthly home visits in the child's first year of life. As in the Australian study, these gains were achieved through the efforts of lay volunteers.

## ROLE OF EVALUATION IN RESILIENCE/FAMILY SUPPORT PRAXIS

In applying the evidence from resilience research in the design and implementation of interventions, Luthar and Cicchetti (2000) specify four conditions which should be observed. There should be:

- attention to theory and research evidence on the group served;
- consideration of the interface between intervention goals and the child's own background;
- provision of integrated services rather than fragmented ones;
- clarity regarding resilience as a phenomenon, not a personal trait.

The implication for evaluative work in the field of family support seems to be the importance of incorporating perspectives based on detailed knowledge of the context, the cases, and the specific issues that the support is addressing.

In thinking about the potential impact of family support, we may need to think of possible longer-term as well as short-term gains. There is a gathering body of research evidence that shows that, at least under certain conditions, family support interventions can impact on longer-term development and foster resilient outcomes in key domains of functioning in children experiencing multiple adversity in their home or community context (Karoly et al., 1998).

In the field of family support, resilience as a concept can influence the design of both intervention and evaluation. Resilience-informed evaluation of family support can serve two purposes. It can explore the extent to which existing evidence about resilience processes is being applied in practice. In particular, the researchers may wish to examine how well existing knowledge about what may be protective for the vulnerable target population is being applied in the design or conduct of the programme under study. In addition, resilience-informed evaluation may also help to shed new light on factors, mechanisms, processes or contexts within which resilience operates or is released, within the given population and under the conditions in which the programme operates.

There are a number of key resilience-informed questions which family support evaluations should be asking.

- Does the intervention promote resilience-enhancing qualities in the child, in key family members or in the social contexts within which the child and family live out their lives?
- Does the intervention identify and tap into strengths and competencies in the child, family or surrounding contexts?
- Is the intervention part of an integrated, multifaceted approach to the known vulnerabilities and adversities facing the target population?
- Does the intervention (and indeed the evaluation design itself) have a developmental perspective which takes into account the long-term effects of things done or happening today ?
- Does the intervention attend to the role played by different stakeholders in sustaining or promoting family support and resilience, and to the nurturing of critical relationships between these stakeholders?

More specifically one might seek, through evaluation, to explore whether the intervention:

- builds the morale and capacity of individual family members;
- enhances the connectedness of individual family members to key sources of support within or outside the family unit;
- influences positively any perceptions or stories which block the person's inclination or capacity to seek or use help;
- enhances the responsiveness of key adults outside the family to the needs of family members.

From a resilience-led perspective there are a number of formats or features of service evaluation which are particularly appropriate. Luthar and Cicchetti (2000, p. 878) argue that it is important to use 'flexible, integrative evaluation strategies which combine both quantitative and qualitative approaches'. Karoly et al. (1998, pp. 120–121) identify a number of strategies for improving the quality of evaluation: by long-term follow-up of participants in existing samples; by 'expanding the range of outcomes measured in ongoing evaluation; and by 'making more effort to collect measures that are comparable to those of other studies'. The complexity of what promotes resilience and what constitutes effective family support implies the need for evaluative efforts concerned with resilience to have the necessary breadth and depth: breadth in terms of a long-term perspective and depth in terms of multiple contexts, sources and methods to be employed.

While funding may allow a single evaluation to employ only a cross-sectional approach, the resilience perspective highlights the importance of prospective studies which allow the unfolding story to be told. A cross-sectional study can ultimately become one part of a prospective study if practitioners, planners and researchers are alert to the importance of this kind of evidence. Evaluations need to gather data on the experiences of service users and stakeholders, the multiple contexts in which children and families live their lives, on the impact of intervention in those different contexts, on the developmental progress of children and families, on the natural history of interventions, and on the relationship between structured and spontaneous influences on the unfolding lives of children and families.

## CONCLUSION

In conclusion, it may be worth recalling the cautionary comment of Furstenberg and colleagues (1999) about the developmental pressures on young people growing up in situations of adversity. They note that unlike their peers, who have the luxury of conditions more forgiving of errors and more generous with second chances, 'the adolescents in our study are operating with a thin margin of error' (p. 213). Whether children and young people succeed in conditions of disadvantage depends on much more than their own qualities or efforts. As Furstenberg and his colleagues observe: 'personal agency combined with social opportunity is a potent formula for successful development, but implementing this prescription is no easy matter' (p. 215). Family support, and good quality evaluation of family support, which places resilience at the centre of its concerns, has an important contribution to make in helping to implement that none-too-easy prescription.

## NOTE

1. The programmes covered in the study are: Early Training Project, High/Scope Perry Preschool Project, Project Head Start, Chicago Child–Parent Center (CPC) and Expansion Program, Houston Parent–Child Development Center (PCDC), Syracuse Family Development Research Program (FDRP), Carolina Abededarian, Project

CARE (Carolina Approach to Responsive Education), Infant Health and Development Project (IHDP) and Elmira Prenatal/Early Infancy Project (PEIP).

## REFERENCES

Fraser, M., Richman, J. and Galinsky, M. (1999) Risk, protection and resilience: Toward a conceptual framework for social work practice. *Social Work Research*, **23**, 131–143.

Furstenberg, F., Cook, T., Eccles, J., Elder, G. and Sameroff, A. (1999) *Managing to Make It: Urban Families*. Chicago: University of Chicago Press.

Gilligan, R. (2001) *Promoting Resilience*. London: British Agencies of Adoption and Fostering.

Johnson, Z., Howell, F. and Molloy, B. (1993) Community Mothers Programme: Randomised controlled trial of non-professional intervention in parenting. *British Medical Journal*, **306**, 1449–1452.

Johnson, Z., Molloy, B., Scallan, E., Fitzpatrick, P., Rooney, T., Keegan, T. and Byrne, P. (2000) Community Mothers Programme: Seven year follow-up of a randomised controlled trial of non-professional intervention in parenting. *Journal of Public Health Medicine*, **22**, 337–342.

Karoly, L., Greenwood, P., Everingham, S., Houbé, J., Kilburn, M.R., Rydell, C.P., Sanders, M. and Chiesa, J. (1998) *Investing in our Children: What we Know and Don't Know about the Costs and Benefits of Early Childhood Interventions*. Santa Monica: Rand.

Luthar, S. and Cicchetti, D. (2000) The construct of resilience: Implications for interventions and social policies. *Development and Psychopathology*, **12**, 857–885.

Luthar, S., Cicchetti, D. and Becker, B. (2000) The construct of resilience: A critical evaluation and guidelines for future work. *Child Development*, **71**, 543–562.

Taggart, A., Short, S. and Barclay, L. (2000) 'She has made me feel human again': An evaluation of a volunteer home-based visiting project for mothers. *Health and Social Care in the Community*, **8**, 1–8.

Thompson, R. and Ontai, L. (2000) Striving to do well what comes naturally: Social support, developmental psychopathology, and social policy. *Development and Psychopathology*, **12**, 657–675.

Werner, E. and Smith, R. (1992) *Overcoming the Odds: High Risk Children from Birth to Adulthood*. Ithaca: Cornell University.

Yoshikawa, H. (1994) Prevention as cumulative protection: Effects of early family support and education on chronic delinquency and its risks. *Psychological Bulletin*, **115**, 28–54.

# 5

# ISSUES IN EVALUATING FAMILY SUPPORT SERVICES
## An American perspective

*Peter Pecora*

## INTRODUCTION

The terms 'family support' and 'family-centered services' embrace a broad range of family-centered or family-strengthening programs. The underlying philosophy, kinds of interventions, duration of services, size of caseloads, and components of service that characterize these programs vary widely (see Figure 5.1). Some are motivated by the philosophical stance that society should be willing to invest as much in placement prevention as in placement of children, others by commitment to a particular clinical focus. Some programs provide a wide variety of clinical and concrete services to children and families in their homes and neighborhoods and others deliver services primarily in an office setting. One thing they share is that in virtually all of them the family is not seen as deficient but as having many strengths and resources (Kagan et al., 1987). They can also generally be seen to be distinct from primary prevention and child development-oriented family support programs. They can also be differentiated from childcare or other family-focused services where these are characterized by: providing one type of service; working with clients exclusively in an office or classroom; providing treatment over a long period of time; or the planning and monitoring of client services delivered by other agencies.

The diversity of program models complicates any attempt to understand and evaluate family support. This is one of the reasons why research findings on family-centered service programs have been confusing—it is still not clear what services should be included in the category of family support and who

*Evaluating Family Support: Thinking Internationally, Thinking Critically.*
Edited by I. Katz and J. Pinkerton. © 2003 John Wiley & Sons, Ltd.

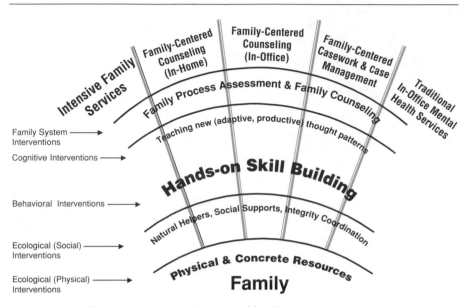

**Figure 5.1**  A sample array of family-centered services

it is or what types of situation can be expected to benefit from them. To enable worthwhile evaluation, it is essential to understand the diversity yet distinctiveness of family support. To help such understanding this chapter proposes a three-part typology of innovative family-centered service models: family support services; family-based services; and intensive family preservation services. It provides American program examples to illustrate the typology and then by a review of existing evaluations, focusing primarily on family-based services, highlights key challenges to evaluation. Particular attention is given to defining effectiveness and outcome measurement. The chapter ends by setting out a list of central questions that future work will need to address.

## A PROGRAM TYPOLOGY OF FAMILY-CENTERED SERVICES

The Child Welfare League of America proposes a three-part typology of family-centered programs.

### Family Resource, Support, and Education Services (FSS)

These community-based services assist and support adults in their role as parents. Services are available to all families with children and do not impose criteria for participation that might separate or stigmatize anyone.

## Family-Centered/Family-Based Services (FBS)

These include case management, counseling/therapy, education, skill-building, advocacy, and/or provision of concrete services for families with problems that threaten their stability. Most are currently found in child welfare agencies; there are a few in mental health centers. Some have recently been started in new service arenas, such as juvenile justice and foster care reunification programs. Some programs actually straddle the definitions presented here. For example, Hawaii's Healthy Start program, an FBS program with a broad public health and family-centered focus, providing services to all newborns and their families irrespective of risk level, but continuing with health care, counseling and concrete services to families judged to be at moderate to high risk of child maltreatment (Breakey and Pratt, 1991).

## Intensive Family Preservation Services (IFPS)

These services are designed for families 'in crisis'—at a time when removal of a child is perceived as imminent or the return of a child from out-of-home care is being considered. This service model is also being applied to chronic family situations, involving child neglect or abuse, which do not involve crisis. Such programs may share the same philosophical orientation and characteristics as FBS, but are much more intensive. They are delivered in a period of 4 to 12 weeks. Caseloads vary between two to six families per worker. Families are typically seen between 6 and 10 hours per week. These services aim to protect the child, strengthen and preserve the family. They focus on preventing the unnecessary placement of children (Whittaker et al., 1990), or on reuniting children with their families (Child Welfare League of America, 1989, pp. 46–47). IFPS include programs such as HOMEBUILDERS™ in Washington, Intensive Family Services in Maryland, and certain types of Families First programs in other states. Although programs may share core features, treatment models vary.

## FAMILY RESOURCE, SUPPORT, AND EDUCATION SERVICES (FSS)

In order to understand what is involved in FSS it is worth considering some examples of innovative programs.[1] A promising development has been the voluntary use of home visitors for families with newborns and young children at-risk. Some of the better known and successful programs of this type have been operating since the 1980s in Elmira (New York), California, and the state of Hawaii. A recent cost/benefits analysis of the Elmira program showed that the net benefits of the program exceed $24 000. This was more than four times the cost of the program—$3246 in 1980 dollars and $6083 in 1996 dollars when the proper economic adjustments are made (Karoly et al., 2001). There are significant savings for low-income families in terms of long-term social costs. Programs vary widely in terms of the coherence of their conceptual model and the rigor with which they are evaluated. Some programs try to take a comprehensive approach. For example, the Supportive Child Abuse Network (SCAN) uses a community-based approach with lay therapists and self-help groups as part of an effort to mobilize public awareness and support (Grazio, 1981).

Some of the recently developed preventive efforts address both physical abuse and other forms of child maltreatment. Hawaii's *Healthy Start* has a multidimensional approach to both supporting and educating families to improve family coping skills and functioning and also to promoting positive parenting skills, parent–child interaction and optimal child development. Home visitation services are offered to families of all newborns deemed at-risk via screenings performed in hospitals at the child's birth. Follow-up visits occur until children reach age 5 (school age).

Nine complementary components make up the Healthy Start approach (Breakey and Pratt, 1991, pp. 16–19):

- systematic hospital-based screening to identify 90% of high-risk families of newborns from a specific geographic area;
- community-based home visiting family support services provided as part of the maternal and child health system;
- the intensity of service based on each family's need and level of risk;
- families linked to a 'medical home';
- coordination of a range of health and social services for at-risk families;
- continuous follow-up until the child reaches age 5;
- structured training in the dynamics of abuse and neglect, early identification of families at risk and home visiting;
- collaboration with the Hawaii Coordinating Council serving environmentally at-risk children;
- staff selection and retention.

Preliminary evaluation results showed very few cases of abuse or neglect among the families served and a significant reduction of the modifiable risk factor. Of the 2254 families served between July 1987 and June 1991, 90% of 2-year-olds were fully immunized, and 85% of children were developing appropriately. Among the 90 families in the program already known to child protective services, no additional reports occurred during the families' participation in the program (Earle, 1995).

A study undertaken in New York City (Hess et al., 1997) examined some of the results of the well-known Sunset Park neighborhood services center—the Center for Family Life's 'Preventive Services Program'. The Center's mission is to help the families of Sunset Park, Brooklyn to remain intact. All families with a child under the age of 18 are eligible for services. All services are free to family members. Open seven days a week from 8 a.m. until 11 p.m., and accessible 24 hours a day, the Center's primary aim is

> ... to sustain children and youth in their own homes by enhancing the capacity of parents, providing developmental opportunities for family members, addressing crisis in parent–child or spousal relationships, or intervening in a variety of ways to bring stability (social and economic) to the family household. The continuum of our activities embraces a large amount of preventive work and early intervention, as well as crisis management and remediation in instances of serious family disorganization and dysfunction.
>
> (Center for Family Life, 1997, p. 1)

Using a prospective sample of 189 families who received comprehensive yet individualized services provided directly and through referrals by a social worker in the preventive program, the evaluation found evidence of program effectiveness. Of the 423 sample children, 98.6% remained with their families. All five families where a child had been placed continued to receive Center services and 87.9% of the families' service needs had been addressed. In the 92 closed cases, statistically significant positive effects were found on five of the eight child-centered problem/behavior factors.

The authors found three elements differentiating the Center's preventive program approach from other family preservation programs:

- broad accessibility to non-categorical services through multiple routes, including self-referral;
- the comprehensive nature of the available within-Center community-based services provided through the preventive program;
- flexibility in service duration, including continuing access to preventive program services.

This program model provides one prototype for delivering comprehensive, integrated, and individualized services required by families with complex and diverse needs and problems (Hess et al., 1997).

The benefits of these types of program parallel other programs that use in-home teaching and other supportive interventions. Evaluation results have been less positive for other child abuse prevention programs—particularly those of short duration, with a less tightly specified parenting curriculum, which target families who have already been referred to child protective services (Barth, 1991). There is also the question of whether to continue periodic bursts of services to vulnerable families with older children, given recent findings that older children are also at risk of child maltreatment, and are under-served by the child protective service delivery system (Sedlak, 1991). Finally, Daro provides an important caution that prevention efforts must be multifaceted in design:

> Just as one treatment strategy is insufficient for all maltreating families, no one prevention effort can adequately address the various causal factors of maltreatment or provide effective inroads to all families at risk of different forms of maltreatment. Some families will respond to educational efforts, while other families initially will be more responsive to offers of material support. While some families will welcome a service provider into their homes, others will prefer to attend classes or support group meetings in a local community center or church.
>
> Certain at-risk families or individuals, recognizing that they need assistance, will voluntarily enter a prevention program; other families will need more encouragement. Effectively preventing child abuse is a tall order and one that requires a differential and flexible local response system. The most useful systems will be ones that address the multiple causal factors associated with various types of maltreatment, target services to both the potential perpetrator and the potential victim, and build on the experiences of others in designing specific prevention services. (Daro, 1988, p. 128)

Well-designed family support services to prevent child maltreatment can be cost-effective in terms of the costs incurred by society, not to mention the most important (and difficult to measure) costs of emotional harm to children. The challenge is to identify the most important areas for attention. For example, is it poor housing conditions, lack of a parental social network, or parental sense of self-esteem and social skills that should be addressed? What family strengths and resources can be built upon? We need to avoid 'single-variable' interventions in a complex area like child maltreatment (Olds and Henderson, 1989).

## FAMILY-CENTERED/BASED SERVICES (FBS)

While design and specific interventions differ, it has been suggested (Bryce and Loyd, 1981) that most Family-Centered/Based Service programs share some, or all, of the following characteristics:

- a primary worker or case manager establishes and maintains a supportive, nurturing relationship with the family;
- a wide variety of helping options are used including 'concrete' or supportive services such as food and transportation, together with clinical services;

- caseloads of 2 to 12 families;
- one or more associates serve as team members or provide back-up for the primary worker;
- workers (or their back-ups) are available 24 hours a day for crisis calls or emergencies;
- the home is the primary service setting and maximum utilization is made of natural helping resources, including the family, the extended family, the neighborhood, and the community;
- the parents remain in charge of and responsible for their family as the primary caregivers, nurturers, and educators;
- society is willing to invest the necessary resources in the family to prevent amount of home placement for the child;
- services are time-limited, usually one to four months.

In the United States, the target population for FBS programs (and for the more intensive IFPS programs) is generally families who can no longer cope with problems that threaten family stability. This includes situations in which a decision has been made by a public social service agency to place a child outside the home. An FBS program may also be appropriate where children in temporary out of home care are being reunited. Although 'crisis orientation' may be emphasized by some programs, many of these families are not in crisis, but trying to cope with an abusive or neglectful family member, child mental illness, juvenile delinquency, or other chronic problem. Thus, these services may be appropriate for families seen by the day care (Moore et al., 1998; Roditti, 1995), child welfare, juvenile justice, or mental health systems, as well as adoptive or foster families facing potential disruption (Barth, 1991; Briggs and Hawkins, 1993; Dore, 1991; Fraser et al., 1996; Haapala et al., 1988; Hodges et al., 1989; Whittaker and Maluccio, 1988). Accordingly, service delivery context and client characteristics may vary significantly.

Although some FBS program results have been shown to be positive, the limitations of these programs also need to be recognized. They cannot replace other types of child and family services or broader societal and service system reforms (Halpern, 1990). While some case situations can be addressed by FBS programs alone, some families will always need other child welfare services, such as day treatment, family foster care, residential treatment or adoption, and most will need other preventive or support services, such as income support, childcare, parent education, substance abuse treatment or job training. Studies of FBS, and indeed of other types of program, indicate that many families need assistance with housing, food, medical care, employment and basic financial support. Many families served by public systems live in communities with few other resources to help parents or support healthy child development. Some experience internal family problems, such as ineffective communication among family members, poor self-esteem, mental illness, lack of social support and pronounced deficits in parenting or basic social skills. Responding effectively to these difficulties requires recognizing that they stem from a mix of larger societal problems and significant psychological or social impairment (Polansky et al., 1981, 1992).

FBS programs must not be oversold as a cure-all for families because of their emphasis on family strengthening instead of fundamental systems reform, and mixed reports of cost-effectiveness, nor must services such as public assistance, housing, health care and others essential to child and family well-being be cut to fund FBS programs. While significant foster care and residential treatment program savings may be realized in some cases, FBS programs are just one of the services that must be available to support families. Without a broad network of support available in the local community, families may not be able to maintain gains made during the FBS, and children may be vulnerable to continued abuse or neglect. Researchers and program staff need to emphasize to policy makers that both the short- and long-term success of FBS programs depends on the family's ability to access a range of community services and other societal supports. More immediately, how the availability of these services affects the success of the program must be evaluated.

## DEFINING EFFECTIVENESS

The major outcome criteria for evaluating programs, in particular Family-Based Programs, have been listed (Pecora, 1994, 1995) as follows:

- placement prevention
- number of placement days used
- reduction in the restrictiveness of placement location
- reports of child maltreatment
- changes in child, parent, and family functioning
- family reunification
- consumer satisfaction ratings.

As discussed below (and summarized in Table 5.1), the evaluation results for each of these outcomes, with the exception of placement prevention, have been mixed. This variability is partly due to the limitations in the research methods and measures used but also to the lack of analyses of findings by subpopulations of families. The lack of stability in some of the programs has also contributed to this problem.

**Table 5.1** Outcome criteria and findings from selected studies

An experimental or case overflow research design was used in the studies marked by an asterisk (*).

*Days in Placement and Case Closure*

- Children in the IFPS treatment group spent significantly fewer days in placement than comparison group children (e.g. AuClaire and Schwartz, 1986, pp. 39–40*; Nelson, 1984*; Yuan et al., 1990, p. v*).
- The likelihood of case closing for the FBS cases was 46% greater than for the control group cases (Littell and Fong, 1992; as cited in Rzepnicki et al., 1994, p. 61*).
- There is some evidence that FBS may shorten the placement time of children served by the program. In one Connecticut study over half the children placed were home within 12 months compared to the state-wide average placement duration of 31 months (Wheeler et al., 1992, p. 5.10).

*Changes in Placement Rate*

- In Michigan where IFPS programs were established in stages, some counties which did not have the program were used as comparison sites. Out-of-home placement rates grew more slowly in the counties with IFPS than those in non-served counties. In counties where IFPS programs were implemented later, placement rates diminished, resulting in considerable savings by government agencies in those counties (Visser, 1991, as cited in Bath and Haapala, 1994).

*Restrictiveness of Placement*

- Treatment group children used a larger proportion of shelter care days than other forms of placement (e.g. Yuan et al., 1990*).
- Treatment group children used 'less restrictive' placement options (e.g. Kinney and Haapala, 1984*; Willems and DeRubeis, 1981, pp. 16–25*).

*Further Reports of Child Maltreatment*

- Treatment group children from chronically neglecting families had fewer subsequent reports of child maltreatment than control group children (Littell et al., 1992, pp. 8 and 16*).

*Improving Child, Parent, and Family Functioning*

- Improvements in child and family functioning were found, with the treatment group rated as better in several areas than the control group (Feldman, 1991a, pp. 30–33*). In some studies, however, differences in improvement found at about seven months after FBS services began, lessened over time, with few differences reported by parents at a 16-month follow-up (Rzepnicki et al., 1994, pp. 67–68*).
- In a quasi-experimental study, ratings by workers and clients indicated improvement in caretaker parenting skills, verbal discipline, knowledge of childcare, child school adjustment, child oppositional or delinquent behavior, and child's oppositional behavior in the home (Spaid et al., 1991, pp. 139–156).
- In a Los Angeles study of two IFPS programs, there were improvements in parent-child interactions, family living and financial conditions, financial conditions, supports available to families and the developmental stimulation of children (Personal Communication, J. McCroskey and W. Meezan, January 4, 1994*). →

- Parental use of new skills at six-month follow-up was higher in a recent family reunification study using an experimental design ($E = 62, C = 58$) (Walton, 1991, pp. 113–114; Walton et al., 1993*).

*Family Reunification*

- When behaviorally-specific case planning to achieve more permanent plans for children in family foster care was emphasized, more experimental group cases were closed (50%) than comparison group cases (29%), and a greater number of experimental group children were returned to their birth families (Stein et al., 1978*).
- When special efforts were made to provide services to birth families, 66% of the treatment group children either returned home or were adopted, compared to 45% of the comparison group children (Lahti, 1982, p. 558*).
- A recent experimental study of IFPS focused on children who were in foster care for more than 30 days and had been randomly assigned to receive a three-month IFPS intervention. They were reunited more quickly, in higher numbers, and remained in the home for a greater number of days during a 12-month follow-up period than the control group (Walton et al., 1993*).

*Consumer Satisfaction*

- Primary caretakers reported relatively high satisfaction levels with most aspects of the FBS service (e.g. Hayes and Joseph, 1985; Magura and Moses, 1984, p. 103), including studies that involved comparison of the FBS-served parent ratings with those of parents receiving traditional child welfare services (McCroskey and Meezan, 1997, p. 6; Rzepnicki et al., 1994, p. 77*).
- Primary caretakers mentioned as positive the workers' ability to establish good rapport with them, together with the teaching of communication, problem-solving and chore chart/reward systems (Pecora et al., 1991).
- In a recent family reunification study using an experimental design, consumer satisfaction ratings in a number of areas were significantly higher for the experimental group families (Walton, 1991, pp. 106–109*). (Also, see Walton et al., 1993.)

*Juvenile Delinquency Reduction*

- In a quasi-experimental study of a home-based service program, based on Alexander's behavioral systems family therapy (Alexander and Parsons, 1982), the FBS treatment group participants were assigned, based on the need to prevent placement or reunify and a high likelihood of recommitting a delinquent offense within one year. Recidivism in juvenile delinquency differed between the FBS and comparison groups (11.1% treatment, 66.7% comparison group). When the recidivism rates were adjusted for different follow-up periods, the differences were maintained (5%, 25%). (See Gordon et al., 1988, p. 250*.)
- A home-based FBS program using the Multi-systemic Treatment (MST) model was used to treat 43 youths (an additional 41 youths were in the control group) to reduce rates of institutionalizing young juvenile offenders. At 59 weeks post-referral, youths who received MST had:
  statistically significant lower arrest rates
  an average 73 fewer days of incarceration
  less self-reported delinquency (Henggeler et al., 1992*).

## Placement Prevention

Although this has been the focus of much research there are problems with using placement prevention rates as a primary measure of success. To start with, placement prevention is an imperfect proxy for the outcomes being sought, namely improvements in child, parent and family functioning. In addition, early studies did not include comparison or control groups. Forming these groups in a rigorous manner has been difficult because of problems in risk assessment, referral patterns, and organizational problems (Feldman 1991b; Rzepnicki et al., 1991; Tracy, 1991; Yuan et al., 1990). Intake criteria, client screening methods, treatment models, program stability, client characteristics and other critical factors also vary across programs. Placement definitions, family monitoring methods and follow-up periods differ between studies thus making comparisons difficult. The appropriateness of placements must also be considered as not all placements may be in the best interest of the child and family in the first place. If the comparison group was found to have a higher number of 'inappropriate/undesirable' placements than the treatment group, this clearly has implications for any evaluation of effectiveness.

Literature reviews indicate mixed findings about placement prevention rates (Bath and Haapala, 1994; Frankel, 1988; Jones, 1985; Magura, 1981; Pecora et al., 1995; Rossi, 1992; Stein, 1985; Wells and Biegel, 1991). However the full reports, as opposed to summary data, must be read to understand the particular objectives, findings and limitations of each study. Nevertheless, in some recent large-scale evaluations, placement prevention rates were not significantly different between the treatment and control groups. While subgroup analyses by child age, type of case or other variable might reveal significant differences, other measures of placement-related outcome, more sensitive to variations in service are needed. Days in placement therefore remain an important supplementary outcome criterion as several studies found that children in the FBS (and also in Intensive Family Preservation Service programs) treatment groups spent significantly fewer days in placement compared with those in the control group.

## Restrictiveness of Placement

Reducing the restrictiveness of the placement is an important but infrequently used outcome measure. This applies to both FBS and Intensive Family Preservation Service programs. Treatment foster care rates are much lower than the $40 000–80 000 annual costs of residential treatment. An IFPS program may be very beneficial if it can safely divert youths from psychiatric hospitalization, juvenile corrections facilities, or residential treatment to relative, foster family or group home care. A home-based program in Milwaukee, Wisconsin, has provided such a service for over five years. Clearly, the optimal outcomes are some form of permanent care—ideally, return home or adoption, but in others, diversion from residential treatment to family foster care can be both cost-effective and the best alternative for the child.

A few studies have looked at the proportion of shelter care days used compared with other forms of placement (Yuan et al., 1990). Others have considered the use of less restrictive placement options overall (Kinney and Haapala, 1984; Willems and DeRubeis, 1981, pp. 16–25). There are serious methodological challenges to overcome; for example, developing a credible means of determining that a youth should be (or would have been) placed in a particular setting so that placement diversion can be validly assessed. There are however, successes such as 'wrap around' placement diversion programs for a small group of highly disturbed youths, and the many long-term family foster care programs which maintain youths in foster families rather than in institutional settings (Fanshel et al., 1990).

## Preventing Further Reports of Child Maltreatment

From a child advocacy perspective, programs have little value if they do not protect children from further serious maltreatment. Few studies have measured whether these programs reduce further reports of child abuse or neglect (Littell et al., 1992; Theiman and Dail, 1992; Yuan et al., 1990) and there are a number of methodological challenges. There is often greater 'surveillance' of FBS families than of comparison group families because of the nature of the service, especially if it is home based. Also self-reporting by the parents or children may be more likely if they have confidence in the worker's ability to help them. Criteria for 'substantiation' of reports require operational definition and close monitoring to ensure reliable data. This is a critical outcome measure with significant methodological problems and little current research data. Given relatively high recidivism rates in child neglect, physical abuse and sexual abuse, the total elimination of subsequent reports is unrealistic. Moreover, many chronic neglecting families and other families in difficulty may need more ancillary and follow-up services than are typically provided by FBS programs. Nevertheless, further studies should show that, compared to other forms of treatment, FBS programs effectively reduce further reports for certain types of cases.

## Improving Child, Parent, and Family Functioning

This is for many the primary area of focus for assessing program effectiveness. One challenge is matching the program objectives, intervention methods and areas of functioning to be addressed. For example, it is important not to focus on improvements in child academic functioning if the primary goals of the intervention are improving of specific parenting skills and increasing the family's use of neighborhood social supports. The preliminary findings of the experimental studies in this area are mixed, while the quasi-experimental and qualitative research is more positive. A New Jersey study noted improvements in child and family functioning for both treatment and comparison groups, with the treatment group being better in a few areas (Feldman, 1991a). Another quasi-experimental study indicated that improvement had occurred in caretaker parenting skills, verbal discipline, knowledge of childcare, child–school adjustment, child oppositional or delinquent behavior, child oppositional behavior in the home (e.g. Spaid et al., 1991, pp. 139–156). It is interesting to note that a Los Angeles study of two Intensive Family Preservation Service programs also shows indicators of improvement in these areas, but they vary by agency and type of functioning (McCroskey and Meezan, 1997). There are differences in the service model across the participating programs, necessitating a number of special analyses by type of program model. Developing the social support networks of families has also been recognized by a few FBS agencies (Tracy, 1991).

## Family Reunification

The use of FBS for family reunification has not been extensively evaluated. The outcome is important, as providing FBS to children already in foster care for more than 30 days eliminates the problem of trying to ensure whether or not the referral criterion that the child is at risk of 'imminent placement' has been met (Stein et al., 1978; Lahti 1982; Walton et al., 2001; Fraser et al., 1996). While further research is needed, this may be an area where IFPS is effective, including, perhaps, in kinship care cases, where children are remaining in care for longer periods of time.

## Consumer Satisfaction

Conceived as both satisfaction studies and methods for gathering client views on what made the service effective or ineffective, such studies are producing intriguing information when a focused set of questions is used. In one of the oldest studies to combine both qualitative and quantitative methods in evaluating an Intensive Family Preservation Service, Haapala (1983) asked consumers about critical incidents that helped in their work with the therapist. These incidents were then clustered into eight themes and correlated with child placement. The provision of concrete services and session interruptions (which may have provided the worker with opportunities to teach or demonstrate problem-solving and other skills) were most strongly associated with placement prevention (Haapala and Fraser, 1987). Elsewhere, primary caretakers reported relatively high satisfaction levels (e.g. Hayes and Joseph, 1985; Magura and Moses, 1984, p. 103). However, satisfaction ratings varied from program to program. While these initial results are positive, consumer ratings from treatment and control groups must be examined to determine if these services are more effective than traditional or other types of child welfare services.

## OUTCOME MEASUREMENT

While much can be learned from reviewing existing findings, it still has to be acknowledged that, as with early child development studies, researchers faced, and continue to face, major difficulties in undertaking effective evaluations of family centered services. In many studies the intervention model being evaluated did not include explicit statement of desired outcomes and required interventions. It was not clear what the core interventions were and what worker behaviors were expected. In some studies the intervention model or independent variable was not consistently implemented. In others intake screening procedures were not well developed. Some programs measured long-term outcomes but could not specify interim indicators of change that led to those outcomes, and did not clarify costs of the services.

It is undoubtedly the case that too often family support programs are shown to produce poor results because the intervention model is neither implemented consistently nor faithfully. Effective programs require supervisory and consultant support and continuous attention to fidelity. However these poor outcomes also reflect the difficulties that inadequately designed and implemented programs pose for evaluation. For example, where program design and implementation are loose there is much greater likelihood of the evaluator choosing an assessment measure that does not match the treatment model, or using instruments that are not appropriate to the consumer population or are not clinically sensitive to change. Where that occurs evaluation will miss changes that may be occurring and outcomes that are being achieved, with the resulting negative judgement of the program. It is also worth noting that outcome indicators that are important for program monitoring and service refinement may not replicate those needed for more formal research—even measurement tools may vary.

At the core of these issues lies the question of outcome measurement. Success takes many forms and there needs to be clarity about how outcomes are being conceptualized. Service effectiveness in terms of child, parent or family functioning can be viewed in at least four ways:

- increases in functioning—e.g. cognitive functioning;
- maintenance of functioning—e.g. maintaining emotional health during a stressful time;
- prevention of another problem or relapse prevention—e.g. teen parents who are at risk of another pregnancy;
- slowing of a progressively deteriorating condition—e.g. certain health conditions.

(Adapted from an outcome measures discussion group, The Behavioral Healthcare Quality and Accountability Summit, Oak Brook Illinois, chaired by William Bermon, June 14, 1996.)

In addition to being clear about which of those views apply, it is important to link statements about outcomes to process. It needs to be recognized that programs are based on practice wisdom, research and theory, which together go to make up an understanding and specifying of a process of change. Often there is a failure to articulate the 'change model' that describes how and why a particular set of interventions will meet the child or family needs and produce certain outcomes. It is important to specify these theories of change. They can be documented through a program snapshot summary or a logic model. These models specify the needs of the population being served and how these needs can be addressed by achieving specific short-term, intermediate, and long-term outcomes using a particular intervention at a determined cost (see Table 5.2). The latter point on the need to be able to tie key outcomes to service costs is worth emphasizing. There is an appalling lack of benefit–cost and cost-effectiveness data about program interventions in child welfare. This stems, in part, from a lack of well-specified interventions that have been validated through rigorous outcome research. Benefit–cost analysis is an important evaluative approach because of the importance of funding social programs with the largest net benefits (Plotnick, 1994).

Specifying reasonable outcomes is also a key challenge to both program planning and evaluation. Outcome criteria beyond prevention of unnecessary placement and shortening lengths of stay should be considered. Such criteria could include school attendance and performance, behavior at home,

**Table 5.2**  Major program logic model components[a]

| Who are we serving and what are the needs and problems? | Short-term, intermediate, and long-term outcomes | Service delivery model and theory of change | What are the costs of these services? |
|---|---|---|---|
| • Risk factors (e.g. family history, poverty) | • Program outcomes/Case statuses | • Kinds of interventions | • Per child service cost |
| • Social problems or mental illness—severity, chronicity | • Individual outcomes such as development or demonstration of skills and competencies | • Modality of service e.g. theoretical orientation, mode of service delivery | • Per family cost |
| • Family strengths/tolerance for stress | • Stakeholder satisfaction | • Intensity, frequency, and duration of services | • Cost-effectiveness data |
| • Social supports | • Aspects of quality service linked to positive outcomes, e.g. worker engagement of parents or children in services | • Location of services | • Benefit–cost data |
| • Skills of each family member in mediating the service delivery system | | • Variety and sequencing of services | |
| • Ability and motivation of parents and youth to implement intervention methods | | • Integrity of services (e.g. how much consistency is there to the service, to the treatment model, program 'drift', and treatment 'fidelity'?) | |

[a] Adapted from Hernandez and Hodges (1996) and Savas (1996) by Pecora et al. (1998).

employment, having at least one positive relationship with a peer and with a caring adult. To achieve the necessary specificity child and parent outcome data should be linked to age, gender, ethnicity, geographic area, neighborhood and any other pertinent factors. Other forms of 'risk-adjusted' outcomes may need to be applied to understand how success rates are affected by the impact of risk and protective factors on youth, families and service effectiveness. The key is to negotiate reasonable outcomes tailored to the individuals, families and communities being served. Specified mini-indicators of change or progress can be linked to more long-term outcomes. When, for example, a family improves their communication skills, it can lead to reduced parent–adolescent conflict and then to fewer runaway incidents. It is worth repeating that it is important to make explicit the conceptual maps that lay out the change theory underlying the program and the process linking the mini-indicators of progress and the long-term outcomes.

## CONCLUSION

In the United States, family support and family-based services research data gathered from a number of studies is producing a growing body of evidence about their effectiveness. The program evaluation results, while promising, are far from conclusive. Evaluation needs to match measures to treatment objectives and methods. Outcome criteria beyond placement prevention must be incorporated. Information is lacking about which particular types of programs are most effective for different client groups and which program components are most important. Studies are just beginning to look at subpopulations and estimating the value of various intervention components (Bath et al., 1992; Fraser et al., 1991; Lewis 1991; Haapala, 1983; Nelson and Landsman, 1992). A number of Family-Based Service programs are experimenting with special assessment and intervention methods for engaging substance-abusing families. There is also a need for 'life-course' studies of families and youth involved in the various types of family support services. What brought them to the attention of the child welfare, public health, juvenile justice or mental health systems? What services have been provided and what placements have occurred before, during, and after the family support services or FBS?

Family support programs are not a panacea, merely part of the larger array of services that must be available to families. There is some evidence of their effectiveness but there is other information that must be considered as future programs and evaluation studies are implemented. The effects of these programs will be better established only as the various types of family support programs are refined, the follow-up services necessary for some situations are identified, and additional rigorous quantitative and qualitative studies are conducted. Listed below are some key questions that need to be addressed in future work.

- Will outcomes assessment form part of a larger organizational commitment to continuous quality improvement?
- What key outcome domains and indicators will be focused upon?
- What data should management information systems collect?
- When does it become essential in program evaluation work to use more rigorous research designs?
- Can the use of functional outcomes be maximized and assessment scales used strategically?
- Should inexpensive data collaboratives be formed?
- Can consumer satisfaction measures be moved away from merely being process-focused surveys with poor response rates?
- How quickly can data about child, parent, family and community characteristics, services, outcomes and costs be obtained?

It is time for social services program administrators, researchers and university faculty members to make a renewed commitment to careful process and outcome evaluation. There is an urgent need to pursue a rigorous long-term agenda of research, seeking to document how well-implemented programs, with theory-based interventions, have meaningful effects with specific populations of children and families. While many challenges remain, the American experience to date suggests that there is every reason to be optimistic about family-centered service delivery approaches and the partnerships between families and service delivery systems that are necessary for success.

## NOTE

1. For additional examples of family support programs, see Jones (1985, pp. 27–34); Kamerman and Kahn (1995); Kosterman and Hawkins (1997); Marcenko et al. (1996); Reynolds (1998); Schorr (1997); Yale Bush Center in Child Development and Social Policy, and Family Resource Coalition (1983); Zigler and Black (1989).

## REFERENCES

Alexander, J.F. and Parsons, B.V. (1982) *Functional Family Therapy*. Monterey, CA: Brook/Cole Publishing.

AuClaire, P. and Schwartz, I.M. (1986) *An Evaluation of the Effectiveness of Intensive Home-Based Services as an Alternative to Placement for Adolescents and Their Families*. Minneapolis, MN: Hennepin County Community Services Department, and the University of Minnesota, Hubert H. Humphrey Institute of Public Affairs.

Barth, R.P. (1991) An experimental evaluation of in-home child abuse prevention. *Child Abuse and Neglect*, **15**, 363–375.

Bath, H.I. and Haapala, D.A. (1994) Family preservation services: What does the outcome research really tell us? *Social Services Review*, **68**(3), 386–404.

Bath, H.I., Richey, C.A. and Haapala, D.A. (1992) Child age and outcome correlates in intensive family preservation services. *Children and Youth Services Review*, **14**(5), 389–406.

Breakey, G. and Pratt, B. (1991) Healthy growth for Hawaii's *Healthy Start*: Toward a systematic statewide approach to the prevention of child abuse and neglect. *Zero to Three* (April).

Briggs, F. and Hawkins, R.M.F. (1993) Follow-up data on the effectiveness of New Zealand's national school-based child protection program. *Child Abuse and Neglect*, **18**(8), 635–643.

Bryce, M. and Lloyd, J.C. (Eds) (1981) *Treating Families in the Home: An Alternative to Placement*. Springfield, IL: Charles C. Thomas Publishers.

Center for Family Life (1997) *Center for Family Life Annual Progress Report*. New York, NY: Author.

Child Welfare League of America (1989) *Standards for Service to Strengthen and Preserve Families with Children*. Washington, D.C.

Daro, D. (1988) *Confronting Child Abuse: Research for Effective Program Design*. New York: The Free Press.

Dore, M.M. (1991) *Family-based Mental Health Services Programs and Outcomes*. Philadelphia, PA: Philadelphia Child Guidance Clinic.

Earle, R. (1995) Helping to prevent child abuse—and future criminal consequences: Hawaii Healthy Start. *National Institute of Justice Program Focus Brief*. Washington, D.C.: US Department of Justice.

Fanshel, D., Finch, S.J. and Grundy, J.F. (1990) *Foster Children in a Life-Course Perspective*. New York: Columbia University Press.

Feldman, L.H. (1991a) *Assessing the Effectiveness of Family Preservation Services in New Jersey within an Ecological Context*. Bureau of Research, Evaluation and Quality Assurance. Trenton, NJ: New Jersey Division of Youth and Family Services.

Feldman, L. (1991b) Target population definition. In Y.T. Yuan and M. Rivest (Eds), *Evaluation Resources for Family Preservation Services*. Newbury Park, CA: Sage.

Frankel, H. (1988) Family-centered, home-based services in child protection: A review of the research. *Social Services Review*, **62**, 137–157.

Fraser, M.W., Pecora, P.J. and Haapala, D.A. (1991) *Families in Crisis: The Impact of Intensive Family Preservation Services*. Hawthorne, NY: Aldine de Gruyter.

Fraser, M.W., Walton, E., Lewis, R.E., Pecora, P.J. and Walton, W.K. (1996) An experiment in family reunification: Correlates of outcome at one-year follow-up. *Children and Youth Services Review*, **18**(4–5), 335–361.

Gordon, D.A., Arbuthnot, J., Gustafson, K.E. and McGreen, P. (1988) Home-based behavioral-systems family therapy with disadvantaged juvenile delinquents. *American Journal of Family Therapy*, **16**, 243–255.

Grazio, T. (1981) New perspectives on child abuse/neglect community education. *Child Welfare*, **60**(5), 679–707.

Haapala, D.A. (1983) *Perceived Helpfulness, Attributed Critical Incident Responsibility, and a Discrimination of Home-based Family Therapy Treatment Outcomes: Homebuilders Model*. Report prepared for the Department of Health and Human Services, Administration for Children, Youth and Families (Grant #90-CW-626 OHDS). Federal Way, WA: Behavioral Sciences Institute.

Haapala, D.A. and Fraser, M.W. (1987) *Keeping Families Together: The Homebuilders Model Revisited*. Federal Way, WA: Behavioral Sciences Institute (mimeograph).

Haapala, D.A., McDade, K. and Johnston, B. (1988) *Preventing the Dissolution of Special Needs Adoption Families Through the Use of Intensive Home-based Family Preservation Services: The Homebuilders Model*. (Clinical Services Final Report from the

Homebuilders Adoption Services Continuum Project.) Federal Way, WA: Behavioral Sciences Institute.

Halpern, R. (1990) Fragile families, fragile solutions: An essay review. *Social Service Review*, **64**, 637–648.

Hayes, J.R. and Joseph, J.A. (1985) *Home-based Family Centered Project Evaluation.* Columbus, OH: Metropolitan Human Services Commission.

Henggeler, S.W., Melton, G.B. and Smith, L.A. (1992) Family preservation using multisystemic therapy: An effective alternative to incarcerating serious juvenile offenders. *Journal of Consulting and Clinical Psychology*, **60**, 953–961.

Hernandez, M. and Hodges, S. (1996) *The Ecology of Outcomes.* Tampa, FL: University of South Florida, Florida Mental Health Institute, Department of Child and Family Studies, The System Accountability Project for Children's Mental Health.

Hess, P., McGowan, B. and Botsko, M. (1997) *Final Report of a Study of the Center for Family Life in Sunset Park: Greater than the Sum of its Parts.* New York: Authors.

Hodges, V.G., Guterman, N.B., Blythe, B.J. and Bronson, D.E. (1989) Intensive aftercare services for children. *Social Casework*, **70**(7), 397–404.

Jones, M.A. (1985) *A Second Chance for Families: Five Years Later.* New York: Child Welfare League of America.

Kagan, S.L., Powell, D.R., Weisbourd, B. and Zigler, E.F. (1987) *America's Family Support Programs: Perspectives and Prospects.* New Haven, CT: Yale University Press.

Kamerman, S.B. and Kahn, A.J. (1995) *Starting Right: How America Neglects its Youngest Children and What we can Do About It.* New York: Oxford University Press.

Karoly, L. Kilburn, R., Bigelow, J.H., Caulkins, J.P. and Cannon, J.S. (2001) *Assessing Costs and Benefits of Early Childhood Intervention Programs. Overview and Application to the Starting Early Starting Smart Program.* Seattle: The Casey Family Programs; Santa Monica: Rand.

Kinney, J. and Haapala, D. (1984) *First Year Homebuilders Mental Health Project Report.* Federal Way, WA: Behavioral Sciences Institute (Mimeograph).

Kinney, J.M., Haapala, D.A. and Booth, C. (1991) *Keeping Families Together: The Homebuilders Model.* Hawthorne, NY: Aldine de Gruyter.

Kosterman, R. and Hawkins, J.D. (1997) Effects of a preventive parent-training intervention on observed family interactions: Proximal outcomes from preparing for the drug free years. *Journal of Community Psychology*, **25**(4), 337–352.

Lahti, J. (1982) A follow-up study of foster children in permanent placements. *Social Service Review*, **56**, 556–571.

Lewis, R.E. (1991) What are the characteristics of intensive family preservation services? In M.W. Fraser, P.J. Pecora and D.A. Haapala (Eds) *Families in Crisis: The Impact of Intensive Family Preservation Services.* New York: Aldine de Gruyter.

Littell, J.H. and Fong, E. (1992) Recent findings on selected program outcomes. In J.R. Schuerman, T.L, Rzepnicki and J.H. Littell (Eds), *An Interim Report from the Evaluation of the Illinois Family First Placement Prevention Program.* Chicago, IL: The University of Chicago, Chapin Hall Center for Children.

Littell, J.H., Kim, J.L., Fong, E. and Jones, T. (1992) *Effects of the Illinois Family First Program on Selected Outcomes for Various Kinds of Cases.* Chicago, IL: The University of Chicago, Chapin Hall Center for Children (Mimeograph).

Magura, S. (1981) Are services to prevent foster care effective? *Children and Youth Services Review*, **3**(3), 193–212.

Magura, S. and Moses, B.S. (1984) Clients as evaluators in child protective services. *Child Welfare*, **63**(2), 99–112.

Marcenko, M., Spence, M. and Samost, L. (1996) Outcomes of a home visitation trial for pregnant and postpartum women at-risk for child placement. *Children and Youth Services Review*, **18**(3), 243–259.

McCroskey, J. and Meezan, W. (1997) *Family Preservation and Family Functioning.* Washington, D.C.: CWLA Press.

Moore, E., Armsden, G. and Gogerty, P.L. (1998) A twelve-year follow-up study of maltreated and at-risk children who received early therapeutic childcare. *Child Maltreatment*, **3**(1), 3–16.

Nelson, J.P. (1984) *An experimental evaluation of a home-based family-centered program model in a public child protection agency.* Unpublished doctoral thesis. University of Minnesota, School of Social Work.

Nelson, K. and Landsman, M.J. (1992) *Alternative Models of Family Preservation: Family-Based Services in Context.* Springfield, IL: Charles C. Thomas.

Olds, D.L. and Henderson, C.R. Jr (1989) The prevention of maltreatment. In D. Cicchetti and V. Carlson (Eds), *Child Maltreatment: Theory and Research on the Causes and Consequences of Child Abuse and Neglect.* New York: Cambridge University Press.

Pecora, P.J. (1994) Are family preservation services effective in terms of placement prevention and other outcomes? Yes. In E. Gambrill and T.J. Stein (Eds), *Controversial Issues in Child Welfare.* Needham Heights, MA: Allyn & Bacon. (Con argument written by T.L. Rzepnicki.)

Pecora, P.J. (1995) Assessing the impact of family-based services. In B. Galaway and J. Hudson (Eds), *Child Welfare in Canada: Research and Policy Implications.* Toronto, CN: Thompson Educational Publishing.

Pecora, P.J., Adams, B., Le Prohn, N.S., Paddock, G. and Wolf, M. (1998) Accessing Casey youth outcomes: A working paper and list of indicators. Seattle, WA: Casey Family Programs.

Pecora, P.J., Bartlome, J.A., Magana, V.L. and Sperry, C.K. (1991) How consumers view intensive family preservation services. In M.W. Fraser, P.J. Pecora and D.A. Haapala (Eds), *Families in Crisis: The Impact of Intensive Family Preservation Services* (pp. 225–271). Hawthorne, NY: Aldine de Gruyter.

Pecora, P.J., Fraser, M.W., Nelson, K., McCroskey, J. and Meezan, W. (1995) *Evaluating Family-Based Services.* New York: Aldine de Gruyter.

Plotnick, R.D. (1994) Applying benefit–cost analysis to substance abuse prevention programs. *International Journal of Addictions*, **29**(3), 339–359.

Polansky, N.A., Chalmers, M.A., Buttenweiser, E. and Williams, D.P. (1981) *Damaged Parents: An Anatomy of Neglect.* Chicago, IL: University of Chicago Press.

Polansky, N.A., Gaudin, J.M. Jr and Kilpatrick, A.C. (1992) Family radicals. *Children and Youth Services Review*, **14**, 19–26.

Reynolds, A.J. (1998) Developing early childhood programs for children and families at risk: Research-based principles to promote long-term effectiveness. *Children & Youth Services Review*, **20**, 504–505.

Roditti, M.G. (1995) Child day care: A key building block of family support and family preservation programs. *Child Welfare*, **74**(6), 1043–1068.

Rossi, P.H. (1992) Asssessing family preservation programs. *Children and Youth Services Review*, **14**(1–2), 77–97.

Rzepnicki, T.L., Shuerman, J.R. and Littell, J.H. (1991) Issues in evaluating intensive family preservation services. In E.M. Tracy, D.A. Haapala, J.M. Kinney and P.J. Pecora (Eds), *Intensive Family Preservation Services: An Instructional Sourcebook.* Cleveland, OH: Case Western Reserve University, Mandel School of Applied Social Sciences.

Rzepnicki, T.L, Schuerman, J.R., Littell, J.H., Chak, A. and Lopez, M. (1994) An experimental study of family preservation services: Early findings from a parent study. In R. Barth, J. Duerr-Berrick and N. Gilbert (Eds), *Child Welfare Research Review* (Vol. 1; pp. 60–82). New York: Columbia University Press.

Savas, S.A. (1996) What are we intending to do with those we work with? In P.J. Pecora, W. Selig, F. Zirps and S. Davis (Eds), *Quality Improvement and Program Evaluation in Child Welfare Agencies: Managing into the Next Century.* Washington, D.C.: Child Welfare League of America.

Schorr, L.B. (1997) *Common Purpose: Strengthening Families and Neighborhoods to Rebuild America.* New York, NY: Doubleday.

Sedlak, A.J. (1991) *National Incidence and Prevalence of Child Abuse and Neglect: 1988.* Rockville, MD: Westat, Inc. (Original report published July 1988, US Department of Health and Human Services, under Contract 105-85-1702.)

Spaid, W.M., Fraser, M.W. and Lewis, R.E. (1991) Changes in family functioning: Is participation in intensive family preservation services correlated with with changes in attitudes or behavior? In M.W. Fraser, P.J. Pecora and D.A. Haapala (Eds), *Families in Crisis: Findings from the Family-Based Intensive Treatment Project* (pp. 131–148). Hawthorne, NY: Aldine de Gruyter.

Stein, T.J. (1985) Projects to prevent out-of-home placement. *Children and Youth Services Review,* 7(2/3), 109–122.

Stein, T.J., Gambrill, E.D. and Wiltse, K.T. (1978) *Children in Foster Homes: Achieving Continuity of Care.* New York: Praeger.

Theiman, A.A. and Dail, P.W. (1992) Iowa's family preservation program: FY 1991 evaluation. *The Prevention Report* (Fall, 1992), pp. 14–15.

Tracy, E.M. (1991) Defining the target population for intensive family preservation services: Some conceptual issues. In K. Wells and D.E. Beigel (Eds), *Family Preservation Services: Research and Evaluation.* Newbury Park, CA: Sage Publications.

Visser, K. (1991) *Original Families First counties versus original Non-Families First counties.* Lansing, MI: Michigan Department of Social Services. Unpublished memorandum.

Walton, E. (1991) *The reunification of children with their families: A test of intensive family treatment following out-of-home placement.* Unpublished PhD Dissertation, University of Utah.

Walton, E., Sandau-Beckler, P. and Mannes, M. (Eds) (1993) *Family-Centered Services.* New York City: Columbia University Press.

Wells, K. and Biegel, D.E. (Eds) (1991) *Family Preservation Services: Research and Evaluation.* Newbury Park, CA: Sage Publications.

Wheeler, C.E., Reuter, G., Struckman-Johnson, D. and Yuan, Y.T. (1992) *Evaluation of State of Connecticut Intensive Family Preservation Services: Phase V Annual Report.* Report prepared for Division of Family Support and Community Living, Department of Children and Youth Services, Hartford, CT. Sacramento, CA: Walter R. McDonald & Associates, Inc.

Whittaker, J.K. and Maluccio, A.N. (1988) Understanding families in trouble in foster and residential care. In F. Cox, C. Chilman and E. Nunnally (Eds), *Families in Trouble, Vol. 5: Variant Family Forms.* Newbury Park, CA: Sage Press.

Whittaker, J.K., Kinney, J.M., Tracy, E.M. and Booth, C. (1990) *Reaching High-Risk Families: Intensive Family Preservation in the Human Services.* Hawthorne, NY: Aldine de Gruyter.

Willems, D.M. and DeRubeis, R. (1981) *The Effectiveness of Intensive Preventive Services for Families with Abused, Neglected or Disturbed Children.* Trenton, NJ: Bureau of Research, New Jersey Division of Youth and Family Services.

Yale Bush Center in Child Development and Social Policy, and Family Resource Coalition (1983) *Programs to Strengthen Families: A Resource Guide.* Chicago, IL: The Family Resource Coalition.

Yuan, Y.T., McDonald, W.R., Wheeler, C.E., Struckman-Johnson, D. and Rivest, M. (1990) *Evaluation of AB1562 In-home Care Demonstration Projects, Volume 1: Final Report.* Sacramento, CA: Walter R. McDonald & Associates.

Zigler, E. and Black, K. (1989) America's Family Support Movement: Strengths and limitations. *American Journal of Orthopsychiatry*, **59**, 6–20.

## Further Reading

Henggeler, S.W., Schoenwald, S.K., Borduin, C.M., Rowland, M. and Cunningham, P.B. (1998) *Multi-systemic Treatment of Antisocial Behavior in Children and Adolescents.* New York: Guilford.

Hess, P.M. and Proch, K.O. (1988) *Family Visiting in Out-of-Home Care: A Guide to Practice.* Washington, D.C.: Child Welfare League of America.

Levine, R.A. (1964) Treatment in the home. *Social Work*, **9**(1), 19–28.

Mrazek, P.J. and Haggerty, R.J. (Eds) (1994) Reducing risk for mental disorders: Frontiers for preventive intervention research. Washington, DC: National Academy Press, p. 23.

Olds, D.L. and Kitzman, H. (1993) Review of research on home visiting for pregnant women and parents of young children. *The Future of Children—Home Visiting*, **3**(3), 53–92.

Winterfeld, A., Hardin, M., Field, T. and Pecora, P.J. (in preparation) *A Philosophical and Conceptual Framework for Child Welfare Services.* American Humane Association, Children's Division; American Bar Association, Center on Children and the Law; Annie E. Casey Foundation; Casey Family Services; Institute for Human Services Management; and The Casey Family Program. Englewood, CO: American Humane Association. (Mimeograph)

# 6

# COMPARATIVE RESEARCH AS A METHOD OF EVALUATING SYSTEMS

*Rachael Hetherington*

Comparative research has usually been seen as the tool of large-scale, top-down, 'macro' programmes looking at difference between social systems in terms of officially measured rates of, for example, employment, or expenditure on various services, or take-up of services. However, comparison can be used as an adjunct of many different levels and types of research. It always brings its own problems, but it also has its own advantages, particularly in throwing a new light on recurrent problems and encouraging the reframing of the familiar.

At the macro level, there is a long tradition of using comparison between countries as a way of investigating welfare systems. The comparative approach has been used by researchers such as Esping-Andersen (1990, 1996, 1999), Castles (1993) and Sainsbury (1996) for building categorizations or taxonomies of welfare systems, or investigating the responses of welfare states to global capitalism. It has also been used at an intermediate level to compare topics such as benefit systems or unemployment; Øyen (1990), Hantrais and Mangen (1996) and Clasen (1999) assemble a range of such studies. Øyen described the aim of cross-national research as being 'to reduce unexplained variables and find patterns and relationships' (Øyen, 1990, p. 3), and the unexplained variables, the difficulties of finding true equivalence, are a central problem in cross-national research. Baistow (2000) discusses the obstacles that will be encountered in making comparisons across linguistic and cultural boundaries, and points to the initial and fundamental problem of establishing whether there is an equivalence which can serve as the basis for comparison. Finding an equivalence entails the consideration of linguistic differences, conceptual differences and developmental differences. This is a matter not only of language and usage, but also of time and historical development. She points

*Evaluating Family Support: Thinking Internationally, Thinking Critically.*
Edited by I. Katz and J. Pinkerton. © 2003 John Wiley & Sons, Ltd.

out that 'The terms we use and the ways in which we use them do not have an absolute meaning even in our own countries but change over time, relative to the contexts in which they occur'. Thus, for example, studies of benefit levels may become mired in differences over definitions of need, retirement age, and in differences of structures in health services and taxation to the point when the attempt at comparison loses its way in a description of the details of difference.

The objectives of micro-level research in the social sciences, and in particular of research into social work or social welfare policy and practice, are initially very different from those of macro-level research. They are likely to be more specific and to focus on practical applications. They will, however, have to face all the same problems of non-equivalence as macro-level investigations. Cross-country comparison of social work practice starts with problems of definition because social work is differently defined in practical, professional and legal terms in different countries (Lorenz, 1994; Adams et al., 2000). When we wished to investigate social work practice in child protection in other European countries, we had to find a way of giving ourselves a sound basis of comparison. Drawing on approaches developed in social work education and training, a micro-level methodology was evolved using a case vignette as the fulcrum of the investigation, the shared point to which other things could be related. To put it another way, comparison requires that there is a reliable similarity between the things compared, as well as differences. Lacking either of these, there is no basis for comparison.

The case vignette, which has to be agreed as being a possible and likely scenario by all the countries taking part in a project, forms the similarity, the thing that is held in common, the same in all the countries. The differences are differences in structures (such as laws and the organization of government and service delivery), professional ideologies (built on accepted theories and practice experience) and culture (attitudes and values). These differences lead to different outcomes. Because there is a shared starting-point, the case vignette, the relationship between differences in structures, professional ideologies, culture and outcomes can be investigated. This methodology makes use of the fact that within Europe there are identifiable common problems (at the micro-level) to which different countries have developed a range of responses. We can compare the responses of different countries to see what outcomes their different strategies achieve, and thus evaluate the outcome of different ways of structuring welfare services. This is not an evaluation in terms of ranking or judging what is *best*. It is evaluation in terms of establishing what the *value* of a particular approach may be.

Using comparison to create a hierarchy of what is best, what has succeeded and what has failed is not useful. It is also illegitimate. It is illegitimate because of the difficulty, perhaps impossibility, of establishing comparability in the measure of outcomes. There is nothing new, of course, in saying that the definition of a successful outcome is fraught with difficulty. It requires subjective decisions about the aims of the intervention as well as the collection of information about the outcome of the project to be evaluated. The information on outcomes may be factual and objective, but in the field of social welfare it rests on subjective assessments about what is important, what is relevant, what is measurable and what is reliable. As we will see later, countries may value, and therefore measure, different outcomes, and this will affect their evaluation of similar projects.

It is not useful to use comparison to create hierarchies because it ignores the subjective element of assessing value, and limits what can be learnt from comparison. It may be a good way of learning about another system, but it tells you nothing new about your own. To explain this it is necessary to consider what can be learnt from making comparisons and what the nature of this learning is. It could be said that all research is both comparative and evaluative; any thing described is implicitly comparative with another, and it is extremely hard (and usually not desirable) to exclude evaluation from even the most exploratory and descriptive research. Explicit comparison, however, makes active use of the description of difference in a number of ways. Thus comparison between two similar objects (or systems, or happenings) stimulates questioning about the reason for difference. On the other hand, comparison between several similar objects makes it possible to identify (or try to identify) what is most important and fundamental in the similarities and what is superficial in the differences, thus to begin to disentangle the intrinsic aspects of a problem from the extrinsic factors.

Comparison, and this applies particularly to cross-country comparison, is likely to raise questions about the reliability of factual information, and it underlines the subjectivity of much that we assume to be objective. It requires that we question our use of words and the meaning that we give to words, how we conceptualize the thing that the word represents. This soon leads to questions about the implications of that conceptualization for policy and practice. For example, the word 'family' is similar in French and English. But, even though in both countries 'the family' is highly valued, this does not mean that we are talking about the same thing. Cooper et al. (1995) suggest that the family is conceptualized as a much more robust and resilient institution in France than in England, which has important implications for both policy and practice. This difference creates a greater confidence in France that families can be rehabilitated, which in its turn leads to different developments for children in the care of the state, and a different approach to family support. Thus, to compare the outcome of a particular welfare intervention in France and in England is highly complex, because the intention may have been different, and the definition of success may be different.

Inter-country comparison heightens awareness of the subjectivity of aims and of the assessment of outcomes. Reflection on the practice of other countries leads to questioning of our own practice. This questioning and reflection does not necessarily lead to change, although it may; but it leads to a deeper understanding of practice, of the influences on practice that impinge on the practitioner from outside or from the practitioner's own value system and experience. It develops awareness of alternative possibilities and of the impact of culture and circumstances on action. To summarize, comparison develops new perspectives, which makes facts seem less secure, and it creates new information, by informing one about different ways of understanding things.

A West African novelist, Chinua Achebe, illustrates both these points. He is writing about West Africa in the 1950s, and he describes how different perspectives affect reality, making facts contingent on individual experience. Events are seen through the different understandings not just of African and English, but of different people within these groups, people from different villages or in different parts of the colonial service, with differences of social position, of age, sex and religion. The following quotation illustrates two points: firstly, that facts are not straightforward and, secondly, that out of comparison you can find new information.

An Englishman is speaking, a young colonial official who has recently arrived in Africa, starting his first job. He is reflecting to himself about his work.

> Did knowledge impose a handicap on one? Perhaps it did. Perhaps facts put you at a great disadvantage; perhaps they made you feel sorry and even responsible.... Perhaps this was the real difference between the British and the French colonial administrations. The French made up their minds about what they wanted to do and did it. The British, on the other hand, never did anything without first sending out a commission of enquiry to discover all the facts, which then ham-strung them. (Achebe, 1964, p. 105)

Later the young man says to a colleague:

> You know, I was thinking the other day about our love of commissions of enquiry. That seems to me to be the real difference between us and the French. They know what they want to do and do it. We set up a commission to discover all the facts, as though facts meant anything. (Achebe, 1964, p. 109)

Achebe's point is, firstly, that facts can be understood in many different ways and, secondly, that by making a comparison between two systems you learn not about the unfamiliar system but about the familiar one. Whether this opinion of the French system was correct is not, at this point, what matters. What matters is that standing back and looking at an alternative changed the young man's perspective. His comparison between the French and English responses gave him a new and different understanding of the English approach. And this comes about because he begins to look at facts differently. In using comparison to evaluate welfare systems, we are aiming to understand these systems better and, as far as possible, accurately, whether our own or other people's. But any evaluation we make is likely to lead us to question *facts* and ultimately to tell us most about our own system.

## THREE EXAMPLES OF COMPARISON

The first two of the following examples of the use of comparison are drawn from comparative research coordinated by the Centre for Comparative Social Work Studies (CCSWS) at Brunel University. The third makes use of research carried out in other countries.

### Example I  Users' Views of Services

Our earliest comparative researches at CCSWS had been approached with a child-protection focus. One of our first findings was that a sharp distinction between child protection and child welfare is not shared in other countries. The phrase 'integrating family support and child protection' was not meaningful elsewhere—they had never been separated. When we moved on to look at the point of view of families in different countries, we therefore focused on child welfare rather than child protection, covering the potential range of interventions from none to adoption against a parent's wishes. The first of the two CCSWS studies described in this chapter used a variant on the methodology of the case vignette described above. This was a small project in which we sought the views of the parents in 13 families in England, France and Germany on their experience of child welfare interventions. The equivalence, the human situation that was the same for all countries, instead of a case vignette, was the fact that the parents we interviewed had experienced difficulties with their children for which they had sought help from official child welfare agencies. The method was similar to biographical methodology in sociological research (Chamberlayne and King, 1997; Chamberlayne et al., 2000).

The aim of the project was to disentangle what was particular to policy and practice where the parents lived, and what was felt in common by parents in difficulties in all three countries, by comparing the subjective stories of the parents. We wished to identify what was determined by the system, and what was part of the experience of seeking help. The findings of this research are discussed in detail in Baistow and Hetherington (1998), Hetherington (1999) and Baistow and Wilford (2000). The methodology is described in the research report (Hetherington et al., 1996).

In all three countries, parents placed a very high value on being listened to. This included being given time, and 'having your view of your problem taken seriously'. Using similar imagery and language, parents valued 'someone who is there for you', someone who is 'a friend', 'a shoulder to cry on', 'someone who makes you feel you can do things'. This did not necessarily mean that their social worker had to agree with the parents' views, but that their views were heard and received serious attention.

What was different in each country was the subjective experience of seeking help and support. Comparing these differences gave us a new picture of the support that is offered to families in England, and one which challenged the reality of integrating family support and child protection. This difference between countries was not about good or bad social work practice. The parents described good and bad work equally in all three countries.

It appeared that, in France, parents seeking help were supported by an assumption that seeking help from the state is a reasonable thing for a citizen to do. The state belongs to the citizens, and both workers and the families they worked with seemed to consider that asking for help was not, of itself, a negative action. The structures of services are such that it is very clear where you should first go for help. The parents did not always agree with the help that they were offered and sometimes rejected it. Sometimes they took their disagreement with the social worker to the children's judge, and the judge might or might not agree with them. There was much that was chancy (resources, for example), and some judicial decisions seemed strange to us (and to French social workers), but the actual asking for help was not the problem.

In Germany, there was the same feeling of an underlying right to help, but parents were faced with a very different situation. In Germany there are many non-profit-making and non-governmental organizations involved in the provision of services, and parents have a wide choice of where to go for help. This means that they can, to some extent, define their view of their problem by their choice of which agency to go to. Some parents in difficulties with their child might see this as a need for personal support, or for practical help or for therapy for the child, and would choose the appropriate source of help. If they did not succeed in getting the help that they wanted in the first place, they could try elsewhere. It is a very flexible system, but it was confusing for some families. Freedom of choice entails, for some, the risk of falling through the net.

The most consistent complaint of the English families was the difficulty in getting help. Those who had the most serious problems, and had children on the child protection register, got help, but not until that point. Those with less critical needs did not, and felt rejected by the system. They felt that to get help you had to make yourself out to be a bad parent. They were, however, clear about how the system worked. In a crisis the services were there, the support was there and the procedures were clearly explained.

How, between these different experiences, would one define a good outcome; how could the systems be evaluated? How would these parents have defined a successful outcome to being supported? Would their definition have been shared by their social workers? Or by the elected members of their local authority? You could argue that the English system should be positively evaluated because it appeared to target resources at those most in need. But for someone accustomed to the French system, it would appear to fail, because it was unresponsive at the stage when problems could have been prevented. And, for someone accustomed to the English system, the German system appeared dangerously fragmented. Their criteria were different from those of the professionals, and the outcomes that they identified were dependent on the functioning both of systems and of individual practitioners. The parents who told us their stories were evaluating their individual experiences. We were able to interview some of the English parents a second time and (with the help of our French colleagues) we were able to outline to them how their request for help might have been met in France. This gave them the opportunity to compare systems from their own experience and evaluate the aspects of the systems that mattered most to them. This aspect of the research, the reflections of the participants, was not fully developed (because of resource constraints), and did not provide enough information for generalization, but it should be an important part of any comparative project involving user participation.

## Example 2   Professional Responses

This example demonstrates the close relationship between evaluation, the perspective from which it is undertaken and the system within which evaluation takes place. A larger cross-country comparative study, the *Icarus* project, focused on family support from the perspective of the professionals (*Icarus* stood for *Interventions for Children with Adult Relatives under Stress*). In this project, professionals in different countries were asked for their responses to the same case vignette which tracked the experiences of a family with a mentally ill parent. The case hinged on the provision of support for the family at different points of time and in different levels of crisis. In each country there were two groups of professionals, one group made up of professionals working in adult mental health, the other of professionals working in child welfare and child protection. The countries that took part in the project were (from north to south), Norway, Sweden, Denmark, the UK, Ireland, Germany, France, Luxembourg, Italy, Greece and Australia (Victoria). Within the UK, England, Northern Ireland and Scotland were treated as separate countries. For details of this research see Hetherington et al. (2000) and Hetherington et al. (2001).

The vignette presented three stages of the family's problems. At the first stage, the mother was in a state of acute anxiety following the birth of her second child. The level of her distress raised the possibility that she would need hospital treatment, and that she might have a puerperal psychosis. Three years later, the mother was four months pregnant. Her husband was unemployed, her eldest child was having difficulties, which were being noticed at school, and she was finding her 3-year-old son a problem. At the third stage, a month after she gave birth, the children were reported by the school to be thin, unkempt and stealing food. The mother said that people were trying to poison the baby. The father had been drinking and left home three days previously; they had no money.

The groups were asked what they thought would happen, and what resources and services would be brought in at each stage. In spite of quite
similar assessments of the problems that the family faced and similar views
on, for instance, the importance of keeping mother and baby together if possible, the experience of the family would have differed considerably from one
country to another. In England, the pairs of groups were run in three different locations, and their responses were very similar. This suggested that the
differences in the family's experience were connected to the resources and
service structures of the country, rather than differences in the attitudes or id-
iosyncrasies of the individual groups. It was very clear from the discussions
that resources varied greatly from one country to another. Some countries
were better resourced than others, and the nature of the resources differed.
The German groups could count on the service of an intensive family support team but, at the time of the research, had no mother-and-baby facilities
in psychiatric hospital care. In contrast, the Danish groups could not count
on such intensive family support, but there was a very well-established unit
for mentally ill mothers and their babies. Structures also affected the family's
experience, and could determine whether they were likely to be supported,
and by which service. In Italy, the mental health centres are the lynch pin of
the adult mental health system, and provided an important service that was
not replicated elsewhere.

There were differences within countries between the discussions of the
groups made up from adult mental health professionals and the groups made
up from child welfare professionals. In some countries, this was mainly a difference in emphasis. The adult mental health groups were focused on the
mother's illness and the mother as a patient. The child welfare groups were
focused on the mother as a parent, and the needs of the children. Two countries stood out as different in this respect. In Italy, there was much more
emphasis in both groups on the family as a unit, and the needs of different
family members within that whole. In England, there was much less agreement between mental health and child welfare groups on the seriousness of
the mother's mental illness. This difference in estimation of the illness polar-
ized the patient/parent split. The level of agreement between the two groups
of professionals affected the experience of the family. Where the professionals were working with different conceptualizations of the problem, the family
was more likely to receive conflicting or confusing responses from the services. The evaluation of the success or effectiveness of a service would also
be affected.

As well as differences in the level and nature of resources to support the
family, there were differences between countries in attitudes towards family
support. In England there was an expectation that the wider family would
provide support at the first stage, and that social services would not be involved. In Germany, while the wider family was expected to play a part, it
was not thought that they should be the only source of support. There was

an assumption by the German groups that it would be right for formal family support services to play a part, not only in giving practical help but also in giving emotional support to the father and the children. If help from the wider family was not forthcoming, the input that could be given in Germany was extensive—if necessary, several hours daily for weeks or months. This was seen by the English and other English-speaking professionals as enviable but intrusive and likely to be unacceptable. Thus, although the focus of this project was on families with a mentally ill parent, the responses of the participating professionals were relevant to wider issues of family support and the prevention of family breakdown.

Any evaluation of the services offered to the family has to take account of the attitude and expectations of the policy makers. Where policy is predicated on a high valuation of preventive work, the definition of successful intervention will be that further problems are prevented. Where policy is predicated on a high valuation of rapid and effective crisis intervention, the definition of successful intervention would be that nothing was done until it was clear that there was a dangerous situation, and that the response would then be swift and efficient. Whether you evaluate positively the responses of the different countries therefore depends on the values implicit in the policies to which your evaluation relates. Thus the German and the Swedish groups, working within a preventive policy framework, all put in extensive services from the start, when the mother was first ill. When, three years later, the family was once more in difficulties, they considered that their earlier response had been ineffective in some way and that they had failed. The UK groups put in very few resources at the start and, in England, were clear that children-and-families teams would not be involved. When the family were in difficulties three years later, there was no sense that the system had failed. Rather there was a confident practical reaction to assessing the current problems, and an assessment of need would be made even though there were few resources to offer. At the final stage, when the children appeared to be starving, the mother seemed to be severely ill and the father had left the family, the German and Swedish groups refused to believe that the scenario was possible, because of the services that would have been in place. Apart from anything else, in Sweden there are universal free school meals, so the children would not have been starving. The UK groups had clear procedures for dealing with an emergency, and did not seem to be surprised by the turn that events had taken. The child protection conference system provided a structure of inter-agency communication. If it were thought that there was no time to set up a conference, a strategy meeting would have been called to coordinate work between the children-and-families team and the mental health team. The English teams regretted that they had not been able to do more at an earlier stage but, in terms of their own procedures, they had correctly delayed intervention until it was clearly necessary, and they had been able to respond successfully to a crisis situation.

Comparison that focuses on similarities provides new information about the object of comparison, the thing that is constant, in this case the situation described in the case vignette. If all the countries shared a particular problem in working with the situation, it was likely that this problem was inherent in the situation. All the groups had difficulty in keeping the children's needs in focus and in maintaining a *whole family* approach when faced by the manifold and pressing problems of the adults. Thus it is likely that this is a problem that is always going to be met when working with a family with a mentally ill parent. Comparison that focuses on difference provides new information about individual countries. If one country has a particular problem with the case, which is not shared with all countries, that problem is likely to be related to the functioning of the structures of that particular country. Thus in France and England the groups talked about difficulties in communication between mental health and child welfare services, which were not shared by the groups in Northern Ireland. France and England both have a structural division between health and social welfare services, Northern Ireland does not. The evaluation of services needs to take into account the effect of different structural frameworks on service delivery, so that services are not held accountable for problems deriving from structures.

## Example 3   Intensive Family Support Projects

On the basis of the two examples discussed above, we can hypothesize that the structures within which services operate fundamentally affect the functioning of services. It would follow that, if we have confidence in the theoretical approach of a service and in the professional practice within the service, the functioning of the service can be used as a way of evaluating the effectiveness of the structures within which the service functions. Our third example of inter-country comparison is concerned with this possibility.

Comparisons can be made on the basis of studies which are not themselves comparative, but which are studying the same thing in different countries. The sources for such studies are not extensive. Descriptions of services and structures in different countries, even when collected by editors trying to impose similar formats, are usually too different in their approach, and cover too wide a field to provide comparable information. The problems of equivalence raised at the beginning of this chapter make it very difficult to develop detailed comparisons. Gilbert (1997) provides very interesting accounts, written by authors in the countries concerned, of several European and North American child protection systems. These are broadly comparable, and lead him to the interesting conclusion that the dividing systemic difference between these countries is not whether they have mandatory reporting of child abuse (his original thesis), but whether the underlying rationale is family support or child protection. However, these comparisons are made at a broadly descriptive level of policy and there are problems of equivalence. While they suggest useful categorizations, they do not have the detail of actual operation that is needed for micro-level comparisons.

An opportunity to look at more detailed information, where the problems of equivalence are less acute, is provided by Hellinckx et al. (1997) in their collection of papers on family support. This includes some papers evaluating intensive family support programmes in the USA and in the Netherlands. Whittaker, surveying the situation in the USA, states that the purposes of his paper are:

> 1. To review the value base, objectives and essential components of a major service initiative in the United States known as Intensive Family Preservation Services. 2. To identify critical challenges this initiative has posed in three interrelated domains: evaluation research; the development of clinical practice protocols; and the refinement of public policy. (Whittaker, 1997, p. 124)

He reviews the current debates on how family support is best provided, and distinguishes 'intensive family preservation programmes' from more general family support. They are 'brief, highly intensive services generally delivered in the client's home with the overarching goal of preventing unnecessary out-of-home placement' (Whittaker, 1997, p. 128). In listing the characteristics of such services, the first is 'imminent risk of placement'. However, his reflections are pessimistic; in considering the research findings on such services, he concludes, 'some studies show a modest advantage to intensive family preservation for preventing placements over regular services. Others do not' (Whittaker, 1997, p. 131). He lists the methodological problems in evaluating family preservation services, the conflict between qualitative and quantitative methodologies, the difficulties of giving practitioners ownership of the evaluation, and the problems of *selling* the results to policy makers when the financial gains are unclear or delayed. In discussing the policy-making context, he points to the need for a positive and flexible use of placement, and the importance of the basic substructure of employment, housing, health and education services in supporting families.

Jacobs, Williams and Kapuscik, also writing about the USA, review the evaluation research on family preservation programmes:

> The central goal of family preservation is to improve the family's child-rearing abilities to the point where the family unit may be maintained without endangering the child. Unnecessary out-of-home placements should be reduced as a result. Many programme participants, providers and supporters are convinced of the effectiveness of this approach, though relatively few of these efforts have been evaluated successfully by conventional methods. (Jacobs et al., 1997, p. 206)

They describe three *waves* of evaluation. The first wave 'boasted wildly positive findings' (p. 207); the second wave was less optimistic. 'They turned up few statistically significant results', and 'the only somewhat consistent statistically significant positive results were modest improvements in certain discrete aspects of child and family functioning' (p. 207). The third wave had not yet reported its findings; but Jacobs and colleagues conclude that 'a kind interpretation of the findings available to date is that they are equivocal' (p. 213). However, after presenting this bleak picture, the authors go on to make very similar points to Whittaker. They question the focus on avoiding out-of-home placement and suggest that the measurement of more modest and intermediate goals, such as getting a child to school every day, might provide a more useful way forward. Like Whittaker, they emphasize the importance of the context, in terms of available community services and other available services.

In the same publication, researchers report on the evaluation of intensive family support programmes in the Netherlands. These programmes are referred to as *home training*, a designation which covers a range of family support initiatives where work takes place in the family home. The projects surveyed by Van den Bogaart, like the family preservation services in the USA, focused on families where children were at risk and might be placed out-of-home. He describes the development of *home training* since 1945, and the evaluation studies set up by the government during the 1980s. Of particular interest is the evaluation programme set up by the government and carried out by the Leiden Institute for Social Policy Research (see Van den Bogaart, 1997), which studied 10 projects using a combination of qualitative and quantitative measures. The research programme took into consideration the context within which the agency operated, as well as the different treatment approaches and the character of the families. The result was unequivocal. '*The most important result* of the evaluation research was a distinctive affirmative answer to the main research questions: Is home training effective?' (Van den Bogaart, 1997, p. 90; original emphasis).

Positive results were not achieved in all families; it was less effective with older children, with children with more severe problems and with children in families who did not cooperate willingly. However, the evaluation demonstrated that home training 'can be effective in multi-problem families with children at risk for placement, and that the success of home training seems to be systematically influenced by factors that can be established and measured beforehand' (Van den Bogaart, 1997, p. 92). Since that research was completed, home-training programmes of various kinds have multiplied, and Van den Bogaart comments that it has 'played an important role in the development of thoughts on coherent, connected, individualised treatment paths for children and their families' (Van den Bogaart, 1997, p. 99).

In the same publication, Baartman looks at some different approaches and methodologies of home training, focusing on preventive home training. Reviewing research in this area, he identifies the need for further research to establish preferred approaches for different target families. His conclusions in relation to preventive home training are similar to those of Van den Bogaart. 'Preventive home training is demonstrably effective in tackling family problems and child-rearing problems in high-risk families, and there are indications that this effectiveness is increased when more intensive programmes... are employed' (Baartman, 1997, p. 119).

The researchers in the USA and the Netherlands seem to be evaluating similar programmes with similar aims targeting the same families, but reaching very different conclusions. There is a stark contrast between the evaluations of intensive family support programmes in the two countries compared. In the USA, there are considerable doubts; in the Netherlands there is confidence, government support and a rapid development of new applications and a more detailed analysis of theory and practice.

There are two possible explanations for this difference. The first is that they are evaluating similar programmes, but valuing different outcomes and therefore asking different questions. The second is that differences in context, the structures within which the services operate, dominate the outcome. There is some evidence that both these factors operate.

Whittaker questions the use of placement prevention as a criterion of success, pointing out that placement is not easy to predict and that, in some circumstances, it may in any case be a positive outcome. Jacobs and her colleagues ask for a shift in evaluation to a consideration of the attainment of lesser, intermediate but very important goals. This appears to be more in line with the evaluation criteria used in the research in the Netherlands. The apparent difference in success between the similar programmes in the two countries may be partly explicable in terms of the use of different criteria of success.

However, although the point is not specifically made in the papers in this collection, the authors are writing about similar services taking place within very different systems. Both Whittaker and Jacobs refer to the importance of the system as the context of the service but it remains a background factor. Similarly, in the contributions from the Netherlands, the structural background of welfare provision is taken for granted. But it is well known that the Netherlands has an extensive and well-financed welfare regime, while the USA has the reverse, and we would hypothesize that the differences in outcome related to the differences in the contextualizing systems. The difference in the criteria used for judging success or failure can be seen as an aspect of the differences in welfare regime. Different outcomes are valued so that if, in the Netherlands compared to the USA, there is a lesser drive to save the costs of placement and there is a greater acceptance of state intervention in the family, the criteria for success will be different. If there is less family poverty, better public health provision, more support for single parents, it may be possible for intensive family interventions to be successful. In a context of family poverty and limited social services, they are likely to fail.

This then re-orientates evaluation towards a different target. If we hypothesize that intensive family interventions can be expected to have a certain level of success (as the Netherlands' research suggests) then the effectiveness of welfare regimes could be evaluated in terms of how far they enable programmes of intensive family interventions to succeed. Rather than evaluating the programmes and disregarding the structures, we would be evaluating the structures, and using the experience of the programmes as a means of measuring the success of the system. This approach would hold the family intervention programme as the fixed point, the *equivalence*, and evaluate different welfare regimes in relation to their ability to facilitate the effectiveness of the family intervention.

## CONCLUSION

The three examples discussed demonstrate how inter-country comparison can be used to uncover the characteristics of social welfare structures, and the values and unspoken assumptions that help to determine both how welfare systems are structured and how they function. In the first two examples, comparison provides a means of widening our understanding of the range of options available for policy makers in constructing welfare systems. Comparison demonstrates the subtle connections between policies and practice, and the role of values and cultural assumptions in influencing or determining both policy and practice. It also enables us to see our systems through other eyes, and see them differently.

The final example suggests a proactive use of comparison, whereby the micro-system, the individual service, can be used as a way of evaluating the nature of the macro-system. The successful functioning of the face-to-face service demonstrates the values that determine the nature of the macro-system and becomes the criteria by which the effectiveness of the welfare regime is evaluated. The micro-system can only be used to evaluate the macro-system if there is confidence in the theoretical underpinning of the micro-system and in the professionalism of the workers and managers. The intensive family support service would be a good candidate because it has a solid theoretical base and has been extensively tested. (Another possible basis for a comparative evaluation of macro-systems would be the functioning of home-hospital treatment in the mental health field). The policy makers in the Netherlands set up a very thorough evaluation and piloting of the use of intensive family support services before committing themselves to promoting their development on a national basis. Their support for this policy rests on the fit between the outcomes offered by intensive family support services, the way the rest of their child welfare system works and the underlying values of family support and preventive intervention that their macro-system demonstrates. Gilbert (1997) points out that the Anglo Saxon systems (North American and English) prioritize child protection and delay intervention while the northern European systems (his examples include Denmark, Germany and Belgium as well as the Netherlands) prioritize family support and preventive intervention. A comparison of the different expectations of intensive family support services demonstrated in the Netherlands and North America suggests that these services may not be a resource that fits with low intervention, child protection orientated systems. England and Wales share with the USA a child protection orientation, so any evaluation of intensive family support services is likely to be skewed. These services do not offer the outcomes that we prioritize.

The use of comparison in evaluation thus tends to produce more questions than answers. Comparison undermines certainties about facts and about the interpretation of facts, and challenges assumptions about values and about the connections between values and action. This can feel risky but also exciting; and the risks are well worth taking.

# REFERENCES

Achebe, C. (1964) *Arrow of God*. London: Heinemann.

Adams, A., Erath, P. and Shardlow, S. (Eds) (2000) *Fundamentals of Social Work in Selected European Countries: Historical and Political Context, Present Theory, Practice, Perspectives*. Lyme Regis: Russell House Publishing.

Baartman, H. (1997) Home-based services: Each to his own? In W. Hellinckx, M. Colton and M. Williams (Eds), *International Perspectives on Family Support*. Aldershot: Arena.

Baistow, K. (2000) Cross-national research: What can we learn from inter-country comparisons? *Social Work in Europe*, 7(3), 8–13.

Baistow, K. and Hetherington, R. (1998) Parents' views of child welfare interventions: An Anglo-French comparison. *Children and Society*, **12**, 124–133.

Baistow, K. and Wilford, G. (2000) Helping parents, protecting children: Ideas from Germany. *Children and Society*, **14**, 343–354.

Castles, F. (Ed.) (1993) *Families of Nations*. Aldershot: Dartmouth.

Chamberlayne, P. and King, A. (1997) The biographical challenge of caring. *Sociology of Health and Illness*, **19**, 601–621.

Chamberlayne, P., Bornat, J. and Wengraf, T. (Eds) (2000) *The Turn to Biographical Method in Social Science*. London: Routledge.

Clasen, J. (Ed.) (1999) *Comparative Social Policy. Concepts, Theories and Methods*. Oxford: Blackwells.

Cooper, A., Hetherington, R., Baistow, K., Pitts, J. and Spriggs, A. (1995) *Positive Child Protection: A View from Abroad*. Lyme Regis: Russell House Publishing.

Esping-Andersen, G. (1990) *The Three Worlds of Welfare Capitalism*. London: Polity Press.

Esping-Andersen, G. (Ed.) (1996) *Welfare States in Transition*. London: Sage.

Esping-Andersen, G. (1999) *Social Foundations of Postindustrial Economies*. Oxford: Oxford University Press.

Gilbert, N. (Ed.) (1997) *Combatting Child Abuse: International Perspectives and Trends*. Oxford: Oxford University Press.

Hantrais, L. and Mangen, S. (Eds) (1996) *Cross-national Research Methods in the Social Sciences*. London: Sage.

Hellinckx, W., Colton, M. and Williams, M. (Eds) (1997) *International Perspectives on Family Support*. Aldershot: Arena.

Hetherington, R. (1999) Getting help and having rights. In P. Chamberlayne, A. Cooper, R. Freeman and M. Rustin (Eds), *Welfare and Culture in Europe: Towards a New Paradigm in Social Policy*. London: Jessica Kinglsey.

Hetherington, R., Baistow, K., Spriggs, A. and Yelloly, M. (1996) *Parents Speaking: Anglo-French Perceptions of Child Welfare Interventions. A Preliminary Report*. London: Centre for Comparative Social Work Studies, Brunel University.

Hetherington, R., Baistow, K., Johanson, P. and Mesie, J. (2000) Professional intervention for mentally ill parents and their children: Building a European model. Final report on the Icarus Project. Centre for Comparative Social Work Studies, Brunel University.

Hetherington, R., Baistow, K., Katz, I., Mesie, J. and Trowell, J. (2001) *The Welfare of Children with Mentally Ill Parents: Learning from Inter-Country Comparisons*. Chichester: John Wiley & Sons.

Jacobs, F., Williams, P. and Kapuscik, J. (1997) Evaluating family preservation services: Asking the right questions. In W. Hellinckx, M. Colton and M. Williams (Eds), *International Perspectives on Family Support*. Aldershot: Arena.

Lorenz, W. (1994) *Social Work in a Changing Europe*. London: Routledge.

Øyen, E. (1990) Comparative research as a sociological strategy. In E. Øyen (Ed.), *Comparative Methodology, Theory and Practice in International Social Research*. London: Sage.

Sainsbury, D. (1996) *Gender, Equality and Welfare States*. Cambridge: Cambridge University Press.

Van den Bogaart, P. (1997) The application of intensive programs: Hometraining in the Netherlands. Evaluation and its impact on practice. In W. Hellinckx, M. Colton and M. Williams (Eds), *International Perspectives on Family Support*. Aldershot: Arena.

Whittaker, J.K. (1997) Intensive family preservation work with high-risk families: Critical challenges for research, clinical intervention and policy. In W. Hellinckx, M. Colton and M. Williams (Eds), *International Perspectives on Family Support*. Aldershot: Arena.

# Part III

## 'CASE STUDIES' FROM AROUND THE WORLD

# 7

# NATIONAL POLICY MAKING AND THE NEED TO EVALUATE FAMILY SUPPORT IN THE REPUBLIC OF IRELAND

*Catherine Hazlett*

In recent years there has been a growing appreciation in government and among policy makers of the value of high-quality research and evaluation in the development of family policy and family support initiatives. In Ireland, this development has taken place against a background of rapid social and economic change which poses huge challenges for policy makers in responding to new and emerging needs. As elsewhere in Europe, Ireland is experiencing major changes in the traditional values and norms which for generations have underpinned the development of the State's response to families. Recent years have seen a growth in marital breakdown, a fall in the rate of marriage and in fertility rates, a growth in lone parenthood and a continuous rise in births outside marriage. On the economic front, there has been radical transformation with unprecedented growth, record levels of employment, and unemployment falling dramatically. A population boom, the phenomenon of returning emigrants together with immigration as more workers from abroad are attracted to Ireland, has brought about a situation where the population is now at its highest since 1881. At the same time these major improvements in economic well-being and personal wealth also bring into sharp relief the plight of those who have not benefited from the 'Celtic Tiger' economy. A National Anti-Poverty Strategy has highlighted the situation of children in families who are poor. Recent figures show that while there has been a reduction in the number of children living in households which can be described as consistently poor,[1] it is clear that much needs to be done to address the needs of these, the most vulnerable families.

*Evaluating Family Support: Thinking Internationally, Thinking Critically.*
Edited by I. Katz and J. Pinkerton. © 2003 John Wiley & Sons, Ltd.

The pace and scale of economic change, along with that taking place in society, at community level and in family behaviour, bring major challenges for policy makers in developing appropriate responses. Change has prompted a new appreciation of the need for soundly based empirical data and a new commitment to systematic evaluation of policies and programmes. This has been most evident in the fields of social inclusion and family support. There have been a number of important policy catalysts for the growing consensus about the importance of these matters to proper planning and development. These include: the introduction of formalised systematic reviews of public spending programmes throughout all government departments; the success of the Living in Ireland Research Programme[2] in informing policy development through the provision of high-quality data on topics such as poverty, the labour market, tax and welfare; the work of the Combat Poverty Agency in researching the nature and causes of poverty in Ireland and in promoting greater public understanding about these issues; and the report of the Commission on the Family *Strengthening Families for Life*, published by the Irish Government in 1998. The latter highlighted the central importance of high-quality research and ongoing evaluation to underpin the development of family policy and family support programmes.

This chapter will consider the place of research and evaluation within the development of support to families as a key objective of national government within Ireland. It will describe the work of the Commission on the Family that was established by the Government to produce a comprehensive and in-depth analysis of the issues affecting families in contemporary Ireland. Attention will be given to the use of research alongside public consultation as forms of evaluation that informed the work of the Commission. The establishment of a strategic research programme, with an important emphasis on evaluation studies, by the Department of Social, Community and Family Affairs as a result of the Commission will be described. Finally the potential of the Families Research Programme as one of the means to drive forward the policy of family support in Ireland will be explored.

## A NEW FOCUS ON FAMILIES

The Commission on the Family was established by the Irish Government in October 1995 and completed its work in July 1998. Its brief was: 'to examine the effects of legislation and policies on families and make recommendations to the Government on proposals which would strengthen the capacity of families to carry out their functions in a changing economic and social environment.' The detailed terms of reference of the Commission included a remit to raise awareness and promote understanding about issues affecting families and to carry out research to assist with its work.

The setting up of the Commission had both an international and national context. Initiatives to mark the UN designated International Year of the

Family in 1994 encouraged a new focus on family issues throughout the world. The concerns raised in the Year of the Family carried through to the UN World Summit for Social Development in 1995. The plan of action that followed contained a number of commitments regarding the obligation of the State to help families in their education, support and nurturing roles. Also at this time arrangements were in hand for a referendum to amend the Constitution of Ireland to permit the legalisation of divorce. Comprehensive legislative provision in respect of judicial separation and the matters that arise on marital separation had been in place since the late 1980s providing the legal remedies equivalent to divorce in almost every respect except one—the right to remarry. The lead-up to this referendum in November 1995 was characterised by a widespread debate not only about the institution of marriage but also the general issues and challenges facing family life (Government of Ireland, 1995). The referendum was carried by a narrow majority and the Family Law (Divorce) Act 1996 came into effect in 1997. The results of the vote (50.28% of people voted for change and 49.72% voted against) reflected the central dilemma of many voters—how to protect the family and the institution of marriage while at the same time providing remedies for the increasing number of couples whose marriage had broken down and who wanted to move on with their lives.

The Houses of the Oireachtas (the Irish Parliament) set up a Committee on the Family, representative of the membership of both Houses of Parliament. Their work provided a forum for political debate about the need for public policy to provide greater support to build strong and stable family relationships in society. The setting-up of the Commission provided the means for further addressing these concerns. Its work received additional impetus when the Government, in June 1997, expanded the remit of the Department of Social Welfare to make family policy and family services central to its activities. The new title of the Department of Social, Community and Family Affairs was seen as reflecting the new emphasis in public policy on promoting a modern society in which the family and community are key elements.

## STRENGTHENING FAMILIES FOR LIFE REPORT

The final report of the Commission on the Family, *Strengthening Families for Life*, published by the Irish Government in July 1998, was the culmination of three years' work by a group of experts in family matters.[3] It sets out a comprehensive and in-depth analysis of the issues affecting families in Ireland at the start of the twenty-first century. It made recommendations across several different areas of public policy and aimed to lay the foundations of a national family policy to strengthen families in Irish society. The overall thrust of its recommendations centred on the need for public policy to focus on preventive and supportive measures to strengthen families in carrying out their functions. The Commission set out its views on the policy approach which

should be pursued towards this objective and made some preliminary recommendations as to how to make a start on this.

The Commission's main findings and recommendations are presented in
terms of desirable outcomes for families. The pursuit of these desirable outcomes are the core themes of the report. They relate to:

- building strengths in families;
- supporting families in caring for children;
- promoting continuity and stability in family life;
- protecting and enhancing the position of children and vulnerable dependent family members.

The individual themes cover a number of different policy areas. This is
in line with the Commission's contention that there is a need for greater
coherence in the approach to family support and for a shared vision about
what the State is trying to achieve through family support measures. The
Commission recommended that the institutional framework within which the
State's response to families is developed should be strengthened. The series
of recommendations to achieve this included a strategic Family Affairs Unit
to be located in the Department of Social, Community and Family Affairs
and a system of family impact statements to routinely audit the effects of
government policies, programmes and services on families.

## BUILDING STRENGTHS IN FAMILIES

In addressing the question of how to build strengths in families, the Commission recommended greater investment in family support work at a preventive
level in the statutory health boards through which both health and welfare
services are delivered. It also recommended the introduction in all health
board areas of family support workers for families who are experiencing difficulty in caring for their children and the extension of Community Mothers
Programmes, which offer support and guidance to parents in the child's early
years, to reach 10% of all children in Ireland under two years (some 10 000
children in 1998). The Commission considered the delivery of health services
to children and in particular the difficulties facing families when a problem
arises with a child's development. Recommendations were made for consistent support for these families, better information for parents and a single
contact point with the professional services. It was also recommended that
there should be a nationwide network of family and community services resources centres, with a national target of 100 centres. As a means to provide a
gateway to a range of services for families at a local level, the transformation
of local offices of the Department of Social, Community and Family Affairs

into 'one-stop-shops' was recommended. The report also documented the importance of close cooperative links between all local agencies, including State agencies and community-based services, in pursuit of shared family and community objectives.

## SUPPORTING FAMILIES IN CARING FOR CHILDREN

The Commission considered the role of the State in supporting families in carrying out their responsibilities. The level and structure of statutory income support arrangements are of central importance having both direct and indirect effects on the incomes, living standards, life choices and welfare of all citizens. It was the Commission's view that policies should support parents in their choices in relation to the care of their children, enable them to be the best parents they can be by giving them practical help with child rearing and equipping them with parenting knowledge and skills. Sharing with families responsibilities for caring should underpin the approach in promoting a family-friendly work environment which values families' caring roles and provides equal opportunities to get access to the labour market.

The report recommended a substantial investment package for pre-school children. Recommendations included: an Early Years Opportunities Subsidy, which could be used in a wide range of high-quality pre-school settings to ensure that 3 year olds can enjoy the benefits of early education services; and a substantial investment in the care of children aged under 3 years, through a combination of financial support for parents caring for their own children in their own home, and a subsidy for parents using purchased childcare. Various payment options were considered as to how this might be delivered to families and the Commission suggested that the cost of this very significant investment might be met through a review of the tax arrangements for married persons. The recommendations for childcare support were put forward in the context of a range of recommendations for the development of quality standards in services for children and for more support for community-based childcare and for facilities for children with special needs. Further support for parents was recommended through the introduction of a national, accessible programme of parenting information to be available to anyone encountering the ordinary challenges of parenting and family living.

## PROMOTING CONTINUITY AND STABILITY IN FAMILY LIFE

The Commission suggested that family policy must have regard to the principle that continuity and stability are major requirements in family relationships. The report goes on to say that continuity and stability should be recognised as having a major value for individual well-being and social stability, especially as far as children are concerned. The point is made that for many people marriage represents their commitment to long-term continuity and stability in their relationship and that in this context there is a valid role for public policy in supporting marriage. The need for better preparation for marriage and relationships, for promotion of the benefits of marriage counselling and for greater use of family mediation as a non-adversarial approach, which is in the interests of children, and the resolution of issues on the breakdown of couples' relationships are all highlighted in the report. The Commission expressed the view that joint parenting, where this is in the child's best interest, should be encouraged and that public policy has a key role in promoting the children's interests. A range of recommendations is made in the report to achieve these objectives, including recommendations for substantial investment in counselling and family mediation services.

## PRIORITISING THE MOST VULNERABLE

The Commission made a series of recommendations prioritising the needs of families who are trying to do the best they can for their children in difficult circumstances. These circumstances may arise because of unemployment, low incomes, parenting alone or living in communities that are contending with social and economic disadvantage. One recommendation was a concerted drive to achieve employment objectives for long-term unemployed men and women and their families. Another was that there should be a new focus on support for parents rearing children without the support of a partner. Continued improvement in the various programmes to support lone parents' participation in the workforce, increased access to schemes and training and one-to-one advice and assistance in finding a placement and in arranging childcare were also among the recommendations to support lone parents and their children.

Recommendations were also made for a comprehensive policy response to teenage parenthood. These included:

- a prioritisation of support services for teenage mothers and more initiatives to keep them in school;
- strengthening the role of youth services in support for young parents and a specific budget for them to expand services;
- the development of a strategy which encourages young people to defer parenthood, by improving life choices through training, education and offering young women a realistic hope that they may succeed in education and in securing employment;

- information for young people which seeks to influence their behaviour and their choices in relation to their futures;
- greater resources for social, personal and health education type programmes to reach young people who are out of school;
- the introduction of programmes for young men about sexuality and the responsibilities of parenthood.

The report examined the role of the education system in preparing young people for family life and for parenthood. The Commission recommended a radical approach to the introduction of family-life education throughout the school curriculum and made suggestions to ensure that these studies are accorded a high status by students, parents and teachers. It also made the case for greater investment in primary-level education to benefit all children. Along with endorsing existing national policy objectives to tackle educational disadvantage and early school leaving, the report highlighted a number of measures to enhance the attractiveness of staying in school. These included extra resources for the day-to-day running costs of schools in disadvantaged communities and a national strategy in relation to sports for school children. The Commission prioritised action to improve educational facilities for children with disabilities and action to help Traveller children stay in education and complete second-level studies.

Recognising the importance but also the vulnerability of older people within the family, the report documented the situation of this group within Irish society and acknowledged the contribution that the generation entering retirement had made to the country's present economic prosperity. The Commission made recommendations to improve the levels of pension payments and promote occupational pension coverage for the future, to develop health care and community supports for older people and for carers and to increase coordination in the delivery of these services.

## A CENTRAL ROLE FOR RESEARCH

Throughout the report the Commission highlighted the importance of research to underpin development of policy in different areas. It also emphasised the need for ongoing evaluation of the effects of policy and programmes in the longer term on the well-being of families. The Commission noted the dearth of original research in many of the key areas which are of interest to families in Ireland. The growing emphasis in recent years in the management of public services on the evaluation of programmes was considered a welcome development. The Commission called for a similar emphasis on high-quality quantitative research to underpin the development of appropriate policy responses which will be effective in securing desired outcomes for families. In one of its most significant recommendations the Commission set out the case for a national child development study which would follow through a cohort of children from birth to adulthood and provide reliable data for researchers, analysts and policy makers. Such a study has never been carried out in Ireland. Preliminary costings were indicated in the report and the Government was urged to explore further the possibility of undertaking the project.

The Commission recommended that government departments concerned with family policy should be allocated a budget to carry out innovative research into the difficulties families experience and the responses required to meet their needs. The Commission further suggested that any future investment in family support services should include specific allocations for the development of new initiatives and for evaluation of the effectiveness of measures in terms of outcomes for families. A research budget which would allow for the funding of pilot studies (with an emphasis on quantitative approaches) which could be developed within a specific framework was recommended. Health and welfare agencies were urged to put in place mechanisms to ensure continuing evaluation of programmes. The Commission cited the exchange of experience and widespread dissemination of information about what works best in different situations and information about models of good practice as being critical to the successful use of evaluation findings. The Commission's commitment to the research agenda was also evident in the extent to which its own deliberations were informed by the small number of innovative projects which it commissioned during its terms of office.

## THE WORKINGS OF THE COMMISSION

Two distinct elements in the way the Commission went about gathering information to inform its task enabled it to put forward with confidence the authoritative and ambitious programme for the development of family policy and family support services outlined in the previous sections. First, the Commission decided early on to adopt an open and inclusive approach to carrying out its task. The objective was to encourage contributions from all those who had an interest in families and the challenges they are facing today. The Commission received some 540 submissions from every part of Ireland as well as a small number of submissions from abroad. The submissions came from individuals, families and small groups (which formed the majority), national organisations and voluntary and community groups that work with families and children. Leading experts in the fields of family law, the Constitution of Ireland, childcare and services for children, employment and workplace policies, parenting and healthcare also offered advice and expertise. The overriding concern of families and the organisations that work with them was to promote family life and to tackle the problems that families encounter in carrying out their responsibilities for children. Contributors were keen to see partnership between families, statutory agencies and the voluntary sector in achieving these objectives.

The contribution of hundreds of individuals, families and community and national organisations that work with families were considered. Contributors covered a wide range of themes in their submissions but there was a consensus about the core issues that needed to be addressed. The growth in marital and family breakdown was raised and there was concern about the effects of these changes on family. Almost half of all submissions commented on the importance of education in relation to a range of family concerns. Education was seen as particularly important in equipping young people for life. Partnership with parents in educating their children was considered the most productive way forward. The effect of educational disadvantage on children from poor families was a particular concern. Other prominent themes included: counselling support as a preventive measure to assist families in time of difficulty or stress; early access to marriage and relationship counselling; childcare as a fundamental support, particularly for families on low incomes; improving health and social welfare services (including income support payments), which was a concern in about one-third of all submissions. There was also a focus on the needs of children in a changing society, especially those living in poverty or with a disability. Improving their health and well-being were priority concerns. The role of the State, it was generally agreed, was to support families, fund services adequately, ensure access to services for all and put in place the framework for the well-being of families and society. Many contributors commented on the role of the media in supporting values important to family life such as stability and dependence on one another. The common theme of all submissions was the importance of family life to the social fabric, the essential contribution that it makes to all our lives and how families can best be supported and strengthened for the future.

The issues and concerns which emerged from this widespread consultative process were an important reference source for the Commission. The Commission took the view that there is a case to be made for evaluating family policy measures not only by reference to their practical efficacy (although this is a key concern) but also by reference to the aspirations and ideals of family life which they entail. Thus, the response from the public and their interest in the work of the Commission were particularly appreciated by Commission members. It was the Commission's assertion that the validity of this type of public evaluation should be acknowledged alongside other forms of evaluation such as those based on scientific research or technical/professional expertise.

The second distinct feature of the Commission's work was its determination to ensure that its exploration of the needs of families would be underpinned by high-quality research. The Commission was realistic about what could be achieved in the short timeframe available to it to complete its work.

A pragmatic decision was taken to instigate research projects exploring a small number of themes of interest to families and on which little quantitative or qualitative information was available. The priority themes that were identified were: the nature of the development of family policy in Ireland; an exploration of the role of fathers in family life; and a national survey of care arrangements which families make for children.

The paper 'Family policy in Ireland: A strategic overview' was produced for the Commission by the Economic and Social Research Institute (ESRI) in Dublin (Fahey, 1998). It examines demographic, economic and social changes and assesses the impact these have brought about in the role and functioning of families in Irish society. The report traces the development of State provision for families and identifies the issues which are pertinent to the future direction of family policy.

The ESRI report provided an analysis of the historical context within which family policy in Ireland has developed. In doing so it identified the key principles which the Commission was later to adopt as fundamental to the development of a coherent, progressive and effective family policy. The principles are described in the Commission's report as the 'essential truths' about families which should inform policy thinking:

- Principle No. 1: The family unit is a fundamental unit providing stability and well-being in our society. The experience of family living is the single greatest influence on an individual's life and the family unit is a fundamental building block for society.
- Principle No. 2: The unique and essential family function is that of caring for and nurturing all its members. It is in the family context that a person's basic emotional needs for security, belongingness, support and intimacy are satisfied. These are especially important for children. Individual well-being has a high priority as a measure of family effectiveness and as an objective of family policy.
- Principle No. 3: Continuity and stability are central requirements in family relationships. These characteristics have a major value for individual well-being and social stability, especially for children, and should be promoted by public policy. Joint parenting should be encouraged with a view to ensuring, as far as possible, that children have the opportunity of developing close relationships with both parents. However, it needs to be recognised that this may not always be available or indeed optimal—for example, where violence, abuse or extremes of conflict are involved. For many people marriage represents the expression of their commitment to long-term continuity and stability. Accordingly, it should be supported by public policy.
- Principle No. 4: Equality of well-being between individual family members should be recognised. This means that there is a necessary limitation and constraint on an individual's freedom of behaviour and expression within

family life. In practice, this constraint would be effective in the area of children's rights and would be implemented by particular legal guarantees of children's rights within society. Similarly, family membership and the concept of family privacy and autonomy should not be misused to cloak oppression of weaker members by the strong within the family. In areas of apparently conflicting rights children, because of their vulnerability, must be particularly protected.

- Principle No. 5: Family membership confers rights, duties and responsibilities. There is, as a prerequisite for healthy family relationships, a fundamental obligation on family members to recognise and serve each other's interests as well as their own. Tension between these interests will often arise, and families may need outside support and help to resolve such tensions. This is an area where well-directed public policy is of paramount importance.
- Principle No. 6: A diversity of family forms and relationships should be recognised. The fundamental human activity of care, intimacy and belonging can take place in a variety of family forms. Policy should recognise the diversity and provide appropriate supports where necessary.

In publishing the principles, the Commission drew particular attention to the contribution of research work in informing its thinking:

> The principles and objectives which emerge from the process of clarification need not be radically new. We would hope that they would capture and project forward the essence of developments which have emerged in Ireland in recent decades and are valued by Irish people. Family policy we consider should retain a strong popular base while at the same time protecting minority rights and recognising the real diversity of family life in Ireland today. Family policy should acknowledge and reflect the social work of long-established traditions of family centredness and family cohesion in social life in Ireland while at the same time taking cognisance of new awareness and new concerns for individual well being in family life which have emerged in recent years.
> (Commission on the Family, 1996)

A literature review of national and international work on the role of fathers in family life was also commissioned (McKeown et al., 1998a). The report presented a range of perspectives on the growing literature on fathers, particularly in the fields of psychology and sociology but also in psychoanalysis, social policy and some areas of the law in Ireland as it affects fathers. The report also provided information about some of the experiences of fathers as highlighted in submissions made to the Commission during the consultation phase of its work.

The report on fathers provided much needed information in relation to the emerging concerns about the role of fathers in family life today. Firstly, it enabled the Commission to address in a meaningful way in the report the issues to do with the pressures on families in balancing work and family life, the sharing of care responsibilities, and the often neglected issues to do with the mutual benefits to fathers and children of active engagement in parenting by fathers. Secondly, the report, which has since been published for a wider audience by the authors under the title *Changing Fathers? Fatherhood and Family Life in Modern Ireland* (McKeown et al., 1998b), has done much to provoke discussion and set in motion a reappraisal of attitudes to fathers and parenting, particularly in the field of family policy.

In a third area of interest to the Commission, the Economic and Social Research Institute produced a report, *Childcare Arrangements in Ireland* (Williams and Collins, 1998), which presented the findings of a national survey of over 1300 families with children aged 12 years or less. The survey collected information about the different care arrangements that children experience throughout the day, and the services used by parents working full time in the home as well as those who work outside the home. This was the first time that this type of data had been collected in Ireland. Thus the Commission's recommendations on support for parents with child rearing were grounded in the realities of families' day-to-day experiences in providing care for their children.

A wide range of information about State provision relevant to families, including family income support, labour market policies, education and family life, and health policy for families was drawn together for the Commission by the Family Studies Centre, University College Dublin (Kiely et al., 1996). The work covered recent policy developments in relation to families with caring responsibilities for an older member or a member with a disability, marital separation and lone-parent families and families under stress.

In summary, the findings of the research undertaken by the Commission strengthened the arguments for a radical new approach in family support. It enabled the Commission to put forward an approach to family support that reflects the essence of what was good about traditional family life while recognising new concerns about individual well-being. This approach affirms parents, both fathers and mothers, in their important parenting role; and is responsive to the dynamic changes that are taking place in family life and in society while placing children centre stage.

## ESTABLISHMENT OF THE FAMILY AFFAIRS UNIT

The Commission's work was completed in the context of a new Programme for Government committed to a 'families first' approach to the development of policies and services. This included a broadening of the remit of the Irish Government's Department of Social Welfare to take on new responsibilities in family policy and services; the establishment of a Family Affairs Unit to coordinate family policy; and new investment for the development of a range of family services and support initiatives. The Family Affairs Unit of the

Department of Social, Community and Family Affairs commenced work in July 1998. It has responsibility for pursuing the findings in the report of the Commission on the Family, following their consideration by Government, coordinating family policy in cooperation with other departments of State, undertaking research and promoting awareness about family issues and the development of a number of family services. Considerable extra resources have been allocated by the Government for the development of these services. Key developments include:

- a major programme of support for the provision of marriage and relationship counselling and child counselling;
- the establishment of a nationwide Family Mediation Service, free and available to all couples who have decided to separate;
- the launch of a Families Research Programme to support independent research into family issues.

A parenting information programme is also planned and some hundred Family and Community Resource Centres are to be funded. A pilot programme to provide a local family information service through 'one-stop-shops' is underway. In addition the Government have set up a National Children's Office and published a national strategy to enhance the status and further improve the equality of life of Ireland's children. The Government has enacted legislation to establish a Family Support Agency. This Agency will further the development of programmes and services to support and promote the well-being of families. It will provide information about issues of interest to families and it will have an advisory role to the Minister for Social, Commmunity and Family Affairs.

## FAMILIES RESEARCH PROGRAMME

The Family Affairs Unit has responsibility for a Families Research Programme. This was seen as a major step forward in furthering the objective of the Commission on the Family to promote the use of research in debates on issues about families and in the development and shaping of future family policy. The Programme complements the work of the Combat Poverty Agency (which has a particular function in relation to examining the nature, causes and extent of poverty and, for that purpose, the production, commission and interpretation of research) and the work of the Economic and Social Research Institute in the field of social research. The Families Research Programme can both support independently identified themes for research and provide funding for evaluation studies undertaken by voluntary organisations in order to critically assess the quality of their own services. The Programme has a strong emphasis on evaluation studies, particularly in relation to family services and pilot programmes. The Programme is an important strategic instrument.

The potential of the Family Research Programme strategic role is perhaps best illustrated by taking a closer look at the detailed criteria for inclusion in the Programme and a brief description of those research projects which have been successful in securing backing. Two distinct categories of research are eligible for consideration. At one level the Families Research Programme aims to attract innovative research proposals from researchers and academics, working in the field of family policy and family support within universities and other academic institutions. A second strand of the Programme is designed to support the evaluation of policies and services for families. Proposals were particularly sought from national organisations that work with families.

For both strands the overriding criterion for inclusion in the funding programme is the potential of the proposed research to inform the future development of aspects of policy relating to families and family services. Other important considerations were: the quality of the proposal; the level of research and evaluation experience and expertise involved, and the proposed management arrangements to deliver the project on time to the Department of Social, Community and Family Affairs. In the event, the proposals received were on the whole of an exceptionally high standard and highly pertinent to the family themes.

Agreements with proposers for staged payments over a two- to three-year period meant that it was possible to undertake funding commitments for 13 projects for completion over the period from 2000 to 2002. The themes being researched capture a range of issues which are increasingly challenging to established policies and practice. They include: an exploration of children's experience of parental separation; an assessment of the need for parenting support; a study of couples in the first five years of marriage focusing on what helps or hinders, the development of relationships; a study of grandparenthood in modern Ireland; an examination of the causes and effects of men's marginalisation from family and community; a study of the nature of marital problems and the predicative ability of pre-marital screening to determine couples likely to break up; a nine-year psychosocial follow-up study of children and families; an investigation of the processes of family formation in Ireland; and a study to identify good professional practice in working with vulnerable fathers.

Although it is still early days in terms of testing the resolve by policy makers to take on board the findings that may emerge from the Programme, two recent developments augur well for the future. The first project to be completed under the Families Research Programme concerned flexible working arrangements, and it coincided with the establishment of a committee, representative of government and social partners, charged with the formation of a national framework for the development of family-friendly policies at the level of the enterprise. Thus the findings of the research are very timely with considerable potential opportunity to inform the future policy approach to be adopted by social partners in enhancing the opportunities for workers to reconcile work and family life.

The announcement by the Minister for Social, Community and Family Affairs and the Minister for Health and Children that the possibility of a National Child Development Study or Birth Cohort Study for Ireland was to be explored was further evidence of the growing appreciation of the role of high-quality research to underpin future family support initiatives. A Cabinet Committee had agreed that a feasibility study to explore all the issues involved in such a major study should be undertaken. It was part funded under the Families Research Programme. The feasibility study set out the scope, methodology and management arrangements which would be appropriate for a full National Child Development Study in Ireland, the estimated costs and the options open to the Government as regards funding. That feasibility study has now been completed and the Government has announced that a full study is to go ahead.

The findings from other projects in progress also have strong potential to influence development. The work underway in relation to the processes of family formation in Ireland is expected to provide, for the first time, sound data about possible trends in lone parenthood and cohabitation, which are relatively recent phenomena in Ireland. Two studies, both concerned with the effectiveness of marriage and relationship counselling, were initiated in 2000. The findings of the studies will be of immediate interest to the two major providers of these services to families in Ireland, Accord—the Catholic Marriage Advisory Council and Marriage and Relationship Counselling Services Ltd. The studies, which are part sponsored by those organisations, both aim to assess the effectiveness of services on their respective clients.

The Accord client study will follow 3000 clients through counselling to assess the impact of the service on them. The analysis of the data will endeavour to explore the similarities between clients of the services and other populations and tease out the differences between social class, gender, stage in life cycle and other aspects of personal circumstances. The size of the sample involved and the scope of the evaluation study will break new ground, and without doubt has the potential to yield important results about the effectiveness of counselling intervention and indicate more effective ways of developing support programmes for personal relationships.

The Families Research Programme is still at an early stage of development. Nevertheless, the evidence to date is that it is filling an important niche in the publicly funded research environment in Ireland. It is opening up new possibilities for researchers in the field of family support. In particular the emphasis in the Programme on evaluation studies should help to take forward the case for a coordinated, systematic programme of evaluation for services and initiatives in family support across all statutory and non-statutory services, as envisaged by the Commission on the Family. Improving access for practitioners, researchers and policy makers to information about studies underway, and better mechanisms for the dissemination of findings as they become available—particularly on 'what works' and models of good practice—remain the major challenges for the future development of the

Families Research Programme, and indeed for all agencies with an interest in family support.

## CONCLUSION

In concluding, mention must be made of the role of the Government Public Expenditure Review process as a driver for better evaluation of family support. From the beginning of the 1990s, evaluation studies have been undertaken to assess particular aspects of programmes funded by individual departments reflecting their own concerns. So, for example, the Department of Social, Community and Family Affairs undertook studies mainly concentrated on services provided in the community and voluntary sector which were largely dependent on government grant aid. A more formalised programme of comprehensive expenditure reviews was then introduced in 1997 across all Departments of State involved in public expenditure. The reviews are aimed particularly at major expenditure programmes; for example, income support schemes.

The aims of the review Programme are to provide a systematic analysis of what is actually being achieved by expenditure in each programme and to provide a basis on which more informed decisions can be made on priorities within and between expenditure programmes. The guidelines issued by the Department of Finance (1997) explain that implementation of the conclusions of reviews has to be viewed as an essential part of the success of the review process. The reviews are carried out under the aegis of a specially established Steering Group comprising representatives of the Department of Finance and the spending departments. The review process involves identifying the objectives of the Programme, their validity in the contemporary context, evaluating the extent to which the objectives are being achieved and commenting on how efficiently and effectively the Programme is meeting its objectives. The reviews often include an independent evaluation of effectiveness of services in meeting client needs. In the field of family support, as in all areas of public policy in Ireland today, it is likely to be within this process of assessing public expenditure effectiveness that the best opportunity exists to realise the potential of research and evaluation as a catalyst for more responsive and effective services.

## NOTES

1. *Consistent poverty* is defined as below 50–60% of average household disposable income and *experiencing enforced basic deprivation* described as being without basic necessities such as a warm waterproof overcoat and two pairs of strong shoes.
2. The Living in Ireland survey began in 1994 interviewing a large sample (3000–4000) of Irish households as part of the European Community Household Panel. It

is carried out by the Economic and Social Research Institute (2000) with the core sponsorship of Eurostat, the Department of Social, Community and Family Affairs and the Combat Poverty Agency.
3. The Commission membership comprised experts in the following fields: social policy (specifically health, education and welfare), family law, mediation and counselling, medical expertise from both general practitioner and psychology disciplines, economics, taxation and income support policies.

# REFERENCES

Commission on the Family (1996) *Strengthening Families for Life: Interim Report of the Commission on the Family*. Dublin: The Stationery Office.

Commission on the Family (1998) *Strengthening Families for Life: Final Report of the Commission on the Family*. Dublin: The Stationery Office.

Department of Finance (1997) *Expenditure Review: Framework and Guidelines*. Dublin: Department of Finance.

Department of the Taoiseach (1999) *Programme for Prosperity and Fairness*. Dublin: The Stationery Office.

Fahey, T. (1998) Family policy in Ireland: A strategic overview. *Strengthening Families for Life: Final Report of the Commission on the Family*. Dublin: The Stationery Office.

Family Affairs Unit (1999) *Families Research Programme*. Information available from the Department of Social, Community and Family Affairs, Dublin.

Government of Ireland (1995) *The Right to Remarry: Information Paper on the Divorce Referendum*. Dublin: The Stationery Office.

Government of Ireland (2000) *Social Inclusion Strategy: Annual Report of Inter-Departmental Policy Committee*. Dublin: The Stationery Office.

Kiely, G., Richardson, V. and Grattan, S. (1996) *Issues in family policy in Ireland*. Unpublished paper prepared for the Commission on the Family.

McKeown, K., Ferguson, H. and Rooney, D. (1998a) Fathers: Irish experience in an international context. In *Strengthening Families for Life: Final Report of the Commission on the Family*. Dublin: The Stationery Office.

McKeown, K., Ferguson, H. and Rooney, D. (1998b) *Changing Fathers? Fatherhood and Family Life in Modern Ireland*. Cork: Collins Press.

Nolan, B. (2000) *Child Poverty in Ireland*. Dublin: Oaktree Press in association with Combat Poverty Agency.

Williams, J. and Collins, C. (1998) Childcare arrangements in Ireland. In *Strengthening Families for Life: Final Report of the Commission on the Family*. Dublin: The Stationery Office.

# 8

# A CULTURALLY RELEVANT MODEL FOR EVALUATING FAMILY SERVICES IN HONG KONG

*Monit Cheung and Chi-Kwong Law*

Strengthening the family has been positively noted in the literature as a mission and foundation for the development of family services (Kaplan and Girard, 1994, Kumpfer, Molgaard and Spoth, 1996; Walsh, 1998). However, there is not a specific prevention or treatment programme that can fit the needs for all families. In order to adequately assess and meet family needs, social workers need to view cultural considerations as one of the most important criteria, especially when they provide services to at-risk families to enhance their strengths during a time of crisis (Dunst, Trivette and Thompson, 1994). This strengths-based concept is not uniquely applicable to any one culture, but applies equally well across cultures.

This chapter focuses on describing a public–private partnership model for developing family services in Hong Kong, a Special Administrative Region of China. It analyses the history and philosophy of family service development, and critically reviews the collaborative efforts of the government and non-government organizations (NGOs). Consideration is given to the multifaceted culture of Hong Kong as a driving force in determining the format and style of service delivery. In this way Hong Kong's Family Services are considered as a case example through which to explore how best to provide and evaluate a culturally relevant model of family support.

Self-reliance has always been the acclaimed value of Chinese families. Voicing concerns about family problems and seeking professional help are usually the last resort. Chinese families tend to try to solve their problems by themselves. If the problems cannot be resolved, they will then seek help from their extended family members, followed by friends and relatives. A study

*Evaluating Family Support: Thinking Internationally, Thinking Critically.*
Edited by I. Katz and J. Pinkerton. © 2003 John Wiley & Sons, Ltd.

conducted by the Hong Kong Family Welfare Society (HKFWS, 1991) indicated that on average clients approached the Family Service Centre 28.5
months after they felt the emergence of the major presenting problem. At the
same time social workers, and other helping professionals who work with
Chinese families, must have ethnically sensitive competencies and sensitivity to the issues faced by these families.

## STUDY FOCUS

Hong Kong provides an interesting site for study because it is a multicultural
environment connecting the east (Chinese) and the west (European, British,
and North American). This chapter provides information about family services and their evaluation efforts in Hong Kong. It is organized under five
major headings:

- family service history and philosophy
- types of family services in Hong Kong
- family service review and evaluation
- lessons learned
- suggested next steps.

In the historical analysis, guiding principles of family services will be described with an emphasis on their evolution within socio-economic and
political changes. An integrated family service typology based on shared
governmental and NGO service delivery will be presented, and this typology
system described to identify new service trends as an influential force.

The discussion of evaluation will include an analysis of a recent development in reviewing family services in Hong Kong. It will address the emerging
need to analyse outcome-based data, to promote family-focused services, to
close the service gap for hard-to-reach populations, and the priority-setting
process in the service delivery system. A list of lessons learned from the
evaluation process will be included to identify long-term service goals, frameworks for analysis, limitations and strengths of the Hong Kong family service
model, and future research strategies. Arising out of those lessons an evaluation framework will be proposed from the analysis of the public–private
partnership model, which can be implemented within the culturally diverse
environment of Hong Kong. This framework is built around five major concepts: credibility, creativity, cultural sensitivity, feasibility, and result utility.

## FAMILY SERVICE HISTORY AND PHILOSOPHY

It is imperative to note that Hong Kong was a British colony for 97 years
and the history and philosophy of family services have been affected by that

experience. Most residents of Hong Kong are ethnic Chinese: 95% in the 1996 census. As an open port and the eighth largest trading community in the world, Hong Kong takes its cultural influences not only from China but also from across the international community. Cultural practices in Hong Kong exemplify an interesting and generally harmonious blend of Chinese and western cultures. People in Hong Kong celebrate their Christmas holidays as joyfully as their Mid-Autumn and Dragon Boat festivals.

The Hong Kong population has been considered as more traditional in their family values than their counterparts in China. A comparative study conducted in Hong Kong and in two other major cities in China, Guangzhou and Beijing, showed that though over half of the working women in the three cities would consider work and family as equally important, 28% of the working women in Hong Kong considered family as more important than work, while only 8% in Guangzhou and 3% in Beijing thought so (Chan, Law and Kwok, 1992). However, the political uncertainty during the 1990s has gradually reduced the significance of the family value of maintaining a solid and stable family life. It also promoted a sharp increase in the rate of family migration to European and North American countries. Nevertheless, family services, which are perceived as a means of maintaining harmonious family values, are still in great demand.

Since the return of Hong Kong to China there has been a massive influx of new migrants from the mainland for family reunification, and a great number of immigrants returning to Hong Kong. The daily quota of 150 migrants from the mainland and the countless number of returning immigrant families mean more newly arrived families in need of family services to assist with cultural adjustment and integration. In a study of elderly Chinese living in the United States, Cheung (1989) found that the traditional family values held firmly by elderly Chinese immigrants have affected their receptivity to social services. To help migrant families to adjust to a new environment, it is suggested that 'services should focus on the person's need for a cohesive family structure by providing services in a simulated family setting' (Cheung, 1989, p. 459). In addition, to work effectively with families from different ethnic backgrounds, social workers should be equipped with four ethnic competencies:

- ethnographic knowledge base—understanding what is salient in the family's culture and the client's help-seeking behaviour;
- professional preparedness—assessing one's own biases and prejudices, developing appropriate language skills, and learning from the client system;
- comparative analyses—understanding the importance of cultural relevancy and the reality of diverse world views;
- appropriate interventions—expanding the horizons of culturally sensitive practice by working with the client system (Green, 1995).

The Hong Kong Council of Social Service, which is a coordinating body for social services providers, has been advocating the development of a coherent family policy for years. It supports the need for family policy in preserving the function of Chinese family culture in Hong Kong. The Council has drawn attention to some of the characteristics of Hong Kong's family culture and some of its recent changes emphasizing that, despite the sweeping changes that have occurred in the past several decades, the family has still remained the most basic social unit of solidarity and sentiment, and this ought to continue. The changes that the family have undergone include size, form, authority structure and role expectations. All have repercussions for the family's capacity to provide personal care to its members and on the demand for social services. What is of great concern is the presence of many social problems in relation to families, such as unattended children, marital and family breakdowns, drug abuse among the young, juvenile delinquency, student truancy, child abuse, spouse battering and many family tragedies that involve neglect or cruelty to, and even death of, family members (HKCSS, 1995).

These significant demographic and cultural changes have led to the suggestion by a Family Service Review Team that Hong Kong should adopt five principles for government intervention recommended by the UK Government (Home Office, 1998):

- ensuring that all parents have access to the advice and support they need, improving services and strengthening the ways in which the wider family and communities support and nurture family life;
- improving family prosperity, reducing child poverty, and ensuring that the tax and benefit systems properly acknowledge the costs of bringing up children;
- making it easier for parents to spend more time with their children by helping families to balance work and home;
- strengthening marriage and reducing the risks of family breakdown;
- tackling the more serious problems of family life, including domestic violence and school-age pregnancy.

Other guiding principles, as outlined by the Steering Committee of the Consultancy Study on Review of Family Services (2000), are related to the nature of the service required to enhance outcome effectiveness. These principles, which are supported by the international literature, state that family services must be:

- family-oriented, to maximize the involvement of all members;
- community-based, to address the relevance and responsiveness of service provision;
- user-friendly, to encourage service utilization and engage participants in the decision-making process;
- strengths-based, to build family competency and self-sufficiency;
- resources-based, to help families to identify their own potential to solve problems;

- preventive in nature, to avoid the need for crisis intervention;
- barrier-free, to integrate community services to assist all families;
- cost-effective, to measure needs and goal accomplishments;
- integrative in nature, to coordinate other relevant services and avoid service duplication.

A tenth principle, seen as essential by practice-oriented researchers such as Pithouse, Lindsell and Cheung (1998), needs to be added: accountability in service design and implementation. A Consultancy Team reviewing family services stressed that both process and outcome evaluations should be incorporated in service planning and implementation, as a means of identifying needs and assessing outcome effectiveness.

## Historical Development of Family Services in Hong Kong

How the 10 service-orientation principles fit with Hong Kong's current cultural situation can be learned from considering the development over the years of Hong Kong's Family Service. This historical perspective illustrates how the mixed culture in Hong Kong has played a significant role in service planning and design.

### Pre-war Years: 1931–1945

Before World War Two, welfare services were provided mainly by small mutual help groups from clans, Kai Fong (neighbourhood) associations, and missionaries. Welfare provision concentrated on meeting the needs of poor families who had deserted their homes due to economic difficulties or had moved to Hong Kong to escape the plague of wars. There were no formal family services established in that era. Nevertheless, services were user-oriented and needs-based.

### Germination Years: 1945–1965

In the immediate post-war years, Hong Kong received an influx of new immigrants. The population of Hong Kong grew rapidly from 600 000 in 1945, to 1.6 million in 1951, then to more than 3.1 million in 1961. The inability of the economy to provide employment opportunities resulted in a large number of families who were unable to provide adequate food, shelter and education to their children. Family Service Centres were established to meet basic needs by providing financial aid and free food rations to needy families, and educational sponsorships for children. Although the Hong Kong government agreed that families played an important role in relieving the distress of individuals, limited services were delivered in the hope that families would be self-sufficient once they had settled. Family Service Centres were organized by NGOs to reduce the suffering of families through tangible services aimed to meet their basic survival needs. These services were community-based to fulfil the mission of providing assistance for families within the community. Given the limited financial and human resources available to the NGOs for providing direct tangible services, it is not surprising that documentation let alone service evaluation is non-existent.

### Establishment Years 1965–1980

The gradual development of the Hong Kong economy enabled the government to put more resources into family welfare services. In 1965, the first White Paper on the Aims and Policy of Social Welfare in Hong Kong was announced. The White Paper stated that:

> In Chinese tradition, social welfare measures which individuals may need on account of poverty, delinquency, infirmity, natural disaster and so on are regarded as personal matters which at least in theory ought to be dealt with by the family (if necessary the 'extended family'). It is clearly desirable, on social as well as economic grounds, to do everything possible in Hong Kong to support and strengthen this sense of family responsibility.
>
> (Hong Kong Government, 1965, p. 7(c))

In the 1960s, while living standards improved, new social problems emerged such as juvenile delinquency, overcrowded living conditions, relationship conflicts, and unemployment. The aim of family services was to strengthen family functioning and support the well-being of family members. The Family Casework Service was localized in 1965 and became more accessible at the district level. In 1971, the government implemented the social security scheme to provide financial assistance to the poor. New types of service, such as home help, school social work, and family life education began to emerge and grow. Within the Social Welfare Department, social workers also took on a number of statutory responsibilities, for example the care and protection of children. These services were clearly family-oriented and focused on remedial work.

### Development and Innovative Years: 1980–1994

In the 1980s, the standard of one Family Service Centre for every 150 000 people was established. The service domain expanded rapidly to include counselling, referring clients for practical advice and assistance, and empowering and supporting individuals and families to help themselves in coping effectively with personal and social problems. Home-help services and family-aid services were also developed to provide relief to family caregivers and to help the vulnerable to stay in the community rather than being institutionalized. As the economy grew and society became more complex, new social problems emerged requiring more services and new methods of intervention. Thus, Family Service Centres constantly reviewed their domain and expanded to deal with new areas of need. There were also studies on the needs of single parents (HKFWS and Law, 1991), the profile of families affected by extra-marital affairs (Caritas Family Service, 1995), and the social welfare needs of white-collar workers (Caritas, 1987).

The objectives of Family Service Centres were reiterated in the 1991 White Paper: *Social Welfare into the 1990s and Beyond* (Hong Kong Government, 1991):

> The overall objectives of family welfare services are to preserve and strengthen the family as a unit to develop caring interpersonal relationships, to enable individuals and family members to prevent personal and family problems and to deal with them when they arise and to provide for needs which cannot be met from within the family. With these objectives in mind, support services have been developed to assist families when they are unable to discharge their caring and protective functions satisfactorily.
>
> (Hong Kong Government, 1991, p. 19)

In the early 1990s, many NGOs launched innovative projects and services such as the Emergency Foster Care Service (HKFWS and Cheung, 1994), the Senior Social Work Practitioner Project to provide high-quality family services to clients with multiple needs requiring intensive intervention (HKCSS, 1989), and specialized group work services for adults with mental health problems (HKFWS, 1989). Innovative services associated with marital dissolution included mediation services (Catholic Marriage Advisory Council, 1991), and family drop-in services at Family Service Centres providing a wide range of services using an integrated approach (HKFWS, 1991). A refuge service for women suffering domestic violence was also established to provide support to these vulnerable women. Services for separated families and immigrants from China were first initiated by NGOs. The major concern in the evaluation endeavour focused on service impacts and the learned experiences from these pilot projects. This was particularly important as the NGOs had taken the role of identifying and rendering services to meet specific needs. The government would then provide support if these services proved to be necessary and viable. Much of the government subvention went into remedial work, though funding was also available for preventive and resource-oriented services.

## Consolidation and Evaluation Years: 1995 Onwards

In the mid-1990s, Family Service Centres began to concentrate more on service quality and accountability. Currently, performance pledges have been developed to protect clients' rights to services. These cover issues such as the client right to complain and the number of days for Family Service Centres to initiate contacts after receiving applications from clients, and so on. Funding bodies, including the Social Welfare Department, are increasingly concerned with accountability. Furthermore, the public has raised service expectations, and the demand for quality services is increasingly high. Evaluation has an important role to play in equipping Family Service Centres with information in order to identify areas for improvement in order to achieve better results. It also facilitates the Family Service Centres in monitoring service quality and improving service effectiveness and public accountability by promoting a new focus on outcome and client satisfaction. Services are to be strengths-based, outcome-oriented, and integrative in nature.

The rapid social, economic and political changes in Hong Kong, coupled with technological advances and family structural changes, have altered the focus of services away from traditional families to a diversity of families, including single-parent families and new and returning migrant families. Newly arrived families from the mainland are faced with more than financial and economic adjustments; many of these migrants face problems that deal with cultural adjustment and discrimination. If self-sufficiency was the vision of family services in the 1990s, the vision in the new millennium has to be expanded to include self-reliance and empowerment. Family services in this era are assessed against the criteria of strengths, barriers, effectiveness and cost.

## TYPES OF FAMILY SERVICES IN HONG KONG

Since the establishment of the first Family Service Centres in Hong Kong, the government has put tremendous effort into providing support for the development of family services, in both the public and private sectors. The primary function of the Family Service Centres is to provide family casework and counselling to assist families and individuals to understand and deal with family problems, to care and protect young children, to obtain support to deal with illness, disabilities, finance, accommodation and interpersonal relationships, and to provide support for the family caregiver. In conjunction with the Family Service Centres, services such as home help, family aid, family life education, and school-based social services are also provided.

Family and child welfare services are inseparable for many families. The Social Welfare Department (2000) lists 17 service areas for families: family casework, post-migration support, childcare, services for families and children experiencing domestic violence, child custody, family mediation, residential childcare, adoption, foster care, family life, compassionate rehousing, temporary shelter and urban hostels for single persons, day relief centres for street sleepers, departmental hotlines, family aid, charitable trust funds, and family care demonstration and resource centres. According to the Social

Welfare Department (www.info.gov.hk), the major objectives of family and child welfare services in Hong Kong are:

- to preserve and strengthen the family, through services such as family life education and family activity and resource centres;
- to support families which are unable to fulfil their functions, through services such as day nurseries and day crèches for children under 6, occasional childcare, extended hours services, fee assistance and family aid;
- to help families in trouble, through services dealing with family casework, child protection, child custody, residential care for children (including foster care, small group homes and other residential homes), and battered spouses;
- to carry out other statutory and non-statutory responsibilities, such as the adoption service, the Child Care Centre Advisory Inspectorate, hotline services, and services for street sleepers and bed-space apartment lodgers.

In Hong Kong, a public–private partnership model is always in place when family services are planned and delivered. It is important that evaluation should focus on this partnership. Attention should be given to the dynamics of the relationship and the process and outcomes that result. In addition, Hong Kong culture and its population density have enriched the experience of establishing neighbourhood organizations, community networks and self-help programmes. It is important to evaluate these collaborative efforts as a crucial aspect of the way in which family-centred services deliver a continuum of community-based support for families.

## Public–Private Partnership Model

Family services are provided through Family Service Centres that are established by both the Social Welfare Department and NGOs. In the current system (see Figure 8.1), services are provided on a continuum covering remedial, supportive, preventive and developmental functions. At one end there is casework which is remedial in nature and involves the self-referral of families, outreach activities, and collaborative efforts between various agencies. Family Life Education (FLE) by contrast lies at the other end of the continuum, laying stress on the importance of prevention and the developmental tasks of families. Group work and community work are delivered to all families and in conjunction with service provision in individual and family counselling.

A useful brief summary of services was prepared as a Consultancy Brief (2000) for a Review of Family Services. It identified seven different types of services.

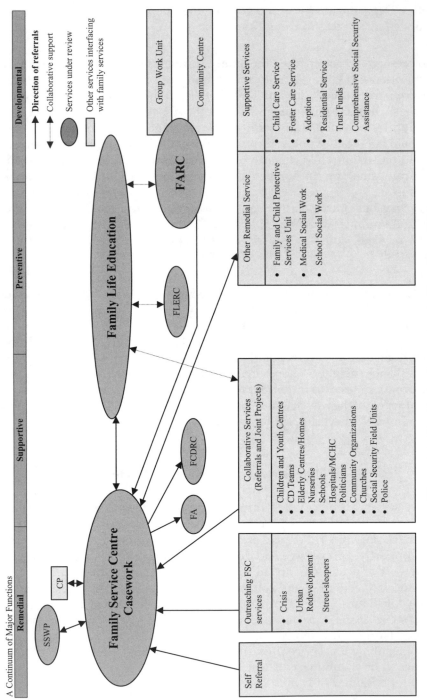

**Figure 8.1** Family services system in Hong Kong 2000

### Family Casework Service

The purpose of family casework is to empower and strengthen families' potential to resolve difficulties. It aims to obtain a long-range goal of self-reliance. Services include counselling, assistance in meeting basic needs, and referral on to other services. Services in Family Service Centres are supervised by a Social Work Officer and provided by registered social workers at the rank of Social Work Assistant, Senior Social Work Assistant, and Assistant Social Work Officer. As of the year 2000, there are more than 800 social workers serving 65 Family Service Centres, 42 operated by the government's Welfare Department and 23 by NGOs which are funded by government subvention. The current workload ratio is 1 caseworker to 65 cases. Case management is the monitoring model adopted by these agencies to ensure that needs are being met.

### Senior Social Work Practitioner Service

The Senior Social Work Practitioner post was first introduced in 1995. It allowed for the appointment of a senior social worker to provide intensive casework for families at a Family Service Centre. Their duties range from therapy to consultation and clinical supervision.

### Family Aid Service

The Family Aid Service, first introduced in 1990, provides support to needy families so that they can acquire basic skills in self-care and household management. Structural programmes and transitional home care services are provided to enhance learning. The service is targeted at families with young children, the elderly and the disabled. This service is similar to home health aid and homemaker services, all of which are used to ease transitional adjustment.

### Family Care Demonstration and Resource Centre

The Family Care Demonstration and Resource Centre was established in 1994 to provide support and training to caregivers. It is operated by the Social Welfare Department with the aid of a caregiver support centre. Families with a life crisis learn caring skills for their sick, aged or disabled members in a simulated environment. They also receive tangible and emotional support to empower their actual practice at home.

### Family Life Education

Family Life Education (FLE), introduced in 1977, is a form of community-based service to provide educational and preventive information for the entire society. Its wide-ranging services include promotional programmes on life tasks and educational materials on family life issues, such as communication, parenthood and drugs. It targets primarily adolescents, parents, parents-to-be, married couples and couples-to-be. The target ratio for each FLE worker is 50 000 people in the age range of 10 to 50 years. With plans to reach seven million people, the government aims to launch an average of 5000 programmes annually to engage at least 250 000 participants each year.

### Family Life Education Resource Centre

Since 1979, the FLE Resource Centre has been developing printed and audio visual materials to help to support family life education. The provision of library resources also links learning to the professional community in the hope that educational materials will be distributed with professional assistance. The Centre provides support to produce publicity programmes that aim to promote public awareness on the importance of family life. To enhance service utilization, an FLE website has been available since 1999 to disseminate information about marriage, parenting, child development, and public programmes about family life. A 'Q&A' section is available to help to answer questions on such issues as childcare, couples' communication and sexuality (www.family-land.org). In addition, a Child Care Services Resource Centre and a Child Abuse Resource Centre have been established in each of the 13 districts in Hong Kong to provide resources for citizens and professionals.

### Family Activity and Resource Centres

Based on the idea of coordinating Family Service Centres' direct services, Family Activity and Resource Centres (FARCs) were established in 1994 in both government-run Group Work Units and NGO-operated community service centres. The mission of these Centres is to promote family cohesiveness and identify families at risk. They are focal points in the community for families to drop in and make use of the services provided. Support and mutual aid groups are among the most popular activities organized in these Centres. Networking with others is an effective way to break the silence of abuse, and gain the power and support to resolve difficult problems.

## FAMILY SERVICE REVIEW AND EVALUATION

In Hong Kong, there is a growing demand for accountability in social services. Whether the resources come from taxation or private donations, the funders and the general public demand that services should be cost-effective. Summative evaluation of social welfare programme effectiveness bloomed in the late 1980s. To develop any new service programme required conducting a pilot project together with a programme evaluation.

The heavy workload of 70 to 80 cases per social worker has placed a serious barrier in the way of effective practice. The ratio has improved since the early 1980s when it was expected that a social worker would carry 100 cases. An improved ratio not only allows social workers to closely examine the effectiveness of their own practice, but also takes away the 'lack of time' excuse for the 'non-evaluating' practice. If the ratio is reduced to 50 cases per social worker within the next decade, more published documentation of service effectiveness could be expected.

The Social Workers Registration Bill was passed in April 1997. Statutory registration of social workers represents a clear landmark for the social work profession after approximately 50 years of development in Hong Kong. To establish their professional status, social workers have to demonstrate that social services work. Practice research is germinating in clinical practice. There is growing interest in the application of single-subject or single-system design and the employment of qualitative methods for self-evaluation of clinical practice. With the slowly improving worker-to-case ratio, it is becoming more feasible for social workers to use research techniques in their own practice.

In the subvention review conducted in 1995–1996, a set of 19 Service Quality Standards was proposed for adoption:

- The service ensures that a clear description of its purpose, objectives and mode of service delivery is publicly available.
- The service should have available current, documented policies and procedures describing how it will approach key service delivery issues.
- The service maintains accurate, current records of service operations and activities.
- The roles and responsibilities of all staff, managers, management committee and/or other relevant committees are formally noted.
- The service implements effective staff recruitment, development, training, assessment and deployment practices.
- The service has an effective mechanism by which clients, staff and other interested parties can provide feedback on the service's performance.
- The service regularly reviews and evaluates its own performance.
- The service demonstrates financial management.
- The service complies with all relevant legal obligations and professional codes of practice.
- The service takes all reasonable steps to ensure that it provides a safe physical environment for its staff and clients.
- The service unit ensures that clients have clear, accurate information about how to enter and leave the service unit.
- The service unit has a planned approach to assessing and meeting client needs (whether the client is an individual, family, group or community).

- The service ensures that, as far as is practical, it coordinates its activities with other services to promote the best quality outcomes for clients.
- The service supports the maintenance of client–family relationships and social relationships.
- The service respects the client's right to self-determination as far as is practicable.
- The service respects the client's rights in relation to private property.
- The service respects the client's rights for privacy and confidentiality.
- Each client and staff member is free to raise and have addressed, without fear of retribution, any complaints he or she may have regarding the agency or service.
- The service takes all reasonable steps to ensure that clients are free from abuse.

These standards provide a framework of process audits to examine the structures and procedures of service delivery to improve the quality of services. The idea of implementing process evaluation or process audits is not new to Hong Kong, but it does take time and can be costly. As a result of the growing attention to evaluation, the New Millennium Family Services Review will focus on five tasks:

- assessment of service needs and target groups;
- evaluation of service provision and mode of delivery;
- identification of culturally relevant outcome measures that address both client needs and measure biases;
- recommendations of long-term strategies and future directions;
- development of action plans.

These tasks are currently being developed and discussed.

The Social Welfare Department completed an information technology strategic study at the beginning of 1997. This study will draw up a blueprint for future developments in utilizing information technology in the management of social welfare services in the next decade. Client information systems and subvention systems will be integrated into the future information network. Social workers expect that the social welfare field will take advantage of advances in information technology to improve the collection, compilation, analysis and dissemination of service information to employ better management and delivery of social welfare services in the future. Though this rate of change is much slower than that in the commercial sector, information technology will eventually become available at the fingertips of social workers to assist their evaluation of practice.

In 2000, the Hong Kong Council of Social Service published social indicators to identify historically vulnerable population groups in Hong Kong. These indexes are divided into five major areas of concern: women's status; low income; child status; youth status; and elderly status. It is important to note that domestic violence, single-parent households, unemployment, education, and suicide are among the many important indicators of family vulnerability.

Pithouse, Lindsell and Cheung (1998) suggest that a comprehensive evaluation framework should include needs assessment, formative evaluation, efficiency analysis, implementation study, summative evaluation, outcome study, and impact analysis. To evaluate family-centred services, they also suggest that an evaluation plan should be included when a service plan is proposed. When services are ready for delivery, programme evaluation should begin. Based on this comprehensive framework, and with Hong Kong culture being seriously considered, an evaluation framework is proposed here. It integrates information from the typology suggested by Manalo and Meezan (2000) and the community-awareness model suggested by Pithouse and his associates (1998). Four major evaluation goals are proposed: needs identification, community awareness, staff involvement, and needs attainment. Content, process and outcome measures are integral to programme evaluation. In this evaluation framework, added components include various routes for measuring service utilization, serving hard-to-reach populations, and evaluating service philosophy, strategies and the priority-setting process (see Table 8.1).

## LESSONS LEARNED

The provision for family services in the new millennium includes three major developments. The first provision is an expansion of family education. With prevention being at the forefront of service planning, the Hong Kong government has learned that family education is essential to enhance effective service delivery. It provides greater learning and service support to parents. It helps parents to learn and develop their life skills so that parent–child communication can be improved and child protection can be promoted. It also provides support to parents and children, empowering them to learn socially integrated skills to promote a healthy family life. On a publicity level, this service expansion also delivers a clear message to citizens that families are important for child development, and that mutual support and family life can be learned and enhanced through the support of both internal and external resources.

Another provision is long-term service planning on support services that target directly the promotion of the self-reliance strategy proposed by family practitioners. This service provision must include multidisciplinary collaborations and professionals' active involvement. Currently, the Social Welfare Department is requesting additional resources to support this strategy with two major target populations in mind: single-parent and new-migrant families. Post-migration services are required to help maintain harmonious family

**Table 8.1**   A framework for evaluating family services

| Evaluation goal and tools | Agency variables | Individual/family/community variables |
|---|---|---|
| *Needs identification*<br>• Service recipient<br>• Service provided<br>• Potential collaborative services<br>• Community indicators | *Content of programmes/services*<br>• Philosophy<br>• Goals<br>• Strategies<br>• Activities that are family focused<br>• Staff qualifications<br>• Programme preparation and evaluation planning | *Needs of children*<br>• Survival needs<br>• Sense of security<br>• Health<br>• Self-esteem<br>• Personal competence<br>• Academic-cognitive competence<br>• Social competence<br><br>• *Needs of families*<br>• Values and goals<br>• Patterns of social interaction<br>• Resources and strengths<br>• Social and emotional support<br>• Financial support<br>• Cultural and spiritual support<br>• Stability and safety |
| *Community awareness and staff involvement*<br>• Service target<br>• Service utilization<br>• Advocacy effort<br>• Publicity effort<br>• Training effort | *Process of programme development*<br>• Intensity of services<br>• Duration and length of service utilization<br>• Programme comprehensiveness<br>• Collaboration with other programmes<br>• Input from families<br>• Staff input | *Community variables*<br>• Values<br>• Resources and support<br>• Constraints and risks<br>• Priority-setting<br><br>• *Staff's competencies*<br>• Informational competencies<br>• Intellectual competencies<br>• Interpersonal competencies<br>• Intrapersonal competencies<br>• Intervention competencies |
| *Needs attainment and programme success*<br>• Recipient input<br>• Staff input<br>• Community awareness measures<br>• Community need indicators<br>• Special needs<br>• Cultural and public awareness measures<br>• Coalition building | *Outcomes expected*<br>• Programme adaptation to family needs<br>• Crisis intervention<br>• Prevention of child abuse and neglect<br>• Family-focused outcomes<br>• Reaching hard-to-reach populations | *Effectiveness measures*<br>• Maximization of needs obtainment<br>• Family participation in services<br>• Better family relationships<br>• Better communication skills among family members<br>• Improved health (less illness, improved health status, fewer birth complications, improved nutritional status)<br>• Improved mental health status<br>• Increased opportunities for education and/or training<br>• Increased employment and earnings<br>• Improved quality of life<br>• Decreased family problems<br>• Improved family stability |

life, especially when the family has to manage children's school-related issues, while at the same time dealing with their cultural-adjustment difficulties and discrimination.

The third new provision is the development of service coordination mechanisms. Coordination efforts among the 18 Hong Kong Districts are to be periodically evaluated to learn the various aspects of identifying service needs and fulfilling service goals, with a focus on the uniqueness of demographic distributions in each of these districts. There are three major directions for promoting interdisciplinary collaboration: needs assessment in the districts; evaluation of community-based family life education; and coordination between the Social Welfare Department and NGOs.

In the new millennium, several initiatives are being implemented to enhance the development of family service efforts in Hong Kong. Three major lessons that were learned from previous studies should be considered when social workers are planning service implementation and evaluation. First, overemphasis on cost-effectiveness measures can slow down service development due to the cutback of resources and reserved use of advanced technology or practice methods. Although it is a current trend to evaluate the cost–benefit and cost-effectiveness of all services, a culturally relevant evaluation model should also consider significant cultural barriers as complicating factors. Resistance to seeking external help, for example, is considered a cultural barrier against achieving full participation and maximizing service utilization. As a result, input and output measures (such as regular attendance) in family treatment programmes cannot be the sole evaluation indicators. Process evaluation, including perception of support, should be emphasized.

A second lesson learned is that impact analyses should focus on both children and their families, even though many services are delivered directly to children in their school environment. Bailey and his colleagues (1998) identify an evaluation framework that consists of eight major areas:

- appropriateness for the family in making a difference in their child's life;
- appropriateness in making a difference in the client's own family's life;
- positive view of professionals and the special service system;
- helpfulness in enabling the family to help their child grow, learn, and develop;
- enhancement of the family's perceived ability to work with professionals and advocate for services;
- level of assistance provided for the family in building a strong support system;
- helpfulness in enhancing an optimistic view of the future;
- enhancement of the family's perceived quality of life.

This framework suggests that quality of life can be measured in both absolute and perceptual terms, and that different methodological approaches should be used with various types of formats to enhance the accuracy of data representation.

A third lesson learned is that family service evaluation should be integrative and comprehensive in design to include: mutual exchanges between practitioners and researchers; direct input and observations from clients, service providers and other constituencies; and a comprehensive view of service effectiveness. In the field of evaluation research, evaluation should be planned prior to the inception of service delivery to avoid design biases (Calsyn and Winter, 1999). It is also important to address: units of analysis; service priorities; culturally sensitive assessment tools and procedures; family involvement; and outcome variables. When designing evaluation, social workers and service planners should list the major variables and plan the design in advance without presuming what the results should be.

## SUGGESTED NEXT STEPS

To reiterate, family service planning in Hong Kong is based on principles that aim to ensure that services are: family oriented; community based; user friendly; strengths based; resources based; preventive in nature; barrier free; cost effective; integrative; and accountable. Also, the Consultancy Team that reviewed services at the end of the 1990s stressed that evaluation of family services should focus on the needs-based and community-based orientation of service delivery. Accordingly, there are three particular approaches that suggest themselves for measuring the effectiveness of family services in Hong Kong:

- using a networking approach to involve NGOs and other grassroots organizations in collecting and providing needs-assessment data;
- assessing a wide range of services which address needs and developmental formations of families, obstacles in preventive and early intervention, and the establishment of remedial crisis interventions;
- evaluating family life education programmes in terms of community involvement.

In Hong Kong, the definition of the family is traditionally based. Although it is important to include children in family life education or intervention, it is equally important for the childless couple to learn about family life. However, most family life education programmes assume the inclusion of children, either currently or in the future, in the service-delivery framework. It will only defeat the purpose of learning when some of the couples, such as the childless, gays and lesbians, feel that the learning is not designed for them. In adopting a framework for evaluation, the evaluator must allow for the inclusion of five key dimensions: credibility; creativity; cultural sensitivity; feasibility; and resulting utility of the evaluated service.

## Credibility

Family services, subvention or government-run, should be accountable to meet the public's needs. It is essential to have both input–output measures and outcome–impact measures so that taxpayers are well informed of the service provision and its effectiveness. It is critical not only to evaluate the clinical effectiveness of family services, but also to develop strategies to assess the three levels of family service commitment: casework, group work, and community involvement. Further, in order to increase the credibility of evaluation data, a variety of approaches or evaluation procedures should be designed and implemented.

## Creativity

Demands on services are increasingly diverse due to cultural changes in migration patterns and family formations. Family service evaluation should be creatively designed to encompass the increasing demands and the measurement of service outcomes for new users. Cost containment may not be an appropriate measure when, for example, services are designed to accommodate the needs of a migrant population or a newly defined family population.

## Cultural Sensitivity

Input, process, output, outcome and long-term impact are the five major processes in programme evaluation. When evaluating Hong Kong's family services, one must bear in mind several factors that may hinder effectiveness. These factors include cultural adjustment, educational reform, welfare reform, languages and dialects, resistance to external interference, family values, and culturally competent social work practice. Since seeking help may be considered 'losing face', the designated result indicators should include individual and community attitudes to seeking help, perceptions about obtaining support, client and community definitions of family life improvement, as well as service utilization and its longitudinal continuity.

## Feasibility

It is important to identify the feasibility of implementation and to suggest ways to overcome barriers. Practitioners in family support have heavy workloads and it is likely that evaluation would be implemented in practice only when evaluation plans are required. The establishment of a mandatory evaluation system should be accompanied by both financial and technical support.

## Resulting Utility

It is also important to develop exchange processes between practitioners and evaluators as part of any programme evaluation. The results should be utilized by practitioners for planning and delivering better services, not used as a punitive or negative measure against their practice. It should be related to practice-enhancement as a priority. Therefore, one of the evaluation measures should be on results, focusing on how practitioners will utilize the results to design future programmes to meet the goals of the agency/department, address the unmet needs of the users, and evaluate the implementation of innovative ideas to maximize client participation and minimize cost.

## CONCLUDING REMARKS

There are three common driving forces in developing service evaluation, namely service development, administrative requirements, and professional development. The one-shot evaluation studies are primarily driven by the service development purposes, while ongoing programme evaluation is fuelled by administrative requirements and professional development. As discussed earlier, Family Service Centres before 1965 were established to meet the basic needs of poor families by providing practical assistance. Programme evaluation was non-existent. During the rapid economic development in the late 1960s and 1970s, they began to provide personal and psychosocial services. Needs assessment studies were performed to help them define the direction of their future development. Moving into the 1980s, one-shot programme evaluations were used to justify the development of new services. Community-based and outcome-based practice research is the new evaluation trend for the new millennium.

Demands for accountability grow as the social welfare budget grows. In 1970–1971, social welfare spending constituted only 1.5% of total government spending. In 1995–1996, social welfare spending grew to 10.8% of total government spending. The spending of taxpayers' money has to be justified. While Family Service Centres are primarily financed by public funds, effective means of monitoring service quantity and quality become necessary. The developments of the subvention information system and a user-friendly client information system are part of this growing demand on information to meet the requirement for management efficiency.

Heavy caseloads in the 1970s and early 1980s prevented any real concerns about the development of professional practice from being addressed. However, with the growing professionalism among social workers since the early 1980s, the demand to improve the quality of services has been the driving force for family service workers who must better equip themselves with the necessary clinical and practice research skills. The development of advanced training to social workers at the universities in the 1990s was a response to the growing demand for clinical skills in dealing with the ever-increasing complexity seen in many family cases. Although this developmental process is still evolving, it will accelerate when researchers and practitioners are jointly evaluating the impact and effectiveness of family practice.

It is wise to use existing needs and estimated demographic shifts to project the future directions of the social services. In Hong Kong, approximately 200 million US dollars have been allocated in the 2000–2001 fiscal year to fund family and child welfare programmes. Self-reliance strategies are ranked top of the list to move the services ahead. It is also expected that advanced technology will help Hong Kong to develop an ongoing evaluation system to identify service strategies for managers and social workers. Accountability demands will push the development of process audits to ensure that Family Service Centres have in place monitoring and feedback mechanisms to generate information and make use of such information to improve the quality of their service. With effectiveness in mind, impact analysis will become a frequently utilized approach to justify the continuation of existing services. Finally, the growth of professionalism in the field of social services will help the Hong Kong government and NGOs to develop a systematic plan of action for practice-oriented research and research-oriented practice.

## REFERENCES

Bailey, D.B., McWilliam, R.A., Darkes, L.A. et al. (1998) Family outcomes in early intervention: A framework for program evaluation and efficacy research. *Exceptional Children*, **64**, 313–328.

Calsyn, R.J. and Winter, J.P. (1999) Understanding and controlling response bias in needs assessment studies. *Evaluation Review*, **23**, 399–417.

Caritas (1987) *A study on the Working Pattern and Welfare Needs of the Clerical Staff Working in Central District*. Hong Kong: Hong Kong Caritas.

Caritas Family Service (1995) *Study on Marriages Affected by Extramarital Affairs*. Hong Kong: Caritas Family Service and Department of Social Work and Social Administration, University of Hong Kong.

Catholic Marriage Advisory Council (1991) *Evaluation Research Report on the Marriage Mediation Counselling Project*. Hong Kong: Hong Kong Catholic Marriage Advisory Council.

Chan, C., Law, C.K. and Kwok, R. (1992) Attitudes of women toward work in socialist and capitalist cities: A comparative study of Beijing, Guangzhou and Hong Kong. *Canadian Journal of Community Mental Health*, **11**, 187–200.

Cheung, M. (1989) The elderly Chinese living in the United States: Assimilation or adjustment? *Social Work*, **34**, 457–461.

Dunst, C.J., Trivette, C.M. and Thompson, R.B. (1994) Supporting and strengthening family functioning: Toward a congruence between principles and practice. In C.J. Dunst, C.M. Trivette and A.G. Deal (Eds), *Supporting and Strengthening Families, Volume 1: Methods, Strategies and Practices*. Cambridge, MA: Brookline Books.

Green, J.W. (1995) *Cultural Awareness in the Human Services: A Multi-Ethnic Approach*. Boston: Allyn & Bacon.

HKCSS (1989) *A Report on an Evaluation of the Project on Utilization of the Senior Social Work Practitioner*. Hong Kong: Hong Kong Family Welfare Society. (Hong Kong Council of Social Service.)

HKCSS (1994) Social service hotlines in Hong Kong. *Welfare Digest*, **238**(6), 1–4. (Hong Kong Council of Social Service.)

HKCSS (1995) Family policy in Hong Kong. *Welfare Digest*, **245**(1/2), 4–5. (Hong Kong Council of Social Service.)

HKCSS (2000) Social development in Hong Kong: The unfinished agenda. *Welfare Digest*, **307**, 1–6. (Hong Kong Council of Social Service.)

HKFWS (1989) *A Research Report on Cognitive-Behavioural Group Therapy for Adults with Mental Health Problems*. Hong Kong: Hong Kong Family Welfare Society.

HKFWS (1991) *An Evaluation Research Report on Family Resource Centers. A Twin Project of a Family Drop-in and Single Parent Families Service Unit*. Hong Kong: Hong Kong Family Welfare Society.

HKFWS and Cheung, S.K. (1994) *An Evaluation Report on Emergency Foster Care Service*. Hong Kong: Hong Kong Family Welfare Society.

HKFWS and Law, C.K. (1991) *Needs of Single Parent Families: A Comparative Study*. Hong Kong: Hong Kong Family Welfare Society.

Home Office (1998) *Supporting Families: A Consultation Document*. London: The Stationery Office.

Hong Kong Government (1965) *Aims and Policy for Social Welfare in Hong Kong*. Hong Kong: Government Printing Office.

Hong Kong Government (1991) *Social Welfare into the 1990s and Beyond*. Hong Kong: Government Printing Office.

Kaplan, L. and Girard, J. (1994) *Strengthening High-Risk Families: A Handbook for Practitioners*. New York: Lexington Books.

Kumpfer, K.L., Molgaard, V. and Spoth, R. (1996) The strengthening families program for the prevention of delinquency and drug use. In R. DeV. Peters and R.J. McMahon (Eds), *Preventing Childhood Disorders, Substance Abuse, and Delinquency*. Thousand Oaks, CA: Sage.

Manalo, V. and Meezan, W. (2000) Toward building a typology for the evaluation of services in family support programs. *Child Welfare*, **79**, 405–429.

Pithouse, A., Lindsell, S. and Cheung, M. (1998) *Family Support and Family Centre Services*. Aldershot: Ashgate.

Social Welfare Department (2000) *Family and Child Welfare Services*. Hong Kong Government. Available: www.info.gov.hk/swd/

Steering Committee, Consultancy Study on Review of Family Services (2000) *International Review of Family Issues and Family Services* (preliminary draft). Hong Kong.

Walsh, F. (1998) *Strengthening Family Resilience*. New York: Guilford Press.

# 9

# LESSONS FROM THE EVALUATION OF FAMILY SUPPORT IN NEW ZEALAND

*Jackie Sanders and Robyn Munford*

## INTRODUCTION

This chapter provides a New Zealand perspective on family support. It will also explore some of the issues involved in evaluating and researching family support programmes. Family support services in New Zealand can be broadly defined as intensive home-based support for families wanting to make changes in various aspects of family life, such as family relationships and parenting. Support work focuses upon defining issues and problems, setting goals to be achieved and working with the client to achieve these goals. Work is often carried out with just the primary caregiver, but may include other family members and those living within the extended family network. Attention is paid to identifying sources of informal support and the worker may focus on these in the intervention and assist the client to strengthen his or her naturally occurring networks of support (Munford and Sanders, 1999). Family support supervisors carefully match workers to clients in order to maximize the synergy achieved when people are able to connect effectively with each other. Family support work generally has the following characteristics:

- Work is based in the home of the client rather than on agency premises.
- Visits from support workers take place according to client need and can occur several times per week for extended periods of time per visit.
- Interventions are goal-oriented and involve a mixture of practical and supportive strategies. Interventions include interpersonal support, practical assistance, advocacy, referral and liaison, development of family strategies and provision of parenting support, household management skills

*Evaluating Family Support: Thinking Internationally, Thinking Critically.*
Edited by I. Katz and J. Pinkerton. © 2003 John Wiley & Sons, Ltd.

development, development of communication skills and strategies, self-esteem development and support with assessing options, and development of problem-solving skills.

- Work acknowledges the cultural, social and economic context of the family.
- Client strengths are acknowledged and harnessed in the intervention process.
- Client participation in goal-setting is an important part of the support process. Realistic outcomes are focused upon in assessment, planning and intervention.

A range of non-governmental agencies provide family support in New Zealand. These agencies are, usually partially, funded by the State to provide services to children and families, including family support, childcare, counselling and parenting courses. Funding is always a challenge for these agencies as they work to obtain enough financial resources to provide responsive and intensive family support services. These agencies work closely with the statutory agency, the Department of Child Youth and Family, which has responsibility for providing child protection services and has a legal responsibility to investigate suspected cases of emotional, physical and sexual abuse. This agency has also managed the contracts with non-governmental agencies which provide family support services in communities throughout New Zealand. In New Zealand, therefore, child protection work and family support work are functionally separated even though the funding for both of these activities is administered through the same agency.

In New Zealand, issues of bicultural practice and the maintenance of cultural safety in relationships with clients are central to the work of social service agencies. There is a statutory obligation for social service organizations to work under the principles of the Treaty of Waitangi. The Treaty of Waitangi is a constitutional document and specifies that the relationship between Maori (currently the Maori population comprises 14.5% of the total population) and the Crown will be based upon the three principles of partnership, protection and participation. Social service providers are required through their contracts with the State to ensure that their work incorporates the principles embodied in the Treaty. This means that they must be able to demonstrate how they consult with Maori, how they tailor their services to the particular needs of Maori clients and how Maori participate in decision-making within their organizations. Some providers work exclusively with Maori families and clients, others work with clients who come from a range of ethnic backgrounds, but all are required to demonstrate how they take account of Maori cultural practices and beliefs in their work with clients.

There are particular issues of social exclusion for Maori within New Zealand which are traceable to the colonization experience. Disputes over land are still taking place and Maori still struggle to retain their language and to practise their own cultural beliefs in this country. Maori struggle to share equally in national wealth and well-being. Current social, health, education and economic statistics suggest that many Maori remain marginalized and do not experience full participation in their communities. However, in striving for social change, Maori have developed a range of innovative social service initiatives as a response to the needs of children and families. Many of these embrace the family support philosophy and mode of delivery by providing intensive and home-based services that reinforce key values around family life and the care of children. The models for best practice developed within social service organizations providing services to Maori clients have influenced the provision of services for other ethnic groups and have a significant impact on the strategies developed to achieve cultural safety in social service and related organizations, for example health and education services.

## EVALUATING FAMILY SUPPORT IN NEW ZEALAND

Since 1994 the authors have been involved in an extensive programme of research relating to families, children and well-being. A key aspect of the research programme has involved research on a large national family support agency. The family support research involved three distinct stages. Stage One provided a foundation for the subsequent phases and involved the analysis of 232 client files (this represented one year's completed caseload). The analysis of files revealed descriptive material about the families who used the family support service and the presenting problems they brought to the service. This analysis also examined the variables that contributed to the achievement of positive change for families (Munford et al., 1996). Stage Two extended this analysis and involved in-depth fieldwork with a sample of 14 clients, their support workers and service supervisors. This research followed clients throughout the intervention and involved regular interviews with clients, workers and supervisors. It identified common themes in support work and provided detailed information about the interventions with families. This enabled us to pinpoint key characteristics of interventions that were related to the achievement by clients of positive change. The in-depth nature of the research also allowed us to identify family characteristics and to document the complex interplay of these with the support process (Munford et al., 1998). Stage Three involved a survey of 245 clients, which represented one year of service. It built upon information gathered in Stages One and Two and in so doing tested the relationships between a range of variables and the achievement of positive change. A set of data-collection forms was developed to measure client characteristics, intervention characteristics and positive change. These were developed in conjunction with support workers and were used to track clients as they moved through the service (Sanders et al., 1999).

The next section will discuss the lessons from the field and identify some key issues associated with carrying out research in social service organizations.

## KEY ISSUES: LESSONS FROM THE FIELD

Researchers involved in researching social service agencies and interventions will be presented with a unique range of issues. The research team was sensitive to how clients and workers might have experienced the research and the activities carried out by the research team. It was important that any disruption caused by the research for workers, clients, supervisors and the agency itself was kept to an absolute minimum. Disruption is an inevitable part of agency research because it usually involves introducing new people into relationships and it also usually requires that agency staff dedicate time to providing information and access. This is disruptive. It is therefore important that care and attention is paid by research teams to minimizing these disruptions and to working actively with staff to resolve the issues that inevitably arise in a timely and responsive fashion. These factors were acknowledged at the time that access to the agency was negotiated. The research team had some familiarity with the agency and they were able to use this knowledge to establish an effective relationship with participants. We recognized that, at all times, the needs of clients came first and that situations could well arise when the research team would need to take a step back to allow the agency to *get on with* service delivery. Managing the interface between the research and service delivery became a significant part of this research programme and it is likely that this will be the case in most similar sorts of research programmes.

The research team spent time with the agency identifying the importance of evaluation research and securing support and commitment to the research programme in general terms. The team spent considerable time clarifying the research questions and the focus on identifying what intervention processes and strategies contribute to positive change for clients. The research programme was not assessing the work of individual practitioners or the general work of the organization, but was focused on exploring the intervention process in detail to discover what made a difference for clients. However, in this kind of research the boundary between these can become blurred in practice and there is a degree to which practice, policy and organizational issues are considered by the research team. The research team took time to discuss these challenges in the processes used to negotiate access to the research site(s). Opportunities for reflecting on these challenges were provided throughout the research programme.

Access was negotiated with the agency as a whole but also with each participant involved in the research. The research team spent a large amount of time preparing the research site once access had been granted. This included explaining the methods to be used; the time commitment required from participants (this was particularly important in Stage Two, which included a number of in-depth interviews with clients, workers and supervisors); protocols for informing participants of progress throughout the research programme; ideas about how the research would be reported and disseminated and the role of participants in this process. The research team readily made themselves available to meet with staff whenever necessary throughout the research programme and attempted to resolve any difficulties as they arose. It is important for those carrying out evaluation research to understand that access may need to be renegotiated at different stages in the research programme and that they must be continually monitoring the impact of the research on the family support service. This is important for the smooth running of the research or evaluation programme. It is also important if the results of the research/evaluation are to have ongoing value in the day-to-day operation of family support services and their long-term development. Here, the relationships that evaluators and researchers are able to build with practitioners and service managers are crucial. These relationships can facilitate the transfer of valuable, grounded knowledge back into programmes and in this way research and evaluation can make a major contribution to the ongoing development of family support services.

## DOING RESEARCH: METHODS, TEAMS AND KEEPING ON TRACK

The research team spent considerable time identifying the methods to be used for the research. It was decided to use a multi-method approach given that there was a range of information that needed to be collected. The team was aware of the shortcomings and the strengths of both quantitative and qualitative methods in evaluation research (Denzin and Lincoln, 1994; Shaw and Lishman, 1999) and took all of these factors into account in the process of clarifying the research questions and the methods that could be used to explore these questions and identify the nature of family support work.

The research team used quantitative methods in Stage One of the research in order to generate a description of the family support service and the clients utilizing the service, and to identify some of the factors that might have contributed to the achievement of positive change for clients (Munford et al., 1996). In this stage we reviewed existing client files from the organization as a whole and analysed a 12-month caseload. This procedure was valuable because it provided a comprehensive overview of the services provided and the interventions with clients, and it also generated some of the questions to be asked in the interviews with clients, workers and supervisors in Stage Two of the research programme. The information collected from an analysis of client files over a period of a year included: demographic information; hours and months spent with the family; previous use of services; referral source and reasons for referral; assessment of need; interventions used; changes achieved; informal/personal support available to the family; non-service factors contributing to changes (such as resolving custody issues in the family courts); and other agencies involved with the family.

Qualitative methods, semi-structured interviews with all participants and focus groups with workers/supervisors were used in Stage Two to explore the family support relationship and to understand the meanings clients and workers attributed to the intervention process (Munford et al., 1998). Information included reflections on assessment processes, discussion about the context of the clients and the challenges with which they were faced, feedback on the intervention strategies used and their effectiveness as they related to the achievement of positive change, reflection on the client/worker relationship, and any other information the participants wished to share about the intervention process. Rich data was generated from the interviews. These interviews were carried out with clients, workers and supervisors at several points during the intervention. This meant that data sets could be compared with one another. Client confidentiality was maintained by removing all identifying information from the data during the transcription of the interviews and before analysis took place. Client and worker perspectives were compared and the supervisors of the family support service were also interviewed in order that the client work could be located within an agency context. There were no focus groups with clients given the need to maintain anonymity. The discussion groups with workers and supervisors focused on their perspectives of the intervention processes and the factors that contribute to positive change. Participation in these groups also meant that staff were able to make comments about the progress of the research and any research issues that required resolution. During this stage, ongoing research management meetings were held with workers to provide a regular forum for the raising and resolving of any issues created by the research for practice with clients.

The quantitative methods used in Stage Three of the research programme built on the findings from Stages One and Two (Sanders et al., 1999). In this stage a set of data-collection forms was designed specifically for tracking clients as they moved through the intervention process. The forms were developed with support staff who had considerable experience in the service. The forms were pre-tested and categories modified accordingly. Guidelines were established to assist staff in the use of these tools and regular contact with the research sites (20 sites across New Zealand) was maintained. Data was collected on four areas, intake information including presenting problems, demographic and household income information goal reviews with clients; changes in severity of presenting problems, intervention strategies (including hours of support), and the changes in clients' coping styles and parenting strategies over time. Likert-type scales were used to measure change in addition to the yes/no questions included on the data sheets. At the conclusion of the research programme, workers evaluated the data-collection forms and reported that the forms required more textual and descriptive information about the intervention process. The agency reviewed data-collection forms, and the research team was able to contribute to this process by recommending that client-information forms used in the agency be developed so that they could capture client information in this manner.

This feedback from staff raised an important issue of evaluation and research methodology, and in so doing it also demonstrated the value of reflective research practice and the involvement of practitioners in research and evaluation processes (Munford and Sanders, 1999). We consider that it is important that systems for collecting research and evaluation information from agencies should be designed so that they fit practice, rather than practice being required to fit a predetermined set of forms. It can be expected that the quality of research and evaluation data will be enhanced considerably if the systems for generating that data, which will always involve practitioners, fit comfortably with the ways in which staff work with clients. From a methodological point of view, it highlighted the fact that practitioners, who deal daily in the struggles of people to make a better life for themselves and their children, may have difficulty when asked to reduce this complexity and variability in human pain into neat categorical measurements. It clearly suggests that in order to generate valid and reliable measures it may be preferable for researchers and evaluators to develop data-recording methods that have a higher text content and that these text records then either be analysed qualitatively or be converted into statistical measures as part of the research process rather than as part of the client management system.

Text-based systems provide a recording approach that is more consistent with the ways in which agency staff usually work with clients and are able to thoroughly capture the characteristics of a particular intervention. This example demonstrates the important links between research practice and social service delivery. Researchers can remain responsive to service providers by ensuring that workers have opportunities to provide feedback on the data-collection methods. The findings of the research, both in terms of the methods used and the data on the family support process itself, can thereby contribute more to the family support intervention by highlighting the factors that contribute to effective practice.

During the research process researchers must be prepared to modify their techniques if these are not effective or if participants' feedback suggests that these should be modified. For example, in Stage Three, procedures for collecting information from the sites were modified in response to time pressures on agency workers. In Stage Two the researchers modified the timing of interviews so that these did not interfere with assessment processes and relationship building between the worker and client. Once the intervention process was underway the interviewer would check on the timing of subsequent research interviews. Interviews would also be postponed at any time in the research process if participants were unavailable or if other personal or family issues became pressing. This is a key point given that the interviews could last up to an hour and a half and the nature of the information covered was often of a sensitive nature and required much emotional input from the participant.

The nature of the interviews also required a high level of energy and commitment from the interviewer. Interviews were timed to enable interviewers to debrief if necessary with a research team member before moving to the next interview. Interviewers had to be available at times to suit the participants and they needed to prepare themselves well for the interview, given the sensitive nature of some of the interviews. Interviewers were provided with training and support throughout the research process. They became familiar with the interview schedule before beginning their interviews and had a *rehearsal* before their first client and worker/supervisor interview. As with the agency matching of worker to client, interviewers were also matched to participants, and clients and workers were asked about their preferences regarding interviewers at the time of signing the consent form. Interviewers were also assisted in differentiating between a research interview and a social work interview. Given that several members of the research team were social workers, it was important to support them in the transfer into a role of research interviewer. It was also important to reinforce this point with clients so that they could differentiate between the roles of researcher and family support worker.

These issues were regularly discussed in the research team meetings. The research team met fortnightly and reviewed the progress of the research and the key tasks. These meetings were used to:

- develop and refine research questions, methods and data instruments;
- define plans for research-site preparation;
- provide training and support to researchers;
- identify appropriate mechanisms for providing feedback to all stakeholders and ensure that all research participants were being kept informed of progress;
- meet with the family support agency staff to discuss ongoing issues and share feedback on the progress of the research;
- clarify the role of research participants, for example the role of the family support workers and their contribution to the research;
- monitor the impact of the research on the participants;
- ensure that accountability was being met and that protocols such as ethical procedures were being followed;

- review research methods;
- prepare for data analysis and report writing;
- connect the three stages of the research programme and make links between the findings;
- situate the research within the broader context of the family support literature and practice in New Zealand and other countries;
- provide opportunities for critical reflection on all aspects of the research programme;
- arrange discussion meetings on particular aspects of the findings and involve the agency staff in these discussions, providing them with an opportunity to reflect upon their practice.

Research tasks were divided between team members. One key role in the qualitative phase of the research programme was to ensure that methodological, data and investigator triangulation was achieved (Morse, 1994; Opie, 1995). This was accomplished by having multiple interviews with a range of participants (client, worker, supervisor) and also having a number of team members analysing each of the interviews. Methodologically the results from this stage of the research programme were triangulated through data collection and analysis in the other two stages of the programme, which both involved the application of a range of statistical measures to research data. Throughout the research programme the research team gave seminars to practitioners, professional groups, academics and policy analysts as a way of providing information on the research and to receive constructive feedback on the research programme. Strong links were maintained with the practice community—something that the researchers believed was essential if applied research and evaluation of social service delivery was to make a difference in practice settings.

Evaluation research is complex and time consuming. Research teams are an effective mechanism for handling the complexities of the research and ensuring that the research remains on track and focused on its identified tasks and goals. As it is often a challenge to keep the team focused on the research tasks in team meetings, the facilitator of these meetings (often shared) provides a key role. Team members need to make a commitment to attending meetings and to making a sustained, ongoing contribution to the research programme throughout its life. The team leader has a key role in keeping the research going and research team members actively involved. One should not minimize this aspect of evaluation research in that the team leader has an important task in ensuring that all research tasks are completed, including the administrative tasks associated with carrying out site preparation, data collection and data analysis. The team leader has a significant role in ensuring that the research team members can bring a diversity of perspectives to the research programme and that these are used to enhance the quality of the research programme.

## ETHICAL CONCERNS

Evaluation research takes place alongside interventions with clients and this presents researchers with some unique challenges. There are many ethical issues to address, such as those relating to safety, privacy, confidentiality and anonymity. These relate to family support workers, clients and to the host organization. Researchers must be clear about the ethical issues with which they may be confronted and be equally clear about how they will effectively address them. For example, in an interview situation are they prepared to respond to a disclosure of abuse, or a client's criticism of the worker's competence? Are protocols in place to address such situations? Are they prepared to modify their research programme, including data-generation instruments, if it becomes apparent that these methods are inappropriate, excessively intrusive or getting in the way of the support being provided?

In order to ensure that ethical issues were adequately covered in the research design and execution, the research proposals for each stage of the programme were submitted to a university human ethics committee. Procedures for recruiting and protecting participants throughout the research programme were included in the application for ethical approval prior to the commencement of the research. Throughout the research regular updates were provided to the ethics committee.

The qualitative stage of the research programme raised a number of ethical dilemmas. These related to the fact that such work involved tracking in a detailed manner aspects of human experience as it unfolded. The research interviews had the potential to be intrusive and would inevitably have an impact upon participants. The nature of the data being collected posed ethical issues because of the need for privacy of information and the protection of participants' individual rights. There were also issues of the potential harm to participants as they discussed painful experiences and talked of their struggles to make big changes in their lives. Clarity was required about the uses to which the information would be put and what would happen if researchers were confronted with a situation where the client and/or worker were at risk of harm or where their safety might have been compromised. Research participants were made aware at the beginning of the research programme that if any of these events arose the research team would act according to established protocols. This involved providing information to the appropriate body so that these matters could be addressed. Participants would be kept informed about this process.

Care was taken to ensure that adequate safeguards for participants were put in place and individuals were clear that they had the right to freely decide to participate and to withdraw during the course of the project. If a client chose to withdraw, he or she would still continue to receive a service from the agency. If a worker chose to withdraw there would be no consequences with respect to that person's employment status. The research team spent considerable time with the workers, responding to their ethical concerns and reinforcing the fact that information obtained in research interviews would not be passed on to the employer. It was also made clear that if issues of safety of clients and competence arose these would be discussed with the worker and a process for informing the employer would be put in place. In the event, none of these situations arose throughout the research.

The research team was quick to respond to any ethical issues clients and workers raised about the research. One that did arise in Stage Two related to finding ways to minimize the disruption to family support interventions and the intrusion into participants' lives. Six weeks into the Stage Two interviews, family support workers asked for a meeting to discuss these issues. They were concerned that the research interviews were having an impact on their ability to establish relationships with their clients (Munford et al., 1998). As a result of these discussions modifications were made to the timing of the interviews. Workers also wanted an opportunity to speak regularly to the team about the research so that any issues could be resolved quickly. This opportunity was provided and communication lines were kept open. The research team's approach was to remain open and responsive to the needs of all participants and to recognize that fieldwork within practice settings is challenging for staff whose practice is under the spotlight. The team recognized that there would be times when they might have to take a step backwards and cease gathering data to allow staff and clients time to review issues. These factors were built into the research design and the research timelines.

Research teams must provide clarity about the role of participants in the research programme. For example, are they part of the research team involved in designing the project or are they participants in a more traditional sense where they contribute information about the research questions being studied? The team was clear from the outset that, while the workers would have some input into the questions to be addressed, the research team would take responsibility for the other aspects of the research programme, such as data gathering and analysis. For this project we wanted clients and workers to be able to share fully their experience with the service and we did not want this information contaminated by their involvement in the other roles of the research team. It is important to note that, in some research, clients and workers will be members of the research team and will perform key roles in the team. This role should be clarified from the outset so that all research participants are clear about their role on the team. This is particularly important if the research is carried out within the worker's own agency.

The team also had a commitment, in the qualitative stage of the programme where participants provided in-depth material, to gain consent from the participants for the use of their material in the research reports (Munford et al., 1998). Participants viewed their transcripts and had the opportunity to modify, extend, or delete information from them. Specific consent was obtained for the quotations that were to be used in the research reports and other publications. Although these processes were time consuming, we saw them as essential if research participants were to feel comfortable in sharing their experiences with the interviewers. In this sense, we recognized that in addition to the ethical issues these approaches resolved, there was a methodological benefit to being willing to work collaboratively with participants and to provide them with access to information throughout the research process. The researchers provided clear guidelines as to the purpose of transcript-checking by clients so that the integrity of the data was preserved. For example, given that a key component of the research was to track the intervention process it was important that transcripts were checked and returned prior to the next research interview so that data about each stage of the intervention process could be clearly delineated.

Ethical concerns will always be present in research on families and family services. Open and honest communication between participants and researchers provides opportunities to respond to any ethical issues that may arise. It behoves the researcher to remain vigilant about ensuring that ethical guidelines have been established and are conformed to throughout all phases of the research programme.

## RECIPROCITY: GIVING BACK

Reciprocity is a key component in research, and in this research programme the team acknowledged in a variety of ways the essential contribution that participants made to the research. In Stage Two the researchers were acutely aware of the significant contribution participants were making and the need to *give back* to these participants (Munford et al., 1998). Reciprocity, to be effective, must be specific to the research situation and may at times require researchers to change the direction of the research process (Munford and Sanders, 1999). For example, while researchers may feel it is important to return transcripts, participants may see this as time consuming and wish only to see the direct quotations to be used in the research report. In evaluating family support agencies the researchers may wish to meet regularly with workers to provide ongoing feedback. The workers may see this as unnecessary and would prefer to wait until the end of the evaluation to meet with researchers. For the workers, reciprocity is not about attending feedback sessions which place an additional burden on them in terms of a time commitment. For them reciprocity may occur through other forums such as meetings with researchers to reflect on issues they see as important and at times that suit them.

It is the responsibility of the researcher to find the most appropriate way in which to say thank you to research participants. This reciprocity should not create additional burdens for participants. In Stage Two of the research programme reciprocity was achieved in several ways. Clients reported that being listened to was valuable, as they had an opportunity to tell their story to someone who had respect for their situation. Many of the workers found it affirming to have their practice evaluated and to receive feedback about the interventions that were successful and to have these documented. Some of the workers have attended the presentations given by the research team and have commented on how important it has been to have family support acknowledged as an important service for families who are working to achieve positive change. They have been active participants in the feedback workshops the research team has given to the organization, and they continue to be advocates for carrying out research alongside practice.

The guiding principle in achieving reciprocity in this research programme on family support has required that researchers say thank you in ways that are of direct benefit to clients and that require no ongoing obligations on their part. The team found ways of saying thank you throughout the project and endeavoured to ensure that reciprocity with clients did not interfere with the ongoing intervention process. They listened to what workers were saying about providing feedback and modified their strategies accordingly.

Researchers need to understand the potential impact their research can have on participants. These participants may be asked to disclose previously hidden experiences and researchers must have strategies in place to address this situation. At all times researchers must be aware that any research practice that poses a threat to participants will need to be discontinued. This is why time is such an important component of successful research programmes, and why researchers must be honest about the time commitment required of participants throughout the research programme (Munford and Sanders, 2000). Research is intrusive and relies on the goodwill of participants, which means that researchers must have time to respond to participants and address any concerns they may have. It also means that researchers must have time to reflect on the progress of the research meetings and to modify research agendas when necessary.

Given all the factors addressed in this discussion about what is likely to constitute effective research, the research team have taken a lesson from the family support workers and have engaged in reflective research practice (Munford and Sanders, 1999). In their current research on families and well-being the researchers remain committed to carrying out reflective research practice which enables them to take time to reflect critically on the progress of the research. Regular meetings are organized and each research team member is expected to report and reflect on the progress of the research. The researchers believe that, as with good family support practice, opportunities for reflection and support lead to good research practice.

## CONTRIBUTING TO MORE EFFECTIVE
## FAMILY SUPPORT SERVICES

We argue that research is only successful if the findings can add to the knowledge of family support and the factors that contribute to its effectiveness in bringing about positive change for families. Both the findings and the research process should be reflected upon by researchers, and effectiveness evaluated not only in terms of identifying whether the research has produced good outcomes but whether, in the process of carrying it out, good research practice was followed. Good research practice involves both attention to methodological details and to the maintenance of good relationships with stakeholders. Paying attention to this latter factor helps us to ensure that results will be transferable because, en route to the findings, researchers have developed mechanisms for technology transfer.

The research team has a commitment to linking research to practice, which involves disseminating the research findings to other researchers, and to practitioners and those who have a responsibility for developing and managing family support services and policy, and for training practitioners. The research team has been guided by such questions as:

- How can evaluation research enhance practice in family support services?
- How can family support interventions and outcomes be improved?
- How are research participants involved in the research programme and how can researchers ensure that research does not disrupt the daily operation of the family support agency?
- How can research be incorporated into the modus operandi of an organization so that it becomes an expected part of the operation of this agency?

Integrating research into practice, or ensuring good *technology transfer*, to use the language of the present, is not easy. Often, towards the end of a project, researchers find themselves under pressure to complete the work and move on to the next project. In many situations researchers are employed outside of the service delivery organization—in universities, for example—and so there is no easy obvious route for channelling results back into practice settings. Researchers also do not usually have the authority to drive results and findings into the structure and policy frameworks of organizations, and in some cases this type of input is actively resisted at various levels within organizations. All of these issues influence the extent of uptake of research and evaluation findings in practice settings and ultimately the degree to which research and evaluation can make a positive difference to the lives of families and children. These are very real constraints on the capacity of research and evaluation to make a difference and their impact upon research and evaluation should not be underestimated.

There is no magic formula for ensuring that our research does make a difference to practice and, from there, to the lives of families. However, our experience suggests that several factors will increase the likelihood of such uptake. We have noted elsewhere in this chapter that developing and maintaining effective relationships with all key stakeholders does facilitate the completion of agency-based research and evaluation. We have found that these relationships also enable the uptake of research and evaluation results because they provide a channel through which results can be passed back into organizations. The structures through which research and evaluation are conducted also influence the level of uptake of research results. Here we have found that technology transfer can also be strengthened by situating research within service delivery organizations and incorporating into the research team researchers from education and training courses in institutions such as universities and technical institutes. We have taken every opportunity available to interweave the research programme into practice settings. We argue that effective researchers and evaluators have a commitment to seeing themselves as making a contribution to the development of service delivery and the creation of change. They should not stand aside from practice and act merely as external commentators who move in and out of organizations with no ongoing responsibilities or interest in the long-term impact of their work.

The length of the programme, the use of a range of methods and the willingness for workers and clients to be involved in this research has enabled the researchers to generate a database which captures the experience of family support from a range of perspectives. The research programme has demonstrated that research can be successfully carried out in family support agencies alongside the daily work with clients. While presenting many challenges, this kind of research can contribute to our knowledge about what constitutes effective work with clients.

The following section will outline some of the key findings of the research programme under discussion in this chapter. The researchers have had a strong commitment to ensuring that staff have been involved in the research process and that findings are reported to support workers at regular intervals.

## KEY RESEARCH FINDINGS

A number of key factors contributing to building effective family support services emerged from the three stages of the research programme.

### Presenting Problems

Clients generally come to family support agencies seeking support in a number of areas:

- to develop more effective social support networks;
- to establish more appropriate problem-solving strategies;
- to strengthen the parenting role (over 60% of parents in the research programme were parenting alone);
- to address the problems that result from inadequate material resources.


## Client/Worker Relationship

The research identified that the relationship between client and worker was of critical importance in the achievement of positive outcomes. The family support agency emphasized the importance of careful matching of client and worker in order to maximize the potential for the development of the relationship. The findings clearly demonstrated that time, flexibility and responsiveness are key ingredients in the changes achieved by clients. The worker expended considerable time building a strong and supportive relationship and this often constituted a discrete part of the first phase of the intervention. This relationship provided the foundation from which difficult issues could then be addressed.


## Client Contexts

The family support workers spent considerable time developing an understanding of the family context and identifying how factors such as conflict and problem resolution had been addressed in the past. The worker also attempted to develop an understanding of the way in which wider issues impacted upon the family. The family support services were able to work on both the individual issues and challenges which faced clients, and also focus upon the wider contextual factors which influenced the capacity of both client and family to function well. This meant that workers would recognize and respond to issues such as inadequate housing, financial worries, struggles with the education system and so on, in their support work. In these situations, a combination of instrumental support and community development strategies were often effective. The worker had a key role to play here in assisting the client to establish and strengthen naturally occurring support networks. One of the biggest challenges facing family support workers was how to achieve positive changes in families where both personal and material resources were limited. Many of these families lived in communities that were impoverished and this often had an impact on the ways in which support workers could work. These workers built strong links with workers in other agencies in order to develop effective helping mechanisms and to strengthen their work with families and find creative solutions to difficult challenges.

## Multi-levelled Interventions Increase Effectiveness

A key strength of the family support service was the ability to provide multi-levelled interventions. The combination of a range of intervention strategies, such as practical support, emotional support and advocacy, with different delivery methods, such as individual and group work, and the ability to work simultaneously on a number of issues, was an important aspect of successful interventions. Workers also developed strong links with other agencies and if other resources needed to be contacted (such as a community mental health service) the worker would provide support to the clients while they made contact and then for a period of time while the new support relationship was becoming established. The worker was the central point for developing connections with other agencies and interventions and the family support work often reinforced what was being learned in other settings. For example, the worker provided opportunities for the clients to practise the parenting strategies they had learned in their parenting group. The worker assisted the clients to address their emotional issues and, at the same time, supported them in trying different strategies in their relationships with others, especially their parenting role.

## Developing Positive Parenting

A key area of work involved actively supporting clients to identify with the parent role and to develop their own styles of positive parenting. Workers often described clients as being 'unavailable to parent' when they first came to the agency. The workers explained that rather than not knowing how to parent effectively, clients often found that the intensity of past or current experiences were such that they were not able to put this knowledge into practice on a consistent basis. In these situations family support staff focused on the wider issues at the same time as supporting the client to implement new strategies within the family. The clients talked of the value of having a worker who could listen to them and work through the issues of being a parent and other issues they faced. The worker assisted them to identify and practise new strategies and make significant changes in their approach to parenting. Success in this area enabled the client to gain confidence to address challenges in other areas, such as issues associated with custody and separation.

## Strengths-based Approach

Family support workers viewed clients as partners in the change process. Their work focused upon enhancing clients' problem-solving skills and strengthening their naturally occurring support networks so that they could sustain the positive change they had achieved during the intervention. In many cases, clients did not have networks that provided them with emotional and instrumental support, or they lived at a distance from their strongest supporters. A key focus for support work would be upon developing these networks so that there were people around the clients who could continue to provide support once the intervention was complete. The worker aimed to ensure that the clients maintained their integrity despite facing difficulties and that they remained in control of the change process (Munford and Sanders, 1999). Their work recognized the importance of client dignity and self-respect and was founded upon the knowledge that long-term change can only be achieved when individuals are supported to have a stake in the changes they are working towards. The worker assisted the clients to gain confidence and to develop mastery over important dimensions of family life in order to achieve self-determination. The strengths-based approach is a focus for family support work in many countries (Dunst et al., 1988; Lee, 1994). This approach guides the work in the following ways:

- The worker has unconditional positive regard for clients, views them as partners in the change process and acknowledges their willingness to achieve change and make things better for themselves and their children.
- The worker focuses on clients' strengths and competencies, not on the *deficits* of clients. It identifies clients' past achievements and reinforces the idea that no matter how difficult a situation may appear, clients can develop strategies to address the difficulties.
- The worker finds ways to develop and advance clients' strengths and competencies.
- Strengths and competencies are used to expand the coping repertoire of clients. Workers assist clients to gain confidence in using strategies that will contribute to successful problem resolution in the future.

The family support workers had a strong commitment to practising strengths-based work and encouraged clients to develop self-determination and a more positive sense of self, to identify and develop new strategies, and to gain more control over their lives.

## FUTURE DIRECTIONS: BUILDING EFFECTIVE RESEARCH PROGRAMMES

The family support research has pointed to other areas that require further investigation. The research programme focused upon the primary client and the relationship between support workers and parents. Although the research examined how the parent viewed the changes in their parenting strategies as a result of the intervention, the researchers were not able to observe this directly. The researchers are developing procedures for examining in more detail the ways in which positive parenting strategies can be developed and maintained. Future research should also include a detailed examination of how relationships outside the home are a contributing factor to the way in which parenting is carried out. For example, we know that custody issues have a major impact on family life and these require further investigation in the context of family support research. The research programme was not able to provide detailed information on how the relationships between social service agencies (and other agencies, such as health services) will contribute to effective outcomes for families. In New Zealand there is a strong focus on inter-agency collaboration, but as yet little research is being carried out on the link between this collaboration and positive outcomes for families. Further research is also required on how practice models can incorporate interventions that respond appropriately to a range of cultural groups. In New Zealand research is emerging in this area (see Walsh Tapiata, 2000, for a discussion on indigenous models of practice).

The family support research discussed in this chapter was carried out within an organizational context. Its focus was upon identifying the key intervention factors that contributed to positive family change. This research was located within a broader research programme that explores family well-being more generally. The evaluation of family support interventions was one aspect of this. The part of the programme that focused upon family support held some valuable lessons for us as teachers and evaluators. These lessons have relevance for those researching family support services in a range of social service contexts in countries that view family support as a key component of support services for families. The lessons suggest a model of research and evaluation practice that is closely aligned with the strengths-based model of social work service delivery. Key components of a research and evaluation approach which embodies these sorts of principles includes a recognition that relationships are crucial for the smooth and effective conduct of evaluations and research into family support practice. We suggest that in the past, and also in many evaluations being conducted today, evaluators and researchers pay insufficient attention to the development of relationships that will facilitate and support the ongoing research process. This seems to be partly as a result of concerns about contamination by the site of the results of the research. We argue that rather than contaminating the research, sound interactive relationships between researchers and practitioners enhance data quality and the depth of understandings that research can generate about interventions.

It has been our experience that researchers and evaluators will generate higher quality data if they are able to align their methods and systems of measurement, data collection and so forth with the logic of the intervention process. In particular, we have found that when client records are to form part of the data set, textual rather than categorical systems provide a more accurate way of capturing client information. The involvement of practitioners in the development of recording systems, in decision making about how and when data will be collected from clients, and in some interpretive activities increases data quality and the long-term applicability of results. This is not to suggest that practitioners should be involved in every aspect of research and evaluation as the research should not disrupt their support work to families. Rather, we have found that throughout the research process opportunities for staff to have input can be created and that these generally improve the quality of the final research product.

Research teams work well in agency settings and provide the opportunity for people to have different roles and to make differing levels of contribution to the overall research effort. We have found that partnerships between universities, providers, independent researchers and practitioners are a good mix for research in family support agencies. These partnerships provide mechanisms for quality control of research to ensure that standards are met, and they also provide a practical way of involving service staff in the research endeavour. Flexibility is also important in agency-based research as the original plan may need to be modified once fieldwork begins. Researchers and evaluators need to recognize this in their planning so that time will be available to rework plans as the research progresses.

Ethical issues must be given priority in the planning and execution of research and evaluation of family support services. Staff need to feel safe when their practice becomes a focus of research and the organization needs to know that internal issues will not become a matter for public discussion. Clients need to know that their privacy will be protected and that the researchers will ensure that they remain fully informed about research procedures. Our experience has taught us that we need to keep ethical issues under continual review throughout data generation and during the report-writing phase of the research. Ethical issues are a regular item on our research-meeting agendas and, by regularly scheduling these issues for discussion at each meeting, we ensure that any changes to research procedures have incorporated a review of ethical issues.

Finally, we believe that researchers must allocate time and resources to provide effective feedback to participants. If there is to be a positive synergy between research and the development of family support services, researchers need to be available to work with agencies over the implementation of research findings. The challenge for researchers and evaluators is to find ways of establishing an ongoing dialogue with the practice and policy communities so that we can become more effective partners in the development part of the research and development equation. The challenge for researchers of family support services is to ensure that research findings can contribute to the development of effective services and interventions.

## ACKNOWLEDGEMENT

The authors wish to thank the staff of Barnardos New Zealand for supporting the research and allowing access to their services. The research programme described would not have been possible without their support.

## REFERENCES

Denzin, N.K. and Lincoln, Y.S (Eds) (1994) *Handbook of Qualitative Research*. Thousand Oaks: Sage Publications.

Dunst, C., Trivette, C. and Deal, A. (1988) *Enabling and Empowering Families*. Cambridge MA: Brookline Books.

Lee, J. (1994) *The Empowerment Approach to Social Work Practice*. New York: Colombia University Press.

Morse, J.M. (1994) Designing funded qualitative research. In N.K. Denzin and Y.S. Lincoln (Eds), *Handbook of Qualitative Research*. Thousand Oaks: Sage Publications.

Munford, R. and Sanders, J. (1999) *Supporting Families*. Palmerston North: Dunmore Press.

Munford, R. and Sanders, J. (2000) Getting to the heart of the matter—making meaning: Three challenges for family researchers. *International Journal of Qualitative Health Research*, 10, 841–852.

Munford, R., Sanders, J., Tisdall, M., Mulder, J., Spoonley, P. and Jack, A. (1996) *Working Successfully with Families: Stage 1*. Wellington: Barnardos NZ.

Munford, R., Sanders, J., Tisdall, M., Henare, A., Livingstone, K. and Spoonley, P. (1998) *Working Successfully with Families: Stage 2*. Wellington: Barnardos N.Z.

Opie, A. (1995) *Beyond Good Intentions: Support Work with Older People*. Wellington: The Institute of Policy Studies.

Sanders, J., Munford, R. and Richards-Ward, L. (1999) *Working Successfully with Families: Stage 3*. Palmerston North: Child and Family Research Centre, Barnardos, NZ.

Shaw, I. and Lishman, J (Eds) (1999) *Evaluation and Social Work Practice*. London: Sage Publications.

Walsh Tapiata, W. (2000) Te Tau Rau Mano. He aha nga wero inaianei? The year 2000. What are the challenges for Maori social workers now? Te Komako IV. *Social Work Review*, **XII**(4), 9–12.

# 10

# A NATIONAL EVALUATION OF FAMILY SUPPORT SERVICES

## An Evaluation of Services Provided by the NSPCC in the United Kingdom

*Ruth Gardner*

This chapter describes a national evaluation of family support services provided by the National Society for the Prevention of Cruelty to Children (NSPCC), a voluntary organization operating in England, Wales and Northern Ireland. First, the main findings are set out, then the aims, process and implications of the evaluation are considered. In the second part of the chapter, issues of policy and practice touched on in the evaluation are discussed in more detail. Inevitably, as the major part of the work was undertaken in England, the context is English practice and law in relation to family support. The evaluation is reported in detail elsewhere (Gardner, 2002).

The process of the evaluation will be reviewed and its overall impact will be assessed in relation to its aims, which were:

- to identify services and activities which could be shown to support families effectively within their communities;
- to ascertain the extent to which services are valued by key stakeholders as delivering family support.

By 'effective' and 'valued' we mean able to offer robust evidence that the services achieve their stated aims in supporting children and families, in ways that conform to or exceed acknowledged practice, standards, and at optimal cost.

The services under consideration were primarily those provided by the NSPCC, but it was important to investigate and profile other local services,

*Evaluating Family Support: Thinking Internationally, Thinking Critically.*
Edited by I. Katz and J. Pinkerton. © 2003 John Wiley & Sons, Ltd.

to see which (or which combination) appeared to be most effective. We interviewed staff from local agencies as well as comparing demographic data and local authority data such as Quality Protects management action plans[1] and Area Child Protection Committee reports for the evaluation sites.

NSPCC projects were well aware that the evaluation would be independent and would report bad news as well as good. In general, NSPCC staff (practitioners and managers) welcomed the process, for a number of reasons. Some had undertaken similar work, either as part of project development or combined with their own research, and valued an exchange of ideas. Some projects were isolated from others doing similar work, geographically and/or by reporting structures. The evaluation had the potential to offer them a bigger picture of practice in family support and to improve communication. Many staff providing family support thought that they lacked status in an organization that is recognized mainly for dealing with victims of abuse and abusers, evidenced by the fact that staff working in its investigation, assessment and treatment teams were generally better paid. They felt that training and support for staff was very strong in terms of child protection, but weaker in other areas related to preventive work such as project management, developing parent training and evaluation itself. Staff requested opportunities to meet on a national basis and to contribute to the evaluation process. As a result, six staff seminars were held to which service users and external speakers were invited. There were also smaller workshops for the projects directly involved in the evaluation. The cost of this exercise was heavy in terms of time to organize the events, but the benefits outweighed the cost. The evaluation process was more inclusive and the evaluator saw a wider cross-section of NSPCC's work than would otherwise have been possible. Additionally:

- staff and managers gave helpful insights into the organization, its key players, changes underway and areas of possible difficulty;
- much careful evaluation work came to light;
- practitioners and managers started to debate, and set an agenda for further development work.

These outcomes demonstrated the benefits of an open evaluation process for practice learning and staff development, as suggested by the literature on 'research-mindedness' (e.g. Shaw and Lishman, 1999). Practitioners actively engaged in evaluation tended to:

- see family members and colleagues as sources of important knowledge and information, and acquire key skills in questioning, listening, collecting data and reflecting on it;
- continually scan and reflect on their work, relate individual cases to a wider body of knowledge and, as a result, critically appraise progress, avoid drift, and seek appropriate advice and support where necessary;
- develop greater confidence in bringing together and presenting data.

Staff contributed to the evaluation but without compromising its independence. As a result there was generally a positive, rather than a defensive, attitude to mistakes and failures, which could be shared as a rich and legitimate source of learning. This was partly the case, it seemed, because the organization encouraged learning and also because most staff had a fundamental optimism about the work, which allowed criticism to be used constructively. In other words, most staff members did not fear evaluation (or audit, or inspection) as seeking to blame, and so could make use of it. Such practice should be safer and more effective for children than where evaluation skills are not developed.

## THE PROJECT SERVICES

An initial survey of all NSPCC's 140 projects allowed us to pick up these perspectives and to form an overview of the work. About 20% of the projects had a major family support function as defined in Part III of the Children Act 1989: 'services intended to safeguard and promote the welfare of children and, so far as is consistent with that duty, to promote the upbringing of such families with their children'. A further 30% of projects said that while their primary activity was with children in need of protection, they had a complementary role that they identified as supporting families and/or promoting social inclusion, for example 'improving access to local services for families and children' and 'improving community networks'. Such projects offered family support in the form of outings, activities or material help in order, for example, to help families through traumatic court proceedings, to promote safe behaviour in adults and children, or to maintain links between family members.

Variety characterized the projects undertaking family support (Figure 10.1). They had a range of partner agencies including education, health, social services and other charities. Even more varied was the skills mix; while the most frequent qualification was social work, there was a large group with expertise in nursery nursing, play therapy and similar work, and others with nursing and health-visiting experience and/or community work, business, and administrative backgrounds. Of the projects offering only or mainly family support, we selected six across the country as the main sites for the evaluation. They had been established for several years and had a large group of service users, to whom we wrote for volunteers to be interviewed.

One of the projects was located in an inner city and two in metropolitan areas, and are called Inner City, Metropolitan Outskirts and Metropolitan Suburb. Two more were in relatively new, planned estates (Garden City and New Estate) and the sixth in a resort (SeaSide). In others words, there was a range of settings. The services they offered included a mixture of open-access groups and social events run with a crèche, more structured play and activities for older children, and structured support for parents—either one-to-one or in discussion and therapy groups, or interactive sessions. Dependent upon

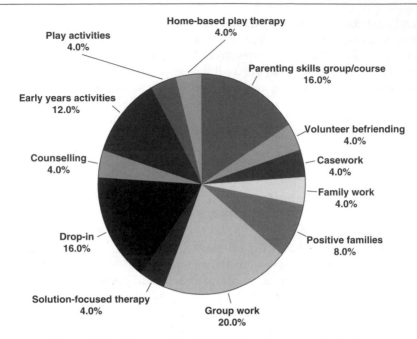

**Figure 10.1**   Range of the NSPCC's family support activities

demand, the latter might offer training in parenting techniques or practical skills and self-development, with links to adult education (Table 10.1). Broadly speaking the projects provide a cross-section of family support services as described in Part III and Schedule 2 of the Children Act 1989.

## FINDINGS ABOUT THE CHILDREN AT FIRST INTERVIEW

*Note: all case examples and quotations have been made anonymous.*

The evaluator interviewed 88 parents. Thirty children were also interviewed directly, either individually or in groups; with 16 of these we used

**Table 10.1**   Similarities and differences in service provision

|                          | MetS | MetO | NewE | SeaS | InnerC | GardenC |
|--------------------------|------|------|------|------|--------|---------|
| Drop-in                  | ×    | ✓    | ✓    | ✓    | ✓      | ✓       |
| Childcare                | ✓    | ✓    | ✓    | ✓    | ✓      | ✓       |
| Twice a week or more     | ✓    | ✓    | ✓    | ✓    | ✓      | ✓       |
| One-to-one counselling   | ✓    | ✓    | ✓    | ✓    | ✓      | ✓       |
| Social worker            | ×    | ✓    | ✓    | ✓    | ✓      | ✓       |
| Group work for adults    | ×    | ✓    | ×    | ×    | ×      | ×       |
| Group work for children  | ×    | ✓    | ×    | ×    | ✓      | ✓       |
| Skills (non-parenting)   | ✓    | ✓    | ×    | ×    | ✓      | ✓       |
| Parenting training       | ✓    | ✓    | ✓    | ✓    | ×      | ✓       |

similar questionnaires to those used with the parents. Of the 105 children about whom we spoke to parents, 77 were aged 3 or over and we used the Strengths and Difficulties questionnaire to ask parents about their behaviour. This is 'a brief behavioural screening questionnaire that provides balanced coverage of children's and young people's behaviours, emotions and relationships . . . designed to meet the needs of researchers, clinicians and educationalists' (Goodman, 1997). The threshold score identifies children who may be at risk of more severe behavioural or mental health difficulties. We used the higher of two possible thresholds to avoid identifying children incorrectly (false positives). On this basis, over two-thirds (68%) of children aged 3 or over whose families were receiving family support had a borderline (17%) or critical (51%) score, as assessed by their parents. At the same time, most children (69%) were seen by their parents as having reasonable prosocial behaviour, such as helpfulness.

We were able to use the same questionnaire, provided in the relevant format, with a small group of children and teachers. Most of these reports were consistent: the children saw themselves as helpful and prosocial and, while identifying their difficulties, saw these as less serious than did their parents. Teachers identified the most severe behavioural problems with graphic examples, but otherwise also tended to see behaviour as less problematic than did the parents.

There were three clusters of behavioural traits among those children perceived as having difficulties. One group (45%) showed hyperactivity and conduct disorders, a second (42%) had fewer overall difficulties and more strengths, and a smaller group (13%) had emotional and peer relationship difficulties with some hyperactivity. These groups did not vary significantly by age or gender. The first group (children with hyperactivity and conduct disorders) exercised parents and schools most. The parents often identified possible causes of the behaviour in the family history. For children, these histories included witnessing domestic violence or abuse; suffering abuse; multiple changes of address; loss of contact with key people, for instance grandparents, father, or siblings; lack of attention from a parent; and being bullied or taunted at school and/or in the community.

A substantial minority of the sample of children, approximately 10% (or 5% of all children in the families), were prescribed Ritalin. Some parents spoke of their child having ADHD (attention deficit hyperactivity disorder) and a few of oppositional defiance disorder, which was described as 'like ADHD but Ritalin doesn't work'. In fact, most of the parents with children on Ritalin spoke of increasingly short-term and inconsistent benefits.

A typical example of such children were Jane and David, spoken about here by their grandmother:

> My grandchild Jane is 9 years old and was in a refuge for three months last year. Her mother has had three violent partners and Jane is now violent to her sister and brothers, or when she is restrained. She kicked in the wardrobes

at the refuge. Even so she is top of her class in reading. Her brother is 7—he has oppositional defiance disorder, it's like ADHD but ritalin doesn't work. He watched his mother being raped. He is in a special unit now, calming down a bit. These problems have been passed on I believe. I was abused as a child and I was so ashamed of myself I married the first man who came along and he did the same to my daughters. Only one of them did the same as I had though. I think it can be stopped for my grandchildren now they are getting help. It shocked me when my grandson came to the workshop here and said, 'What makes me sad? Seeing my dad strangling my mum'.

Nearly half of parents thought their children were being bullied and nearly as many (43%) thought their children were fighting or bullying others. There was an appreciable overlap, with parents seeing over half of possible bullies (55%) also as victims of threats or violence.

As well as the Strengths and Difficulties questionnaire, we asked parents of all age groups of children, general questions about type and degree of any difficulty and the amount and duration of stress on the child and other family members. Of the 29 children aged under 3, 44% were thought to present some difficulties, but only three children were thought to have pronounced difficulties. Assessed in terms of its immediate effect, of stress on the child and family, difficulty differed significantly with age. Over half of children over 3 years old were seen as having pronounced or definite difficulties ($p = 0.000$). There was a significant positive relationship between the age of the child and perception of stress caused by the difficulty ($p = 0.026$). The mean age of children found a burden to the parent is 9 years, whereas the mean age of children *not* seen in this way is 6.7 years; it appears a change in many parents' view of the child's behaviour occurs between these ages, with its effects becoming more disruptive. Across the six evaluation sites, there were patterns in the spread of behavioural difficulty, with only about one-sixth (15.4%) of the sample seen as having fewer difficulties in Inner City, whereas over half (61.5%) were seen thus in New Estate. These patterns were replicated in other findings.

## FINDINGS CONCERNING PARENTS AND CARERS AT FIRST INTERVIEW

Parents and primary carers who were interviewed were aged between 18 and 63, the majority being in their thirties. Seven per cent (six) of those we interviewed were male. Just over 80% described themselves as 'UK White', 4% as 'Irish' or 'other White', 12.5% as of mixed heritage or 'Black African', 'Caribbean', 'British or other Black', with a small group from the Asian sub-continent.

The average family size was 2.4 children but a significant minority (17%) had four or more children. Nearly half (48%) of the parents or carers were alone as parents. In other words, although most lone parents had a partner, this did not include joint, consistent care of the children. Despite this, many lone parents mentioned important practical and/or emotional help from partners, ex-partners and their families. Nearly one-fifth of those interviewed were with second or subsequent partners and children. A few were in another type of family, e.g. with grandparents. Nearly one-third (31%) of carers were with the other parent of their children.

As we have seen, we asked parents about their children. We also asked them about their life experiences: about health, about support networks and their view of the neighbourhood (networks and neighbourhood, when amalgamated, are referred to as the community climate) and of course about local support services including NSPCC.

We used a Stress and Health questionnaire to ask parents about their emotional and physical health. Again this has a threshold score, above which more severe health problems might occur and which therefore suggests a clinical referral. Studies in which this measure has been used (sometimes called the Malaise or Social Malaise Inventory) show a remarkable degree of consistency in terms of the rate of referral and the stress levels of parents. For instance, Jane Gibbons and colleagues (1990), interviewing 144 parents, found that between

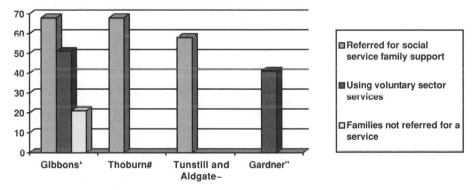

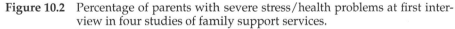

**Figure 10.2** Percentage of parents with severe stress/health problems at first interview in four studies of family support services.
*Gibbons and Wilkinson's (1990) sample included 72 families referred to and receiving a service from social service (all referrals), 72 referred voluntary sector services, 359 families not referred for a service.
#Thoburn et al.'s (2000) sample was 122 families receiving service from social services (including those referred for neglect and emotional harm).
~Tunstill and Aldgate (2000) included 93 families receiving services from social services (excluding child protection and disabilities).
"Gardner's (this) study is 88 families receiving services from the voluntary sector.
Gibbons, Thoburn and Gardner used the 'social malaise inventory' (Gibbons, 1991). Tunstill and Aldgate interviewed parents about their physical and mental health.

one-half and two-thirds of those referred to social services for family support had severe levels of stress, compared to 21% in groups of parents from the same neighbourhoods who had not been referred. June Thoburn and colleagues (2000) used the same measure with 122 parents receiving social services support in cases of emotional maltreatment and neglect. Well over 60%, a similar proportion to that found by Gibbons, had a severe level of stress. Tunstill and Aldgate (2000), interviewing 93 parents about their health in cases of need other than a child's disability or child protection concerns, found somewhat lower levels of serious ill-health.

In our study of the NSPCC's family support services, well over a third (41%) of primary carers had a critical score, and half of these—nearly 20% of carers—had up to twice the critical score. These denote major crises; such parents described suicidal feelings and attempts, post-natal depression and chronic and/or disabling conditions.

There was a significant association between projects and critical levels of stress, with parents in Inner City project four times as likely to have severe problems as those in Garden City (similar proportions as for children's behavioural problems). Lone parents had the greatest proportion of high stress levels and parents in second or subsequent partnerships the lowest (11%).

We asked parents about life experiences such as early parenthood, educational achievement, changes of address, abuse as a child or violence, and whether their child had been a subject of child protection concerns. We scored this using an (arbitrary) cut-off for high vulnerability. Gibbons' research had used similar questions but trawled records for the answers, which were therefore estimates. This combination of particular adverse past experience and disadvantage was associated with several other measures: high levels of stress; children's behavioural problems; a perceived lack of informal or formal (professional) support; higher material disadvantage; and a negative view of the local neighbourhood. While vulnerability did not differ significantly by project, higher levels occurred in those projects offering specialist therapy or counselling.

Parents said that they had used NSPCC's family support services because they gave some choice and control over whether, how and when to disclose a history of abuse and/or violence. They would not have sought help if it had meant talking about this history first. The significance of family support was in allowing the parents to build up confidence both in the project staff and in themselves, and to gain support from other parents as and when they needed it. The special role of the NSPCC service was providing access to specialized help if and when a disclosure was made, without lengthy or traumatic referral procedures.

Severe material disadvantage was not evident from these interviews, although it was observed on a few of the home visits. The questionnaires probably did not take sufficient account of debt; we observed that assets such as mobile phones, cars and other equipment came and went from households over six months. Indicators differed across projects in a familiar pattern, Inner

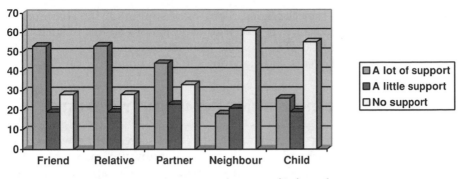

**Figure 10.3** Amount and source of informal support

City project having 40% of interviewees with a wage earner in the household while New Estate and Garden City had nearly 80%; Inner City and Metropolitan Suburb having 20% of parents with access to a car, while projects New Estate and Metropolitan Outskirts had 75% and 85% respectively.

## FINDINGS CONCERNING SUPPORT NETWORKS

We wanted to find out as much as possible about the local context for family support. We asked parents and 37 staff (from both NSPCC and other agencies) for their assessment of the neighbourhood of the project in terms of its child and family friendliness, and its local services. Some of these questions were based on a short survey by Garbarino and colleagues (Garbarino and Kostelny, 1992), who investigate the meaning of risk in relation to areas where there are high, or higher than expected, rates of child abuse. We too were interested in any perceived patterns (differences or similarities) between project areas in terms of children's and families' experiences, their environment and the response by agencies. Parents were asked about sources of support at three levels: informal (family and friends), semi-formal (groups, clubs, activities including the NSPCC's, and work, paid or otherwise) and formal (professional) support.

Because the tools have not been tested, these are very tentative results. The findings on all levels of support were of interest, but only informal support was significantly associated with other measures such as parental stress ($p = 0.000$) and the level of children's behavioural problems ($p = 0.009$). Lack of informal support was associated with higher levels of difficulty on these measures.

Most of those who had a partner—this was 42% of those interviewed—found him or her supportive, but over 50% had a supportive friend (see Figure 10.3). Parents kept in contact with ex-partners' relations and with relatives at a great distance to maintain this close, special support. One in ten of parents interviewed had no source of informal support. The great majority of parents said that the NSPCC project offered them some support at the community (semi-formal) level, and for over half who had only one source of such support, this was the NSPCC. The projects also actively encouraged informal networks, with social events and activities and befriending by volunteers.

## FINDINGS CONCERNING COMMUNITY CLIMATE

We used a basic scoring method, and aggregated scores for networks and views of the neighbourhood to produce a community climate score. We wanted to see if it was possible to differentiate warm climates, where families typically experience support as readily available on a variety of levels and the fabric of local networks is good, through cool where it is patchier, to cold climates where there are holes in social networks and respondents maintain them with difficulty. Levels of perceived informal support correlated with views of the overall community climate. While the methodology did not allow us to measure other effects, there were observable differences and patterns. For example, in two of the project areas, Inner City and SeaSide, measures of children's difficulties and of parental stress were very high. These project neighbourhoods and/or the local authority area contained relatively very high levels of social need, as measured by such indicators as proportion of local authority tenure, proportion of families on benefits and lone parent families, and numbers of children on child protection registers and accommodated. The characteristics of projects where parents and staff saw themselves as making progress, despite high levels of need (compared to those where they were less confident), appeared to be:

- Projects, along with other individuals and groups, had created a supportive community and inter-professional network, in other words, a more benign 'microclimate'. There was a mandate from local parents and/or agencies to address specific needs with specific services, and projects were demonstrably meeting these expectations.
- The support network had to some extent been articulated as an explicit neighbourhood and/or local authority strategy for family support, with well-developed inter-agency relationships. This, for instance, allowed families to obtain specialized help without delays and unnecessary reframing of the case as more serious than it was, in order to meet threshold criteria.

Where these key elements were absent, projects were struggling or even closed down. The local authority itself was sometimes in difficulties in terms of finance or public criticism, but projects could survive such crises if their local systems were strong enough. However, there was a tendency for local services and systems that were not in difficulty to isolate those that were, thus contributing to the overall fragmentation.

## FINDINGS CONCERNING CHANGES AND DEVELOPMENTS OVER SIX MONTHS

We describe various types of change over the six months of the evaluation:

- changes observed by professionals who referred parents and children;
- changes reported by parents, their partners and children;
- changes in test scores;
- changes in relation to a specific threshold such as the stress/health score for a parent or the behavioural score for a child.

One of the tasks of the study was to identify the advantages and disadvantages of these approaches. We compared results for users of more structured, intensive services with those of users of regular services. An example of the former would be a 10-week course on techniques for dealing with difficult child behaviour; the latter might be regular drop-in attendance with occasional advice sessions. We did not have a control group of non-service users and we lost service users between the two groups and had to allow as far as we could for the consequent differences. For example, those still receiving help after six months tended to have had higher stress levels at the first interview. These limitations meant we were unable to attribute changes to a particular intervention with any degree of certainty. But we looked in detail at changes in scores that occurred over six months in relation to the first interview and the threshold score, and found a great deal of consistency.

Within the follow-up group of 55 parents, stress and health difficulties had shifted over six months. On the test scores, over half (53%) of the sample had remained stable, and of these 33% had improved. However, nearly half had deteriorated and almost a quarter (22%) had reached a critical score. When respondents were asked to assess overall changes in their stress levels and health, more said that no change had occurred than the test results suggested was the case (Table 10.2).

While there was no significant association with improvement and type of service, a higher proportion of those receiving a structured service attained or maintained lower stress and ill-health levels at the end of six months. However, as stated above, the methodology did not allow us to identify cause

**Table 10.2** Changes in health over six months

|  | Worse | No change or balance out | Better |
| --- | --- | --- | --- |
| *Changes by questionnaire (%)* | 48 | 19 | 33 |
| *Changes by self-assessment (%)* | 28 | 48 | 24 |

and effect; for instance, motivation of parents attending classes may have contributed to their improvement.

In terms of children's behaviour, there was a clear shift in the scores of the 47 children aged 3 and over whom we followed up. Fifty-eight per cent showed an improvement, 7% no change and 35% deteriorated, in the parents' assessment. If children's behaviour had maintained or attained a score that indicated no major concern, the carers' stress levels were also likely to be within a normal range at the end of six months ($p = 0.026$). Parents with greater vulnerability in terms of their past experiences (see p. 198) were more likely to assess their children as maintaining or developing severe behavioural problems ($p = 0.035$). On the other hand, parents with more perceived informal support and a positive view of their neighbourhood were more likely ($p = 0.000$ and $p = 0.005$ respectively) to see children maintain or develop behaviour indicating no major concerns. Parents whose overall rating of community climate was lowest (in terms of their whole support network and view of the neighbourhood) also found least behavioural improvement in their children ($p = 0.035$).

There were other patterns, short of statistical significance, consistent with these findings. Younger children tended to show more improvement. There were variations in the amount of improvement shown over six months across the six projects. The two projects showing the highest levels of improvement focused on parents with younger children using structured services with strong planning according to a theoretical base. The two projects with the highest proportion of children not improving did most direct work with older children referred by social services, whose problems were unlikely to be alleviated readily. But even their parents thought that between 28% and 50% of children showed some improvement. While we are very cautious about these findings because of the size and methodological limitations of the study, we believe they are of sufficient interest and consistency with other studies to warrant further investigation.

We have reported here some of the quantitative findings in terms of amounts of difficulty presented by parents and children over the period of time during which they received family support. The problem with such findings is that they are rarely hard enough in smaller studies. Any evaluator or researcher in this field is only too aware of the slippery nature of the evidence, and strictures about pseudo scientific methodology: '... (their) research does not tell us anything. Because control groups were not used, there is absolutely no basis upon which to draw any conclusions whatsoever' (Gelles, 1997).

While it is important to be clear about the limitations of an investigation, this should not discourage us from attempting to measure what we find. Alongside the measures we used other methods—for example, open discussions and meetings with parents and children, both individually and in groups. Our approach here was to take detailed notes and to highlight themes that emerged regularly in a number of settings. For instance, for children the main themes were:

- *Trust*—Children had experience of adults being inconsistent if not oppressive. Where this was a loved person the child's confidence and self-esteem were affected.
- *Loss*—Many children had lost a home and local friends by eviction or by multiple moves, and/or had lost a parent by, often violent and acrimonious, separation. These children were often distressed and/or depressed as well as anxious about further changes. Symptoms such as bed-wetting, sleeplessness, hyperactivity and aggression were being treated with little attention to the underlying psychological difficulties.
- *Local neighbourhood*—Children spoke of being frightened on the street, of muggings, sexual assault and/or robbery. Some had been attacked or verbally abused by older children, and had heard about more serious incidents in the local media.
- *Fun and adult attention*—Children enjoyed NSPCC activities because they were designed to offer social and play opportunities without demanding a specific output, such as academic work. Adults listened and engaged with them, attentive to their well-being and the rules but without pressuring them. This was a unique experience for some children. Some had also absorbed, and made use of, the social skills being taught.

> They tell you what to do but in a fun way. We played a game about what is a right and what is a responsibility. I tell my mum where I am going and I think she feels more secure, and I feel safer too. I complained at Burger King because they threw my food away—the person at the counter said, 'So what?' so I asked to see the manager and got a replacement. I think that the workshop here helped me to do that because I thought it through. (Michael, age 12 years)

For parents, key themes were:

- *Social contact in the community*—For many parents, NSPCC was the only or main social support outside the home. This is hard to imagine if you have work, clubs or learning and leisure activities. But parents without work looking after several children alone were unable or lacked confidence to take these up. Many described the project as their only route to such a network.
- *Housing and neighbourhood*—Parents were more settled and positive about the neighbourhood if they had a strong informal network. Few complained about their own accommodation, but all aspired to neighbourhoods where there was little street crime or vandalism, where children could play safely and where shops and amenities were accessible without a car. Such neighbourhoods were identified similarly by all the parents and often bordered those where none of these aspirations could be met.
- *Education*—All the parents, whatever their own history, aspired to better experiences for their children. For pre-school children, they wanted both

cognitive and social skills that would prepare them to do well at school. For older children they wanted verbal and social skills that would help them to cope better with adverse situations such as bullying, frustration or anger. Parents wanted their children to gain life choices and be fulfilled and happy. They saw this as a matter of confidence and social skills at least as much as of academic success.

- *Health and social services*—Parents had positive accounts of individual GPs, health visitors and social workers who they felt had made a special effort to help them. An example was a mother with two children under 5 years old who said:

> I had serious post-natal depression with my first child and was a psychiatric in-patient. I have had bulimia and borderline agoraphobia but I have got better and more confident and have weaned myself off the tablets. My GP and health visitor have been very supportive and so has the community psychiatric nurse. The health visitor had to fight to get me hormone injections after the second child; they cost $26 a day for seven days. The hospital would not fund them. Without them I am sure I'd have another breakdown.

On the whole they thought that professionals appeared unable or unwilling to help them and they blamed systems as much as individuals: 'It is not their fault; I've worked in social services and their desks are full, a lot of them just have too much to do—but it is very frustrating when you tell your story over again and get no further.' Many serious health difficulties did not appear to have been treated promptly or sensitively. Child mental health services were singled out by parents and other professionals as a cause of particular concern because criteria and waiting-list rules were so intransigent that problems were often past remedy by the time the child received treatment. Even when a service was offered, parents often said that they were made to feel guilty and did not want to go back.

## CONCLUSIONS

Taking all the evidence together over the two-year period of the evaluation we here set out some broad conclusions, and indicators for further work.

- Most of the stakeholders we were able to speak to (children, parents, relatives and other agencies) valued the NSPCC's family support service and could identify changes for the better which they attributed to its work. Changes were usually related to improvements in children's behaviour and their own concerns about it, and/or to the project providing help with parents and children's experiences of violence or abuse. The measures we used indicate that children's behaviour had indeed improved, although we cannot attribute this to the project. However, parents tended to underestimate the increasing burden of stress and ill-health they suffered themselves. This suggested serious personal and service costs at a later date. Family support should include more active health assessment and advocacy for parents.

- Children and parents especially appreciated the open, informal nature of access to the service combined with explicit rules of conduct for staff and service users and a choice of more structured forms of support.
- The majority of parents had mixed views about the NSPCC's national image insofar as it suggested that the organization dealt mainly or solely with child abuse. While they were very supportive of the NSPCC's child-centred and child-safe practice, they did not want to be identified with the organization's image of dealing with abusers, and they thought parents might well be put off seeking help because of it.
- A small minority of parents also had difficulty with the group ethos of some of the projects and felt marginalized. Projects need to work on this actively and make group dynamics a more explicit issue, for instance reviewing membership or bringing in outside group workers from time to time in order to question established hierarchies.
- Men using family support services had a similar range of problems (isolation, stress, management of children's behaviour, past abuse) as women did, but services are not geared to their needs, and tend to reinforce gender stereotypes. Developing services for men would have cost implications but these should be balanced against the potential benefits of a group of fathers and partners gaining greater confidence, skills and emotional literacy—and the development should be evaluated.
- In this evaluation, work with families from Black, Asian or other ethnic minorities was limited to specialist projects set up to meet those families' needs, and a minority of other projects that made continual efforts to access the whole of their local community. The projects for Black families appeared to have a more diverse user group than average, because they were also used by White parents with children of dual heritage. The organization as a whole needs to do more to support and promote diversity. In a few projects one group of users tended to monopolize the service and again, the efforts of staff to counter exclusivity and/or prejudice need more active support and leadership.

## Indicators for Further Evaluation

The NSPCC has now commissioned a further stage of evaluation of its family support services. In this stage we would like to follow up the same families (as far as possible) 18–24 months on. We would like to interview more referrers or third parties such as teachers, to obtain their pre- and post-intervention assessment of children's progress. We want to interview more men, both those using the service and partners of women using the service. We would like to interview a sample of parents and children in similar circumstances but not using a family support service and/or a sample using social services support as contrast groups.

The lessons from this evaluation will also be applied to the next phase. In particular, the evaluation pointed towards the importance of constant engagement and dialogue with service providers. Ownership by the practitioners and front-line managers of family support services was an essential prerequisite for keeping the evaluation going, and it is crucial that this continues to be the case. Engagement of senior management within the organization has also been important, and dissemination of the findings to decision makers within the agency has been an important factor in persuading the organization to fund further work in this area. In the next phase efforts to engage families themselves will be increased. While there was some involvement in the first phase, it will be important to involve them more effectively in the research. The evaluation has been influential in refining the family support services provided by the NSPCC and for raising the profile of this area of work within the organization and beyond, and further evaluation will, we hope, continue to improve the services to children and families.

## NOTE

1. *Quality Protects* is a Government initiative aimed at improving children's social services, in particular the health and education outcomes for looked-after children. Money is disbursed to local authorities, and the allocation is dependent on a Management Action Plan which sets out the spending priorities for the following year.

## REFERENCES

Garbarino, J. and Kostelny, K. (1992) Child maltreatment as a community problem. *Child Abuse and Neglect*, **16**(4), 455–464.

Gardner, R. (2002) *Supporting Families: Child Protection in the Community*. Chichester: John Wiley & Sons.

Gelles, R.T. (1997) *Intimate Violence in Families*. Newbury Park: Sage.

Gibbons, J., Thorpe, S. and Wilkinson, P. (1990) *Family Support and Prevention: Studies in Local Areas*. London: HMSO.

Goodman, R. (1997) The strengths and difficulties questionnaire: a research note. *Psychology and Psychiatry*, **38**, 581–586.

Shaw, L. and Lishman, J. (1999) *Evaluation and Social Work Practice*. London: Sage.

Thoburn, J., Wilding, J. and Watson, J. (2000) *Family Support in Cases of Emotional Maltreatment and Neglect*. London: The Stationery Office.

Tunstill, J. and Aldgate, J. (2000) *Services for Children in Need*. London: The Stationery Office.

# 11

# EMPOWERING PARENTS

## A Two-Generation Intervention in a Community Context in Northern Ireland

*Nuala Quiery, Sandra McElhinney, Harry Rafferty, Noel Sheehy, and Karen Trew*

This chapter presents aspects of an evaluation undertaken by a team of university-based psychologists of a family support initiative in Northern Ireland. This initiative, named the Greater Shankill Early Years Project (EYP), is still in existence at the time of writing, although operating at a much lower capacity than in its first three and a half years due to funding restrictions. The aim of the EYP was to enhance educational opportunity in the long term, by means of a two-generation strategy of family support with a community dimension. It did this by providing a home visitor service to all families with children under 5, irrespective of income, education or any other criteria. Out-of-home opportunities for pre-school childcare and education, as well as education, training and employment opportunities for parents, were an integral part of the EYP. Local mothers were recruited, trained and employed as home visitors. This added a peer-education dimension to the EYP and was in keeping with the empowerment model adopted in the EYP's approach to parenting and early child development. The EYP opened in April 1996 and engaged in a process of internal monitoring and evaluation from the outset. The formal, external evaluation, which is reported here, was undertaken between August 1998 and February 2000 with the specific brief of assessing the impact of the EYP on the children of the area.

*Evaluating Family Support: Thinking Internationally, Thinking Critically.*
Edited by I. Katz and J. Pinkerton. © 2003 John Wiley & Sons, Ltd.

## CONTEXT OF THE EARLY YEARS PROJECT

The Greater Shankill consists of some 11 066 households and 25 644 inhabitants, or 5% of the Belfast Urban Area's population. From the mid-nineteenth century, through to the 1960s, it benefited from the industrial development and growth of Belfast. The area has experienced a steep decline in its population since the 1960s due chiefly to a combination of natural and planned migration, and the contraction of many of the larger, traditional industries. The Greater Shankill comprises those areas of West Belfast dominated by the Protestant unionist community. It includes a combination of public housing estates built in the 1960s, older Victorian housing, and some more recent, private sector dwellings. The small proportion of privately owned dwellings on the margins of the Greater Shankill stand in stark contrast to the public sector estates, many of which are drab and poorly serviced in terms of commercial and public amenities. Combined with high levels of poverty, this housing contributes to the social isolation, low uptake of existing services and ill health experienced by many in the area.

As a community, the Shankill developed around a shared political and cultural identity, involving close ties of extended kinship. These extended family and neighbourhood networks provided an informal system of support. In the 1960s and 1970s, this network was severely undermined by the collapse of the area's economic base, the impact of political violence, the process of redevelopment, and the general pace of social change. Left behind is an inner-city area characterized by an ageing population, families locked into poverty and benefit dependence, with community structures all but destroyed.

## ORIGINS AND AIMS OF THE GREATER SHANKILL EARLY YEARS PROJECT

In the early 1990s, community workers in the Greater Shankill decided to tackle the problems presented by community decline, and began the process of developing a long-term economic, social and physical regeneration strategy, drawing together the key players in the governmental, statutory, private and community sectors. The key issue facing a successful regeneration programme is how and where to break into the cycle of deprivation and demoralization. Since low school attainment was one of the many problems identified, investment in the pre-school children of the area and their families was selected for intervention. Recognizing that empowerment is a vital part of regeneration, the process of promoting engagement within the communities that make up the Greater Shankill was considered essential. The Early Years Project aimed to empower parents and reconnect them with their communities by providing social support through home visitors, and opportunities to participate in activities beyond the home. In this way the

EYP hoped to enrich the early experience of a whole generation of pre-school children.

The Early Years Project had five explicit aims:

- to recognize, value, support and empower parents in the parenting role in a widespread process of community engagement;
- to maximize the potential for development of a new generation of early years children as a foundation for life;
- to raise the value placed on education by the Greater Shankill community;
- to enable and support parents to make use of relevant pathways of opportunity in education, training, employment, and community involvement;
- to create a key strategic process of renewal within the community of the Greater Shankill area, which will catalyse the wider regeneration strategy for the area. This synergy is to achieve lasting improvement and change.

Together these aims represent the urban vision for the Greater Shankill area, that is a community network of opportunity, with a regenerative dynamic, based on the early years development of the child and empowerment of the parent(s), leading to economic and social renewal. This was to be achieved by offering support to every parent of a new generation of children in the Greater Shankill, from ante-natal care through the early years of their child's life (at least three years) leading seamlessly into nursery and primary education. This was an ambitious project that was entered into with enthusiasm and vision.

The Greater Shankill partnership was formed and became the means whereby the vision and goals of community regeneration were to be made a reality. In February 1995, it was announced that the European Urban Community Initiative and Making Belfast Work, a Northern Ireland Government programme, would fund the EYP for a period of nearly five years, ending in December 1999. The Director was in post by November 1995, and the first group of EYP workers began their induction and training in April 1996. Four neighbourhood bases came into operation. In addition, two special interest teams (one for young parents and one for fathers) were established, as well as an Infrastructure Team, which operated across geographical areas within the Greater Shankill. The Infrastructure Team provided peripatetic play materials and equipment for events, supported existing groups within the community to initiate pre-school and parenting initiatives, and organized events between neighbourhoods.

## THEORETICAL BASIS OF THE EVALUATION

Given the multi-service approach of the Early Years Project, the complexity of its aims, and the difficulties that could be faced in measuring change over a relatively short time, it was clear that the evaluation would require a sound theoretical foundation to guide the evaluation strategy and on which to base findings and conclusions. The evaluation team looked to existing models within the field of early child development and community intervention, as well as the lessons learned from evaluations of previous interventions of this kind. The evaluation faced a number of challenges. The first was to find an approach that would do justice to the sophistication of the EYP's aims and objectives. The second was to identify ways in which the theoretical concepts underlying the EYP's approach were being applied in practice at the level of the individual. The outcome of this exploration of theoretical models was two-fold. First, it led to the identification of a transactional model of early child development and, secondly, it identified an ecological model of the relationship between the individual and community as the most appropriate.

## A Transactional Model of Development

Arnold Sameroff (1987) comments on 'how theoretical limitations have placed limits on the sophistication of research paradigms' and calls for the expansion of 'our understanding of the environment in order to lay a basis for more complex paradigms in both research and practice' (Sameroff, 1987, p. 167).

He emphasizes the ongoing transaction of influence between child and environment in which the subtle, but nonetheless often potent, impact of a number of factors comes into play. In this view the *progress* achieved by the individual child in development is essentially that of growing self-regulation both biologically and psychosocially. Sameroff (1987) compares cognitive and social development in childhood to the biological model in which:

> one has to think about a system with two levels, the developing organism and a superordinate regulatory system. In biology the regulatory system for physical outcomes is found in the genetic code. For behavioural outcomes there is also a system that regulates the way human beings fit into their society. This cultural code is directed at the regulation of cognitive and social-emotional processes so that the individual will be able to fill some social role defined by society including the reproduction of that society. (Sameroff, 1987, p. 177)

Sameroff breaks the cultural code down into macro-, micro- and mini-regulations. Macro-regulations include, for example, formal schooling as a social institution established for the socialization and training of children. Micro-regulations are at the level of culturally accepted caregiving activities within families, for example, providing for basic needs such as feeding. And mini-regulations refer to the social interaction between parent and child and this early relationship. Problems in development, or less than optimal development, can be due to a failure in the self-regulatory functioning at any of these three levels. To this extent Sameroff notes that developmental outcomes for young children are multiply determined. However, he goes on to state that:

> when one searches for factors that can be easily altered to improve the outcome for children the list is short. . . . What is left are the coping skills of the parents. These include the psychological variables of mental health, parental perspectives, and parent-child interaction patterns. These coping skills are what we have described . . . as the cultural code, the social regulatory system that guides children through their development and buffers them from those aspects of the broader environment with which they are not yet able to cope by themselves.
> (Sameroff, 1987, p. 180)

The aim of prevention or intervention strategies for children and their families is defined by Sameroff as 'the adjustment of the child better to fit the regulatory system or the adjustment of the regulatory system better to fit the child', and he considers that 'models that focus on singular causal factors are inadequate for either the study or manipulation of developmental outcomes' (Sameroff, 1987, p. 186).

## AN ECOLOGICAL MODEL OF DEVELOPMENT

There are two competing models of intervention with children. The more traditional model aims to remediate pathology within the individual child. The other focuses on mitigating the effects of a poor environment by strengthening protective and facilitating factors in a child's environment.

Garbarino et al. (1997) also distinguish between these two models and cite Lofquist's (1983) matrix, which classifies different kinds of intervention according to whether they focus on the individual or community, and whether they are remedial or preventive in their goals. They conclude that the individual/remedial approach has become the predominant model in the USA. The focus of each of these two approaches, individual or community, is fundamentally different. The first is remedial and attempts to assist a maladapted individual, whereas the second attempts to alter aspects of the environment in such a way as to facilitate the development of individuals within that environment. While the first locates the problem at the level of the individual, the second locates the problem at the level of the community, and affirms that a change in environmental circumstance will allow for more optimal development of the individuals within that environment. Garbarino and colleagues argue that in challenging neighbourhoods greater support for the individual is not enough:

> efforts must be designed and implemented that restructure the social and physical environment of the neighbourhood in ways that induce and reinforce

changed individual behaviour. . . . Much of our neighbourhood-based initiative
to help communities has burdened those with the fewest resources with the
task of solving some of society's biggest problems.

(Garbarino et al., 1997, pp. 322–323)

They propose that what is required is a community-focused programme
which increases social support and community integration as well as providing support to individuals. An emphasis on community engagement, as
the context for the empowerment of parents and children, links together the
various aims of the Project and echoes the work of recent intervention attempts in many American cities (Bailey et al., 1998; Garbarino et al., 1997).
A home-visiting programme, with training and back-up support from team
leaders and an infrastructure team, represents a genuine attempt to put the
principles of an ecological model of intervention (Garbarino et al., 1997)
into practice at the level of community, family and individual parent and
child.

The EYP set out to tackle the problems identified by a strategic audit at
each of the four levels, or systems of influence, which Garbarino et al. (1997)
identify to be at work in any community, that is:

- *The microsystem.* This is the level of interpersonal contact between child
  and parents. The EYP attempts to influence this context by means of home
  visitors, and the work of the community bases.
- *The mesosystem.* This is the level of links between the *microsystems* in a
  child's life (for example, home and playgroup or school). The EYP attempts
  to strengthen these links by providing more opportunities to take part in,
  for example, pre-school and after-school activities which involve parents
  and offer them support.
- *The exosystem.* This refers to areas of life which influence the child but in
  which they have no direct role, for example the employment or unemployment of parents, school management, the work of statutory agencies. The
  EYP sought from the outset to empower parents in these aspects of their
  lives.
- *The macrosystem.* This is the broader institutional and ideological base of a
  particular culture or subculture. Some of the work of the *infrastructure team*
  is at this level. The very fact of acquiring funding is evidence of the impact
  of the EYP on the macrosystem level of influence in children's lives. In
  addition, efforts to influence the value of education within the local culture
  also represent an attempt to have influence at this level of the community
  context.

The systems of influence identified by Garbarino can be equated with the
macro-, micro- and mini-regulations which Sameroff (1987) considered make
up a cultural code in which a child develops. Lofquist (1983) offers a matrix
for classifying these different kinds of intervention services. In doing so he

**Table 11.1** Lofquist's matrix and the Early Years Project

|  | Remedial | Preventive |
| --- | --- | --- |
| *Individual* | Home visiting of families with a focus on the concerns specific to individual families | Broad-based child and parent centre-based activities, e.g. playgroups |
| *Community* | More focused work, i.e special interest groups which address specific problems, e.g. post-natal depression, parenting skills classes | Infrastructure team activities, e.g. educational and/or employment opportunities for parents; strengthening school and community links |

(Adapted from Garbarino et al., 1997, p. 321)

provided a framework for examining how the EYP operationalized intervention theory and ideas for young children and their families (see Table 11.1).

Crnic and Stormshak (1997) note the increasing emphasis on families in early intervention programmes and view this to be the result of the emergence of ecological frameworks for the understanding of developmental processes:

> The focus of early intervention efforts has changed dramatically since the 1980s from near exclusive attention to center-based, child-focused interventions to models that consider the broad context of factors influencing development.
> (Crnic and Stormshak, 1997, p. 209)

The EYP has been very much in tune with recent interventions of this kind elsewhere. Together, this ecological model of individuals and the community in which they live and a transactional model of child development, which acknowledges the interactive role of the child, formed the theoretical basis for the evaluation. The EYP chose to focus more on the benefits of enhancing a child's environment than on the individual pathology of the child who fails in the school system. In this way the project adopted an holistic concept of education and development for young children.

The model which the project implemented has two key features: universal access for parents, irrespective of identified need or evidence of family dysfunction; and a multi-service and flexible approach whereby each family is able to draw on the resources offered in whatever way they feel is most appropriate for their particular needs.

## Rationale for the Evaluation

The universal and flexible delivery of services to families and pre-school children presented a number of challenges to the evaluation team, as did the lack of any baseline measures. The evaluation team had to find a way to meet the challenges presented by the nature of the project, with its emphasis on flexibility of provision and universal access; and the fact that the EYP had been up and running some 18 months prior to the beginning of the evaluation. This presented a number of specific problems, namely the absence of either baseline measures or a control group for parents and/or children, and the lack of uniformity of provision to families.

The issue as to whether the use of a control group is appropriate for this kind of evaluation has been discussed elsewhere (Hill, 1998). Hill suggests that a control group should be used only if it is likely to be instructional, and, more importantly, that a method of research is adopted which ensures that the mechanism under study is active and that the research does not interfere with the operation of this mechanism. An evaluation model was adopted to measure change over time, making use of both quantitative and qualitative research methods.

In keeping with both a transactional model of development (Sameroff, 1987) and ecological approaches (Garbarino et al., 1997), the evaluation itself operated at a number of levels, two of which are the focus of this chapter—mothers and children. Quantitative measures were complemented by qualitative research, that is, focus group discussions with EYP staff, school principals and mothers, as well as individual semi-structured interviews with parents and staff. In addition, postal questionnaires were distributed to all participating parents, case studies were carried out which focused on a small number of specific aspects and initiatives within the overall intervention, and voluntary and statutory bodies external to the EYP and active in the area were also consulted. Only some of the findings based on these data are reported here: measures of mothers' well-being, attitudes to education, marital difficulty, parenting stress, and the nature and extent of social support, as a measure of community integration; and child outcomes resulting from the assessment of school readiness.

## METHODOLOGY

The evaluation of the EYP presented methodological challenges characteristic of community-based interventions of its kind. The most significant of these was the absence of baseline measures—measures on children and parents taken towards the beginning of the project. This limitation was addressed in two respects. First, wherever practicable, norm-referenced measures were used, thereby providing a comparison group that permitted valid inferences to be made from any changes that might be detected. Second, a technique was devised to quantify family contact with the project—the EYP Exposure Index. This was used at different stages of the evaluation, for example to draw samples of parents with low, medium and high exposure to the project, and in statistical analysis following the gathering of data. In this way it was possible to make some judgements about the relative benefits of different levels of exposure.

Ramey and Ramey (1998), in their review of early intervention programmes, could find only one study that addressed programme intensity at the level of the individual child. Drawing on existing evidence regarding early childhood intervention, they cite six principles for effectiveness: developmental timing; programme intensity; direct provision of learning experiences; programme breadth and flexibility; individual differences in programme benefits; and ecological dominion and environmental maintenance of development. The EYP Exposure Index attempts to meet some of the limitations of previous evaluations of this kind identified by Ramey and Ramey (1998).

Two broad measures were used to assess the impact of the EYP on the children of the Greater Shankill. The first measure explored the experiences and attributes which characterize the day-to-day lives of mothers in the Greater Shankill, as this is the primary environment for these children, and was the main focus of the intervention. The second of these was a measure of the readiness of children on entering primary school, which included an assessment of their progress at the end of their first year of school. Only the first measure will be dealt with here in the discussion of methodology and findings that follows.

## Questionnaire Interviews with Mothers

The purpose of these interviews was to establish the nature and extent of the challenges and difficulties these mothers face as parents and, further, to explore whether involvement in the EYP impacts upon the interpersonal environment of these mothers and children in a way that is likely to optimize child developmental outcomes. The questionnaires[1] were selected for their relevance to the experiences of mothers of young children and for their sensitivity to change over a relatively short period of time. Questionnaire instruments were also selected for their relevance to the ecological model we adopted for the evaluation.

## Maternal Well-Being

Depression, marital harmony and parenting stress were assessed because previous research has shown that high levels of each of these among mothers can impede effective parenting, and are often associated with poor child performance at school. Life stress, maternal depression and level of spousal support are all predictors of parenting behaviour and child adjustment (Abidin et al., 1992).

## Mothers' Theories of Intelligence and their Aspirations

Mothers' aspirations for their child's attainment at school, and the extent to which they consider intelligence to be malleable during the course of childhood, were also assessed. In doing this, the measures adopted were those used in Kathryn Wentzel's study (1998), which aimed to explore the issues that influence parental, educational-attainment goals for their children. In this study she tackled the difficult issue of parental beliefs and aspirations, how they are determined and the relationship they have to child cognitive outcome—for example, what the relationship may be between parental values for achievement and children's school performance. Her work reflects how research is approaching broad questions about intervention effectiveness in ways that increasingly grapple with quite specific aspects of parenting processes, and how theory can be seen to operate in practice. Wentzel (1998) found that parents' aspirations for their children were significantly and positively related to their confidence in their children's academic ability, their teaching efficacy as parents and their beliefs in the value of achievement. In addition, parents' aspirations for their children were significantly and positively related to the belief that intelligence is malleable.

## Social Support

Crnic and Stormshak (1997) reviewed the outcome of intervention studies which included the provision of social support to parents. They cited a number of studies which demonstrate that social support has direct positive influences not only on maternal self-esteem and well-being, but also on maternal interactive behaviours with young children. In addition, they noted that positive social support to parents in the first two years of a child's life has been found to predict higher cognitive functioning when the child is 5 years old. While a direct relationship between support for parents and enhanced child cognitive performance has proved hard to establish, a number of pathways thought to mediate the effect on child outcome of social support to families have been identified. Melson et al. (1993) found a direct effect of network size and quality on child cognitive outcome and also an indirect effect of quality and size of social support network on peer acceptance among children. Peer acceptance is an important ingredient for early school adjustment (Green et al., 1980), and parenting behaviour is known to enhance or inhibit peer popularity (Peery et al., 1985). Parental social support is therefore thought to have a main effect on parent well-being and ability to parent effectively, and is also thought to act as a buffer against the impact of parenting stressors such as poverty, single parenthood and depression.

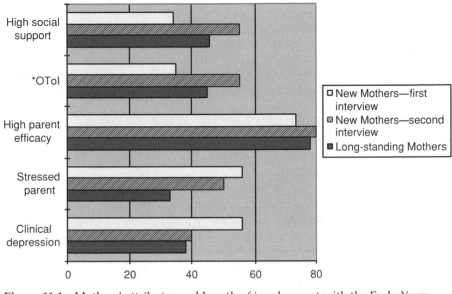

**Figure 11.1** Mothers' attributes and length of involvement with the Early Years
Project
*OToI = optimistic theory of intelligence

## Sample of New and Long-Standing Mothers

Over 60 mothers were interviewed, 34 of whom were relatively new to the
EYP (*new mothers*) and 27 who had a more long-standing involvement with
the project (*long-standing mothers*). In addition, 20 of the *new mothers* were
re-interviewed six months later. This approach allowed comparisons to be
made, not only between mothers when they first joined the project, and after
six months' exposure to it, but also between mothers new to the project and
mothers with a long-standing involvement.

## Findings from the Interviews

The questionnaire responses provide detailed information about the experiences and needs of mothers of young children involved with the Early Years
Project. (Mothers were also interviewed with regard to their experience of
the home-visiting programme and the EYP in general, but this will not be
reported on here.) This survey of the attributes and needs of the mothers
revealed that many of them were rearing their young children under very
challenging conditions (Figure 11.1). High levels of depression and parenting
stress typified the day-to-day experience of many of them. However, despite
these difficulties, the majority of mothers had high educational aspirations
for their children.

- *Depression*: Levels among new mothers at first interview were found to be alarmingly high with more than two-thirds scoring within the range which indicates serious depression. Furthermore, scores indicated that more than half of these mothers experienced clinical levels of depression. At the time of the second interview, levels of serious and clinical depression were down to 40%. Among long-standing mothers, serious and clinical-depression levels were even lower, 38% and 30% respectively.
- *Parenting stress*: 56% of new mothers scored above the cut-off point of 90 for stressed parents on this measure at the first interview. This was reduced to 50% at the second interview. In contrast, only 33% of long-standing mothers scored above this point.
- *Theories of intelligence*: This is a measure of the extent to which parents believe their child's intelligence is malleable and thus open to parents' influence. It comprises a five-point scale, with higher scores indicating more optimistic views of how open to influence intelligence is in the course of development. New mothers' average score was 3.3 at first interview, and 3.8 at second interview. For long-standing mothers the average score was 3.7. At the first interview, only about one-third of new mothers thought of their child's intelligence as open to change in response to their own efforts as parents. This rose to 55% at second interview. 45% of long-standing mothers viewed intelligence as malleable.
- *Maternal efficacy*: This questionnaire is designed to tap into the sense of personal effectiveness of a mother of an infant. Maternal efficacy increased between the first and second interviews among new mothers, from 34 to 34.6. Although this difference may seem small it is statistically significant and suggests that the rise in maternal efficacy is caused by involvement in the EYP.
- *Parent efficacy*: This measure assesses parents' sense of competence in influencing child progress at school. More than a quarter of new mothers at first interview reported low parent efficacy, compared with one in five at second interview, and almost one in five of long-standing mothers.
- *General social support*: In general, levels of social support were very low among new mothers at first interview. New mothers reporting high social support rose from 34% at first interview to 55% at the time of the second interview. High levels of support were reported for 45% of long-standing mothers. Other details about social support are presented in Figure 11.2.
- *Family support*: At first interview, four new mothers had no family support other than their partner. At second interview this was true for two mothers. New mothers at second interview and long-standing mothers typically had good family support.
- *Neighbours' support*: At first interview 66% of new mothers had no neighbour to call on for support. At second interview this figure fell to only 20%. Long-standing mothers typically had one or more neighbours to call on for support.

- *Professional support*: 68% of new mothers at first interview had no professional support of any kind other than the project worker. At second interview, nearly 70% of mothers cited their health visitor, GP or another professional as a support contact.
- *Friends' support*: At first interview 50% of new mothers had no friends outside of their family compared with 20% at second interview. Among long-standing mothers, typically each had at least one friend and many had two or three.

## New Mothers at First Interview

At first interview new mothers were found to have high levels of depression, parenting stress and low maternal self-efficacy. These attributes tended to occur together, like a package, so that mothers who were depressed were also those with high levels of parenting stress and low levels of parent efficacy. New mothers had low expectations of children academically, and they tended to regard child intelligence as a characteristic that is fixed from birth, and thus largely beyond parental influence. In addition, it was found that mothers who scored higher on a measure of optimal child-rearing practices were those with good social support on joining the EYP, and who placed greater emphasis on achievement values for their children.

## New Mothers at Second Interview

At the second interview, six months later, the same relationship between parenting stress, depression and self-efficacy was found for the new mothers. However, levels of parenting stress and depression were generally lower and levels of self-efficacy higher than before. The difference between maternal efficacy at first and second interview was statistically significant. This means that the difference cannot be attributed to chance and is likely to have been caused by mothers' involvement with the project.

The new mothers' degree of social support was found to be related to parent efficacy, parenting stress and theories of child intelligence (whether a parent considers child intelligence to be malleable or fixed). Mothers with higher social support experienced less parenting stress, had higher parenting efficacy and were more likely to view child intelligence as open to change through parent practice and behaviour in the course of childhood. Higher marital dissatisfaction was associated with higher levels of parenting stress at both interviews among mothers in this group. Low expectations of how their child would progress through the school year were also related to either greater depression or parenting stress levels among these mothers at both interviews.

## Long-Standing Mothers

For the long-standing mothers it was also found that high depression, high parenting stress and low self-efficacy occurred together as a package; that is, mothers with one of these tended to have all three. In contrast to new mothers, marital dissatisfaction was not found to be related to parenting stress among the long-standing mothers. Levels of social support in this group were related to parent efficacy so that mothers with higher social support felt better about themselves as mothers.

## Long-Standing Mothers and New Mothers Compared

Comparisons between long-standing mothers and new mothers revealed that more long-standing mothers have significantly lower levels of parenting stress and depression, and significantly higher self-efficacy, than new mothers on first joining the EYP. In addition, mothers in the long-standing group had higher expectations for their child's progress at school in the current year. However, when new mothers were revisited six months later, we found that these differences in depression, parenting stress, parent efficacy and expectations no longer existed. This suggests that exposure to the EYP, and in particular the home-visiting programme, had the effect of quickly reducing levels of stress and depression, and raising mothers' sense of worth as parents.

## Mothers' Social Support

Our analyses reveal a consistent link between social support and self-efficacy among mothers (see Figure 11.2). Social support is a measure of both the level

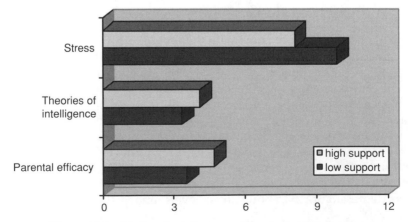

**Figure 11.2**   Mothers' attributes and level of social support

of support mothers feel they got from their project workers, and the amount and quality of support mothers received from others in their families and community. Many mothers said they had been very isolated before becoming involved in the EYP. Having regular visits from a project worker reduced this isolation considerably. Furthermore, mothers who had most exposure to the EYP were also those who had higher levels of social support beyond the project, that is friends, family, neighbours and professionals. The EYP home-visiting programme thus appears to have reduced mothers' isolation and increased how much they related to other people in general beyond the project workers. This of course means that their children also enjoyed a more enriched social life.

## Exposure to the Early Years Project and Self-efficacy

Self-efficacy is a very important mediator between an individual's problems and how they are coped with. Mothers with higher self-efficacy are likely to have more effective coping strategies in dealing with problems in their lives. A comparison between mothers with high exposure to the EYP and mothers with low exposure revealed that mothers with high exposure had significantly higher general self-efficacy than other mothers.

## Parent Efficacy and Quality of Parenting

Many mothers still experienced high levels of depression and parenting stress despite the EYP intervention. There is no magic wand that can completely remove depression and the stresses of parenting. However, what the EYP appears to have achieved is to influence how these mothers cope with their children in the face of depression and stress. In essence, mothers with high self-efficacy relate better—that is, more sensitively and more consistently—to their children despite depression and parenting stress. This is evidenced by the rise in parent efficacy despite the persistence of depression and parenting stress, and by the fact that the mothers who had greatest exposure to the EYP were those with the highest levels of parent efficacy. Thus, the EYP not only reduced depression and parenting stress among many mothers but also improved the quality of the relationship between mothers and their children.

## Links found between Mothers' Attributes and Social Support

A number of the aspects of mothers' lives on which data was gathered by the questionnaire package tended to group together in a kind of parenting package. Figure 11.3 illustrates how mothers' experience of parenting stress, self-efficacy, social support and views of child intelligence were related.

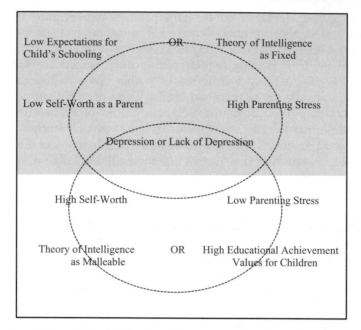

**Figure 11.3**   Links found between mothers' attributes

Mothers who experienced high levels of parenting stress were also those most likely to experience low levels of self-efficacy and low levels of social support. This was true for new mothers at both first and second interview, as well as for long-standing mothers. The figure shows how levels of social support, whether high or low, were associated with more or less optimal parenting experiences. The unshaded area in Figure 11.3 represents the positive blanket effect of high social support on these aspects of mothers' day-to-day experiences.

There were two different patterns of experience for the mothers surveyed. The top half of the figure, the shaded area, represents the experience of the majority of the mothers on first joining the EYP. Social support is often the magic ingredient which allows parents to break out of the cycle of parenting difficulty represented in the shaded, top half of the figure. This is essentially what the EYP's home-visiting programme offered to parents. Mothers who have adequate social support in their lives are more likely to experience greater self-worth and a stronger sense of their own effectiveness as parents. This, in turn, resulted in more optimal parenting behaviours for both parent and child.

## CONCLUSIONS

The links found in the course of the evaluation between social support and a range of parent attributes (parenting stress, parent efficacy and theories of child intelligence) complement the findings of previous research in the field of parenting and child development. Much of the success of the Early Years Project appears to be attributable to the project's effectiveness in raising social support among mothers. Given the levels of isolation and depression among many of these women prior to their involvement in the project, this was a sizeable achievement and one which reflects the quality of relationship which project workers established and maintained with the mothers.

## Summary Points in Relation to the Impact of the Early Years Project

- Long-standing mothers involved in the EYP, when compared with new mothers, had higher parent efficacy and higher expectations for child progress at school in the current year.
- New mothers had significantly lower parent efficacy than long-standing mothers in the EYP, irrespective of whether they had high or low social support. This suggests that it was not the increase in social support alone that raised parent efficacy over time but rather the quality of the relationship between project worker and mother.
- Mothers with high social support had higher *parent efficacy*, lower parenting stress and more optimistic theories of child intelligence than other mothers.

## Evaluating Community-Based, Family-Focused Interventions

There is necessarily a tension between research and evaluation. Evaluation is tied to the aims and objectives of the organization for whom the evaluation is being carried out. As a team of university-based psychologists we were fortunate to find that the aims and objectives of the EYP were in fact grounded in research from previous interventions of this kind, and aimed to bring best practice to the community of the Greater Shankill. If this had not been the case it would have presented us with the problem of identifying outcome measures which would perhaps have evaluated the work of the project, but would not necessarily have added to knowledge and understanding of the processes which contribute to enhanced child and community outcomes. As it was we were able both to build on our general understanding of these underlying processes and provide useful feedback to meet the specific needs of the EYP at a particular point in its development.

Mirroring to the project staff their work in the form of concepts and psychological theory enabled them to understand better their own practice. This resulted in an engagement with the evaluation findings which led to a more focused view of the work being done directly with families and led to changes in the curriculum for the first year at school. Both of these changes were instigated by the project staff and school personnel in response to the evaluation's findings. This effective mirroring, leading to modifications in the work of the project, was a major benefit from the evaluation. It occurred only because members of the evaluation team became sufficiently involved with the various parties to the process of change and development within the community—parents, project management and staff at different levels, and school personnel. This involvement allowed the evaluators to be sensitive to the possibilities for, and resistance to, change in the light of the findings.

Making and maintaining contact at the different project and community levels, while also maintaining the boundaries necessary to carry out research, was challenging for the evaluation team. One potential major difficulty we faced was the fear of negative findings among some of those involved in the EYP. While we could not overcome all of this fear, by clear communication and transparent presentation of our approach and activities, we were able to assure participants that their boundaries would be respected. We emphasized that our findings and recommendations would be presented in a manner which would serve to add to existing understanding in order to improve future work rather than criticize and undermine past work. In this type of evaluation, process can be as important as product. The expressed aim of the EYP was to benefit children through empowering their parents, and in turn it is useful to see the evaluation as a means of empowering those involved in the project in order to benefit the parents and children.

## NOTE

1. Questionnaires administered to mothers: *Theories of Intelligence*: Aspirations and Expectations for Child Attainment at School; Parent Efficacy with Regard to Child Learning (Wentzel, 1998). *Social Support*: The Social Network Map (Tracy and Whittaker, 1990). *Maternal Depression*: Centre for Epidemiological Studies—Depression Scale (Radloff, 1977). *Marital Harmony*: Golombok Rust Inventory of Marital State (GRIMS) (Rust, Bennun and Golombok, 1990). Parenting Stress Index (Abidin et al., 1992). Maternal Efficacy Scale (Teti and Gelfand, 1991).

## REFERENCES

Abidin, R.R., Jenkins, C.L. and McGaughey, M.C. (1992) The relationship of early family variables to children's subsequent behavioral adjustment. *Journal of Clinical Child Psychology*, **21**, 60–69.

Bailey, D.B., McWilliam, R.A., Darkes, L.A., Hebbeler, K., Simeonsson, R.J., Spiker, D. and Wagner, M. (1998) Family outcomes in early intervention: A framework for program evaluation and efficacy research. *Exceptional Children*, **64**, 313–328.

Crnic, K. and Stormshak, E. (1997) The effectiveness of providing social support for families of children at risk. In M.J. Guralnick (Ed.), *The Effectiveness of Early Intervention* (pp. 209–225). Baltimore: Paul Brookes.

Garbarino, J., Kostelny, K. and Barry, F. (1997) Value transmission in an ecological context: The high-risk neighborhood. In J.R. Grusec and L. Kuczynski (Eds), *Parenting and Children's Internalization of Values: A Handbook of Contemporary Theory* (pp. 307–331). New York: John Wiley & Sons.

Green, K.D., Forehand, R., Beck, S.J. and Vosk, B. (1980) An assessment of the relationship among measures of children's social competence and children's academic achievement. *Child Development*, **51**, 1149–1156.

Hill, M. (1998) Effective professional intervention in children's lives. In M. Hill (Ed.), *Effective Ways of Working with Children and their Families*. London: Jessica Kingsley.

Lofquist, W. (1983) *Discovering the Meaning of Prevention; A Practical Approach to Positive Change*. Tucson, AZ: AYD. Cited in Garbarino et al. (1997).

Melson, G.F., Ladd, G.W. and Hsu, H.C. (1993) Maternal social support networks, maternal cognitions and young children's social and cognitive development. *Child Development*, **64**, 1401–1417.

Peery, J.C., Jensen, L. and Adams, G.R. (1985) The relationship between parents' attitudes toward child rearing and the sociometric status of their preschool children. *Journal of Psychology*, **119**, 567–574.

Radloff, L.S. (1977) A CES-D scale: A self-report depression scale for research in the general population. *Applied Psychological Measurement*, **1**, 385–401.

Ramey, C.T. and Ramey, S.L. (1998) Early intervention and early experience. *American Psychologist*, **53**, 109–120.

Rust, J., Bennun, I. and Golombok, S. (1990) The GRIMS: A psychometric instrument for the assessment of marital discord. *Journal of Family Therapy*, **12**, 45–57.

Sameroff, A.J. (1987) The social context of development. In N. Eisenberg (Ed.), *Contemporary Topics in Developmental Psychology*. New York: John Wiley & Sons.

Teti, D.M. and Gelfand, D.M. (1991) Behavioural competence among mothers of infants in the first year: The mediational role of maternal self-efficacy. *Child Development*, **62**, 918–929.

Tracy, E.M. and Whittaker, J.K. (1990) The social network map: Assessing social support in clinical practice. *Families in Society*, **71**, 461–470.

Wentzel, K.R. (1998) Parents' aspirations for children's educational attainments: Relations to parental beliefs and social address variables. *Merrill-Palmer Quarterly*, **44**, 20–37.

## Further Reading

Gomby, D.S. (1995) Long-term outcomes of early childhood programmes: analysis and recommendations. *The Future of Children*, **5**(3), 6–24.

Heller, T.L., Baker, B.L., Hanker, B. and Hingham, S.P. (1996) Externalizing behavior and cognitive functioning from preschool to first grade: Stability and predictors. *Journal of Clinical Child Psychology*, **25**, 376–387.

McGuire, J. and Richman, N. (1988) *Pre-School Behaviour Checklist Handbook*. Windsor: NFER-Nelson.

Pecora, P.J., Fraser, M.W., Nelson, K.E., McCroskey, J. and Meezan, W. (1995) *Evaluating Family-Based Services*. New York: Aldine de Gruyter.

Webster-Stratton, C. (1997) From parent training to community building. *Families in Society: The Journal of Contemporary Human Services*, March/April: 156–171.

**12**

# THE INDICATORS STUDY

## A Cross-Site Implementation Evaluation of the Community Partnerships for Protecting Children Initiative in America

*Stephen Budde*

In 1998 and 1999, Chapin Hall Center for Children at the University of Chicago evaluated the initial implementation of the Community Partnerships for Protecting Children (CPPC) project. This is a multidimensional community-based child protection reform initiative in the USA funded by the Edna McConnell Clark Foundation. This chapter describes and discusses the Indicators Study undertaken to conceptualise and measure progress within four community sites during the initial implementation phase of the CPPC. The evaluation utilised a set of indicators to assess overall progress and compare performance across the four programme sites. The chapter will focus on explicating data collection and analysis strategies that were developed by Chapin Hall to make reasoned judgements about implementation progress across the four CPPC sites.

The primary purpose of the Indicators Study was to provide an empirical basis for assessing implementation progress in four sites that would inform funding decisions. Chapin Hall attempted to provide an approach to making judgements about progress across multiple sites that was comprehensive (i.e. addressed the wide range of strategies advocated by the CPPC), systematic in collecting and analysing data, flexible in understanding and valuing diverse site strategies, and transparent (i.e. evidence and judgements were clear and accessible to stakeholders).

The study faced a set of fundamental evaluation challenges that are common in community-based reform initiatives. These challenges included the

*Evaluating Family Support: Thinking Internationally, Thinking Critically.*
Edited by I. Katz and J. Pinkerton. © 2003 John Wiley & Sons, Ltd.

programmatic complexity of the CPPC, the diversity of CPPC stakeholders, the use of indicators that were defined in general terms and not easily quantified, considerable site variation in implementation strategies, a paucity of systematic tracking information on initial implementation activities, and variability across sites in the information that was available.

Evaluators of Comprehensive Community Initiatives provide a useful conceptualization of fundamental evaluation challenges that mirror those that we faced, including:

- the horizontal complexity of the initiatives (promoting a wide range of different intervention strategies across multiple systems);
- vertical complexity (change efforts are directed at individual, family, and community levels), contextual issues (macroeconomic factors as well as local context);
- flexible and evolving interventions;
- a broad range of outcomes and objectives that are often not easily defined;
- a lack of comparison communities and control groups (Kubisch et al., 1995, pp. 3–5).

A key strength of this study was its ability to address, and in most cases overcome, these logistical and conceptual dilemmas.

Following a brief description of the CPPC initiative, the chapter provides a detailed description of a set of innovative and robust strategies and guidelines for selecting, presenting, and weighting evidence in order to produce meaningful and defensible ratings of implementation progress.[1] This approach offers new ways of thinking about issues of accountability and of providing systematic and useful feedback to planners and funders about implementation progress and challenges during the formative stages of reform initiatives.

## OVERVIEW OF THE COMMUNITY PARTNERSHIPS FOR PROTECTING CHILDREN INITIATIVE

The ultimate goal of the CPPC is to reduce child maltreatment in four target communities of 30 000–80 000 people by encouraging diverse stakeholders to form genuine partnerships devoted to the protection and safety of children within their communities. The initiative is guided by a theory of change that outlines a comprehensive array of strategies (Center for the Study of Social Policy, 1997). The four essential elements of the theory address:

- systematic efforts to individualise practice with families called Individualised Courses of Action (ICAs);
- the development of accessible and responsive neighbourhood service networks;

- organisational and culture change in the child protection system;
- the development of decision-making capacity by community partnership governance groups.

The CPPC is a multidimensional community-based initiative rather than a single programme. The ambitiousness and complexity of the CPPC are illustrated by: its emphasis on both primary and secondary prevention efforts; the inclusion of diverse partners in governance and implementation who have historically had limited or antagonistic relationships; the attention given to effecting change on multiple system levels (frontline practice, organisational, inter-organisational, and community wide); and the importance in community-based initiatives of developing strategies that respond to local needs. Basic differences among the sites in legal and organisational context also contributed to site variability and the development of differential strategies. This complexity prompted our efforts to explore new research methods and strategies that were well suited to the interventions and that did not oversimplify the implementation process.

The initiative's theory of change and essential elements provided a coherent structure for the indicators and our efforts to collect and weight complex information about site progress. Two key features of the theory of change further shaped the basic approach to assessing implementation progress. First, the theory was explicitly viewed as 'work in progress' and further refinement of the ideas and strategies was an important objective of the initiative and the evaluation. In this context, evaluating implementation progress could not be viewed strictly as a study of model fidelity as might be done with more highly specified models of intervention.[2] Second, although the CPPC theory of change provided an overarching framework for structuring the reform effort and numerous illustrations of specific strategies, it purposely did not mandate how local sites should implement strategies. Sites were expected to develop their own local theories of change through self-evaluation and collaborative decision-making processes, including, for example, the identification of site-specific target populations and implementation strategies. This meant that there was considerable room for site variability and interpretation in the implementation process across the four essential elements of the CPPC. To allow for variability in implementation approaches across sites, many important indicators had to be constructed in fairly broad terms, and flexible and robust strategies for assessing progress had to be developed.

In the end, this site variability (in context, choices of implementation approaches and strategies, and levels of progress) provided an important opportunity for knowledge development and cross-site learning, as has been advocated for evaluators of comprehensive community initiatives (e.g. Brown, 1995, pp. 215–216). It was believed that studying how site participants utilised and built on the basic ideas and strategies of the CPPC in four different local contexts would yield research findings that sites could use to refine their strategies and the Foundation could use to assess site progress, refine the conceptualisation of the CPPC, and consider how to implement the initiative in other locations. In addition, it provided a means for better understanding of how complex reform efforts are implemented and for identifying barriers to systemic change.

## KEY INGREDIENTS OF THE INDICATORS STUDY

It is particularly important in initiatives that have long-term goals, such as the reduction of child abuse and neglect, to study implementation steps that can be measured (Gambone, 1999, p. 156). At the outset of the implementation phase of the initiative, the Foundation and the Center for the Study of Social Policy developed a set of expectations that were organised by the four elements in the theory of change. This was followed by a document describing thresholds of site progress, that is, what needed to be accomplished to meet standards of adequate progress on the indicators during a nine-month period of intensive implementation. Chapin Hall played an active role in specifying and refining the expectations and thresholds, and in identifying the evidence that would be used to evaluate implementation progress.

The Thresholds document outlined 53 specific areas for assessing progress. In reviewing these individual indicators, the Foundation established a weighting system in which each indicator was listed as a 'required' element, a 'bonus' element, or an 'other' element which, while important, was considered less essential than required elements. Two types of judgements were used to rate site progress. A yes or no judgement was made on the majority of items. Many of these items were fairly simple, dichotomous questions about whether an implementation activity occurred. The more interesting component, however, involved the application of a five-point rating scale for assessing progress on nine required indicators. This chapter focuses on these indicators because they involved a more in-depth study of important and complex implementation processes that are common in community-based reform efforts, but are not easily measured. These indicators addressed implementation objectives within each of the four essential elements, providing the evaluators with a tool for examining the considerable breadth of the initiative. Data collection and analysis of these indicators formed the backbone of our overall report, in which findings for each indicator were described in detail, as well as for presentations to each site detailing site-specific strengths and weaknesses in implementing a CPPC. These *qualitative* indicators[3] are listed in Table 12.1 and organised by the four essential elements of the theory of change.

The ICA is a process of case planning and helping families that values and seeks family participation in planning and decision making. Since examples

**Table 12.1**    The indicators of progress, organised by the four elements of the theory of change

---

*Individualising practice with families/implementing Individualised Courses of Action (ICA)*
- Clarity of the ICA plan and implementation process

*Developing neighbourhood networks of services and supports*
- Involve key agency and organisational partners (e.g. agencies that address domestic violence and substance abuse problems, primary prevention programmes, juvenile courts, police) in CPPC governance and service networks
- Resident participation in providing direct support and assistance to families in the neighbourhood
- Resident participation in community activities designed to increase awareness of child safety, promote good parenting, or provide family support
- Use of local hubs and welcoming centres to provide recreation, educational activities, and supportive services identified in site proposals
- Outreach to families at risk of child abuse or neglect

*Child protective services policy, practice, and culture change*
- Meeting the needs of chronic maltreatment cases through intensive services
- Decision-making capacity of the community partnerships
- Giving residents representation and voice in decision making
- Use of self-evaluation strategies and data to assess problems, inform decision making, or refine strategies

*CPPC decision-making capacity*
- Giving residents representation and voice in decision making
- Use of self-evaluation strategies and data to assess problems, inform decision making, or refine strategies

---

of this area of implementation will be used frequently, a brief description is provided. Key elements of the ICA involve:

- engaging the family;
- thorough assessment that identifies strengths, safety issues and risks, underlying causes of the family's situation, needs, the family's goals and dreams, and key need areas (substance abuse, mental health, domestic violence);
- developing an action plan that addresses the family's goals and needs by convening a family team meeting that includes people from the family's support system as well as formal service providers, who develop a plan that is the responsibilities of all parties and uses and coordinates available neighbourhood resources;
- tracking of progress by a lead partner for the team;
- sustaining change through continued provision of needed supports (including after formal services cease) by revising plans and reconvening the team as needed (Child Welfare Policy and Practice Group, 1998).

The term *indicators* is used in this study in an unconventional way. In most evaluation contexts, indicators are relatively specific or concrete quantitative measures of a dimension of a broader construct. In the case of social indicators, an indicator is commonly used to help describe or assess the status or well-being of various populations. For example, Coulton (1995) proposes a variety of quantitative community level indicators of child well-being that can be used to study the outcomes of comprehensive community initiatives (e.g. health indicators such as low birthweight rates and social behaviour indicators such as delinquency rates) that can be examined over time to assess the outcomes of comprehensive community initiatives. In contrast, the qualitative indicators used here are not single variables, but rather are broad dimensions of implementation progress. They are indicators in the sense that progress in each area serves as a proxy measure for overall progress in implementing an element of the theory of change.

Using qualitative indicators that are at higher level of abstraction (as opposed to more concrete indicators formulated at lower levels of abstraction) was quite useful. As fundamental objectives of the initiative, the qualitative indicators served as meaningful yet flexible guides to data collection and analysis. Given the formative stage of development of the CPPC, the emphasis on locally driven planning, and the paucity of tracking data on implementation, it was very important not to rely solely on predetermined indicators that were narrowly operationalised.[4] The qualitative indicators allowed researchers the flexibility to examine a wide range of evidence and to allow for site variability in approaches, strategies, and context. However, this broad conceptualisation of a qualitative indicator raised the fundamental challenge of how to measure or assess progress while still keeping these larger objectives and the complexities of programme implementation in the real world in mind.[5]

To address this challenge, Chapin Hall developed a five-point scale to rate progress for the qualitative indicators. The scale focused on site achievements (e.g. specific implementation activities), progress over time, and building capacity to sustain efforts or to increase implementation activity in the future. The emphasis on progress rather than on absolute standards of performance was especially relevant during initial implementation phase of the CPPC because the sites had different pre-existing capacities for many indicators. Therefore, it was appropriate to examine implementation progress in light of where each community started. The specific wording of the scale was:

0 = no or minimal achievements or progress in building capacity
1 = some achievements/progress in building capacity (but not adequate)
2 = adequate progress in building capacity (minimum level of acceptable progress)
3 = substantial achievement/progress in building capacity
4 = excellent achievement/progress in building capacity.

There were important benefits in using numerical ratings for the qualitative indicators. The ratings enabled researchers to summarise complex evidence and judgements in simple tables that could be easily presented and discussed. The numerical ratings were also desirable and useful to the Foundation, which wanted clear judgements from independent evaluators about implementation progress. The ratings also imposed helpful discipline on the data collection and analysis processes. Especially in a context in which the ratings could affect funding decisions, careful attention had to be paid to the completeness of data collection and the credibility of judgements about numerical ratings.

The rating scale allowed for flexibility in assessing site differences in implementation strategies. This was important because, as suggested above, the CPPC theory of change and the expectations did not define or mandate specific implementation processes and strategies that should be undertaken for most qualitative indicators. Instead of defining implementation processes, the CPPC theory of change encouraged sites to adopt self-evaluation strategies that would lead to responsive and effective programme implementation. A crucial distinction was made in this study between variability in approach and variability in implementation progress. The explicit assumption was that sites could make progress in implementing a CPPC on most indicators by employing a range of implementation strategies. As long as site implementation plans and strategies appeared clearly related to overall CPPC objectives, variation was allowed, without making a judgement about value of particular approach. Thus, researchers sought to keep site variability in approach from directly influencing ratings of progress. At the same time, different implementation approaches sometimes led to different levels of activity—which was critical evidence about implementation progress.

In order to guide data collection and analysis, researchers developed a robust set of heuristic guidelines for selecting and weighting evidence of implementation progress that was consistent across sites and relevant to all of the indicators. The guidelines were culled from the theory of change, objectives of technical assistance providers who assisted sites in addressing implementation issues, and evaluation objectives. In addition to clarifying and simplifying data collection and analytic tasks, the guidelines provided useful tools for thinking about the nature of implementation progress.

Three strategies served as primary guidelines, meaning that they were the focus of the selection process and they were given great weight in final decision making. These guidelines included: (1) the amount, scope, and timing of implementation activity; (2) establishing infrastructure to sustain and support CPPC implementation; and (3) the unique role of CPPC site participants and activities in local reforms. Three other strategies served as secondary guidelines in selecting and weighing information: (1) planning, following through, and sustaining activities; (2) problem solving and planful modifications; and (3) creative thinking. The strategies were not independent criteria and one piece of evidence was sometimes important for multiple reasons.

Each guideline and its utility to the evaluation are described below, followed by an illustration of specific evidentiary questions that were addressed in examining practice reform efforts.

The most important type of evidence of implementation progress was the actual amount, scope, and timing of relevant implementation activities by site participants (i.e. professionals and community residents involved in planning and implementation activities in each site). Although implementation activity is ultimately an insufficient measure of implementation progress, change agents are inevitably involved in planning and trying out new approaches and in expanding the scope of new strategies by increasing the numbers of people involved in providing services or supports and the numbers and types of children and families receiving these services and supports. Detailed documentation of such efforts, using as much quantitative data as possible, provided evidence of both progress and variability in implementation across sites and indicators.

Researchers sought evidence about what and how much was done by site participants, and the number and types of people involved in implementation or who were affected by CPPC strategies. Several dimensions of implementation activity were identified, including planning, training, outreach and communications activities designed to heighten awareness of relevant issues, and actual services and supports provided to families. This enriched our descriptions of implementation processes, but planning and training were not valued as highly as the actual implementation of planned strategies. Time dimensions of implementation activity were also identified whenever possible—when it started, how long it lasted, and whether it increased over time. Sustained or repeated activities were usually valued more than one-time events.

The second primary guideline looked for evidence of infrastructure to sustain reforms. The term *infrastructure* was used broadly to refer to any mechanism put in place by sites to help sustain or increase the use of CPPC strategies over time.[6] The importance of site infrastructure in the CPPC was reflected in the consistent efforts of technical assistance consultants to help the sites to build local capacity to support activities and to encourage sites to address sustainability issues. In addition, contractual restrictions were placed on the use of funds from the grant for ongoing expenses. Significant examples of a CPPC infrastructure for a given indicator included the availability and use of building facilities, allocation of existing staff in partner agencies to CPPC tasks, State-level support for CPPC reforms, and regular and productive planning meetings. Some activities, such as training, also provided infrastructure. Of course, evidence of infrastructure was more compelling when accompanied by actual implementation activity.

Understanding the unique role and contributions of the CPPC to overall reform in each site was a critical and sometimes complicated analytical task. For example, all sites had significant service reform efforts and a core group of service providers working on collaborative planning prior to CPPC. The four sites were selected for the CPPC in part because of pre-existing reform activities and local commitment to reform on which the CPPC could build. Sites varied considerably in the types of reforms that pre-dated the CPPC and the extent to which local communities and service providers were already addressing issues relevant to various indicators. Effective planning and implementation in these local contexts necessarily involved efforts to coordinate with consonant reform efforts and to build on existing resources, and such evidence was valued in the Indicators Study. Evidence of stronger and more direct influence on local change efforts was weighted more than less direct involvement or influence.

Interestingly, in early interviews, site participants often responded negatively to direct questions about the influence of the CPPC, viewing these questions as inconsistent with their emphasis on collaboration and their interest in the community as a whole rather than on just specific CPPC activities. Although researchers retained an evaluative interest in the influence of the CPPC, this feedback helped to focus data collection on understanding the *role* of the CPPC within the community and in its relationships with other local reform efforts. Chapin Hall was then able to identify and value connections with other reform efforts and to examine more closely how CPPC sites utilised and built on existing reform efforts.

Evaluators also considered how the involvement of technical assistance (TA) providers in helping sites should affect assessments of site progress. Technical assistance was provided generously to CPPC sites in a wide range of relevant topic areas (e.g. direct practice, community involvement, fiscal issues). In addition, each site had a dedicated TA provider who helped site participants in all areas of the CPPC and in managing their relationship with the Foundation. Chapin Hall found it useful to try to distinguish the role and influence of site participants from that of TA providers. For example, site use of technical assistance through local (rather than national) consultants was explicitly valued in the study, since local TA providers could sometimes be viewed as a part of local infrastructure. The role of national consultants was considered in several ways. First, for some qualitative indicators, TA providers played important roles in implementing actual services and supports to many families. For example, national TA providers facilitated a substantial minority of family team meetings (a fundamental component of CPPC practice reform). For the purposes of the Indicators Study, such activity could not be viewed as being solely or even primarily undertaken by site participants. Second, there were a small number of instances in which site implementation was delayed by the timing of the provision of technical assistance and sites were not penalised for this. Third, since involvement with national consultants was an integral component of CPPC implementation, evaluators examined sites' utilisation of TA opportunities, an important objective of TA providers. While site capacity in this area could not be thoroughly examined, evidence was available about whether site participants sought out and used

**Table 12.2**   Application of the guidelines for selecting and weighting evidence

Illustration of key evidentiary questions that were addressed for one indicator, the clarity of the Individualised Course of Action (ICA) plan and implementation process

*Clarity of the site plan*
- Was the definition of an ICA clear in site plans? Were definitions of an ICA clearly understood by ICA Coordinators and frontline staff? Did site plans clearly identify the types of families to be served and a range of referral sources [including both child protective service (CPS) and non-CPS agencies]? Were numerical goals for conducting ICAs defined for each referral source? Were cases prioritised in any way to try to target the intervention, and, if so, was this a clear and reasonable approach to targeting/selecting cases? Was there a clear process for reviewing and assigning cases? Was there a coherent plan for training facilitators and frontline staff in the ICA approach?

*Infrastructure*
- Did sites hire staff to coordinate ICAs? If so, what did those staff do (i.e. organise and/or facilitate family team meetings, track ICA cases in CPS and non-CPS agencies, and to monitor services and supports to families) and were they hired through grant funds or through funds from partner agencies? How long had ICA coordinators been in place? Were training plans being implemented (creating infrastructure–trained staff)?

*Implementation activity in relation to the plan*
- How many of the identified referral sources met their goals for the number of ICAs conducted? When were ICAs conducted—did the site start to do this early or late in the time period? Were case selection, case review, and case assignment plans implemented systematically and in a thoughtful manner? How many workers and facilitators were trained and involved in implementing ICAs? Were ICA cases identified prospectively (i.e. through a clear referral process) or retrospectively? How many of the ICAs were for families from targeted CPPC neighbourhoods?

*Role and influence of CPPC (other than some items above)*
- How often (on how many cases) did local participants (as opposed to national consultants) assume the primary roles in facilitating family team meetings and coordinating ICAs? Were all ICAs actually done through some connection with CPPC (in most but not all cases)? Did sites build on existing infrastructure (e.g. using existing integrated service teams as a vehicle for promoting implementation, or building on previous and congruent practice reform efforts)?

*Secondary guidelines*
- Were new referral sources identified? Were plans refined as needed? Were case characteristics and services tracked? Were case selection and targeting issues discussed in planning? Were systematic strategies undertaken to inform case selection (e.g. research to examine characteristics of families in which subsequent maltreatment occurred)?

consultants when they needed assistance and whether this was done in a timely manner.

The secondary guidelines (Table 12.2) for selecting and weighting evidence planning, problem solving, and creativity provided a way to value the reflective approach to reform described in the CPPC theory of change and emphasised by TA providers. Planning and planful modifications of site strategies are integral components of the CPPC theory of change and important features of meaningful implementation of community-based reforms. The CPPC theory of change was informed by many creative ideas and strategies that were developed by the sites. Evaluators wanted to note and value innovative and creative strategies by sites, including when site participants raised thoughtful questions about CPPC precepts or strategies.

One important analytical decision made by Chapin Hall was to include 'negative' evidence about implementation. In other words, instead of just trying to document the extent of site achievement and progress, researchers attempted to provide a more complete picture of implementation 'progress' by including evidence of site strategies and activities that hadn't been adequately implemented or sustained over time, and about major challenges or problems (e.g. staff leaving, specific data on delays in implementation, organisational barriers to change that had not been addressed).

## Using Data from Multiple Sources

Chapin Hall utilised both quantitative data (from surveys and available documentation) and qualitative data (from interviews and observation) in studying indicators of site progress. Important methodological questions have been raised about whether qualitative analyses might be more compelling in studying Comprehensive Community Initiatives than the quantitative data usually sought by funders because of the potentially rich narrative data and the opportunity to modify causal assumptions during implementation (Weiss, 1995, pp. 88–89). The triangulation of qualitative and quantitative methods of data collection and data analysis was generally useful here in providing a more complete story about implementation progress (see, for example, Tyson, 1995, pp. 233–234, and Glisson, 1990, pp. 189–193).

Site documentation and some of our early interviews provided critical information about the types of activities that had been undertaken. Interviews with key site participants about local structure, participants, plans and activities, and observation of multiple site planning meetings and cross-site meetings during which researchers attended planning meetings provided a broad understanding of the Partnership and local context in each site. Findings from a survey of 30–60 individuals per site who were involved in CPPC planning efforts, interviews on governance and implementation with multiple participants gave us a good picture of the views and activities of diverse site participants. Interviews and reports from intensive reviews of practice in about 15 cases per site provided a more complete understanding of existing child protective service (CPS) practice and early practice reform efforts. Overall, the use of multiple methods and data sources helped us to have a broad understanding both of context and of specific implementation activities in each site.

Although data collected by Chapin Hall provided a wealth of useful evidence about site progress, there were three significant limitations in the data that were available. First, tracking data on implementation activities (i.e. who was served and persons involved in implementation by type of activity) were not collected as systematically by CPPC sites as had originally been planned. This often forced us to rely on site documentation. However, there was a strong bias in site documentation on evidence of progress and current challenges, but much less information about past problems and planned activities that had not gone well or had not been undertaken. To address this positive bias, other sources of data were used partly to identify 'negative evidence'.

Second, the availability of evidence varied across sites. There were two sources of inconsistency: the level of Chapin Hall involvement and the amount of site documentation. In one site, the Chapin Hall Liaison lived in the area and was able to gather extensive amounts of information from observation, interviews, and ongoing communication with site participants. In two other sites, the study team maintained consistent but less intensive involvement by using a combination of local researchers and an (off-site) Chapin Hall Liaison. To some extent, the information deficit in these two sites was at least partially alleviated by the fact that they had kept much more extensively written documentation of their own implementation efforts than other sites. The fourth site, in which our staffing had been inconsistent and site documentation was weak, was of greatest concern. Researchers addressed some of this deficit through a series of interviews. Concern about inadequate data in this site and our general interest in ensuring complete evidence solidified a tentative decision to review the evidence early and often with informed TA providers and site participants.

Third, in-depth data on the quality of most activities was limited. Even where Chapin Hall had in-depth information about practice reform efforts from case level interviews, the involvement of technical assistance providers and the lack of data on change over time inhibited judgements about site progress. Given these limitations, the evidence and the judgements about the evidence were necessarily somewhat impressionistic. However, these limitations are often present in the early stages of reform, so Chapin Hall's aim was to make optimal use of available data.

## Transparent and Interactive Research Processes

Chapin Hall sought to make the processes of data collection and analysis transparent. In order to present evidence in an accessible format, we developed a strategy for organising and presenting cross-site information. All relevant information on site progress for each indicator was summarised in a table, with each of the four sites constituting a column. In order to maximise the amount of information that could be viewed on a single page, short descriptions of evidence were presented in a landscape format using long paper. Table 12.3 presents an illustration of the cross-site table format and the type of evidence that was summarised for one site on an indicator that addressed practice reform.

Items describing positive and negative evidence were presented in separate rows. Each entry of positive or negative evidence started with a '+' (items in the positive row) or a '−' (items in the negative row). In addition, highly valued items were marked with a '++' or '−−' in order to further explicate judgements processes. The selected content in the first column illustrates some key types of evidence that were presented for the indicator on practice reform, although this is not a presentation of actual findings. This format enabled research staff and stakeholders to easily review the evidence and the judgements that formed the basis for summary ratings, and to suggest other evidence that might be considered.

The tables were reviewed initially (and periodically) by Chapin Hall staff, and subsequently by consultants and site participants. These reviews were important because of the incompleteness of existing data, variability in data collection across sites, and because ratings could affect site funding. Internal reviews of the tables led to considerable improvement in the quality of the evidence. Chapin Hall Liaisons drew on their more detailed understanding of the sites to identify gaps in evidence that had been identified centrally. In addition, cross-site reviews made it possible to identify evidence that was present in one site and could be sought for other sites.

TA providers who worked closely with individual sites on planning and implementation were then given cross-site evidence and tentative ratings. They made substantial contributions in providing additional evidence and in offering thoughtful comments about the evidence they thought should be weighted strongly and the summary ratings. Finally, site participants were provided with evidence in the table and initial ratings for their own site. Most sites were able to identify additional evidence that was included in the tables, although the volume of additional evidence was relatively small. By the end of the review process, researchers were able to confidently assert that the relevant evidence was included. The cross-site tables and the interactive review process helped to demystify the research, reduce anxiety and potential conflict about final judgements, and promote meaningful discussion about implementation progress.

As in all evaluations, particularly in complex community-based initiatives, there were important issues about what the evaluators role could and should be (Brown, 1995). One overriding issue in addressing the role of the evaluator is considering the extent to which the evaluator is engaged with participants in the evaluation, development, and refinement of the initiative, and the potential effects of any involvement on the research findings. In contrast to emphasising the distant and unbiased perspective of the evaluator, some researchers have begun to consider the benefits and challenges of researchers

**Table 12.3**   The selection and organisation of cross-site information

Qualitative Indicator I2a: Clarity of plan and implementation of Individualised courses of Action (ICA)

| Site 1: Name of site | Rating: | Site 2 | Rating: | Site 3 | Rating: | Site 4 | Rating: |
|---|---|---|---|---|---|---|---|
| + Clear plan that identified a range of cases and referral sources and goals for CPS and non-CPS agencies<br>++ 50 ICAs implemented (2nd highest among sites)<br>++ 5 of 6 referral sources met ICA goals<br>++ Hired ICA coordinator with local $<br>++ Consistently implemented case selection process and used thoughtful clinical review process<br>+ Sought national technical assistance as early as possible for initial training<br>++ Developed and implemented plan to use local experts to train workers in target area<br>+ Discussed appropriateness of different types of referrals in ICA workgroup, formulated plan | | | | | | | |
| −− Frontline staff and ICA coordinator struggled without resolution to define the parameters of an ICA case<br>− At least 8 of 50 ICAs identified retrospectively (inadequate case tracking system)<br>− One agency didn't meet referral goals<br>− 25 of the 50 ICA were completed in the last two months to meet funder's goal and deadline—Interpretation: ICA practice not fully integrated and may not yet be sustainable<br>− 13 of 50 ICA cases from outside of target neighbourhood | | | | | | | |

being more involved in programmatic efforts (e.g. Brown, 1995; Tyson, 1995; Weiss, 1995). The process described above involved a high level of interaction with site participants and consultants and definite benefits. Yet, it was also important to Chapin Hall and the Foundation that the study provided an independent evaluation of the CPPC. To maintain independence in the research process, three strategies were implemented. First, evidence was discussed with site participants but not interpretations during the final data collection stages. In other words, there was a willingness and interest in adding relevant information about site progress, but at that time there was no discussion of the interpretation of the significance of the evidence or the ratings of progress. Second, proposed new evidence was reviewed to ensure accuracy and relevance. Finally, by agreement with the Clark Foundation, a record was kept of changes to the tables—both changes in the evidence and changes in the ratings.[7] Having *an independent* perspective in this evaluation ultimately did not mean that the evaluators, the data, or the judgements were completely unbiased. Instead, the credibility, fairness and independence of our work were based on a systematic and transparent data collection process and by a perspective that was not unduly influenced by CPPC advocates or by the less positive views of some stakeholders that CPPC implementation was moving too slowly.

## Explicit and Systematic Judgement Strategies[8]

Although the guidelines for selecting and weighing information provided the foundation for data collection and analysis, evaluators had to devise strategies to address an additional set of issues in making final ratings of site progress. These issues included when to attempt to assign ratings of progress, the use of cross-site comparisons in the judgement process, aggregating evidence, and how to assign specific ratings.

Early in the process of compiling data in the cross-site tables for each indicator, we faced the issue of whether to start making judgements about site progress or to wait until all the evidence was compiled before trying to give ratings. We were concerned that making even tentative judgements early in a complex decision-making process could have an anchoring effect and produce a bias towards initial and superficial impressions (Rosen, 1981). Waiting for all of the evidence to be compiled and analysed before making judgements would also have been a more traditional approach to data analysis and interpretation. However, the principal investigators decided early in the process to offer initial judgements about site progress (along with supporting evidence in the cross-site tables) as tentative hypotheses that were open to refutation on the basis of new evidence or the differing opinions about the interpretation of the evidence. Such discussion did frequently occur. Many ratings were initially presented in the form of a range (e.g. 1–2) and Chapin

Hall purposely attempted to include all potentially below adequate ratings (scores of 0 or 1) in order to make site participants aware of potential areas of concern.

We initially sought to have Chapin Hall Liaisons make judgements about site progress, since each liaison had the most detailed understanding of his or her site(s). However, the Liaisons raised a fundamental concern about making such judgements given the flexibility of the rating scale and their lack of a cross-site perspective—two Liaisons worked with one site each and one Liaison worked with two sites. Liaisons worried they might have different standards for making judgements. This led to the development of the cross-site tables discussed earlier, which facilitated detailed discussions of site comparisons. In addition, a single individual (the author) assumed responsibility for making initial judgements on site progress, drawing on the data arrayed in the tables. Because this researcher had considerable knowledge about all sites and the relevant data, this approach offered a systematic and fair interpretation of the initial evidence.

Some stakeholders suggested that Chapin Hall combine all of the ratings into a single score. One obvious approach to doing this would have been a weighted sum of the ratings and other items. However, given the lack of independence of the indicators, diversity of evidence involved, lack of directly comparable evidence across sites for some indicators, and the rough approach to weighting used in the study, the use of overall scores was not warranted. Researchers also thought an emphasis on a single score would have inhibited fruitful discussions of the findings. Instead, the distribution of scores for each site was examined and this was useful in identifying one site that had consistently lower ratings than the other three.

On a small number of indicators, there was within-site variability in evidence about implementation progress in some sites. The problem was how to rate implementation progress for the whole site (the unit of analysis in this study) given neighbourhood/within-site variability. Site implementation often involved activities in multiple neighbourhoods within a larger targeted community, and the extent and type of implementation progress within neighbourhoods varied considerably. This was not surprising, given the size of the CPPC sites and the emphasis in the CPPC on neighbourhood-based services. Furthermore, the amount of evidence that had been gathered was far from uniform across neighbourhoods in the sites. As evaluators struggled over how to aggregate evidence of implementation progress across neighbourhoods, we noticed that most of the within-site variability occurred in the two sites that were doing the best on indicators of community outreach and developing neighbourhood-based hubs of services and supports for families. In other words, there was more within-site variability largely because some sites had moved more assertively to implement strategies in multiple neighbourhoods within the communities. Averaging across neighbourhoods would have inappropriately penalised these sites. So it was decided instead to value multiple neighbourhood-based implementation efforts and advanced implementation in some of the neighbourhoods.

Assigning numerical scores involved a decision-making process of choosing a score from the 0–4 rating scale of implementation progress. This measurement task was complicated because there were no clear-cut behavioural anchors to the scale scores (except 0) and because the distance between the points of the scale was not defined (this is an ordinal rather than interval level scale). The written expectations on each qualitative indicator, the broader vision of the CPPC laid out in the theory of change, and our work on weighting the evidence provided useful analytic tools for this judgement process. Furthermore, as we began to compile and organise the data, we were increasingly able to identify differences and similarities in levels of implementation progress both across sites and across indicators. We used both deductive and inductive methods of analysis, that is, final scores were based partly on predetermined criteria and ideals, and also by utilising what was learned about site differences while compiling and weighing the evidence.

The initial judgement we made was whether sites had made *adequate* progress. These decisions needed to be clear and unambiguous because ratings of below adequate (less than 2) could jeopardise funding. We wanted to make this decision fairly and were concerned about whether to use site variability in making this judgement. Cross-site differences were often quite apparent in the evidence and provided an appealing and readily available decision aid. However, it seemed unfair to base this critical judgement on evidence of relative progress and, ultimately, site variability was excluded from the adequacy judgement. As a result, we devised alternative strategies for using weighted evidence and the expectations to determine adequacy.

Instances in which judgements about adequacy were an issue when there was minimal positive evidence regarding the amount and scope of implementation activity or the infrastructure to support activity for a site on a given indicator. Once all available evidence was presented, various types of questions were discussed internally to determine adequacy. Although there was no simple recipe for making the adequacy judgement, questions that proved useful included:

- If there was some substantial positive evidence of positive implementation activity, did this evidence outweigh negative evidence?
- Was infrastructure sufficient evidence in and of itself to warrant a judgement of adequate progress? Based on the time that sites had to implement a CPPC, we decided that infrastructure alone, in the absence of substantial evidence of implementation activity, was not adequate.
- How substantial was the negative evidence? There were few instances in which there was consistently negative evidence. If this occurred, it raised serious questions about adequacy.

- Was there evidence of recent improvement? As noted earlier, recent improvements in implementation activity and infrastructure were valued. If both were present, this could offset the lack of prior progress and justify a rating of adequate.
- Did a local community have extensive pre-CPPC or concurrent non-CPPC reform efforts that mitigated the need for concerted implementation activity by CPPC site participants?

Because sites generally met our thresholds of adequacy, most scores ranged from 2 to 4. It was within this truncated range that we made finer grained distinctions among sites. In order to maximise the opportunity to illustrate site variability in implementation progress, we decided to use half-points (2, 2.5, 3, 3.5 and 4). Since the evidence and ratings were repeatedly reviewed internally and with consultants, evaluators had to build strong arguments based on the evidence for subtle distinctions in ratings across sites. Encouraging discussions of differences in site ratings was useful in prompting evaluators and consultants to seek additional evidence and to develop reasonable alternative interpretations of the evidence. In summary, it was difficult and time consuming to make final ratings on each indicator for each site, but the decision-making process yielded what we believe were reasonable judgements. Perhaps more importantly, the process promoted critical thinking about site progress and the nature of implementation progress.

## SITE PROGRESS WITHIN THE BROADER CONTEXT OF INITIATIVE DEVELOPMENT

The Indicators Study was designed in part to contribute to an increased understanding of the developmental progress of the CPPC initiative as a whole. This broader lens for viewing progress was fundamental to the evaluation and provided a counterbalance to the more narrowly focused assessment of individual site progress. Below, we examine how important developmental issues were examined through careful consideration of: cross-site similarities and differences; differences among stakeholders; changes in the overall vision of the CPPC over time; conceptual gaps in the theory; the pace and flow of implementation; and the relationship of implementation progress to the overall goals of reducing child abuse and neglect.

One way of learning about overall initiative development was to examine ratings of progress across sites. Similarities among sites' implementation strengths were evidence that coherent foundations had been built for certain CPPC strategies. For example, all sites enlisted a core group of front-line staff who championed practice reforms and hired coordinators to help to manage time-consuming case management tasks. Similarities across sites were sometimes more apparent and important at higher levels of abstraction rather than in the details of specific implementation strategies. For example, all sites demonstrated strong commitment to the principles of self-evaluation, though their self-evaluation strategies varied considerably.

Areas of consistently weak or even less than exemplary implementation across sites provided evidence about implementation gaps in which actual CPPC activity consistently did not match the expectations or ideals of the initiative. It is a truism in implementation evaluations that implementation will not precisely match plans, since participants always encounter unexpected barriers and complications. However, it was helpful to identify particularly important gaps and then to explicate possible barriers to implementation in these areas. For example, most sites were not able to implement systematic case selection plans that were responsive to specific local needs as had been envisioned. It was possible to provide specific and detailed evidence of this gap, discuss some of the possible reasons why this had been difficult, illustrate a successful approach, and make some suggestions that could be considered in future planning.

Some important lessons about developmental progress came from comparing areas of general strength and relative weakness. For example, in engaging service providers in the partnership, all sites had ratings of 3 (substantial progress) or higher. In contrast, ratings on resident participation were substantially lower. This cross-indicator difference illustrated that CPPC sites had been better able to engage social service providers in partnership activities than community residents. Although this was not a surprising conclusion, quantifying and reporting such differences highlighted developmental challenges, such as how to increase and sustain resident involvement.

Site variability in approach and ratings helped to identify exemplary site strategies from which other sites could learn. Wherever possible, heuristic examples of excellence and creativity were described in reports in which site participants implemented well-planned and innovative strategies. For example, since most sites did not utilise systematic plans for selecting cases from identified risk groups to receive ICAs, attention was given to a thoughtful and organised process implemented by one site. Chronic neglect cases were defined and identified by the CPS agency and a clinical review of the current status of these cases was conducted in order to consider the potential utility of initiating an ICA for the family.

One central finding about developmental progress in the CPPC related more to site variability in approach than to variation in ratings of progress. Different approaches to implementation often posed completely different types of future challenges for sites in their efforts to improve the quality and expand the quantity of implementation activities. There were several examples of this phenomenon. For example, sites that chose to use a small number of specially trained facilitators faced different types of quality and quantity challenges than sites that advocated having all front-line workers conduct family team meetings—an approach that is likely to produce greater numbers of cases but raises more concerns about the quality of implementation.

Given the diverse partners involved in a CPPC, it was essential to identify differences in the perspectives among stakeholders that suggested important developmental challenges. Differences in perspectives within a site could relate to role, agency affiliation, level of attachment to the community, gender, ethnicity, and simply individual points of view. CPPC is committed to bringing diverse stakeholders together in a partnership and important differences in perspective are sometimes difficult to discuss. However, exploring differences in perspectives can be useful both to value the importance of multiple stakeholders and to encourage discussion of priorities in light of those differences. One example of developmentally significant differences in a site was that many social service professionals involved in CPPC governance (primarily agency managers) wanted their local community partnership to focus much more on changing service delivery (such as ICAs). They stressed that providing improved services to high-risk families was the type of activity that was most directly related to the goal of reducing child maltreatment. In contrast, neighbourhood residents and some professionals with close ties to the targeted neighbourhood were more focused on engaging the community and on discussion of broader child safety issues that were of immediate concern to parents in the neighbourhood.

The study interviews and survey data yielded a wealth of information about the perspectives of people who were involved in the CPPC in a variety of roles. Particular attention was given to the views of participants who were most involved in implementing CPPC strategies, such as front-line staff and community volunteers, as they offered a critical perspective about how the actual work of the initiative was implemented. For example, in examining the implementation of practice reforms, emphasis was given to the perspectives of front-line workers, whose practice tendencies often constitute de facto policies (Lipsky, 1980). CPS workers in some sites strongly emphasised the positive benefits of working in neighbourhood-based settings (e.g. access to nearby service providers, worker familiarity with the community) rather than centralised office locations. Many CPS workers also raised important concerns about challenges or barriers to implementing ICAs, particularly related to the time burden of conducting ICAs and conflicts between new role expectations in ICAs (which emphasised helping and therapeutic roles) and current job expectations that required workers to focus on case management and bureaucratic tasks while leaving helping efforts largely to other service providers. These comments illustrated important benefits and challenges of implementation and raised important developmental questions, such as: Do changes in structure (e.g. working in neighbourhood-based settings) have more substantial or immediate effects on front-line practice than efforts to change practice by training workers on new approaches to practice?

Fundamental changes in reform initiatives can occur in relation to goals, intervention strategies, governance structures, the populations being served, or other basic features of a theory or approach. Such changes are not necessarily negative and might be viewed as reasonable adaptations to contextual pressures or responses to opportunities during implementation. However, major changes often go undocumented when participants are caught up in the challenges of implementing reforms. Accordingly the study monitored significant programmatic changes that occurred during the implementation process relative to the original vision of the CPPC. For example, the historical focus of the CPPC was on the front end of child protection efforts (e.g. prevention, improving services to intact families). However, when practice reforms started, all sites began to provide ICAs to many families in which children were in foster care and family reunification was the goal of intervention. This example and other important developmental shifts were noted in order to encourage discussion about why they occurred, whether the changes were appropriate, and, if so, how initiative strategies are best applied to new situations.

Since the theory of change was viewed as a dynamic rather than a finished document, it was very important to consider where the evidence could help to identify areas for further conceptual work or refinement of the theory. The evidence on implementation progress helped to raise some important conceptual and definitional issues. For example, evidence of site variability in approaches to facilitating family team meetings raised important questions about whether all approaches should be considered acceptable within the CPPC. Another important issue related to the common use of the term Individualised Courses of Action (ICA) in two related but very different ways. Sometimes ICA was used to refer to a specific set of activities to individualise and improve services in certain cases, while at other times it referred more broadly to the capacity of workers to individualise the process of service delivery in all cases. Both uses of the term were reasonable, but the dual meanings led to ambiguity about the term and about acceptable parameters of an ICA case (i.e. what could be counted as an ICA) in some sites.

Examining implementation progress over time across multiple indicators and sites provided important information about the pace and flow of implementation. The CPPC sites tended to focus implementation efforts on one area of implementation at a time (e.g. practice or resident involvement). This suggests that an important developmental challenge in multidimensional reform efforts is how to implement multiple and varied tasks concurrently. Existing evidence suggested that the CPPC sites that were best able to address this challenge had well-organised governance structures and processes that included functional subcommittees that oversaw different areas of CPPC implementation. A second key observation about the pace of implementation was that sites had a burst of activity before data collection deadlines for the initial implementation phase. Since the amount or type of work on some indicators during the final months differed markedly from that of previous time periods, it was difficult to determine the extent to which this increase represented genuine progress. Although the considerable efforts of sites to achieve objectives during agreed upon time frames sometimes resulted in significant achievements, these findings also suggested that sites still faced developmental challenges in integrating reforms into everyday practice and sustaining high levels of activity over time.

One of the potential benefits of theory of change evaluation strategies involves the opportunity to systematically examine the links between activities and outcomes (Connell and Kubisch, 1999, p. 35). While the Indicators Study focused on implementation, it was critical, from a developmental perspective, to consider how overall initiative progress related to larger goals of full implementation and reducing child abuse and neglect. A fundamental assumption of the CPPC theory of change was that progress in improving community-wide maltreatment outcomes was dependent on implementing diverse activities and changes that would affect a wide range and number of people. An important function of the Indicators Study was to raise concerns about the quantity (i.e. amount and scope) of implementation activities needed across indicators in order to fully implement the CPPC and in order to have a reasonable opportunity to achieve ultimate outcomes of a reduction in child abuse and neglect. The considerable challenge of improving quality while trying to increase the volume and scope of implementation was also highlighted.

## SUMMARY

It is important to find systematic ways of examining how community-based reforms are put in place in different contexts and the extent to which key strategies have been undertaken. While implementation evaluations cannot determine the effectiveness of an initiative, they can help practitioners and policy makers to understand how far they have travelled down the road to meaningful reform and provide guidance about the future directions of reform efforts. Despite some important limitations, the Indicators Study was generally successful in achieving these purposes. The key ingredients of the Indicators Study included a wide range of qualitative indicators that described complex implementation objectives and were derived from a theory of change; a flexible scale for rating implementation progress in multiple sites; a set of robust guidelines for selecting and weighting evidence; a transparent and interactive process for reviewing the evidence and the ratings with stakeholders; explicit and systematic judgement strategies for making ratings; and an interest in broad developmental issues and the nature of implementation progress for the CPPC initiative as a whole that served to augment and counterbalance the narrow focus on site progress. These strategies helped us to address fundamental evaluation challenges related to the complexity of the reform effort, limitations in the data, and site variability in approach and context. Specific benefits of the study included:

- a systematic approach to examining complex implementation processes that made maximum use of site variability in implementation, diverse data sources, and often fuzzy information;
- cross-site data on implementation of a reform that values local control and responsiveness enriched understanding of the variability and robustness of successful implementation of strategies and implementation challenges across differing local contexts;
- conceptual and practical strategies for presenting and analysing cross-site data;
- a reflective assessment process that assisted funders in ensuring accountability and in making informed funding decisions;
- a set of judgements about site progress that were widely perceived as fair because of the interactive, transparent, and systematic approach to data collection and analysis;
- robust documentation of the considerable accomplishments of sites, including illustrations of innovative approaches that served to promote cross-site learning;
- explication of major implementation challenges and lessons for future planning;
- increased understanding of important developmental issues for the initiative as a whole;
- identification of conceptual issues that require further explication in the theory of change;
- findings that informed the design of a subsequent outcomes evaluation.

## ACKNOWLEDGEMENT

The author wishes to thank Deborah Daro, Robert Chaskin, Jeff Hackett, Sarah Morrison, and Harold Richman for their thoughtful suggestions.

## NOTES

1. While the chapter focuses on explicating the conceptual and methodological strategies used in the Indicators Study, selected findings from the study, culled primarily from studying the implementation of practice reform efforts, will be used to illustrate the research approach and its utility.
2. See, for example, the assessment of program fidelity for assertive community treatment (ACT) for the mentally ill (Teague, Bond and Drake, 1998).
3. The term *qualitative* is used because qualitative judgements were made about progress and to distinguish these indicators from singular quantitative indicators.

Both quantitative and qualitative data were used as evidence in making these judgements.

4. Since the initial implementation stage, technical assistance providers and the Foundation have instituted a more concrete and quantitative approach to tracking implementation progress by sites. It is an open question as to whether this would have been possible or useful in the initial stages of implementation.

5. This perspective draws from the heuristic paradigm which encourages and helps social workers to study the full complexity of social work practice and social change (Pieper, 1989; Tyson, 1995).

6. Infrastructure can be seen as one dimension of capacity, a more global and somewhat more ambiguous term used in the rating scale. Infrastructure refers directly to a base or foundation for supporting ongoing implementation.

7. While these efforts primarily appeared to protect our judgements from positive biases from site participants and others, it is important to note that we worked equally hard to guard against being biased by the negative views of some stakeholders who were critics of the initiative.

8. Our overall approach to making judgements was based in part on cognitive research and related theories of expert clinical decision making. Given multifaceted and sometimes fuzzy diagnostic information, like the CPPC evaluation context, cognitive theorists suggest the need for decision makers to develop multiple and competing hypotheses starting with the most probable, the need to seek out disconfirming evidence (Elstein, Shulman and Sprafka, 1978), and the necessity of flexible decision-making rules that are subject to continuous revision (Cantor, 1981).

## REFERENCES

Brown, P. (1995) The role of the evaluator in comprehensive community initiatives. In J.P. Connell, A.C. Kubisch, L.B. Schorr and C.H. Weiss (Eds), *New Approaches to Evaluating Community Initiatives: Concepts, Methods, and Contexts* (pp. 201–225). Washington, D.C.: The Aspen Institute.

Cantor, N. (1981) A cognitive-social approach to personality. In N. Cantor and J.F. Kihlstrom (Eds), *Personality, Cognition, and Social Interaction*. Hillsdale, NJ: Erlbaum.

Center for the Study of Social Policy (1997) *Reducing Child Abuse and Neglect: Why Community Partnerships will make a Difference*. New York: Draft report to the Edna McConnell Clark Foundation.

Child Welfare Policy and Practice Group (1998) Key elements of an individuated course of action. Unpublished handout, Montgomery, Alabama.

Connell, J.P. and Kubisch, A.C. (1999) Applying a theory of change approach to the evalutaion of comprehensive community initiatives: Progress, prospects, and problems. In K. Fulbright-Anderson, A.C. Kubisch and J.P. Connell (Eds), *New Approaches to Evaluating Community Initiatives, Volume 2: Theory, Measurement, and Analysis* (pp. 15–44). Washington, D.C.: The Aspen Institute.

Coulton, C.J. (1995) Using community-level indicators of children's well-being in comprehensive community initiatives. In J.P. Connell, A.C. Kubisch, L.B. Schorr and C.H. Weiss (Eds), *New Approaches to Evaluating Community Initiatives: Concepts, Methods, and Contexts* (pp. 173–200). Washington, D.C.: The Aspen Institute.

Elstein, A.S. (1988) Cognitive processes in clinical inference and decision making. In D.C. Turk and P. Salovey (Eds), *Reasoning, Inference and Judgement in Clinical Psychology* (pp. 17–50). Englewood Cliffs, NJ: Prentice Hall.

Elstein, A.S., Shulman, L.S. and Sprafka, S.A. et al. (1978) *Medical Problem Solving: An Analysis of Clinical Reasoning*. Cambridge, MA: Harvard University Press.

Gambone, M.A. (1999) Challenges of measurement in community change initiatives. In K. Fulbright-Anderson, A.C. Kubisch and J.P. Connell (Eds), *New Approaches to Evaluating Community Initiatives, Volume 2: Theory, Measurement, and Analysis* (pp. 149–164). Washington, D.C.: The Aspen Institute.

Glisson, C. (1990) Commentary: Distinguishing and combining qualitative and quantitative methods. In L. Videka-Sherman and W.J. Reid (Eds), *Advances in Clinical Social Work Research*. Silver Spring, MD: NASW Press.

Kubisch, A.C., Weiss, C.H., Schorr, L.B. and Connell, J.P. (1995) *Introduction*. In J.P. Connell, A.C. Kubisch, L.B. Schorr and C.H. Weiss (Eds), *New Approaches to Evaluating Community Initiatives: Concepts, Methods, and Contexts* (pp. 1–21). Washington, D.C.: The Aspen Institute.

Lipsky, M. (1980) *Street-Level Bureaucracy: Dilemmas of the Individual in Public Services*. New York: Russell Sage Foundation.

Pieper, M.H. (1989) The heuristic paradigm: A unifying and comprehensive approach to social work research. *Smith College Studies in Social Work*, **60**, 8–34.

Rosen, H. (1981) How workers use cues to determine child abuse. *Social Work*, **148**, 27–33.

Teague, G.B., Bond, G.R. and Drake, R.E. (1998) Program fidelity in assertive community treatment: Development and use of a measure. *American Journal of Orthopsychiatry*, **68**(2), 216–232.

Tyson, K.B. (Ed.) (1995) *New Foundations for Scientific Social and Behavioral Research: The Heuristic Paradigm*. Needham Heights, MA: Allyn & Bacon.

Weiss, C.H. (1995) Nothing as practical as good theory: Exploring theory-based evaluation for comprehensive community initiatives for children and families. In J.P. Connell, A.C. Kubisch, L.B. Schorr and C.H. Weiss (Eds), *New Approaches to Evaluating Community Initiatives: Concepts, Methods, and Contexts* (pp. 65–92). Washington, D.C.: The Aspen Institute.

## Further Reading

Berlin, S. and Marsh, J.C. (1993) *Informing Practice Decisions*. New York: Macmillan Publishing Company.

Patton, M. (1987) The policy cycle. In D. Palumbo (Ed.), *The Politics of Program Evaluation* (pp. 100–145). Newbury Park, CA: Sage Publications.

Patton, M.Q. (1990) *Qualitative Evaluation and Research Methods* (2nd edn). Newbury Park, CA: Sage Publications.

Smith, M. (1994) Qualitative plus/versus quantitative: The last word. In C. Reichardt and S. Rallis (Eds), *The Qualitative-Quantitative Debate: New Perspectives; New Directions for Program Evaluation*, **61**, 37–44.

# 13

# POLICY ROOTS AND PRACTICE GROWTH

## Evaluating Family Support on the West Coast of Ireland

*John Canavan and Pat Dolan*

The last decade has seen rapid and significant change in family support in Ireland. Not only have various projects been initiated throughout the country but also, and more significantly, family support has emerged in Irish State policy as a strategy in the delivery of services to children and families. Part of this rapid transformation has involved a concurrent expansion in the extent and sophistication of the evaluation of family support projects and programmes. Indeed it may now be meaningful to speak of family support evaluation as a particular area of expertise. But developments in these arenas of practice and research occur in the broader context of change in the delivery of care and welfare services by the State. Thus, underpinning the surface-level changes in the technical repertoire are sets of deeper policy shifts.

This chapter seeks to answer two main questions about family support evaluation in Ireland. First, what are the main features of the development of family support and its evaluation during the 1990s? Second, what are the forces that have influenced the direction of these developments? These questions are based on our contention that a major challenge for all working in the delivery of family support services is to be both practice and policy literate. For example, we believe that it is essential to be able to abstract from day-to-day interaction as a family support practitioner or evaluator and engage with the deeper issue of policy change and its value bases; equally, so is the need for policy makers to be engaged by, and properly understand, the reality of practice.

This chapter is based on an analysis of two projects located in a city in the west of Ireland. The first, which began life as a community-based stand-alone intervention for adolescents in 1991, represents the vanguard of the

*Evaluating Family Support: Thinking Internationally, Thinking Critically.*
Edited by I. Katz and J. Pinkerton. © 2003 John Wiley & Sons, Ltd.

new wave of family support interventions in Ireland. The second, a comprehensive multidisciplinary intervention initiated in 1998, represents a relative
maturation of thinking about family support and operates as part of a national programme. In both cases, while having a central role, the style and
nature of evaluation differ somewhat. Although the chapter focuses on these
two projects and their evaluations, it does not propose that these are totally
representative of all family support evaluations in Ireland. Rather, the case
study approach is adopted because it offers a framework from which various values, ideas and practices involved in the evaluation of family support
interventions can be unpacked and analysed.

In order to do this, the chapter begins with brief descriptive profiles of the
projects and how evaluation functioned in relation to them. Following this,
the chapter's first analytical focus is the key dimensions of change in practice.
This is achieved by contrasting the projects and their evaluations. Among the
issues discussed are the shift within family support work towards greater
participation by families in decisions and a concomitant shift in the role of
workers towards being facilitators. In relation to evaluation, a key dimension
of change discussed is the increase in the importance of self-evaluation and
the adoption by family support workers of action-researcher roles.

The chapter's second analytical focus is the major relevant transformations
in the broader policy environment. Among the policy issues analysed is the
extent to which, and the reasons why, family support has moved from a position of being a soft option in child protection work to being a strategic orientation which has the potential to be the dominant trend in work with children
and families. In addition, attention is given to tracing the cultural shift which
has seen evaluation become a normal part of the operation of state services.
This will involve an exploration of such factors as the influence of neo-liberal
ideology on, and the role of evaluation in, EU-funded programmes. The final
part of the chapter will draw together the implications of our analysis for
family support evaluation, and then offer some prescriptions for policy and
practice in the future.

## WESTSIDE NEIGHBOURHOOD YOUTH
## PROJECT: CASE STUDY I

Located in an area of Galway City known as the Westside, the Neighbourhood Youth Project (NYP) is a community-based intervention which aims
to support children and adolescents experiencing adversity. The project was
established in 1990 with the aim of fulfilling the regional health authority's
newly established responsibilities under the Child Care Act (Government
of Ireland, 1991). Moreover, it was intended that, in advance of the full implementation of the Act, 'the project would also allow the board to develop
skills for community-based childcare' (Canavan, 1993, p. 7). The model on

which the project was based had emerged 16 years earlier in the Reports of the Task Force of Child Care Services (Government of Ireland, 1975; National Commitee on Pilot Schemes to Combat Poverty, 1980).

Although similar in some respects to the intermediate treatment model operating in the UK, the Neighbourhood Youth Project had a less judicial and more preventive orientation. The target group for NYPs was identified (Government of Ireland, 1975, p. 16) as children:

- who have lacked stable adult models with whom they could identify and establish relationships of trust;
- whose parents or parent substitutes have been inconsistent, rejecting or disturbed;
- whose parent or parents have become so dependent on their child emotionally or otherwise that they are inhibiting the natural growing up process;
- who have severe personal, family, educational or social problems for which they need outside help;
- who, while not experiencing emotional problems or lacking in stable adult relationships, have established or are likely to establish patterns of persistent and serious delinquency.

While a number of projects were established subsequent to the Interim Task Force report, the Westside NYP represented a recommitment to community-based preventive work with at risk children and adolescents.

Work with young people attending the project was either on an individual one-to-one basis or in group settings. At the time of the evaluation, the project's group-work activities emphasized such areas as providing a constant relationship with an adult; building self-esteem; developing social skills; giving responsibility; task-achievement and providing new experiences (Government of Ireland, 1975, p. 65). The format of the groups ranged from more intensive discussion-based groups focused on specific areas such as adolescent health, through to arts and crafts, games and physical exercise-based groups. Since an important aspect of its overall strategy was to work in a non-stigmatizing fashion, the project ran weekly *open-house* groups for children in the area, including those attending the project along with their peers. Adolescents were referred to the NYP through a variety of sources, but most typically through the social work services of the regional health authority, local schools or as a result of direct contact by concerned parents. The project had a Board of Management comprising representatives from the health authority, local schools, community groups and parents living in Westside. Although changed now, at the time of the evaluation, workers trained in childcare staffed the project, all of whom had previously worked in the residential childcare sector.

The Westside NYP evaluation, undertaken between 1992 and 1993, was commissioned by the funding agency, the regional health authority. Its

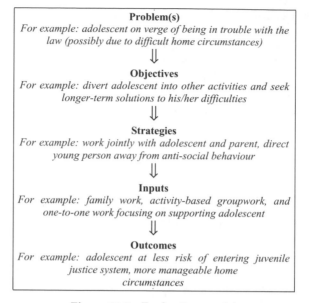

**Problem(s)**
*For example: adolescent on verge of being in trouble with the law (possibly due to difficult home circumstances)*
⇓
**Objectives**
*For example: divert adolescent into other activities and seek longer-term solutions to his/her difficulties*
⇓
**Strategies**
*For example: work jointly with adolescent and parent, direct young person away from anti-social behaviour*
⇓
**Inputs**
*For example: family work, activity-based groupwork, and one-to-one work focusing on supporting adolescent*
⇓
**Outcomes**
*For example: adolescent at less risk of entering juvenile justice system, more manageable home circumstances*

**Figure 13.1**   Evaluation model

primary purpose was to examine the project's effectiveness, with a secondary aim of establishing learning from the experiences at that stage (Canavan, 1993). The wider context of the evaluation was the impending implementation of new childcare legislation, the Child Care Act 1991. For this reason, management in the health authority was concerned with the substantive learning that the evaluation could offer for the future development of the services. There is little doubt too that the evaluation afforded the health authority the opportunity to present itself as a leader in the development of preventive services, in response to the Child Care Act. The evaluation was undertaken by a post-graduate student at the local university under the supervision of a member of the Political Science and Sociology Department with extensive experience in project evaluation. The work was undertaken on a full-time basis for six months and then on a part-time basis for a further six-month period. During this time, the researcher was based at the project premises.

The evaluation model used in the study (see Figure 13.1) provides an example of how it would apply in an individual case.

The model was founded on the assumption that the project was established in response to the existence of a problem or set of problems. The essential problem or challenge in this case was how to meet the needs of adolescents facing various forms of adversity in their lives. Alongside their needs were those of their families and the wider community in which they lived. The project objectives reflected the desired-for situation of the various actors—in particular, the resolution or amelioration of the problems faced by the adolescents targeted by the project. In the evaluation model, the strategies were identified as 'the broad frameworks of methods and techniques' (Canavan, 1993, p. 7) needed to realize the objectives. These frameworks reflected at heart the core strategic orientation towards preventive, community-based provision. The inputs were the various resources required to make the strategy work for example, the skills and experience of the workers and a variety of specific practice tools which they brought to bear.

The methodological approach to the evaluation is best described as mixed, using both qualitative and quantitative methods, plus techniques that combined aspects of both approaches. Underpinning the methodology was a desire to generate a solid base of data from which the overall evaluation aims could be achieved. This involved gathering contextual, attitudinal, outcome and cost data, and information on the ongoing operation of the project. For example, the views of the participating children and their parents were gathered through the use of structured interview schedules, while less-structured interviews were used in interviews with staff, community actors and other relevant personnel. In order to discover the extent to which the project impacted on the children, the main standardized approach was the use of the Coopersmith Self-Esteem Inventory (Coopersmith, 1981). This was judged appropriate given the emphasis within the project on self-esteem as a key aspect of the children's development. Also used for the purposes of developing a case study on the experiences of two of the children attending the project was the Spence Social Skills Inventory (Spence, 1985). Alongside these methods were unstandardized review forms devised by the researcher in consultation with project staff. These allowed both project staff and the original referring agencies to review the children's progress against reasons for their initial referral to the project.

The researcher also worked towards locating the project in its different operating contexts. Setting the needs of children within a community profile and positioning the project within the broad move away from institutional care towards community care and prevention were both important aspects of the evaluation. Also significant was the attempt to elaborate from the project's experience what exactly community-based childcare practice meant—what were its key features and its theoretical and disciplinary roots? Therefore, as well as its effectiveness and learning functions, a basic task of the evaluation was to tell the project, as constituted in particular by its staff and funders, about itself. The evaluation went beyond a mere technical exercise, and attempted to take a more sociological approach to the analysis. That said, the evaluation did not engage in a more critical analysis. Thus, there was no real analysis of how the problem which the project aimed to tackle was socially constructed or the extent to which it simply reflected inequality in access to the resources and rewards available in the society of the time.

In terms of the findings, the evaluation demonstrated a high degree of satisfaction with the project among children, their parents, community members and referring agents. The results from the one standardized measure used in the evaluation failed to demonstrate a relationship between the project and change in the self-esteem of the children attending it. Nevertheless, assessments by parents, referring agents and staff all suggested positive changes in the young people, in respect of the reasons they were initially referred to the project. The evaluation also highlighted the potential saving to the State from the operation of this community-based approach. In terms of process or operational issues, the evaluation report identified a number of areas that required change or greater emphasis by project staff. Of particular importance among these were: recommendations for greater emphasis on assessment and review of the needs of the young people; greater clarity about the function of individual work within the project; and stronger links with the local social work teams for the purposes of identifying children who would benefit from the type of support offered by the project.

## SPRINGBOARD FAMILY SUPPORT INITIATIVE:
## CASE STUDY 2

The Springboard Family Support Initiative, established by the Department of Health and Children in 1999, is a collection of 15 pilot family support programmes scattered around the Republic of Ireland. Three of these projects are located in Galway City in the west of Ireland, and this chapter focuses on one of these, namely the Ballinfoile Neighbourhood Youth Project (NYP). Ballinfoile Park is a local authority housing estate situated on the northern perimeter of Galway City. It suffers from various forms of socio-economic disadvantage, including high rates of unemployment, high referral rates to social work and high levels of juvenile crime.

The Ballinfoile NYP is a community-based day-care support service for adolescents and their families. The project targets young local people known to be experiencing difficulties in their behaviour, drug misuse, early school leaving, those known to be at risk of maltreatment, and those with low self-esteem and poor self-efficacy. The overarching aim of the project is to help young people to become resilient in the face of adversity, in a non-stigmatizing, adolescent-friendly culture. Ultimately, the project aims to prevent family breakdown, and works towards ensuring that young people remain at home and out of the care of the State.

The Ballinfoile NYP places a heavy emphasis on prevention and works with adolescents in the context of their wider ecology including their family, school and community. It provides a range of in-school and in-community diversionary, activity-based programmes to participating young people. In addition, the project works with families through casework and group-work programmes. At any one time, the project works with a cohort of around 60 young people whose average age is 14 years. The project is multidisciplinary and staffed by a project leader, two project workers, a half-time clinical psychologist and a part-time secretary. It is fully funded by the regional health authority but is operated day-to-day by a national youth work organization, Foroige. Both organizations are jointly responsible for its strategy and overall direction.

## Evaluation and Methodology

Running parallel to the operation of the Springboard programme is a national evaluation, which involves the production of interim and final reports (McKeown, 1999). The evaluation format for all projects is identical and focuses on three areas of impact, namely:

- impact on children
- impact on parents
- impact on services.

The methodological approach to the evaluation uses a mixture of qualitative and quantitative methods. The overarching aim of the evaluation is to form a baseline and measure change over a given period of time for participating individual children and families referred to Springboard. Critically, the evaluation seeks to establish the extent to which such change could be attributed to Springboard rather than to any other factors. The focus of the evaluation is about answering the overall question: Does Springboard work for children and their families, and if so how? It is not about which project is doing best.

The first stage in the evaluation involves the collection of baseline data and subsequently data is collected after 6 and 18 months. An interim report has been produced on the basis of the first six months of the programme, while data has now been collected for the final evaluation report. The evaluation takes account of differences between the projects—for example, matters such as differing demographic characteristics of each community site, or the focus in terms of service users, i.e. parents, young children or adolescents. In addition, the research is designed to take account of differences between the project in relation to issues of organizational structures and staffing arrangements.

The researcher uses a variety of standardized research tools in the evaluation. These tools include the Strength and Difficulties Questionnaire (SDQ; Goodman, 1997). This is a checklist that measures resilience to stress over a given period of time and is usually gathered from a number of sources at the time of administration—for example, the child or adolescent completes the questionnaire, which is also completed by the parent. In addition, the SDQ could also be completed by a schoolteacher known to the young person. A second method used is the Parent/Child Relationship Inventory (PCRI; Gerard, 1994), which measures the perceived relationship between the parents and child. In particular, it focuses on the parents' perception of their sense of burden in respect of parenting at a given point in time. Similarly it measures the parents' perception of the status of their overall relationship with their child.

A third data collection tool, a version of the Social Network Map (SNM; Tracy and Whittaker 1990), was used to measure social support. The SNM is an assessment tool that measures perceived social support, including sources of support, strength of the support and quality of support, on offer. This tool takes the format of a circular map representing eight possible sources of support and a grid on which quality of support in respect of these sources is indicated. It is usually administered with children above the age of 10, and can also be used with parents.

The General Health Questionnaire (GHQ; Goldberg and Williams, 1988)—a tool that measures the perceived mental health of a person—was also used. It takes the format of 24 questions in respect of a person's perceived mental health across a range of areas, for example the person's sense of anxiety, current ability to cope with life stress, and personal affect. The tool is usually administered on a one-to-one basis and requires the respondent to answer limited choice questions relating to perceived physical and mental health.

## Other Data Collection Protocols

Apart from the use of standardized tools with service users and their caretakers, the Springboard evaluation design also embodies a commitment to include the views of other key stakeholders. For example, it seeks to incorporate the perspectives of community representatives and local service providers who may interact with the service (through referring children and families to Springboard) but who are not directly involved in the delivery of the programme.

Importantly, staff who work on the Springboard programme are not simply evaluation stakeholders but have been directly involved as active players in the process of collecting data from children, parents and others. In order for staff to be in a position to collect such data they have received training in the use of various research tools, for example the Social Network Map and the Strength and Difficulties Questionnaire. In addition to the collection of data from service users and other agents, staff were requested to identify key case examples. Each project team was asked to write up a case of a child or parent whom they believed benefited noticeably in the course of the evaluation. Thus, the evaluator was able to establish vignettes of best practice and compare scores for each person identified.

Other benefits accrued as a result of the direct involvement of staff in the evaluation, since in the course of using the various research instruments, staff were also able to enhance their work practice. The tools helped to focus their work and enabled them to identify the needs of service users and how best to support children and families.

## Interim Findings

The evaluation seeks to discover changes among children and parents who participated in the Springboard programme. Such changes could relate to child behaviour, improvement in school attendance, reduction in a sense of burden among parents or an increase in perceived social support among the identified social network members of parents. In particular, the evaluation aims to establish the relative merits of direct work with children by staff as compared to work with parents on parenting skills and efforts at building parents' social networks. At the interim report stage—after six months of the programme and based on data from all the projects involving 112 families relating to 192 children—the evaluation suggested 'relatively small but positive impacts on the lives of parents, children and families' (McKeown et al., 2000, p. 97). The evidence showed that:

- for children there was a small improvement in the SDQ scores;
- where changes occurred they indicated improvement rather than worsening of problems;
- while the rate of school attendance did not change, there were less children arriving late at school, hungry or without lunch;
- there was a general perception that children's problems were lessening and, in the assessment of the Health Boards, the percentage of children at moderate to high risk of going into care fell from 24% to 14%.

From the data it appeared that for parents there was a decisive improvement in support networks, a reduction in stress as measured by the GHQ (from 68% to 42%) and a small improvement in parenting capacity. The findings were also interpreted as emphasizing the importance of supporting parents in helping children and possibly even suggesting that working with children alone may be counterproductive. The evaluation at that point also identified the extent to which trust had been developed between services and families and the foundation that this represented for future progress.

## FAMILY SUPPORT: FEATURES AND FORCES

The Westside NYP was established at the time of the implementation of the Child Care Act 1991. This Act did not really commence implementation until 1994 following the report on the Kilkenny Incest Case, which was a major national scandal regarding the failure of State agents to protect a young girl from sexual abuse (McGuinness, 1993). By the late 1990s, aspects of the Child Care Act which relate to child welfare rather than child protection had come more to the fore and, thus, family support had become more of a strategy in its own right. Also at that time, an important government report on family life in Ireland outlined a range of specific rights and measures required by individuals and families experiencing adversity and in need of intervention by services of the State (Government of Ireland, 1998).

By 1999, there had been much change in the development of childcare services both nationally and within the regional health authority. The Ballinfoile NYP, established as part of the Springboard initiative, was the ninth new community youth project to be established by the regional health authority in four years and was also part of 22 family support initiatives either managed and/or funded by the authority. A notable aspect of Ballinfoile NYP is that it is representative of a cultural change within State services and voluntary youth organizations. For the State, this has meant contracting aspects of its service delivery for vulnerable young people to voluntary youth work organizations. For Foroige and other youth organizations, the change has involved working in collaboration with State health services towards specific child welfare objectives.

At a wider level, within health services there had been a marked change of emphasis on valuing family support as an intervention strategy in its own right, and away from seeing it as a soft form of child protection (Gilligan, 1995). Nevertheless, by 1998, family support services were generally relatively few in Ireland and this situation only really began to change as the Irish economic boom began to feed into State expenditure. Thus, in the context of the *Celtic Tiger economy*, and at a cost of £2 million, Springboard was established by the government and funded through its social inclusion budget.

The main point of comparison between the two projects considered in this case study is their instigation as pilot projects, whose continuation was and is subject to proof of success as evidenced in evaluation. The most apparent difference between the two is that the Westside NYP began life as a stand-alone service born in a culture of cutbacks in the health services, while Ballinfoile NYP operates as part of a national programme initiated in the context of an economic boom. In relative terms, because of the national profile of Springboard, Ballinfoile NYP can at least draw on the strength provided by its membership of a national family of projects. In more general terms, Westside NYP began operations in what was the early days of an emerging family support policy context while the Ballinfoile project is rooted in a much more firmly established family support policy context.

## EVALUATION: FEATURES AND FORCES

The main contrast between the current scenario for family support evaluation in Ireland and that existing in the early 1990s is that, while previously there were many individual project-level evaluations such as that of the Westside NYP, there is now a programme of evaluation in place to meet the needs of a national initiative. While self-evident at one level, this is a critical point because the scale of the evaluation reflects the scale of the programme itself. In essence, the resources are available to put in place a sophisticated evaluation model. Moreover, unlike what often happens in project evaluation, the evaluation process was built into the Springboard programme operation from the start with a commitment to have a strong foundation of baseline data.

Given the available resources, the national Springboard evaluation is far more sophisticated than the type of evaluation used in the Westside NYP study. The use of an extensive range of data collection protocols in the form of standardized tests, attitude questionnaires and fieldwork notebooks should allow substantive conclusions to be drawn from the research at both the interim and final stages of the programme's operation. It could be argued that this quite intense level of evaluation is only possible now when the notion of evaluation has far more acceptance among social service professionals. This compares with the climate when the Westside NYP was established, a time when the very notion of community-based provision for young people at risk had just re-emerged as a policy and practice option. In one sense, the Westside NYP evaluation was asking 'What is family support?' while the Springboard evaluation poses the question 'Does family support work?'.

If anything reflects the changed scenario of family support evaluation, it is the adoption of what might be described as an action-research model, with staff directly involved in data collection, both as part of their practice in working with families and as an element of the evaluation data collection process. This scenario presents a sharp contrast with the Westside NYP study, when the very notion of evaluation was new and certainly not something that involved workers as active researchers, despite the use of their assessments of clients as part of the evaluation process. In the Springboard evaluation, project staff have both research and care responsibilities.

### Forces in the Development of Evaluation in Ireland

If these represent some features of the change in the nature of evaluation of family support projects and programmes, what were the forces driving this change? It is clearly beyond the scope of this chapter to specify a causal model for the emergence of the central role of evaluation in policy implementation, but it is possible to identify at least some of the factors that might be included in such a model.

Unlike the situation in the USA, where there is a long tradition of evaluation of social programmes, evaluation in Ireland could be characterized as a relatively immature and underdeveloped discipline. There is little doubt that a major contributory factor in the development of evaluation in Ireland was the European Union and its role in funding various pilot and mainstream programmes. Often, as part of funding agreements, evaluation components were attached, so that in addition to the usual requirements of sound financial and accounting practices, programmes were subjected to detailed analyses of their operational processes and their realized outcomes. For example, this was so in the case of the earliest pilot initiatives sponsored by the EU, the Anti-Poverty Programmes of the 1970s and 1980s (Commission of the European Communities, 1981; O'Cinneide, 1987).

Recent experiences in the vocational training and community and local development areas are also illustrative of the influence of EU funding. In the case of the first round of the Youthstart programme, which operated between 1996 and 1998, each project was required to engage an evaluator to assist with the work, and evaluation plans for each project had to be submitted to the central coordinating body as part of the project's set up. Moreover, a detailed paper was put in place on which these plans were to be based (Employment Youthstart National Support Structure, 1996). In the case of the Local Development Programme, which operated between 1994 and 1999, all of the local partnership companies and community groups funded under the programme had to comply with performance-monitoring procedures. These involved the collection of detailed information about individuals and groups involved, and the completion of qualitative case studies on various aspects of their work.

Although difficult to quantify, there is also the extent to which each new evaluation exercise, as well as impacting on the area in question, had a multiplier effect. There is little doubt that, in some cases, the motivation for evaluation did not derive from deeply held convictions about the need for evidence of outcomes or for practice improvement. Rather, evaluations were put in place because they were seen to be a requirement for new projects. This is not to say that evaluation was simply an issue of fashion, but in some cases the decision to have an evaluation of a project may have been taken before the question was asked 'Do we need an evaluation?' It could be said that over time a culture of evaluation emerged. One general mechanism through which this happened was partnership. At every turn, partnership arrangements provide the backdrop for social interventions, be those in relation to social care of the elderly, youth work, educational disadvantage or the many other domains in which such interventions operate. Thus, personnel from health authorities, local government, youth work and community organizations participate in the joint management of projects. Again, while difficult to quantify, there is little doubt that a certain degree of organizational cross-fertilization takes place in these settings, with evaluation representing one aspect of this process.

However, it would be naive to set out these various factors as operating apart from the wider context of ideological change which has characterized the last 20 or so years. Although less severe in its implications in Ireland, the general move to the right in politics and its attendant implications for a closer scrutiny of the role of the State and the operation of its services has had definite impacts in Ireland. Concrete examples of this are the birth and electoral success of the nominally right wing party, the Progressive Democrats, deregulation in certain policy areas, and a sell-off of State-owned enterprises. The impact on the operation of the State itself is evidenced in two developments. First was the establishment of the Office of the Comptroller and Auditor General in 1992, with the specific brief to examine various State spending programmes for value-for-money. More thoroughgoing has been the Strategic Management Initiative (SMI), which represents an attempt to reorganize the whole public sector in such a way as to increase efficiency and effectiveness in the delivery of services. What makes the SMI notable is the importation of concepts and tactics, formerly more associated with market sector firms, into the operational life of the civil service. Notwithstanding the fact that arguments for greater effectiveness and efficiency by the State in meeting the needs of its citizens can be found equally on the left as on the right of the ideological divide, the significance of the wider context of development of evaluation should not be neglected.

## IMPLICATIONS FOR FAMILY SUPPORT EVALUATION

Thus far, two snapshots of projects and their evaluations operating at different points in time have been presented, with the dynamics of the intervening period discussed in relation to family support and evaluation. In doing so the chapter's two core questions have been addressed. From a situation where family support was a relatively new concept, the chapter has illustrated its emergence in policy in the form of a national programme. Embodied in this shift is the development of more sophisticated and participatory practice. This involves families as lead agents in finding solutions to their own problems, with professional staff as facilitators in this process. In this chapter, it has also been proposed that the nature of the evaluation of family support has changed. Evidence of this change includes a general climate that is more accepting of evaluation as part of family support practice, an increase in the extent and complexity of data collection protocols, and a shift towards practitioners as researchers. In tracing the dynamics of change involved, we have raised many issues, some of which we address in this section.

Overall, the emphasis on good-quality evaluation protocols can only be welcomed. Indeed, the challenge will be to ensure the continuation of this emphasis in State policy beyond the lifetime of the Springboard project. However, in advocating this, we are concerned that the foundations of family support may not yet be as solid as necessary for it to have a long-term future as part of service delivery. A contrast can be made between the ongoing and entirely appropriate commitment to high-quality protection services as part of the mainstream of what services mean to children and families. If the future for family support is not yet certain, the place of evaluation, often perceived as the least necessary part of the expenditure structure of family support projects and programmes, is even more insecure. Without evaluation protocols, family support services will be terminally weakened.

The Springboard programme has facilitated the utilization of various tools in creating baseline needs analyses and assessing the effectiveness of family support interventions. The final evaluation will allow an assessment of their utility both for practice and research. Whatever the findings are, there is the possibility of establishing some level of agreement among family support service providers as to what tools might be used in the future based on the experiences of the Springboard evaluation. If such agreement was possible even, for example, between the regional health authorities, it would increase the chances of comparability between research, and over time the use of meta-analytic research methodologies (Hunter et al., 1982).

There is little doubt that the involvement of staff as practitioner–researchers is a positive development and one that other mainstream services—for example, social work, psychology, the probation service—would do well to emulate. As set out earlier, the adoption of practitioner–researcher roles in the Springboard evaluation has facilitated both family support practice and parts of the data-gathering process for the evaluation. In the longer term, building such protocols should lead to the development of reflective practitioners—i.e. practitioners who not only have no fear of evaluation but can use it strategically for service improvement. One possible negative outcome of a move towards practitioner–researcher roles might be a distraction from the core work of services in meeting the needs of children and families. However, if the emphasis is on the implementation of research methods that have direct utility as practice tools, this problem could be avoided.

One of the positive features in the experience of the Westside evaluation was its use as the basis from which other services developed in Galway City and the region generally. As has been highlighted, the fertile policy context of the time is part of the explanation for this. In the case of Springboard and subsequent evaluations, it will be important to recognize the importance of evaluation utilization. A major strand in the US tradition of evaluation theory is devoted to utilization, and that should be enough of a prompt for those involved in this programme (Weiss, 1998, 1993; Patton 1997). Particularly in the case of a major programme like Springboard, agreeing implementation timetables for evaluation recommendations, and devising and implementing comprehensive dissemination strategies, will be important tasks in enhancing the probabilities that the evaluation report, its findings and insights will be used.

## CONCLUSION

This chapter has highlighted the importance of the wider societal and policy context within which family support evaluation takes place. If evaluation is not related to the wider context in which it operates, it becomes merely a technical matter. Family support projects will either succeed because they are based on proper understandings of the nature of the problem, are well organized, planned and delivered, or they will not because of failure in respect of one or all of these points. Evaluation will be the technique by which this is discovered. At no time will questions that seek to enumerate the role of the distribution of wealth and of access to social goods, for example education and health, in creating stress within families be considered, or if they are, they are accorded a token gesture.

Notwithstanding the points made thus far, in terms of a future research agenda for family support evaluation in Ireland, two areas present themselves readily. The first of these relates to the general nature of services research which is to focus on children and families whose experiences deviate from some generally unarticulated set of norms about what the process of family life and the experience of growing up should be. There is a clear need to undertake research work which has as its focus the experience of children and families who do not come to the attention of State services. Such a process could lead to a greater understanding of the processes that family support interventions aim to address. In a more general sense, such research would be useful as a means of elaborating and testing assumptions about what represents normal family life and a normal process of growing up. A second possible agenda for evaluation is one that focuses on the area of natural support networks. Current emphases on building natural networks for social support assume the involvement of State or voluntary service staff in facilitating this process. Developing systems through which the mobilization of natural support networks occurs outside of, or with minimal prompting by, professional outsiders is an important next step in service development. Devising evaluation procedures to test such networks represents an interesting challenge.

This chapter has contended that thinking about family support evaluation requires an encompassing analytical approach. This ranges across specific psychological measurement instruments to policy and ideological contexts. The interesting question is whether family support evaluation has the capacity to remain on the agenda of social service research in the future. For the moment, the growth in family support evaluation in Ireland is apparent and the foregoing has highlighted areas for potential future growth. But is the visible growth sustainable? Because they are hidden, it is not clear how deep and strong are the roots. Time will tell.

## REFERENCES

Canavan, J. (1993) *Westside Neighbourhood Youth Project: Evaluation Report*. Galway: Western Health Board.

Commission of the European Communities (1981) *Final Report from the Commission to the Council on the First Programme of Pilot Schemes and Studies to Combat Poverty (COM (81), 769)*. Brussels: Commission of the European Communities.

Coopersmith, S. (1981) *Coopersmith Inventory (School Form)*. Paolo Alto, CA: Consulting Psychologists Press.

Employment Youthstart National Support Structure (1996) *Guidelines for Evaluation of European Union Employment Youthstart Initiative Ireland 1996–1997*. Dublin: Youthstart National Support Structure.

Gerard, A.B. (1994) *Parent–Child Relationship Inventory (PCRI) Manual*. Los Angeles: Western Psychological Services.

Gilligan, R. (1995) Family support and child welfare: Realising the promise of the Child Care Act 1991. In H. Ferguson and P. Kenny (Eds), *On Behalf of the Child: Child Welfare, Child Protection and the Child Care Act, 1991* (pp. 60–83). Dublin: A. & A. Famar.

Goldberg, D.P. and Williams, P. (1988) *A User's Guide to the General Health Questionnaire*. Horsham: NFER-Nelson.

Goodman, R. (1997) The Strengths and Difficulties Questionnaire: A research note. *Journal of Child Psychology and Psychiatry*, **38**, 581–586.

Government of Ireland (1975) *Task Force on Child Care Services: Interim Report*. Dublin: The Stationery Office.

Government of Ireland (1991) *Child Care Act, 1991*. Dublin: The Stationery Office.

Government of Ireland (1998) *Strengthening Families for Life: Final Report to the Minister of Social, Community and Family Affairs*. Dublin: The Stationery Office.

Hunter, J.E., Schmidt, F.L. and Jackson, G.B. (1982) *Meta-analysis: Cumulating Research Findings across Studies*. Beverly Hills, CA: Sage.

McGuinness, C. (1993) *Report of the Kilkenny Incest Investigation*. Dublin: The Stationery Office.

McKeown, K. (1999) *Springboard Evaluation System, November*. Dublin: Department of Health and Children.

McKeown, K., Haase, T. and Pratschke, J. (2000) *Does Family Support Make a Difference: Interim Evaluation of Springboard (January to May 2000)—Report to the Department of Health*. Dublin: Department of Health and Children.

National Committee on Pilot Schemes to Combat Poverty (1980) *Final Report*. Dublin: The Stationery Office.

O'Cinneide, S. (1987) *Ireland: First Report of the Programme Evaluation Team*. Bath: Joint Committee for the Second Programme to Combat Poverty.

Patton, M.Q. (1997) *Utilization-Focused Evaluation: The New Century Text*. Thousand Oaks, CA: Sage.

Spence, S. (1985) *Social Skills Training: A Counsellor's Manual*. Horsham: NFER-Nelson.

Tracy, E.M. and Whittaker, J.K. (1990) The Social Network Map: Assessing social support in clinical practice. *Families in Society: The Journal of Contemporary Human Services*, October: 461–470.

Weiss, C.H. (1993) Where politics and evaluation research meet. *Evaluation Practice*, **14**, 93–106.

Weiss, C.H. (1998) Have we learned anything new about the use of evaluation? *American Journal of Evaluation*, **19**, 21–33.

# 14

# THE RESOURCEFUL ADOLESCENT PROJECT

A Universal Approach to Preventing Adolescent Depression through Promoting Resilience and Family Well-Being in Australia

*Ian Shochet and David Ham*

This chapter focuses on one aspect of family support in Australia, the provision and evaluation of mental health support for families with pre-adolescent and young adolescent children. We focus in particular on universal family based and school-based interventions that were developed to promote family well-being and build adolescent resilience with the intention of reducing the incidence of depression in adolescents. It would seem that a universal prevention approach, particularly a school-based approach, could increase engagement and be effective in preventing depression in adolescence. This programme is part of the current Australian Mental Health Strategy and provides an example of the programmes currently being encouraged and funded in Australia for Child and Adolescent Mental Health and Youth Suicide.

Adolescent depression is one of the major mental health concerns and is a mental health priority in Australia because of the incidence, duration and harmful effects of adolescent depression, including youth suicide. There is demonstrated potential for interventions targeting both the adolescents and their families, to strengthen family relationships and develop resilience in adolescents, particularly if they can engage adolescents more widely and without stigmatization. The promotion of family well-being and the development of resilience in adolescence currently have a strong theoretical and empirical basis as vehicles to alter the normal trajectory of the development of

*Evaluating Family Support: Thinking Internationally, Thinking Critically.*
Edited by I. Katz and J. Pinkerton. © 2003 John Wiley & Sons, Ltd.

adolescent depression. Over the past seven years two universal preventive interventions have been developed, trialled and nationally disseminated under the rubric of the Resourceful Adolescent Programme, RAP-A, a school-based resilience-building programme for adolescents; and RAP-P, a programme for the parents of adolescents aimed at promoting family well-being. In what follows we describe the background to the various programmes, the programmes themselves, and the results of the trials and evaluations of the RAP. From the point of view of engagement, de-stigmatization and effectiveness, the results of the controlled trials are very encouraging of school-based universal interventions designed to address risk and protective factors for mental health problems. This approach also appears effective in low socio-economic status (SES) higher-risk environments.

## ADOLESCENT DEPRESSION AND THE AUSTRALIAN NATIONAL MENTAL HEALTH STRATEGIES

There is strong evidence indicating the prevalence and harmful effects of adolescent depression (Fleming and Offord, 1990; Keller et al., 1991; Peterson et al., 1993). It has been estimated in various studies that between 16% and 64% of young people who suicide are clinically depressed, and one Australian study found that over half of the youth who died by suicide in Queensland were depressed (DHAC, 2000). The point prevalence of clinical depression among adolescents in western communities (not including Australia) has been estimated at up to 8.4% (Anderson and McGee, 1994; Fleming and Offord, 1990) and lifetime prevalence for depressive disorders in adolescents may be as high as 20% (Birmaher et al., 1996).

The prevalence of depressive disorders in Australian adolescents appears to be similar to these overseas figures. A large-scale survey of child and adolescent mental health in Australia has recently been completed (Sawyer et al., 2000), providing the first reliable information about the prevalence of depression in Australian adolescents. This survey of 4500 children and adolescents aged from 4 to 17 years found that 4.8% of males and 4.9% of females aged 13 to 17 years were suffering from dysthymic disorder or major depressive disorder at the time. This is close to earlier estimates (DHAC, 1998b) of point prevalence of 5% for any depressive disorder among Australian adolescents and 2.7% for major depressive disorder, although in one Australian survey 12% of adolescents in Western Australia reported feeling depressed most of the time (DHAC, 1998b). After reviewing the available evidence concerning the mental health of Australian children and adolescents, Zubrick et al. (2000) concluded that priorities in efforts to reduce the burden of mental disorders in these groups should include the development and evaluation of preventive interventions targeting those disorders known to be responsive to prevention, including adolescent depression.

Thus in Australia the prevention of adolescent depression has become a major part of the National Mental Health Strategy. In addition, the provision of mental health support for families through preventive intervention programmes, either directly to the families or through schools, is a priority for governments at both federal and State levels. For further information, see the *National Mental Health Policy* of the Australian Health Ministers (AHM, 1992a) and the *National Mental Health Plan* (AHM, 1992b), which detailed actions for implementing this policy for the period 1993–1998; and the *Second National Mental Health Plan* (AHM, 1998), which detailed a coordinated national approach to reform in mental health service and policy over the period 1998–2003.

There has been some pressure to sharpen the focus of mental health prevention on the family and to make research into family risk/protective factors and family preventive interventions priorities for future research (Sanders, 1995). With the prevention of adolescent depression identified as a priority mental health area, and with empirical evidence to show that parents play an important role both in terms of risk factors (e.g. conflict) and protective factors (e.g. supportive care), the family is seen to be a critical setting for preventive interventions aimed at reducing the future incidence of adolescent depression (AHM, 1998; DHAC, 1998b).

## PREVENTIVE INTERVENTIONS AND ADOLESCENT DEPRESSION

Prevention approaches aiming to reduce the incidence of the targeted disorder within the general population, or to prevent the further development of early symptoms of the disorder, are not new. More recently, however, there has been clear empirical support for the effectiveness of some preventive interventions, including those targeting adolescent depression, through controlled trials and systematic evaluations. In addition there has been a development of knowledge of mental health risk and protective factors and concepts in prevention that allows for a clearer understanding of the goals of prevention and approaches to evaluation.

Preventive interventions are currently usually classified with respect to their target groups. Universal preventive interventions target whole populations, for example all families with adolescents, or all Year 8 children in a school, and aim to reduce the incidence of the targeted disorder or problem in that population. Selective interventions target those groups or individuals who, although not displaying symptoms of the problems or disorders, are considered to be at increased risk for particular problems or disorders because of certain predisposing risk factors. Indicated preventive interventions target individuals who display early symptoms of the disorder and are considered at high risk of further development of a more severe stage of the disorder (Mrazek and Haggerty, 1994).

One of the major issues in prevention research is the choice between these strategies of prevention. There is some evidence for the effectiveness of indicated and selective preventive interventions with adolescents in reducing the incidence or severity of adolescent depression. A trial of an indicated prevention programme with 10- to 13-year-old adolescents, using training in cognitive skills, social problem-solving skills, coping skills, negotiation skills and assertiveness (Jaycox et al., 1994), found significant improvements in depressive symptoms for intervention-group participants compared with controls at post-intervention tests and at two-year follow-up (Gillham et al., 1995). A trial of another indicated intervention with 14- to 15-year-old boys (Clarke et al., 1995), based on a treatment approach developed by Lewinsohn et al. (1990), also found significant improvements in depressive symptoms compared to a wait-list control group. These two studies encountered very poor recruitment rates and high attrition rates, indicating that the results may be influenced by a self-selection bias.

The studies reviewed above indicate the benefits of indicated interventions in preventing or reducing depression in adolescents, but also demonstrate the difficulties in recruitment for indicated programmes. One impediment to recruitment to these programmes may be the risk to targeted adolescents of being identified as *different* at a time when peer-group acceptance is critical. This impediment could be overcome if the preventive programmes were offered as universal interventions as part of the school curriculum, if necessary in addition to indicated programmes.

The cost and implementation problems associated with universal programmes are greater than for indicated programmes by virtue of the larger numbers of participants, so a balance between low cost and effectiveness is important for universal programmes (Sanders, 1998; Webster-Stratton, 1996). However, universal programmes can have the added benefit of preventing or inhibiting the development of disorders in adolescents who may not have been identified as at risk but may later develop the disorder without intervention (Tolan et al., 1998).

The Resourceful Adolescent Programme (RAP; Shochet et al., 1999) was developed to meet a need for universal preventive interventions against adolescent depression. The Resourceful Adolescent Programme for Adolescents (RAP-A) was designed for implementation in the classroom as part of the school curriculum for one term. A three-session parallel programme for parents (RAP-P) was designed to address known family-based risk and protective factors for adolescent depression. With the increased knowledge of risk and protective factors of adolescent depression it should ostensibly become more possible to design universal interventions to reduce risk and strengthen protective factors that buffer against the negative effects of the risk factors (Mrazek and Haggerty, 1994; Tolan et al., 1998).

# THE RATIONALE AND CONTENT
# OF THE INTERVENTIONS

## Resourceful Adolescent Programme for Parents (RAP-P)

The RAP-P is designed for parents with pre-adolescents or young adolescent children and is an 8- to 10-hour programme designed to address the family risk and protective factors for adolescent depression. Many identified risk factors for adolescent depression are related to the family environment (see Kaslow et al., 1994; Lewinsohn et al., 1994; Shochet and Dadds, 1997, for research, reviews and discussion on family factors and depression). Family conflict, in particular escalating conflict with parents, and expression of parental over-control are well-established risk factors for social and emotional problems in adolescence, including adolescent depression (Burbach et al., 1989; Lewinsohn et al., 1994). Depressed adolescents who report severe parent–adolescent conflict are at elevated risk for chronic depression or relapse (Birmaher et al., 2000).

As well as risk factors for depression there are also several family-based protective factors against adolescent depression. Strong parental attachments and expressions of warmth and caring have been found to buffer adolescents from depression and anxiety (Papini et al., 1991). A cohesive family appears to be a reliable protective factor against depression (Reinherz et al., 1989), and close relationships with parents lessen the impact of stress (Peterson et al., 1991).

In spite of the evidence outlined above, family environment as a risk and protective factor has been largely ignored in prevention research in adolescent depression. If we focus only on interventions targeting adolescents we fail to recognize the very important role of the family in adolescent development (Kazdin, 1993). The risk and protective factors discussed above indicate that there is also a role for interventions which encourage parents to reduce the levels of parent–adolescent conflict and strengthen family relationships with their adolescents, while also fostering the adolescents' developing independence (Kaslow et al., 1994).

In searching for a technology to develop such a programme we discovered that work with families in adolescent depression has been fraught with difficulties. Some family-intervention approaches that have been used take the form of parent skills training to teach parents conflict resolution and communication skills and to help parents to reinforce the cognitive-behavioural skills taught to the adolescents. The few attempts that have been made to treat depression using this approach have not been particularly successful, with no added improvement attributable to parent involvement (Brent et al., 1997; Lewinsohn et al., 1990). One possible reason for the lack of success is that the conflict-management approaches can result in increased conflict as the conflict is brought into sharper focus (Brent et al., 1997). Thus, while families can play a protective role in adolescent depression and suicide, the technology of how this can be achieved from an early-intervention perspective is far from clear.

In developing the Resourceful Adolescent Programme for Parents (RAP-P) we have examined, on a theoretical and empirical level, some of the factors that underlie the risk factor of conflict, or threaten the protective factor of parent–adolescent attachment, and approach these from a competency and health-promotion perspective. Cognitive-behavioural theory provides a number of strategies which have been found to be useful in helping individuals and families to manage negative emotional reactivity, and some of these are utilized in RAP-P. In RAP-P we integrate a cognitive-behavioural perspective with an understanding of family systems and normal adolescent development. We believe this integration is important if we are to provide an intervention that does not run the risk of being ineffective at best or harmful at worst.

The approach of Bowen (Kerr and Bowen, 1988; Nichols and Schwartz, 1995; Papero, 1990) provides an understanding of the development of chronic and escalating conflict in families with adolescents from a family-systems perspective. In this theory there are two necessary elements in maintaining a healthy self-esteem: a sense of belonging to one's family, and a sense of separateness and individuality. When individuals are able to achieve both elements at once, directing their own functioning and governed by their own independent sense of self and self-worth, they are said to be showing *differentiation of self*. A differentiated person has the capacity, based on a sense of self, to maintain a feeling of self-worth and to respond to the reactions, thoughts and opinions of others.

When people are functioning in an *undifferentiated* way, they are highly anxious and become emotionally reactive both within themselves and in their relationships. In this reactive state they are less able to separate out thinking from feeling, and less able to soothe or manage themselves in the face of conflict and anxiety. They are prone to becoming so flooded with feelings because of perceived threats to their self-worth that they are at times incapable of objective reasoning. People function on a continuum from high differentiation to high reactivity, and differentiation is not a fixed destination that is reached once and for all; rather it is a lifelong developmental process that is achieved relative to the family of origin through resolution of conflicts within individual and relational contexts.

These struggles have their source in the family of origin where family members have a history of being thwarted in their attempts for either more closeness or more distance. Thus they become more vigilant (anxious) in their perception of the behaviour of others in this regard, and ultimately become emotionally reactive in the face of this anxiety as they more desperately try to restore a sense of well-being. Their mechanisms of self-management, self-soothing and self-regulation do not serve them well in these emotionally charged situations.

Normal adolescent development is characterized by a need for both on-going family closeness and developing separation from family members. Consequently, parents are required to adapt to continual changes. In more differentiated families the changes are more easily tolerated without anxiety and emotional reactivity. Ideally, parents are able to feel soothed and gratified by the connection and closeness of their new relationship with their adolescent and are not made anxious by their child's need for autonomy. Ideally, children begin their adolescence from a base of a good connection, and they can optimally differentiate (feel separate but securely connected). When this happens, family members are less likely to react with negative emotions to each other. However, in less differentiated families, this is a time in the family life cycle where the family is at risk of intensive struggles for differentiation and control.

In the development of the RAP-P the aim is to address the issue of conflict and cohesion by layering the Bowenian concepts of reactivity and differentiation of self. The four general aims of RAP-P are to help parents to:

- boost their own self-esteem, differentiation and self-management skills;
- reduce their own negative emotional reactivity to their adolescent;
- boost their adolescent's self-esteem;
- reduce and manage their adolescent's negative emotional reactivity to them.

These aims are achieved through the content of the programme and also through the interpersonal process used by the programme facilitator in proceeding through the programme content.

Four types of interventions related to these aims occur throughout the programme. Interventions for promoting parental self-esteem involve encouraging parents to identify their strengths as people and parents. Interventions for reducing parental emotional reactivity involve encouraging parents to maintain a cycle of positivity, helping parents to reduce their personal stress levels, supporting parents in maintaining a developmental perspective, promoting parents' use of a life-cycle intergenerational perspective, and assisting parents to move beyond the here and now. Interventions for promoting adolescent self-esteem involve promoting parents' use of age-appropriate affirmation and validation, encouraging parents to show confidence and encouragement, and promoting enjoyable and honest time together. Interventions for reducing adolescent emotional reactivity involve reducing conflict by promoting harmony in family interactions, and helping parents to strengthen a new emotional closeness with their adolescent.

The programme has three parts, each with three major themes. Each part occupies one workshop session of two to three hours. Part One, *Parents are people too!*, focuses on identifying what we do well as parents, understanding how stress affects us as parents, and managing stress. Part Two, *What makes teenagers tick?*, includes themes of understanding the teenager better, building up the teenager's self-esteem, and supporting teenage independence with attachment. In Part Three, *Promoting positive family relationships*, the themes are promoting harmony in our families, preventing and managing conflict between our teenagers and ourselves, and looking forward to a positive future.

## Resourceful Adolescent Programme for Adolescents (RAP-A)

There are few family-based prevention programmes directed to improving the well-being of children and adolescents, and participation rates—for preventive parent programmes in particular—have been found to be low (Durlak and Wells, 1997), possibly because there is little motivation to participate when no symptoms are in evidence (Tolan et al., 1998). Many prevention programmes are based on schools where recruitment is easier and delivery is more cost-effective (Tolan et al., 1998) but these still have an effect on the functioning and health of families.

RAP-A is a school-based intervention originally designed primarily for 12- to 15-year-old children (Years 8 and 9), and consists of 11 sessions of 45–50 minutes' duration, conducted weekly by trained facilitators, and intended to occupy one class period per week for one school term. Being offered to all students as a universal programme, RAP-A avoids possible problems of stigmatization associated with selective or indicated interventions.

In addition to the family risk and protective factors outlined above, RAP-A addresses the individual risk factors of stress, low self-esteem, negative cognitive styles, and lack of social support. The content and process of each session of the programme is specified in a Group Leader's Manual (Shochet et al., 1997a). Participant workbooks (Shochet et al., 1997b) are provided to each student in the programme. As the incidence of depression increases sharply from about the age of 15 years (Burke et al., 1990; Lewinsohn et al., 1994), the programme was expected to provide the greatest benefit if introduced just prior to the age when the risk for depression begins to increase.

RAP-A includes many elements of the successful cognitive-behavioural programmes discussed above, but rather than focus on deficits or symptoms, RAP-A emphasizes the recognition and reinforcement of existing personal strengths and the promotion of skills or psychological resources. Cognitive elements in RAP-A include cognitive restructuring, helping adolescents to challenge negative or distorted thinking and develop positive self-talk; stress management, using self-management and self-relaxation strategies; and problem solving based on defining the problems, evaluating solutions and using step-by-step approaches to implementing the solutions. RAP-A also includes interpersonal components (Mufson et al., 1993) related to establishing and drawing on support networks, promoting harmony, and keeping the peace through understanding others' perspectives. These latter components, based on Interpersonal Psychotherapy for depression (Klerman and Weissman, 1993), address known correlates or predictors of depression such as interpersonal conflict (Harter and Jackson, 1993; Lewinsohn et al., 1994).

RAP-A is written around a metaphor derived from the children's story *The Three Little Pigs*. The 'resourceful little pig' built his house of bricks rather than straw or sticks like the other two. When misfortune came his way (in the form of the big bad wolf) his house was strong and resilient, and hence it was able to withstand the onslaught (unlike the houses of the two other little pigs). Each week, participating adolescents develop their own RAP-A house by laying down different personal resource bricks (e.g. *Personal Strength Bricks*, *Keeping Calm Bricks*, *Problem-Solving Bricks*) as the programme unfolds.

In summary, RAP-A is an experiential, resilience-building programme designed to promote positive coping abilities and the maintenance of a sense of self in the face of stressful and difficult circumstances. The common thread that runs through the programme is the teaching of techniques to maintain self-esteem in the face of a variety of interpersonal situations.

## EVALUATIONS OF THE RESOURCEFUL ADOLESCENT PROGRAMS

Whereas the efficacy of treatments is usually evaluated by the reduction in symptoms from before treatment to after treatment, the focus in evaluating preventive interventions is usually on the long-term reduction in incidence of the disorder (Tolan et al., 1998). In the long term the intervention should result in fewer cases of the disorder in experimental groups exposed to the intervention than in comparison groups not exposed to the intervention; however this may not be known for many years. Evaluations in the short-term focus on the impact of the intervention on identified factors which are theoretically and empirically related to the development of the disorder and which are targeted by the intervention. Reductions in factors that predict development of the disorder, and increases in factors that inhibit development of the disorder, may be measurable after the intervention or at follow-up several months later. Many participants will be at little risk and even measured reductions in risk factors may be small; however, achieving a small reduction in risk across a large number of people may be a very beneficial public health outcome (Tolan et al., 1998).

Many different programmes are used in attempts to improve the well-being of adolescents in different ways. However, despite recent significant advances in prevention research (Durlak, 1998), many of these programmes have not been evaluated in properly controlled trials, and often little is known of their efficacy (Kazdin, 1993). Evaluation of the efficacy of the RAP programmes has been a priority, with a number of controlled research trials over the past six years and further evaluations under way.

## Initial Controlled Trial of RAP-A and RAP-P

An initial controlled trial (Shochet et al., 2001) was conducted in 1996. This trial investigated the effects of RAP-A and RAP-P as universal school-based programmes to reduce depressive symptoms in adolescents. The trial used three depression measures to provide convergent data on adolescents' self-report of depressive symptomatology: The Children's Depression Inventory (Kovacs, 1992); Reynolds Adolescent Depression Scale (Reynolds, 1987) and The Hopelessness Scale (Beck and Steer, 1988; Beck et al., 1974). The RAP-A was implemented in the classroom as part of the school curriculum. There were three experimental conditions:

- RAP-A, in which the adolescents received RAP-A only;
- RAP-F, in which adolescents received RAP-A while their parents were invited to participate in RAP–P;
- a no-treatment comparative group.

It was predicted that the RAP-A and RAP-F intervention groups would show fewer depressive symptoms than the non-intervention group after the intervention and at follow-up, with a greater improvement for the RAP-F group.

The results obtained in this first study provided significant incentive for implementing this universal school-based programme aimed at preventing adolescent depression. The predicted improvement in recruitment rates over the indicated programmes discussed above (for example, Clarke et al., 1995; Jaycox et al., 1994) was realized, with 88% of those who had been invited participating in the programme. Attrition was lower than in those studies at 5.8% from pre- to post-intervention, and 19.8% from pre-intervention to follow-up, and was due largely to absences from school on the day of testing and relocations.

The active intervention groups (RAP-A and RAP-F) showed both statistically and clinically significant improvements compared to the comparative group, although the RAP-A and RAP-F groups did not differ significantly from each other. Adolescents in either RAP were found at post-intervention and 10-month follow-up to have significantly lower rates of clinical and subclinical levels of depressive and hopelessness symptoms. At post-intervention and follow-up, initially subclinical adolescents who began with elevated depressive and hopelessness symptoms in the RAP group were more likely to fall in the healthy range, and less likely to fall in the clinical range than those in the comparison group. None of the subclinical adolescents in the RAP programme had moved into a clinical range at post-intervention (five months later) or at 10-month follow-up, while 17.6% of subclinical adolescents in the comparative group fell in the clinical range at follow-up. From the health promotion perspective, 75% of the subclinical adolescents in the RAP group fell into the healthy category at follow-up, compared to 41.2% in the comparative group.

The universal nature of the programme also appeared to be of benefit to adolescents who were initially considered healthy, and who would not normally be recruited into indicated or selective programmes. There was a significant difference between the RAP and comparative groups in the clinical and health status at follow-up for these initially healthy participants, with no initially healthy adolescents in the intervention groups but 10.1% of initially healthy adolescents in the comparative group moving into the subclinical category at follow-up. RAP thus benefited adolescents who were both initially healthy and initially subclinically depressed. Overall, the programme was positively endorsed and all components of the programme were ranked positively. It was not possible to determine which aspects of the programme may have contributed to the change in depression scores.

This initial study does have a methodological limitation that would suggest that we should interpret these encouraging results with some caution. The RAP versus comparative conditions were allocated on the basis of cohort. The results may reflect some error associated with a cohort effect. The positive effects at both post-intervention and follow-up reduce (but do not exclude) an interpretation based on cohort effects. Nevertheless we feel that it is important to conduct a trial that controls for cohort seasonal and school effects. We have developed a school-cohort crossover design that could control for these effects and are currently conducting a large-scale trial implementing this design.

A disappointing aspect of this study was the difficulty in recruiting parents of participating adolescents in the RAP-P component of the programme, which made it impossible to draw any definitive conclusions about the value of incorporating parents in prevention interventions for adolescent depression. It was decided to develop a flexible learning model to avoid relying on stressed parents having to devote precious time to attend after-hours workshops. A videotaped programme and workbook were developed in the expectation that this format would improve recruitment. A pilot trial of the video programme was well accepted but participant feedback indicated that telephone facilitation was an essential part of the process.

## Trial of RAP-A and RAP-P in a Lower
## Socio-economic Area School

Low socio-economic status (SES), belonging to a disadvantaged ethnic minority and stressful life events which may be associated with these, have
been identified as possible risk factors for depression (NHMRC, 1996). This
was supported by the child and adolescent component of the National
Mental Health Survey (Sawyer et al., 2000) which found that adolescent depression was more prevalent in lower socio-economic groups, with 6.5% of
adolescent males and 9% of adolescent females whose weekly family incomes
were less than $580 being depressed, compared with the Australian mean of
4.8% of male and 4.9% of female adolescents. With this relationship between
lower SES and adolescent depression in mind, a further trial of the RAP
(Shochet et al., 1999) evaluated their efficacy in a school serving a very low
socio-economic area. RAP-A was presented during school time as part of the
curriculum.

Although the recruitment rate in the low SES school at 52% was lower
than in the earlier trial it was better than in other reported trials (e.g. Jaycox
et al., 1994). Attrition was low with 91.5% of students completing the programme. Measures of depressive symptoms showed a significant decrease
from pre-intervention to post-intervention and unpublished data indicate
that these effects continued at follow-up. This trial again demonstrated the
value of the wide coverage achieved by presenting a universal intervention
within the school curriculum, particularly when the difficulties encountered
in lower SES living are considered. Again, recruitment of parents to the parent programme was poor, precluding evaluation of any added benefits of this
programme.

## RAP-P Trial

A trial of the RAP-P alone as a universal preventive intervention is currently in
progress. The objective of the trial is to evaluate the effectiveness of RAP-P, as
either a series of three workshops or a videotaped programme with workbook
and telephone facilitation, in reducing the incidence of depression in adolescents through interventions directed to their parents. Reductions in the level of
depressive symptoms and in the incidence of clinical depression in the adolescents are the targeted long-term outcomes, while levels of parent–adolescent
conflict and adolescents' perceptions of interactions with their parents and
attachment to their parents are the proximal or mediating variables predicted
to be influenced by parental involvement in RAP-P. These variables have
been both theoretically and empirically linked to the development of adolescent depression (Kaslow et al., 1994). We also predict that parents' stress levels
will be reduced and their ability to separate rational processes from emotional

responses will be improved, with consequent reductions in parent–adolescent conflict and improvements in parent–adolescent interactions.

Six government schools and five non-government schools with a total Year 8 population (aged 12–13 years) of 1612 agreed to take part in this study. Schools serving similar socio-economic populations were randomly allocated to one of three conditions: (1) RAP-P presented as three parent workshops; (2) RAP-P presented as a videotaped programme with a workbook and telephone facilitation before and after watching the videotape; and (3) a wait-list control condition with participants offered their choice of programme after completing all testing. The recruitment approach included early advice to potential Year 8 parents late in the preceding year in some schools, a two-sided single sheet informal promotional handout enclosed with the *Informed Consent* information letter, school endorsement in school newsletters, and in some cases teacher follow-up of consent forms.

Parent recruitment rates were again low, averaging 15% of school Year 8 populations across the three conditions, with 349 parents and 242 of their Year 8 adolescents signing consent forms. The prediction that a videotaped programme would increase recruitment rates by reducing demands on parents' time was not supported; the recruitment rate for the video programme at 11.6% of families in the relevant schools was the lowest of the three conditions, with the workshop programme attracting the highest recruitment rate of 19.4% and the control condition attracting 13.7% of potential participants.

The Year 8 students and their parents complete questionnaires at pre-test, post-intervention testing and 12-month follow-up. Adolescents complete self-report measures of depressive symptoms, attachment to their parents, parent–adolescent conflict, and separate appraisals of parent–child interactions with their mother and father. Parents complete the same parent–adolescent conflict measures and appraisals of parent–child interactions, as well as a measure of the *Bowen Systems Theory* (Bowen, 1976) construct of differentiation of self, a retrospective measure of adults' attachment to their parents, and a measure of current stress. Parents also completed a demographics questionnaire and evaluations of their allocated intervention programme.

Pre-testing, interventions and post-testing for the control and workshop conditions are now complete. However, the logistics associated with the videotaped condition have proved difficult and demanding of resources. Telephone facilitators found it difficult to contact many parents prior to sending the video package, resulting in multiple phone calls and delays of several weeks in some cases. Arranging phone facilitation after the parents watched the video was even more difficult. Facilitators reported that some parents watched the video in the first few weeks and the process could be completed with these parents very expeditiously, but other parents needed to be contacted several times before they had watched the video and could undertake the post-video facilitation session. Six months after the commencement of

the video facilitation programme the majority of parents in the video condition had not yet completed the video evaluation questionnaire or post-
testing.

Despite these implementation problems with the video programme, early
data analysis indicates that both workshop and videotape programmes were
well received. The mean scores, on a five-point scale, for satisfaction with
the programme, helpfulness of the programme, encouragement from the programme, and how enjoyable the participant found the programme to be, were
4.45, 4.10, 4.41 and 4.43 respectively for the workshops and 3.94, 3.57, 3.89 and
3.57 respectively for the video programme. Although both formats were well
received these figures indicate that participants consistently rated the workshop significantly more positively than the video programme on each scale,
$p < 0.001$ in each case. Although only 67% of the parents who registered for
the workshop condition attended any RAP-P workshop sessions, attrition
rates for the workshops were low with only 5% of parents who commenced
the programme later withdrawing.

Post-intervention data obtained about four to eight weeks after completion
of the intervention do not indicate any changes due to the interventions,
but this is not unexpected; the nature of the changes we predict to occur is
such that significant changes would not be expected over such a short time.
Preliminary analysis of available data (Ham and Shochet, 2001) indicates that
the chosen proximal indicators of parent–adolescent conflict and adolescents'
attachment to their parents are appropriate, with these measures accounting
for significant portions of the variance in adolescent depression.

## National Trial of RAP-A and RAP-P

A large-scale national trial of both RAP-A and RAP-P as universal preventive
interventions has recently been commissioned by the Australian National
Health and Medical Research Council (NHMRC) and commenced in schools
in 2001. This trial is one of two trials currently being conducted as part of the
Australian Government's *Youth Suicide Initiative* to evaluate different school-
based preventive intervention programmes. The national RAP trial involves
at least two pairs of schools matched for socio-economic status and size in each
of Queensland, New South Wales, Tasmania and Western Australia, and will
be conducted with two sequential Year 8 cohorts in each school. Participating
schools are government schools serving lower and middle socio-economic
areas, with Year 8 cohorts of between 100 and 200. A total of about 2500 Year
8 students are expected to be involved.

The interventions are either RAP-A alone or RAP-A for adolescents with
their parents invited to attend RAP-P workshops. This latter condition is
referred to as RAP *for Families* (RAP-F). Pairs of schools are randomly allocated
to either the RAP-A condition or the RAP-F condition. One school in each pair

has been randomly allocated to an intervention condition in the first year of the trial and to a control condition in the second year of the trial. The other school in each pair is in the control condition in the first year and the intervention condition in the second year.

Some of the methodological problems of the earlier RAP-A trials have been addressed in this trial. School effects will be controlled by running the intervention and control conditions in the same school in subsequent cohorts. Cohort effects and seasonal effects will be controlled by running the intervention and experimental conditions in the same school at the same time in subsequent years or at the same time in a matched school. Programme integrity will be measured by facilitator self-reports, participant reports and observation of randomly selected groups.

Self-report measures to be completed by adolescents in this trial at pre-intervention, post-intervention and 12-month follow-up include two self-report measures of depression and measures of hopelessness, optimism, parent–adolescent conflict, attachment to parents, school culture, problem-solving skills, major life events and explanatory style. Adolescent depression and well-being will also be assessed by a structured clinical interview for depression for selected participants at follow-up. Parents complete a measure of parent–adolescent conflict and a behavioural screening questionnaire related to their children at pre-test, post-test and follow-up. Schools will be asked at follow-up to provide a brief report for each child, indicating the frequency of absences and disciplinary problems, and academic performance. This will provide convergent information related to the adolescents' well-being.

We predict that exposure to RAP-A will result in more positive cognitive styles, lower levels of conflict, better approaches to problem solving and lower levels of depressive symptoms in the adolescents, with fewer adolescents in the RAP-A groups displaying clinical or subclinical levels of depression at post-intervention or 12-month follow-up. Adolescents whose parents attend RAP-P are expected to show greater improvement on these measures than those who are exposed to RAP-A alone.

## CONCLUSION

There is adequate evidence of the need for widespread preventive interventions to reduce the incidence of adolescent depression, which is linked closely to adolescent suicide. With very few universal preventive programmes targeting adolescent depression, and even fewer of these having evidence of their efficacy, the *Resourceful Adolescent Programmes* were developed as universal preventive interventions to overcome the recruitment problems associated with indicated or selective interventions and to prevent the development of depression in healthy adolescents who would not be touched by these programmes.

The already mentioned increasing emphasis on the use of evidence-based preventive interventions in Australia (DHAC, 1998a, 1999; Mitchell, 2000) is increasing the pressure for proper evaluation of potential preventive interventions. The careful evaluation of the RAP has been seen as a priority by the RAP project team. The initial trial of RAP-A and RAP-P provided good evidence that RAP-A benefits both healthy and depressed adolescents. It also provided evidence that provision of RAP-A as a school-based universal intervention overcomes the problems of low recruitment rates experienced with indicated preventive programmes. With no evidence from this initial trial for the efficacy of RAP-P, another trial is currently in progress to evaluate RAP-P as a stand-alone preventive intervention, while the forthcoming national trial of RAP-A and RAP-P should provide strong evidence of the efficacy or otherwise of both programmes. The theoretical basis for both RAP-A and RAP-P appears strong, indicating that the programmes should be efficacious; however the problems associated with the implementation of programmes for parents may make it difficult to utilize RAP-P effectively as a universal intervention.

Our work so far has added to the already strong evidence for the efficacy of school-based programmes addressing the well-being of adolescents, adding the new dimension of school-based universal preventive interventions for adolescent depression. However, research into the aetiology of adolescent depression and variables associated with depression indicates that the family environment contains both potent risk factors and potent protective factors for depression. We believe that alongside interventions directed to adolescents there is a place for preventive interventions targeting the family and the family environment.

The two trials involving RAP-P have indicated that the recruitment of parents is a major problem with this family-based programme. Although similar difficulties with the recruitment of parents have been documented by other researchers, we believe that family-based interventions aimed at improving the well-being of children and adolescents have potential, although implementation problems have made it difficult to evaluate these programmes. The RAP-P workshops have been very well accepted and parents have indicated that they found them helpful. The problem with recruitment is seen at this stage as a challenge rather than an indication that parent programmes are to be abandoned; the development and evaluation of improved procedures for the recruitment of parents and subsequent improvement in parent recruitment rates are priorities for the national trial.

RAP-A has been demonstrated to be efficacious even in the face of the difficulties encountered in lower socio-economic environments where risk for depression is higher. By providing the programme as part of the school curriculum we can address the unique needs for resilience of adolescents in these environments. We believe that by doing this we can in the long term make a positive contribution to the mental health of disadvantaged families as well as those from more comfortable environments.

## REFERENCES

Anderson, C.A. and McGee, R. (1994) Comorbidity of depression in children and adolescents. In W.M. Reynolds and H.F. Johnson (Eds), *Handbook of Depression in Children and Adolescents*. New York: Plenum.

AHM (1992a) *National Mental Health Policy.* Australian Health Ministers. Canberra: Australian Government Publishing Service.

AHM (1992b) *National Mental Health Plan.* Australian Health Ministers. Canberra: Australian Government Publishing Service.

AHM (1998) *Second National Mental Health Plan.* Australian Health Ministers. Canberra: Australian Government Publishing Service.

Beck, A.T. and Steer, R.A. (1988) *Beck Hopelessness Scale*. New York: The Psychological Corporation.

Beck, A.T., Weissman, A., Lester, D. and Trexler, L. (1974) The measurement of pessimism: The Hopelessness Scale. *Journal of Consulting and Clinical Psychology*, **42**, 861–865.

Birmaher, B., Brent, D.A., Kolko, D., Baugher, M., Bridge, J., Holder, D., Iyenger, S. and Ulloa, R.E. (2000) Clinical outcome after short-term psychotherapy for adolescents with major depressive disorder. *Archives of General Psychiatry*, **57**, 29–36.

Birmaher, B., Ryan, N.D., Williamson, D.E., Brent, D.A., Kaufman, J., Dahl, R.E., Perel, J. and Nelson, B. (1996) Childhood and adolescent depression: A review of the past 10 years. Part 1. *Journal of the American Academy of Child and Adolescent Psychiatry*, **35**, 1427–1439.

Bowen, M. (1976) Theory in the practice of psychotherapy. In P. Guerin, Jr (Ed.), *Family Therapy: Theory and Practice* (pp. 42–90). New York: Gardner Press.

Brent, D.A., Holder, D., Kolko, D., Birmaher, B., Baugher, M., Roth, C., Iyengar, S. and Johnson, B.A. (1997) A clinical psychotherapy trial for adolescent depression comparing cognitive, family, and supportive therapy. *Archives of General Psychiatry*, **54**, 877–885.

Burbach, D.J., Kashani, J.H. and Rosenberg, T.K. (1989) Parental bonding and depressive disorders in adolescents. *Journal of Child Psychology and Psychiatry and Allied Disciplines*, **30**, 183–204.

Burke, K.C., Burke, J.D., Regier, D.A. and Rae, D.S. (1990) Age at onset of selected mental disorders in five community populations. *Archives of General Psychiatry*, **47**, 511–518.

Clarke, G.N., Hawkins, W., Murphy, M., Sheeber, L.B., Lewinson, P.M. and Seeley, J.R. (1995) Targeted prevention of unipolar depressive disorder in an at-risk sample of high school adolescents: A randomised trial of a group cognitive intervention. *Journal of the American Academy of Child Adolescent Psychiatry*, **34**, 312–321.

DHAC (1998a) *National Mental Health Report 1997*. Commonwealth Department of Health and Aged Care. Canberra: Australian Government Publishing Service.

DHAC (1998b) *National Health Priority Areas Report: Mental Health*. Commonwealth Department of Health and Aged Care. Canberra: Australian Government Publishing Service.

DHAC (1999) *Mental Health Promotion and Prevention: National Action Plan*. Common-wealth Department of Health and Aged Care. Canberra: Australian Government Publishing Service.

DHAC (2000) *National Youth Suicide Prevention Strategy: Setting the Evidence-based Research Agenda for Australia (A literature review)*. Commonwealth Department of Health and Aged Care. Canberra: Commonwealth of Australia.

Durlak, J.A. (1998) Primary prevention mental health programs for children and ado-lescents are effective. *Journal of Mental Health*, **7**, 463–469.

Durlak, J.A. and Wells, A.M. (1997) Primary prevention mental health programs for children and adolescents: A meta-analytic review. *American Journal of Community Psychology*, **25**, 115–152.

Fleming, J.E. and Offord, D.R. (1990) Epidemiology of childhood depressive disorders: A critical review. *Journal of the American Academy of Child and Adolescent Psychiatry*, **29**, 571–580.

Gillham, J.E., Reivich, K.J., Jaycox, L.H. and Seligman, M.E. (1995) Prevention of de-pressive symptoms in school children: Two year follow-up. *Psychological Science*, **6**, 343–350.

Ham, D.R. and Shochet, I.M. (2001, March) *A controlled trial of the RAP Parent Program to foster adolescent wellbeing*. Paper presented at the Australian Infant, Child, Adoles-cent and Family Mental Health Association Fourth National Conference, Brisbane, Australia.

Harter, S. and Jackson, B.K. (1993) Young adolescents' perceptions of the link between low self-worth and depressed affect. *Journal of Early Adolescence*, **13**, 383–407.

Jaycox, L.H., Reivich, K.J., Gillham, J. and Seligman, M.E.P. (1994) Prevention of depressive symptoms in school children. *Behaviour Research and Therapy*, **32**, 801–816.

Kaslow, N.J., Deering, C.G. and Racusin, G.R. (1994) Depressed children and their families. *Clinical Psychology Review*, **14**, 39–59.

Kazdin, A.E. (1993) Adolescent mental health: Prevention and treatment programs. *American Psychologist*, **48**, 127–141.

Keller, M., Lavori, P.W., Beardslee, W.R., Wunder, J. and Ryan, N. (1991) Depres-sion in children and adolescents: New data on 'undertreatment' and a literature review on the efficacy of available treatments. *Journal of Affective Disorders*, **21**, 163–171.

Kerr, M.E. and Bowen, M. (1988) *Family Evaluation: An Approach Based on Bowen Theory*. New York: Norton.

Klerman, G.L. and Weissman, M.M. (1993) The place of psychotherapy in the treat-ment of depression. In G.L. Klerman and M.M. Weissman (Eds), *New Applications of Interpersonal Psychotherapy* (pp. 51–71). Washington, D.C.: American Psychiatric Association Press.

Kovacs, M. (1992) *The Children's Depression Inventory Manual*. North Tonawanda: Multi-Health Systems.

Lewinsohn, P.M., Clarke, G.N., Hops, H. and Andrews, J. (1990) Cognitive-behavioural treatment for depressed adolescents. *Behavior Therapy*, **21**, 385–401.

Lewinsohn, P.M., Clarke, G.N., Seeley, J.R. and Rhode, P. (1994) Major depression in community adolescents: Age at onset, episode duration, and time to recur-rence. *Journal of the American Academy of Child and Adolescent Psychiatry*, **33**, 714–722.

Lewinsohn, P.M., Roberts, R.E., Seeley, J.R., Rhode, P., Gotlib, I. H. and Hops, H. (1994) Adolescent psychopathology II: Psychosocial risk factors for depression. *Journal of Abnormal Psychology*, **103**, 302–315.

Mitchell, P. (2000) *Valuing Young Lives: Evaluation of the National Youth Suicide Prevention Strategy*. Melbourne: Australian Institute of Family Studies.

Mrazek, P.J. and Haggerty, R.J. (Eds) (1994) *Reducing Risks for Mental Disorders: Frontiers for Preventive Intervention Research*. Washington, D.C.: National Academy Press.

Mufson, L., Moreau, D., Weissman, M.M. and Klerman, G.L. (1993) Interpersonal psychotherapy for adolescent depression. In G.L. Klerman and M.M. Weissman (Eds), *New Applications of Interpersonal Psychotherapy* (pp. 130–166). Washington, D.C.: American Psychiatric Association Press.

NHMRC (1996) *Clinical Practice Guidelines: Depression in Young People*. Canberra: National Health and Medical Research Council.

Nichols, M.P. and Schwartz, R.C. (1995) *Family Therapy: Concepts and Methods* (3rd edn). Sydney: Allyn & Bacon.

Papero, D. (1990) *Bowen Family Systems Theory*. Boston: Allyn & Bacon.

Papini, D.R., Roggman, L.A. and Anderson, J. (1991) Early adolescent perceptions of attachment to mother and father: A test of the emotional buffering hypothesis. *Journal of Early Adolescence*, **11**, 258–275.

Peterson, A.C., Compas, B.E., Brooks-Gunn, J., Stemmler, M., Ey, S. and Grant, K.E. (1993) Depression in adolescence. *American Psychologist*, **48**, 155–168.

Peterson, A.C., Sarigiani, P.A. and Kennedy, R.E. (1991) Adolescent depression: Why more girls? *Journal of Youth and Adolescence*, **20**, 247–271.

Reinherz, H.Z., Stewart-Berghauer, G., Pakiz, B., Frost, A.K., Moeykens, B.A. and Holmes, W.M. (1989) The relationship of early risk and current mediators to depressive symptomatology in adolescence. *Journal of the American Academy of Child and Adolescent Psychiatry*, **28**, 942–947.

Reynolds, W.M. (1987) *Reynolds Adolescent Depression Scale*. Odessa, FL: Psychological Assessment Resources Inc.

Sanders, M.R. (1998) The empirical status of psychological interventions with families of children and adolescents. In L. L'Abate (Ed.), *Family Psychopathology: The Relational Roots of Dysfunctional Behavior* (pp. 427–465). New York: Guilford.

Sanders, M.R. (1995) *Healthy Families, Healthy Nation: Strategies for Promoting Family Mental Health in Australia*. Brisbane: Australian Academic Press.

Sawyer, M.G., Arney, F.M., Baghurst, P.A., Clark, J.J., Graetz, B.W., Kosky, R.J., Nurcombe, B., Patton, G.C., Prior, M.R., Raphael, B., Whaites, L.C. and Zubrick, S.R. (2000) *The Mental Health of Young People in Australia*. Canberra: Mental Health and Special Programs Branch, Commonwealth Department of Health and Aged Care.

Shochet, I. and Dadds, M. (1997) Adolescent depression and the family: A paradox. *Clinical Child Psychology and Psychiatry*, **2**, 307–312.

Shochet, I.M., Dadds, M.R., Holland, D., Whitefield, K., Harnett, P.H. and Osgarby, S.M. (2001) The efficacy of a school-based program to prevent adolescent depression. *Journal of Clinical Child Psychology*, **30**, 303–315.

Shochet, I., Holland, D. and Whitefield, K. (1997a) *The Griffith Early Intervention Depression Project: Group Leader's Manual*. Brisbane: Griffith Early Intervention Project.

Shochet, I., Osgarby, S. and Whitefield, K. (1999) *The Resourceful Adolescent Program: Building psychological resilience and decreasing depression in teenagers living in middle or lower socio-economic areas*. Unpublished manuscript.

Shochet, I., Whitefield, K. and Holland, D. (1997b) *The Griffith Early Intervention Depression Project: Participant's Workbook*. Brisbane: Griffith Early Intervention Project.

Tolan, P.H., Quintana, E. and Gorman-Smith, D. (1998) Prevention approaches for families. In L. L'Abate (Ed.), *Family Psychopathology: The Relational Roots of Dysfunctional Behavior* (pp. 379–400). New York: Guilford.

Webster-Stratton, C.H. (1996) Early intervention with videotape modeling: Programs for families of children with oppositional defiant disorder or conduct disorder. In E.D. Hibbs and P.S. Jensen (Eds), *Psychosocial Treatments for Child and Adolescent Disorders: Empirically Based Strategies for Clinical Practice* (pp. 435–474). Washington, D.C.: American Psychological Association.

Zubrick, S.R., Silburn, S.R., Burton, P. and Blair, E. (2000) Mental health disorders in children and young people: Scope, cause and prevention. *Australian and New Zealand Journal of Psychiatry*, **34**, 570–578.

## 15

# EVALUATION OF THE CONTACT FAMILY SERVICE IN SWEDEN

## *Gunvor Andersson*

This chapter deals with a child and family support system called the 'contact person/family'. It is the most frequently used statutory service in child welfare in Sweden, involving 1% of all children (0–18) each year. This is a service provided throughout Sweden in which a volunteer person or family is linked with a child in need. The contact person or family undertakes a range of tasks or activities with the child, including leisure activity, help with homework, and help to the parent with parenting tasks and respite.

In the Social Services Act 1980, and in national statistics, the contact person/family is seen as a single system, intended to be used in a flexible way. However, it is common for contact families to have children staying regularly overnight and taking part in family life, for example, every second or third weekend. It is more common for contact persons to see older children or young people on a daily basis, helping them with their schoolwork or doing activities outside the family. This system marked the introduction into Swedish welfare legislation of the opportunity for children and families to receive social support from volunteers, paid and supervised by social services. Child welfare in Sweden belongs to the public sector, and there are no voluntary organizations serving as alternatives to social services in connection with child welfare. As volunteers, contact persons/families are ordinary people without special training but with the necessary spare time, a feeling of solidarity with people who have social problems, and an ability to provide support.

In Sweden, as in many other countries, family support—in contrast to child protection and out-of-home placements—is seldom evaluated or researched. Far more has been written about how the contact person/family should be used than about how it is used, although it has been a statutory social services

*Evaluating Family Support: Thinking Internationally, Thinking Critically.*
Edited by I. Katz and J. Pinkerton. © 2003 John Wiley & Sons, Ltd.

system for almost two decades, and is increasingly in demand as it is looked upon as an attractive intervention. This chapter will outline the child welfare system in Sweden, including the contact person/family. The chapter will present the results of a study that focused on families with small children, and the results from a more extensive study conducted in Stockholm. In addition, some projects undertaken by social work students will be cited and, in conclusion, the chapter, will discuss some of the main features of the contact person/family system as a preventive and supportive social-services measure to children and families.[1]

## CHILD WELFARE IN SWEDEN

In Sweden there is no specific Children Act because children are included in the Social Services Act 1980 (SSA) and the supplementary Care of Young Persons Act (CYPA). The former provides the framework for regulating several areas of social support and intervention, and the latter regulates the admission of children (0–18 or in some cases up to 20) into care without the consent of parents or without the consent of children over 15 years of age. In Swedish child welfare legislation the main emphasis is on social support and services, rather than on child protection, and there are no strict distinctions between child protection and youth justice (Hessle and Vinnerljung, 1999).

Under the Social Services Act, Sweden's 289 municipalities are responsible for social services and have responsibility for ensuring that children and young people grow up under secure and good conditions. They have local responsibility for the universal welfare system covering all children and families (sometimes referred to as 'primary prevention'). They are obliged to organize neighbourhood services to support vulnerable groups of children and families (sometimes referred to as 'secondary prevention'). They are required to secure children's welfare by providing help and support to individuals and families with identified problems and they have to protect children (sometimes referred to as 'tertiary prevention').

What is included within the remit of child welfare differs from country to country and may vary according to the type of balance which is struck between family and State over the responsibility for children (Furstenberg, 1997). Furstenberg believes that the privatized ideal of family–State relations in the USA, maximizing the authority of parents, stands in contrast to the collaborative model present in varying degrees in most European nations and most fully developed in Sweden and Norway. As Olsson Hort (1997) points out, it is part of the normal course of life in Sweden that children

---

[1] This chapter is an expansion of a paper published in *Social Work in Europe*, vol. 6, no. 1.

receive public health care and welfare services. To provide day nursery or day care at a day-care centre is also part of the universal service to families with children. Consequently, the concept of child welfare in this chapter refers to means-tested services to children and families, additional to the universal services seen as *normal* provision by the State to families in Sweden.

Weightman and Weightman (1995) argue that Swedish culture provides far higher levels of legitimization for State intervention than that found in England, even though there is a controversy regarding compulsory interventions in families (cf. Gould, 1988). In his comparison between countries, Gilbert (1997) points out that Sweden has a family service orientation rather than a child protection orientation, although mandatory reporting of suspected child abuse exists.

There are two statutory means-tested child welfare measures reported in the official statistics every year:

- out-of-home placements
- the contact person/family system.

During 1999 around 17 500 children and young people were in accommodation or care, which means 7.35 in 1000 children/young people 0–20 years of age. Three-quarters of them were in out-of-home care under the SSA and one-quarter under the CYPA. In 1999 around 21 500 children and young people had a contact person/family under SSA, which means 10 in 1000 children/young people 0–20 years of age (National Board of Health and Welfare, 2000). The CYPA provides for the legal possibility to force a young person who has committed a crime to keep in contact with a *contact person*, but that is used only on very rare occasions and not dealt with in this chapter. The concept of *contact person* is also used in the legislation for severely disabled people, to guarantee them the right to support and service, but that also is not dealt with in this chapter.

## CONTACT PERSON AND CONTACT FAMILY

While the Social Services Act (SSA) provides guidance on how to support children and families, the municipalities are free to plan various activities and programmes of their own. However, they are required to include contact persons/families in their repertoire of measures. Contact persons and contact families are seen as a system that can be used flexibly and referred to as a preventive measure. Everybody has the right to request a contact person/family, but the local social welfare committee decides on the need and appoints the contact person or family. It is also common for social services to suggest the system after an assessment of the needs of the child and family.

Different categories of people can be seen as in need of a contact person/family (Svenska Kommunförbundet, 2000):

- families with children—for example, single mothers (or fathers) with an insufficient network and in need of support and relief as parents;
- families in crisis—for example, because of divorce, or physical or mental illness;
- young people with difficulties at school or with psychosocial problems and in need of adult support;
- families from other countries without a functioning network in Sweden.

This system marked the introduction into social welfare legislation of the opportunity for children and families to receive social support from *volunteers*. Child welfare in Sweden belongs to the public sector. There are no nongovernmental or voluntary organizations serving as alternatives to social services offices in connection with child welfare (see Lundström and Wijkström, 1997). Social services are responsible for recruiting contact persons and families. The client family can suggest a family or person known to them, for example, a teacher, a neighbour or a relative. The social services agencies have specific rules for accepting relatives as contact persons/families but it is usually seen as positive if the contact person is known to the child. Contact persons/families are volunteers, but must be officially approved by social services who pay their expenses and supervise them. As volunteers, contact persons/families are ordinary people who have no special training in psychology or social work, but they have the necessary spare time, an adeptness in establishing contact and a feeling of solidarity with people who have social problems, and an ability to provide support to the parents and children in question.

It is common for a child to stay overnight regularly with contact families and for contact persons to undertake various activities with children outside the home, such as helping them with schoolwork. The system must not be used as a resource for supervising and maintaining control of clients. It is not seen as appropriate to use this system if the family's problems are so severe or the home situation is so negative for the children that out-of-home placement should be considered. On the other hand, the problems should not be so minor that the child's needs could be met in other ways, for example by relatives or others with whom the family or children have close emotional ties, or through different forms of group activity. The contact process is reviewed twice a year and can last for a number of years.

## A STUDY CONCERNING FAMILIES WITH SMALL CHILDREN

What do social workers do in cases involving small children? That was the main question in a research project concerning all 0–3-year-old children, in 14 local social welfare offices in 10 municipalities, who had been considered as child welfare cases during a particular year (Andersson, 1992). For the 189 children in the study, the intervention used most often was appointing a contact family. As I was unfamiliar with this system, I looked for research reports and evaluations but realized eventually that, since the Social Services Act 1980 was implemented (1982), the contact person/family facility was being used more and more often without being evaluated or attracting researchers. So I went back to the social services agencies involved in my study and interviewed the social welfare inspectors. I wanted to find an answer to questions such as how they used the system for families with small children (0–3 years old) and what they thought of it. I then interviewed the children's contact families in three of the 10 municipalities (Andersson, 1993).

## From the Point of View of Social Agencies

The following information was given by the 16 social welfare inspectors (leaders of the groups of child welfare workers) in the 14 local social welfare agencies in the 10 municipalities who were handling the cases of the 189 children, all of them 0–3 years old, in my above-mentioned study.

The inspectors agreed that contact families are most frequently used to support single mothers with social problems, especially young mothers and mothers with many children. Making it possible for the children to spend one or two weekends every month, and/or certain afternoons during the week, away from home gives the mother some time for herself. It enables her to get some rest and some breathing space, which may help her to take better care of her children. About half of the social welfare inspectors also pointed out that a contact family provides the parent(s) with an extended network and with the opportunity to receive advice and support in their parenting.

Less than half of the inspectors made any mention of the possible benefits of this service for the children. Those that did mention the benefits to children maintained that it could give the children the opportunity to meet adults (as role models) other than their parent(s), to have peace and quiet not experienced at home, to receive stimulation, and to partake in new activities and experience a more structured everyday life than was possible at home. Some of the inspectors stated explicitly that they tended to take the perspective of the adult and not that of the child. Some also doubted whether it was good for children under 3 years of age to be moved to another family. A few of the inspectors also mentioned a control aspect or a sense of security in knowing that the contact family would call if something serious were to happen to the child—particularly in cases where the inspectors were doubtful of the parenting ability of the parent(s). Most of the inspectors had some critical comments on the use of contact families. These included:

- The system was being routinely applied without adequate consideration of its purpose.
- It was being used for lack of a better alternative, or to avoid taking a child into foster care.

Most of the inspectors who were interviewed emphasized the importance of not placing too great a burden on contact persons/families. Often, undue advantage was taken of them, considering the difficult tasks they faced and that they sometimes had to assume full care of the children, even if they had no intention initially of becoming foster parents. There was consensus that cooperation between the social worker and the contact family was far from satisfactory because they seldom met, and usually only when it was time for the twice-yearly review. The possibility that contact families might report to social workers matters which the clients wished to be kept confidential—a reasonable fear in a system involving control—was not considered a problem at all, since no such reporting appeared to occur. Instead, the fact that contact persons/families often seemed to be left to themselves could explain their taking sides with client families as strongly as they did. It was felt that they reported very little to the social workers. Contact persons/families were clearly seen as being closer to the client family than to the social worker. Surprisingly, contact persons/families seldom complained about the difficulty of the tasks they faced. The system was considered to be in great demand and appreciated by the clients. The demand was so great that the costs had become considerable, even if the pay was low.

The social welfare inspectors differed in their opinions on what this form of intervention meant for the child, and they were unclear about what it meant for a very young child to have a contact family. Some inspectors felt that it might not be particularly good for a young child to spend every second or fourth weekend in another family. Others considered it to be so normal for a child to spend both days and nights with grandparents or with a divorced father that doing so with a contact family would not seem strange at all. Still others pointed out that having an extra family could be an enriching experience for a child if its own family had the kinds of shortcomings characterizing many of the client families. Most of the inspectors stated that they thought about the parent(s) more than the child in connection with the system and that they assumed that what was good for the mother (or in a few cases the single father) was also good for the child. If the mother was given support and was relieved of some of her duties, it would have a positive effect on the child.

### The Views of Contact Families

There were 16 contact families for the 21 children in the sample (from three of the 10 municipalities in the original study). In the interviews carried out with the contact families, attention was largely devoted to the contact with the particular child in the sample and his or her parent(s), but some of the questions also pertained to experiences with other children and their parent(s). All those interviewed were women, except for one man who took part in the interview with his wife. It was quite obvious that the women carried out most of the contact work even if they had a husband to help. For their paid employment all the women worked in care or nursing, except for one librarian—none of them was simply a housewife. Their reasons for becoming a contact person/family were quite similar: a desire to be with children; a desire to help other people; being brought up in a family with great openness towards other children or young people; and having a lifestyle that allowed scope for this sort of work in one's spare time. None of them reported doing this sort of work for the money, although they felt that they would not take on the job if there was no remuneration at all. A few of them had continued their contact with the client after social services were no longer involved.

The 21 children in the sample belonged to 16 families. In 10 of the families the children had a single mother, in three a single father, and in three both parents. According to the interviewees, half of the parents had drug problems, others suffered from mental illness or learning disabilities, and in a few cases there were other kinds of problems which reduced parental strength and capacity. The interviewees clearly felt themselves to be closer to the client family than to the social worker. Asked to compare their feelings of closeness to parents or children, they all replied 'both the parent(s) and the child' or 'the child'. Most of them felt that they meant a lot to the child, but there appeared to be no contradiction between having insight into family problems and serving the interests of both the children and the parents, as is sometimes the case in foster care.

Many of the contact persons and families complained that social workers were often replaced and that they did not know which social worker was responsible at the moment. Their remarks regarding cooperation with the social worker could be summed up as 'there is no cooperation, we never have meetings'. Some of them were less dissatisfied than others with this state of affairs. However, many of them had little experience of the problems they encountered, and they would have liked to have had someone to discuss the issues that arose, offer advice and appreciate what they were doing. Most of them wanted supervision, either from the social worker or some outside person.

## THE STOCKHOLM STUDY: FOUR DIFFERENT PERSPECTIVES

In a large-scale study from Stockholm (Sundell et al., 1994) one-third of contact families (200 families) received a questionnaire to complete, after which 50 of the client families were interviewed as well as the 50 social workers involved. Lastly, 30 of the children involved were interviewed. This study is an evaluation of the contact family facility from four different perspectives: the contact families, the parents, the social workers, and the children.

Of the contact families, 158 answered the questionnaire. It was shown that most of them were Swedish, married or cohabiting couples, and two-thirds of them were aged between 40 and 59 years. Compared with the population in Stockholm as a whole, more of the sample had been in higher education and more lived in private housing. A majority of the women in the contact families worked in social services, in medical and health services, or in school or pre-school provision (including day care). The men in the contact families had a variety of other professions. About half of the contact families had expressed an interest in this work to social services, and about one-third had been asked by the client family whom they knew beforehand. Their main motive for being a contact family was to give help and support. The most common frequency of contact was for the child to stay with the contact family every third weekend. They described what they did as 'ordinary everyday life' plus some activities such as cinema and sports. The length of contact with the children in the study was between eight months and 11 years, with a mean of three years.

The interviews with the 50 client families showed that most of them were lone-parent families (compared with a fifth of the families in Stockholm), and most of them were single mothers. Only two children lived with both parents and 80% of the absent fathers had infrequent or no contact at all with their child. Of the 57 children with a contact family, one-third were 2–6 years old, more than half were 7–12 years old and the rest were 13–18 years old. When they were introduced to the contact family, the children were on average not quite 5 years old, and one-third of them were under 3. Immigrant families were under-represented, while families living in apartment buildings were over-represented. Parents with severe social problems, such as drug addiction, mental-health problems and domestic violence, were also over-represented.

Most of the parents (84%) thought that their situation had improved since they got their contact family and only three (6%) thought that their situation had worsened. Two-thirds of the parents thought that getting a contact family was the intervention best matching their needs, and a fifth of them said it 'partly' matched their needs. Some mentioned that a responsible father or supportive relatives had been better. The parents (80%) mentioned advantages for the children, such as getting to know other adults and adults serving as role models for them. Having new experiences and learning new things were also mentioned as advantages for the child, as well as the opportunity to get a little break from parents and siblings. The most frequently mentioned advantage for the parents (84%) was a break from the children: they could rest, see other people or have more time for the siblings at home. Only a small group mentioned disadvantages, for example that the father in the contact family was not a good role model for the child because he was not involved, that siblings at home got envious if they did not have a contact family, or that they themselves felt inadequate or degraded. Three-quarters of the parents wanted to keep in contact with the contact family after a formal termination of the intervention.

Of the 30 children chosen at random to be interviewed, one-third were 4–6 years old, more than half were 7–12 years old and a few were teenagers. Most liked to go to the contact family and, when asked what they did there, most of them mentioned play and sports activities. A third mentioned outings and picnics, and some to intellectual activities, such as reading books and going to museums. Those who had complaints referred to the food, bedtimes or not having enough to do. When asked about differences from home, almost half described difference in a neutral way, such as there were more family members in the contact family, that they lived in a private house, and did other things with the children or had more time for them. When asked why they had a contact family, one-third of the children had no answer and almost half thought of their mother's need for a break. A smaller group said it was because of problems in the family. Only three children (10%) said it was because it was sometimes nice for them to have an opportunity to come away from home. Asked whom they would talk to about problems if their parents were not available, a third of the children said they would turn to the contact family, a third to other adults (for example, in school or pre school) and a third said they would talk to nobody.

All four groups taking part in the study were asked to describe the purpose(s) or aim(s) of the system. Their replies fell into three categories:

- To stimulate and support the children
- To give the parents advice and support
- To relieve the parent(s) by taking care of the children.

There was little agreement among the social workers, contact families, parents and children about the main aim. While most of the social workers and contact families took relief for the parents into consideration, they primarily emphasized support for the parental role and the children's upbringing. The parents emphasized relief and did not want the contact family to take part in the raising of their children. Only a few of the parents mentioned support in the parental role. The children were quite unclear about the aims. Either they had no idea at all or believed that the aim was relief for the mother. However, there was considerable satisfaction with the system, and the most satisfied were the contact families. Only one-third mentioned problems at all and in these cases they referred most often to the lack of support from the social workers. Most of the parents were satisfied too, and believed that the family situation had changed for the better since they were assigned a contact family.

Three-quarters of the parents, primarily those with severe social problems, wanted continued contact with the support family after the formal ending of the facility. Most of the children liked to go to the contact family, wanted to go there more often, or were satisfied with the arrangements. The researchers, however, raise three objections to the system:

- There is a risk that social workers will not try hard enough to activate the families' informal networks: the relatives, and the father of the child.
- Contact families were often used as the only support for families with considerable social problems—and not as a supplement.
- Many social workers (as well as contact families) set their expectations of the contact family service too high, not only for relief for the parent but also for social and emotional support and parental education.

However, the conclusion is that the contact family could be an important relief for parents and a valuable supplement to families with an insufficient informal network. A contact family also focuses on the child in a way that is unusual for social services provision for families in need. Social services contact tends to be short term and focus on problems rather than providing a stable one-to-one relationship to the child.

## TWO PAPERS ON CHILDREN'S PERSPECTIVES

Two student dissertations were undertaken in this area. They are based on interviews with ten 4–10-year-old children (Börjesson and Held, 1994) and nine 7–12-year-old children (Ottosson and Persson, 1995). The children's views were quite similar in both studies, but fewer in the first study knew why they had a contact family. It was common for those who could give a reason to mention the mother's need of relief (from the child). Some of the younger children said that they went to the contact family because they wanted to and liked going there; others said that their experience had not been positive at the beginning but they now liked to go there. The positive aspects mentioned were the contact family's pets or the animals at the farm where the contact family lived, playing and playmates and/or sports and recreational activities. The negative aspects were homesickness and rules that differed from those at home, for example earlier bedtimes. Most of the children believed that the mother had arranged for the contact family herself and were unaware of social services' involvement. Apparently, the social workers had not asked the children about their views or attempted to involve them in the family support provision. In one of the studies the students also read through the client files and could find no evidence of the social workers having talked with the children about the arrangement or the wishes of the child.

## Child Welfare Files

Some student dissertations are based on studies of child welfare files and usually these studies had to be combined with interviews, because the files gave very little information. Nygaard (2000) stresses the fact that the documentation in the files was brief and unsystematic, when she was trying to find details of the 27 children and young people with a contact person/family during 1999 in a small municipality (less than 15 000 inhabitants). Half of the children were under 13, and 10 were girls. The boys (age range 2–20) were on average younger than the girls (age range 5–23). The majority of the children and young people had a single mother (22 of 27) and the father was largely absent. There were also a few young people in independent living.

Family conflicts were mentioned in 10 cases and parents' drug abuse in five cases. The child's own criminal behaviour, or concerns about his or her use of drugs, were referred to in five cases, and four cases mentioned the child's aggressiveness and school difficulties. The age of the child seemed to be a significant factor in the decision to appoint a contact person, because none of these children was under 12. However, the age of the child seemed less significant for the process of arranging a contact family. For children under the age of 13 their own behaviour was seldom mentioned as a factor; instead, the needs of the mother were noted. The author points out that, on the whole, children not yet in their teens are quite invisible and the needs of the child were mentioned only in relation to older children—for example, the need for adequate adult support or a male role model. The task for the contact person could be to do activities with the child or to support the child's or young person's everyday life and keep him or her away from drugs, although it was usually not very precisely formulated. Whether the contact person/family had already been part of the child's extended network could not be ascertained from the files. The concluding question is: How can the contact person/family be understood as a protective factor if the children's needs and voices are absent from the files?

## DISCUSSION

A contact person/family is a statutory support measure in child welfare with the purpose of preventing identified family problems deteriorating. The support is officially provided to the children but is in reality intended for the whole family and looked upon as a preventive measure (on a tertiary level). The contact person/family is seen as one measure, possible to use in a very flexible way, although it is more common for younger children to have a contact family and for older children and young people to have a contact person. The system has been used increasingly every year since the Social Services Act came into force in 1982, and by 1999 covered 1% of all children and young people aged 0–20. It is hard to believe that it has been evaluated so little by social services and has attracted so few researchers. However, it seems to be the case in many countries that research is less common for family support than for more far-reaching interventions, such as out-of-home placements. It is also less usual to evaluate routine and ordinary measures than new projects and well-defined programmes. It is also complicated to characterize the supportive process or define outcome criteria. Satisfaction can be seen as one outcome criterion. From the few studies presented in this chapter, we can conclude that the contact person/family is surprisingly satisfactory for all parties concerned, although the reasons vary.

The importance of the child's perspective, and of considering children's views in decisions affecting their lives, has been strongly reaffirmed in recently revised legislation in Sweden, as it has in many other countries. Increasing attention is also being paid to research from the children's perspective. A paradigm shift is underway with respect to children (James and Prout, 1990; Tiller, 1991; Qvortrup et al., 1994), whereby children are seen as subjects, active co-creators and valuable informants on their world and their relationships. There is also a greater interest in the everyday circumstances of the child's life in the here-and-now. However, as Ann Oakley (1994) asks: What would it *really* mean to study the world from the standpoint of children both as knowers and as actors? This is a relevant question for social work. The lack of a child orientation in social work—and in social work research—is a fact not only in Sweden (Andersson et al., 1996) but also in other countries (Butler and Williamson, 1994; Hill and Aldgate, 1996; Hill, 1997; Sinclair, 1998).

Although the child is the client within the contact person/family system, it is not absolutely clear who the service is really aimed at. Family support is often seen as relief for the single mother, who sends the children to a contact family every second or third weekend. That seems to be enjoyable for the children, too. They appreciate being away from home at times, going to the countryside, busying themselves with the other children in the contact family, or with the pets, and taking part in play, sport, picnics and other outings and activities. However, most of them think it is for the mother's benefit, because she needs a break, and they would rather be at home. Not until the children are in their teens do social services seem to think of them as separate people with needs of their own. The service has the potential to be an important protective factor, strengthening the resilience of vulnerable children or children at risk (cf. Gilligan, 1999; Rutter, 1990; Werner and Smith, 1992). The children get adult support or an alternative adult role model, a supplementary or extended family, support in their school work, stimulating activities and encouragement for leisure-time interests. The few voices of children presented here seem to show that the system is satisfactory for children. It is, without doubt, desirable to learn more about children's and young people's perspectives on having a contact person or contact family, and what it means to them in the short and long term.

The family is of crucial importance for a child and, of course, supporting the mother has a supportive function for the child, too. If a single mother (or father) with social problems and without a natural supportive network receives some relief to gain new strength, the children will benefit. When children are in their teens, it seems more common to think the other way round, that support for the child has a supportive function for the mother. There is a widespread practice in social work to focus on the mother in the family and look upon her as responsible for the children—and neglect to involve the absent father. There is also a tendency for contact families to focus on the mother, although the child has a pronounced need of a father figure or a male role model. The focus on mothers in child welfare is commented on by several researchers (Farmer and Owen, 1998; Hutchison, 1992; Smith, 1991; Swift, 1995; Turney, 2000).

The contact family system seems to a great extent to be an arrangement between mothers, but there is less certainty about contact persons, because even less is known about them. Most of the parents (i.e. mothers) interviewed seem to be satisfied with the service and look upon it as supportive and as contributing to improvements in the family situation. Many would like to keep in touch with the contact family after the formal arrangement ends. So, from the clients' point of view, the system seems to be supportive and satisfactory, although the contact families have commented that clients appreciated the relief more than the advice and support for their parenting.

Contact persons are volunteers in the public sector; they are people without special training but are approved of, paid (a small sum) and supervised by social services. The assessment for being accepted as a contact family differs, but it has been more common for social services agencies to be as careful as in the selection of foster parents, because it often happens that children may require their contact family to act as a foster family. The need for the facility is reconsidered twice a year and that seems to be the sole contact with the responsible social worker for most of the contact persons/families. Most of them tend to rely on their own competence and do not request a more frequent contact with social services for solving problems, but they do express the need for some encouragement and appreciation of their work. There is no doubt that those interviewed feel closer to the child and his or her family than to social services. There appeared to be no contradiction between gaining insight into the social problems of a family and serving the interests of both children and parents. No such conflicts as those encountered in foster care between the foster parents and the natural parents were reported.

It seems that the contact person/family facility in the Social Services Act has succeeded in breaking the connections with its roots in the probation measures in the old law. It is surprising that there should be no mechanism for finding out what contact persons/families, as well as clients, are saying about the system. It seems to be family support rather than child protection. Contact persons and families have the potential to be part of the extended family of children and families in need, although objections have been raised that, as a result, social services possibly fail to work hard enough to involve the natural networks. There are many research questions to be answered from the perspectives of contact persons and contact families: what the system means to them, how they perceive their relationship with children and parents, and what they do to support their clients. There are also questions to be answered about the role they play in the social services system, and between the family and the State.

The social workers interviewed emphasized the importance of not placing too great a burden on contact families, even if they thought they did. They also said that their cooperation with the contact families was far from satisfactory, because they seldom met. The possibility that contact families might report matters to social workers, which the clients wished to keep confidential, was not considered to be a problem. On the contrary, some social workers had the feeling that the contact families were too close to the client family and worked too hard before reporting an unsatisfactory state of affairs. Although social workers and team leaders had some doubts about the increasing use of the system, they had a positive view on its supportive function and it was clearly in great demand. However, they could not clearly specify how it was used because of the lack of evaluation. The small study on social work files showed that often no working plans were drawn up, documented or followed up. Perhaps this is a way to avoid the controlling aspect and accentuate the supportive role? It seems natural to think that as long as the parties involved are content and do not make complaints, and the intentions of prevention and support are not called into question, why worry or make up bureaucratic rules and guidelines?

When research is undertaken on social work practice in Sweden, social workers often feel criticized for their carelessness in documentation and lack of assessment, follow-up work and evaluation. That must be seen against the background of the Social Services Act as a legal framework without de-tailed guidelines and leaving much social work to professional discretion and the decisions of social services committees (politically chosen boards) in the 189 different municipalities. Social workers are also criticized for not con-tinuously informing themselves about research or using research results in their professional work. As a researcher, of course I would like research to be used to a greater extent than is currently the case. However, I would be very careful when doing evaluations and research work on the contact per-son/family system to reflect on the areas to be studied, whether focusing on the support process or the preventive outcome. It is important to pay atten-tion to aspects of class, ethnicity, age, gender and rural/urban environment to understand support and explain outcomes. I have a positive perception of the system through the few studies presented in this chapter and have not found any evidence of damaging effects. The system has the potential to focus on children and their best interests, while still including the whole family and contributing to an extended network for vulnerable children and families. There is a need to augment the knowledge of the system from different perspectives and explore its values beyond the discourse of costs and benefits.

## REFERENCES

Andersson, G. (1992) Social workers and child welfare. *British Journal of Social Work*, **22**, 253–269.

Andersson, G. (1993) Support and relief: The Swedish contact person and contact family program. *Scandinavian Journal of Social Welfare*, **2**, 54–62.

Andersson, G., Aronsson, K., Hessle, S., Hollander, A. and Lundström, T. (1996) *Barnet i den sociala barnavården* (The Child in Child Welfare). Stockholm: CUS/Liber.

Börjesson, A. and Held, C. (1994) *'Jag tycker om att vara hemma också.' Intervjuer med 10 barn som har kontaktfamilj* ('I like to be at home, too.' Interviews with 10 children who have a contact family). Lund University: School of Social Work (paper).

Butler, I. and Williamson, H. (1994) *Children Speak. Children, Trauma and Social Work.* Essex: Longman.

Farmer, E. and Owen, M. (1998) Gender and the child protection process. *British Journal of Social Work*, **28**, 545–564.

Furstenberg, F. (1997) State–family alliances and children's welfare. A research agenda. *Childhood*, **4**, 183–192.

Gilbert, N. (1997) Conclusion. A comparative perspective. In N. Gilbert (Ed.), *Combatting Child Abuse. International Perspectives and Trends.* New York: Oxford University Press.

Gilligan, R. (1999) 'It's just common sense isn't it?' Exploring ways of putting the theory of resilience into action. *Adoption and Fostering*, **23**, 6–15.

Gould, A. (1988) *Conflict and Control in Welfare Policy. The Swedish Experience.* London: Longman.

Hessle, S. and Vinnerljung, B. (1999) *Child Welfare in Sweden—An Overview.* Stockholm University: Department of Social Work, Stockholm Studies of Social Work, 15.

Hill, M. (1997) Participatory research with children. *Child and Family Social Work*, **3**, 171–183.

Hill, M. and Aldgate, J. (Eds) (1996) *Child Welfare Services. Developments in Law, Policy, Practice and Research.* London: Jessica Kingsley Publishers.

Hutchison, E.D. (1992) Child welfare as a woman's issue. *Families in Society: Journal of Contemporary Human Services.* CEU Article 19, February: 67–78.

James, A. and Prout, A. (Eds) (1990) *Constructing and Reconstructing Childhood: Contemporary Issues in the Sociological Study of Childhood.* London: Falmer Press.

Lundström, T. and Wijkström, F. (1997) *The Nonprofit Sector in Sweden.* New York: Manchester University Press.

National Board of Health and Welfare (2000) *Insatser för barn och unga 1999* (Measures for Children and Young People 1999). Stockholm: Socialstyrelsen, Socialtjänst.

Nygaard, K. (2000) *Kontaktperson/familj. En insats för vem?* (Contact person/family. A measure for whom?) Lund University: School of Social Work (paper).

Oakley, A. (1994) Women and children first and last: Parallels and differences between children's and women's studies. In B. Mayall (Ed.), *Children's Childhoods: Observed and Experienced.* London: Falmer Press.

Olsson Hort, S.E. (1997) Sweden. Toward a deresidualization of Swedish child welfare policy and practice? In N. Gilbert (Ed.), *Combatting Child Abuse. International Perspectives and Trends.* New York: Oxford University Press.

Ottosson, A.L. and Persson, M. (1995) *'Vi har det bra hemma också.' En undersökning om barns upplevelser av att ha kontaktfamilj* ('We have a good time at home, too.' A study about children's perception of having a contact family). Lund University: School of Social Work (paper).

Qvortrup, J., Bardy, M., Sgritta, G. and Wintersberger, H. (Eds) (1994) *Childhood Matters. Social Theory, Practice and Politics.* Aldershot: Avebury and European Centre Vienna.

Rutter, M. (1990) Psychosocial resilience and protective mechanisms. In A.J. Rolf, A.S. Masten, D. Ciccetti, K.H. Neuchterlein and S. Weintraub (Eds), *Risk and Protective Factors in the Development of Psychopathology.* Cambridge: Cambridge University Press.

Sinclair, R. (1998) Involving children in planning their care (research review). *Child and Family Social Work,* **3**, 137–142.

Smith, B. (1991) Australian women and foster care: A feminist perspective. *Child Welfare,* **LXX**, 175–184.

Sundell, K., Humlesjö, E. and Carlsson, M. (1994) *Att hjälpa sin nästa. En undersökning av kontaktfamiljer i Stockholm* (To help your neighbour. A study of contact families in Stockholm). Stockholm: Socialtjänsten FoU-rapport 15.

Svenska Kommunförbundet (2000) *Kontaktperson/familj/vänner 2000. En insats enl SoL* (Contact person/family/friends 2000. A Measure according to SSA). Stockholm: Svenska Kommunförbundet.

Swift, K. (1995) *Manufacturing 'Bad Mothers'. A Critical Perspective on Child Neglect.* Toronto: University of Toronto Press.

Tiller, P.O. (1991) Barnperspektivet: Om å se og bli sett (The child perspective: Seeing and being seen). *Barn. Nytt fra Forskning om Barn i Norge,* **1**, 72–77.

Turney, D. (2000) The feminizing of neglect. *Child and Family Social Work,* **5**, 47–56.

Weightman, K. and Weightman, A. (1995) Never right, never wrong: Child welfare and social work in England and Sweden. *Scandinavian Journal of Social Welfare,* **4**, 75–84.

Werner, E. and Smith, R. (1992) *Overcoming the Odds.* New York: Cornell University.

# Part IV

# TOWARDS AN INTERNATIONAL AGENDA

# 16

# INTERNATIONAL CONVERGENCE AND DIVERGENCE

## Towards an Open System Model in the Evaluation of Family Support

### Ilan Katz and John Pinkerton

This chapter returns to the questions posed at the end of Chapter 1: What seem to be emerging as key themes of convergence and divergence internationally? Is it desirable and feasible to work towards a unified global view of family support? What has evaluation to offer the future development of family support world wide? Taking into account the contributions to this book from various perspectives and national contexts, it will be suggested that there is a recognisable, shared global phenomenon which can usefully be termed 'family support'. It is a phenomenon that is expressed both in terms of characteristics of need, reflecting the pressure and change being experienced by the family as a social institution across the globe, and a service response to that need which expresses shared features of style and format reflecting a growing international agreement that certain ways of providing support to families can be demonstrated to work.

For family support to be considered a global phenomenon there needs to be agreement that it can be defined as a coherent set of means and ends and shares a coherent value base. Such agreement should not deny the complexity and contested aspects of both the purposes and outcomes associated with family support. Fundamental to reaching the necessary international consensus on these matters is arriving at a shared theory base. It will be argued here that the appropriate way forward for achieving that is to use international experience to generate an integrated theory of family social ecology expressing an open system perspective, and recognising power, conflict and unintended

consequences. Such a theory would both value and require continual evaluation of family support policy and practice through international comparison
in order to ensure the critical reflexivity it must have at its core.

In the light of the material on family support and its evaluation shared in
Parts I and II of this book, this final chapter attempts to develop a rationale for,
and the beginnings of, an open system theory of family support. It considers
the implications of such a perspective for the evaluation of family support
policy and practice. Thus the chapter aims to be a further step on a road that
has been described in various ways from different national vantage points
by the other contributors—the road to understanding the challenges faced
by families and the interventions which best help them to rise to meet those
challenges. It does not attempt to suggest where the end of that road might
be, and indeed the open system perspective being argued for would suggest
that there is no such end point.

## INTERNATIONAL PERSPECTIVE

An important aim of this book was to provide a wider variety of perspectives
on the evaluation of family support than would have been possible if the contributions all came from one country. If kept within purely national contexts,
discussions of family support and its evaluation quickly get caught up in arguments about the political and administrative contingencies of the moment.
This means that the debates, while important, become well-rehearsed, repeti-
tive and predictable. In the United Kingdom such discussions tend to revolve
around such issues as levels of resource, government expectations of cost
effectiveness, and unease about the implications for existing child protection
systems. These are crucial concerns, but it requires the re-framing of a global
perspective to move them on through suggesting new ways of thinking and
identifying new opportunities for development (Hetherington, Chapter 6 in
this volume).

Within the material brought together in this book there is clear evidence
that, in all the countries covered, at the core of family support lies concern
with pressures and change in family life. This global concern includes such
issues as:

- increasing diversity and fragmentation within family life and of communities;
- the breaking down of traditional support systems for parents;
- increasing degrees of behaviour and emotional problems in children;
- the changing role of men in relation to family life.

It is also apparent that these issues manifest in particular ways in different
countries, and in different cultural contexts within countries. The degree of

policy attention addressed to different family problems, and to the family as an institution, also varies between different countries at different times. However the types of issues raised by contributors to this book—such as child abuse, teenage pregnancy, lack of fathering, single parenthood, teenage delinquency and crime and cultural erosion—all appear to be causes for global concern. There also appear to be common themes in the characteristics of the delivery of services to troubled families. In the past 20 years, the major trend in the delivery of services has been managerialism. This is characterised by:

- the view that users of public services are 'consumer citizens' and that public services are (or should be) seen as similar to services or products delivered by the private sector to its customers;
- the need to demonstrate that services are effective and cost effective;
- reduction in universal services and increased targeting on vulnerable groups, therefore increasing the use of assessment as a gatekeeper to services.

Another seemingly global pattern is that the delivery of these services and policies are subject to tensions which constantly undermine any straight-forward solution to the issues confronting families in modern life. For example:

- the promotion of day care outside the family to facilitate a flexible workforce in pursuit of ever-increasing productivity versus the pressure on parents to spend more 'quality time' with their children;
- targeting services at the most needy, deserving or likely to benefit as opposed to the provision of open access universal services;
- tailoring services to meet local need and take into account local traditions versus the development of services incorporating internationally proven methods;
- implementing centralised 'joined up' strategies to ensure consistent quality and equality, or operational flexibility to meet variation in local circumstances;
- the increasing professionalisation of family support versus the impetus to involve users and community members in policy development and service delivery;
- the tension between 'care' and 'control' in the delivery of welfare to children and families.

These tensions, while global, are manifested differently according to the particular circumstances of countries or systems. The national responses to these tensions also take different forms. These variations in need, and service responses to that need, reflect national differences in civil society and State structure. They provide a rich stock of cultural, economic and political variations across the world. This book has shown how some of the global dilemmas relating to families and family support are addressed in a number of different parts of the world and how evaluation can contribute to the development of responses to what are at core similar problems. Within these rather random national snapshots of the development of family support and its evaluation at a particular moment in its history, it is clear that there are areas of confusion and underdevelopment. Implicit in every chapter and explicit in some are two core questions:

- Is a unifying, global definition of family support emerging?
- Is there a developing consensus about how best to evaluate family support?

## DIRECTION WITHIN DIVERSITY?

If those two core questions are addressed through trying to locate the material presented in the preceding chapters within the combined family support evaluation framework presented in Chapter 1 (see Figure 1.1), both convergence and divergence become apparent. Divergence or, perhaps more accurately, diversity is expressed in the emphasis given in the various accounts of evaluation to the different policy frameworks, types of service, forms of service delivery, target populations and programmes about which the contributors chose to write. In some countries the national strategic priorities set by the State are apparent, and so the evaluation frame included within Figure 1.1 (Chapter 1) encompasses all the components of family support shown in the figure—from civil society and the State down to outcomes. In other countries family support is fragmented and localised, thereby largely restricting evaluation to a focus on particular aspects of programmes or projects. Diversity is also apparent in the wide range of activities undertaken in the programmes and projects covered: drop in programmes, practical help, volunteer outreach, centre-based parent training, group work, crèche facilities, preparation for employment, benefits and budgeting advice, community development, intensive therapeutic work, structured preventive child protection interventions, and advocacy all appear in the previous chapters. These are used to engage many different types of service user, from socially isolated pregnant women, to children from deprived communities in their first years at school, and to troubled and troublesome young people, in processes to achieve outcomes to meet their varied needs.

Within all this diversity, however, there are also signs of an underlying convergence. For example, there is an increasing commitment to move from fragmented responses to expressed need towards strategic responses to assessed need and from local to nationally driven policy and practice interventions. The national case studies drew attention to how in some countries, such as Hong Kong, Sweden and Ireland, national strategies or frameworks for service delivery have been put in place, while in others, such as the USA and the UK, where policy on family support has historically been fragmented and piecemeal, policy making is beginning to be developed coherently at a national level.

Another area of convergence is the adoption of ecological models, either explicitly or implicitly, as the theoretical basis for understanding needs and services and developing theories of change. This suggests that there is a basis for family support to become a field of enquiry in its own right. There is also a great deal of consistency about the values that underpin family support work. Most of what is described and discussed in the previous chapters is rooted in an empowering, voluntaristic and preventive value base.

The experiences and ideas shared in both the general perspective and the case study sections show that the policy, practice and evaluation of family support are inextricably bound to each other but not in a straightforward way. A number of contributors drew attention to the growing emphasis on evidence-based policy and practice in which evaluation is playing an increasingly important role. It was also pointed out that this development not only holds out the possibility of benefits but also represents a major challenge. The benefits are more or less self evident:

- The growth of a body of literature of rigorously evaluated family support programmes and policies shows that family support 'works', in that it achieves the objectives of the policy makers, practitioners and service users.
- Evaluation will refine and develop services so that more effective and cost-effective methods can be utilised to achieve these policy and practice objectives.
- Evaluation will help ensure that the views of users, both adult and children, will be taken into account when developing new services and policies.

## Effectiveness

But what of the challenges? The most obvious challenge is that evaluation will demonstrate that family support does not work. This fear accompanies any rigorous focus on programmes, and is entirely understandable. It is also justified to the extent that it is by no means yet clear that family support is effective. This was acknowledged in those chapters where this question was addressed either in general terms or for specific evaluations, and this mixed picture is supported by others in the field. Some large-scale analyses of the results of evaluation have shown positive outcomes for children (Karoly et al., 1998; Buchanan, 1999; Olds et al., 1986; Statham, 2000; Webster-Stratton, 1999). In terms of early intervention, research indicates that programmes which target first-time mothers during pregnancy and continue until after the first year of the baby's life are most effective (Olds et al., 1997; Seeley et al., 1996). They also show that the more rigorously a programme is implemented, the better the outcomes. However, as illustrated in earlier chapters, most programmes are adapted and changed to meet local needs or conditions in the field. This is appropriate from a practice point of view but lessens their effectiveness—or at least the capacity of evaluators to demonstrate their effectiveness. Evaluations of 'field' as opposed to 'clinical' programmes have consistently shown them to be less effective (Weisz and Wiess, 1993). For example a recent overview of five home visitation programmes in the USA concluded that:

> Several home visiting models produced some benefits in parenting or in the prevention of child abuse and neglect on at least some measures. No model produced large or consistent benefits in child development or in the rates of health-related behaviors such as acquiring immunizations or well-baby check-ups. Only two program models included in this journal issue explicitly sought to alter maternal life course, and, of those, one produced significant effects at more than one site when assessed with rigorous studies.
>
> (Gomby et al., 1999, p. 4)

From a UK perspective, Little and Mount (1999, p. 86), while concluding that early intervention does benefit children, say of the prevention of health problems:

> Possibly because they have been more open to evaluation, the known effects of prevention and social activity to improve children's health are frequently disappointing.... Activity around the birth of the child has an effect on rates of delinquency, maltreatment, family breakdown and educational failure. What is not known, however, is whether still more problems would be prevented if these resources were better targeted. Evaluation on these lines is much needed.

Overall the results of evaluations of family support show a high level of satisfaction by users and some evidence of at least short-term modest but beneficial outcomes. But the fact is that it is difficult to change people's lives, and that short-term interventions are likely to have short-term benefits. Nevertheless the evidence even for that conclusion needs more confirmation and could be greatly strengthened by cross-national comparison. To be useful, such investigation would require something that is currently conspicuously absent: theory and evidence identifying the mechanisms and constituent factors that lead to positive outcomes. Insofar as research has addressed this issue, it would seem to indicate that some of the factors which practitioners and policy makers have thought to be important are not the main determinants influencing the success of programmes. Freude-Lagevardi and Barnes (2002) conclude that such issues as the method of work, the training of the practitioners and the model of intervention have relatively little effect on the outcomes, and that even intensity and duration are of secondary importance.

They conclude that:

> ... the participants' perceptions or beliefs, rather than other factors such as professional versus paraprofessional status or programme intensity/duration may ultimately determine programme outcome and success.

The indications are that it is the process of engagement between the programme and its potential users rather than the details of the intervention itself which are the most significant factors. Once participants are engaged, then other factors such as the type of intervention and its duration become more salient. Ball (2001) found that the most effective services were those offered in consultation with the local community, and where there are a combination of services offered. She also found that the earlier a service is offered, the more effective it tends to be. Budde (Chapter 12 in this volume) showed that evaluations of programme implementation can be as sophisticated and as relevant as outcome evaluations, and that techniques for rigorously evaluating implementation will have to develop alongside the development of more rigorous outcome measures.

## Definition

Trying to answer the questions of whether, and how, family support works, constantly resurrects the problem of definition. In several chapters of this book there are useful discussions of this issue and indeed recognition that the term 'evaluation' is also open to different interpretations. Although definitional issues do pose problems, they are not insurmountable. Indeed, definitional issues dog many other areas of evaluative endeavour, including child abuse (Hacking, 1999), parenting (Henricson and Roker, 2000) and day care (Belsky, 1990), and this has not prevented rigorous evaluation or effective policy making in these areas. Nevertheless it is important not to take a complacent view of the difficulties. The definitional problems are not simply technical but reflect different ideological stances and are illustrative of the different views about the relationship between children, the family and the State. Similarly the definitions of 'evaluation' reflect different and competing views about the nature of 'evidence' and 'outcomes'.

## Outcomes

Finding agreement on the vexed issue of what are or should be the desired outcomes of family support is central to making progress in unifying the field. From the overviews provided by a number of the contributors it would seem that there is a fair degree of consensus about the generic aims and objectives of family support programmes. Broadly these are to:

- help parents to become more effective in their parenting task;
- improve family functioning;
- prevent family breakdown and child maltreatment;
- improve the educational, social and emotional functioning of children and to help them maximise their own potential.

These outcomes can be seen as universal. It is hard to envisage a family support programme (or any family-based intervention) having aims which contradict them. Of course individual projects may have specific aims, such as the prevention of teenage depression or the promotion of learning through pre-school provision. They may also emphasise some of the aims rather than others, or add on aims not included in the list above. Parenting education programmes, for example tend to emphasise the first two aims whereas child welfare programmes emphasise the second two. Also, as illustrated in a number of the evaluations discussed in earlier chapters, there are taxing problems for the evaluator in finding appropriate operational indicators.

None of the above contradicts the general consensus about the desired outcomes of family-based interventions. Indeed it is tempting to regard this as an area of 'phoney wars'. An anecdote will serve to illustrate this point. Several years ago, one of the authors conducted an exercise with a number of projects providing family support, assessment and treatment services. The aim of the exercise was to develop common outcome measures that would serve as the basis of an evaluation of outcomes in the teams. Some of the teams were dominated by psychoanalytic thinking and technique, while most of them described their theoretical basis as 'systemic' or 'eclectic'. The psychoanalytic teams strenuously asserted that their work was not comparable to that of the other projects, and insisted that the outcomes of psychoanalytically based interventions were too subtle and complex to measure. Yet when asked how they would know that they had succeeded in therapy with a child they provided virtually identical criteria to those cited above, as did the other projects.

It is important to acknowledge the extent of convergence around outcomes and the opportunities which this convergence provides for drawing together the various aspects of family support. After all, as presented in Figure 1.1, outcome is the point to which all aspects of family support lead. But this general agreement also hides significant disagreements and debates. Some of the issues are as follows.

- To what extent is family support a means by which the State manages the social costs of an exploitative social and economic system?
- Is family support essentially normative and thereby restrictive or can it encompass and promote diversity?

- Does family support promote a particular model of parenting to the exclusion of others, particularly those associated with ethnic and other social minorities?
- Is family support intrinsically gender bound or is its apparent failure to engage with fathers simply a problem of finding appropriate methods of reaching out to men?
- To what extent is family support necessarily part of the 'care' component of a child welfare system rather than the 'control' side and can it be provided under compulsion or must it always be voluntary?

Crucial to answering these questions is a further issue of whether family support can be defined in terms of its methods or activities, or whether it is rather defined by its philosophy and attitudes. All of this is open to debate and contest and will have a bearing on what are defined as outcomes of family support.

## Purpose

A fourth challenge to consolidating family support and its evaluation as a coherent field of activity and study is that evaluation is not necessarily undertaken for benign purposes. There may be 'hidden agendas' attached to particular evaluations. This is a different issue from that discussed as the first challenge—that evaluation may undermine family support by demonstrating it to be ineffective. The point here is that evaluation emerged as part of the growth in 'managerialist' thinking about the delivery of public services (Clarke et al., 1994). This promotes the view that within the public sector the lack of competition creates a tendency for unnecessary rising costs which can only be curbed through the constant pursuit of demonstrable cost-effectiveness and the discipline of reduction in budgets. Several factors increase the vulnerability of family support in this context:

- the difficulty of displaying clear and measurable inputs or outcomes;
- the absence of politically important statutory responsibility for the provision of specific family support services;
- the limited capacity of family support users to defend their services as they are often the most excluded and powerless members of the community;
- the reliance on projects run by small voluntary agencies which are dependent on statutory funding;
- many family support services are short term or pilot projects and lack long-term guarantees of funding.

Although the particular evaluations reported in this book are all undertaken from a stance which is broadly sympathetic to family support in particular and welfare provision in general, the wider administrative political context is not so sympathetic. Evaluation (along with audit and inspection) can be part of a cost-cutting process, and findings could eventually be used for purposes which neither the evaluators nor those being evaluated expected when they undertook the research.

## Culture and National Policy

A fifth challenge facing family support and its evaluation is the extent to which these services can be replicated in different national and cultural contexts. It is clear from a number of the chapters dealing with general perspectives and from some of the national case studies that to evaluate specific family support projects and programmes requires understanding the broader national policy. The national policies adopted by particular States are, in turn, related to the cultural perceptions and expectations about family life and about help-seeking and support, as aspects of their national civil society. While there is this variation between countries on a strategic policy level, family support falls within the general ambit of welfare systems and there are well-known ways of grouping these, as noted in this volume by Hetherington (Chapter 6). However, at the level of practice it is more difficult to tell the extent to which services are determined by the national or cultural context. Practitioners in different countries can be describing the 'same' activity, but it can have very different meanings. Conversely people can believe that they are describing a practice unique to their own cultural context, but which is in fact very similar to something within another country. However, it is very difficult to predict the services or practices that will be easily transferable from one context to another. In the UK, family group conferencing from New Zealand (Marsh and Crow, 1998), video home guidance from the Netherlands, and Parent Training from the USA (Webster-Stratton, 1999) have caught on, whereas family preservation services, as described by Pecora (Chapter 5 in this volume), have not—despite the same expressed need to keep children out of care. Diversity and conversion are therefore not easy to describe geographically, and the evolution of services is likely to continue to display local, national and international facets.

One of the important factors associated with effective family support in Chapter 1 was cultural sensitivity. Most users of family support come from socially excluded groups, and it is therefore likely that minority ethnic groups will be well represented in the clientele—or potential clientele, because, as Butt and Box (1998) show, many families from minority ethnic communities are ill served by and do not trust mainstream services. Some of the answers to improving services to minority ethnic families are easy to identify (if difficult to implement). For example, information in different languages, culturally appropriate food, more staff from minority communities are all important for improving the quality of services to this client group. Nevertheless, there are some dilemmas which research and evaluation have still not resolved. Perhaps the most important of these is whether there should be specific targeted services for particular communities or whether there should be more emphasis on mainstream services becoming more inclusive. Of course the easy answer is that both these approaches should be taken, but this is not necessarily always appropriate or possible, for example, in areas where there are many different communities in one area. There is also a risk that too many specialist services aimed at minority communities can damage community cohesion, further marginalising some communities and creating the impression of resources being unfairly targeted.

## Gender

While the term 'family support' expresses the aspirations of services, it does not express the reality of service provision—the vast majority of service recipients are mothers rather than fathers. Parenting and parent training are similarly somewhat misleading terms, because in reality the services are aimed primarily at mothers and mothering (fathering being a recently made-up term with a rather forced meaning to it). The focus on mothers is partly due to practical considerations (mothers still undertake the vast majority of parenting tasks, and are often more available when services are delivered), but is also ideological (a focus on self-help and empowerment for women initiated by the feminist movement in the 1970s and 1980s). However, recent policy and research have resurrected the importance of fathers and positive male role models as being key to positive outcomes for children. But attempts to involve fathers in family support have not proved to be particularly successful (Henricson and Roker, 2000, Ghate et al., 2000), and this poses the question of whether the problem is one of engagement (i.e. making services more attractive to fathers, for example, by making them feel more welcome in family centres, evening opening, etc.) or whether altogether new modes of delivery need to be developed so that family support itself will look rather different.

## Theoretical Base

A seventh challenge to be addressed in the development of family support and its evaluation is anchoring it in an appropriate theoretical base. Most of the contributors in this book either explicitly or implicitly use an ecological model as the basis for describing and evaluating family support. In the UK the ecological model has now been incorporated into government guidance through the *Framework of Assessment of Children in Need and their Families* (DoH, 2000) (Figure 16.1). This is required to be used in all referrals and assessments of children by social service departments.

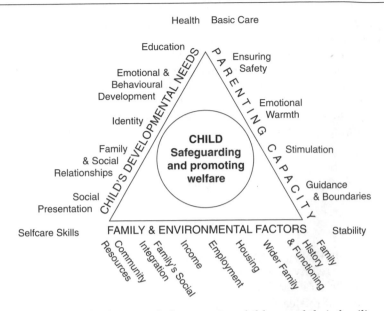

**Figure 16.1**   The framework for assessing children and their families

In a set of readings written to accompany the framework, Jack (2001) gives an insightful account of the ecological model. However, there are some differences of interpretation of this model, and these have implications for the evaluation of family support. The 'weak' version of the ecological model asserts that children should be seen in the context of their family and community, and that work with children should, as far as possible, be sensitive to the enabling and restricting aspects of this context. This view is commonplace among people engaged in family support and has a long history within both social work and social psychology. Indeed, as long ago as the 1940s Winnicott declared that 'There is no such thing as a baby' (Winnicott, 1965). What he meant was that without the mother the baby could not survive, and that it is the mother–infant dyad rather than the infant herself that should be the focus of both research and clinical work.

The 'strong' version of the ecological model sees the interactions between the different levels being as important as the characteristics of the levels themselves. This means that, for example, a family's perceptions of community safety and support are as important to both the upbringing of their children and their involvement in the community as the actual 'objective' level of safety. Interventions have to address the quality of the interaction as well as the characteristics of the layers of the system.

Although the ecological model seems well suited for understanding the relationships between individuals, families, communities and society, it has not actually been rigorously tested, and certainly not in regard to its application in evaluative research. It is relatively well established that child abuse, for example, is more prevalent in children of low socio-economic status (Cawson, 2002) and there is some evidence to show that neighbourhood variables account for some abuse (Garbarino and Eckenrode, 1997; Korbin et al., 1995), but there is little research evidence to show that intervening at the community level reduces the prevalence of child abuse, or improves the level of parenting.

The problem with both the strong and weak versions of the ecological approach is that they are based on a 'closed system' model of society, and this can lead to a rather deterministic way of thinking about need, services and evaluation. This encourages the view that changes at higher levels of the ecology will have direct effects on the lower levels and that it is in principle possible to change behaviour by changing the environment in which it occurs. However, if account is taken of concepts such as resilience and social exclusion it becomes clear that it is the dynamic interaction of forces at different levels, coming from different sources, that deliver outcomes for children and their families. For example, looking at the relationship between resilience and self-esteem, it is possible for resilience to be seen as an outcome partly caused by high self-esteem, but, conversely, high self-esteem can be seen as an outcome of resilience. Although at one level this may be seen as a logical flaw in the analysis of resilience, it can also be seen as a function of the dynamics of development in which outcomes are always contingent and transitory, and every outcome is also an input.

The resilience model can also be taken a step further. Services themselves could be seen as vulnerable or resilient, and many of the factors which determine resilience at the individual level of the child may well apply at the level of the service (or indeed the community). Services could thus be described as 'vulnerable' or 'resilient' at certain points in time. Like individual resilience, 'service resilience' would not simply be a description of certain traits inherent in the service itself, but would be seen as a function of the relationship between the service and its environment. Drawing on both the idea of social exclusion and that of resilience, three important elements need to be added to the ecological model so that it can better describe the processes involved in family support and its evaluation. These are open system, conflict and power relationships and unintended consequences.

## Thinking Open System

The closed system model is based on the notions of homeostasis and equilibrium, in which action by the system involves either adaptation to or accommodation of the environment (Bateson, 1973). In the past two decades there have been developments in systemic theorising which have moved beyond this model towards the open or complex systems approach. According to this way of thinking, most biological and social systems are not basically driven by equilibrium but rather are driven by complex and constant change. Interventions at any point in the system will create consequences, but these are not easily predictable from the initial parameters of the system, and are not necessarily proportionate to the input itself. The analogy often used to evoke this process is the butterfly flapping its wings in Tokyo causing a hurricane in Texas. In effect this model asserts that chance events can magnify the effects of small inputs into the system (and can diminish the effects of large inputs). Some policy makers accept this view, but still believe that the system can be controlled. To extend the analogy they believe it is possible to engineer the system so that the butterfly flaps its wings in a way that causes the hurricane the policy maker wishes to create. However, complexity theory suggests that this is not possible, even in principle.

It is important to recognise that this way of thinking does not imply that all outcomes are random, or that all processes are completely uncontrollable. What an open systems perspective does is to show that the process is never entirely controllable or predictable, and that there are theoretical limits to our understanding of these processes. This has profound implications for the research and evaluation of family support. It means that the processes being evaluated, and the methods used to evaluate them, are constantly changing. Factors outside the control of the evaluator and the operational staff of the programme will intervene to affect the phenomena under scrutiny, and it is very unlikely that these phenomena will be the same at the end of the evaluation from what they were at the beginning. In some cases the whole meaning of the evaluation can change.

An archetypal example of this process (although slightly outside the world of family support) occurred with Gill and Jackson's (1983) evaluation of the British Adoption Project. This was a project set up in the 1960s in response to research findings which showed that black children were very hard to place for adoption. The project set out to find adoptive homes for black children who were in care. The philosophy behind this project was that these children were hard to place because of prejudice, and that by placing black children in white homes they would be demonstrating that people from different races can live together harmoniously. Gill and Jackson followed up these children when they were teenagers. They found that the adoptees were doing well. They were achieving at school, related well to their peers and adoptive families and had high self-esteem. Almost as an aside, Gill and Jackson mentioned that these children tended to live in all white areas, did not identify with black communities and had little to do with those communities.

There was a furious reaction to these findings. Gill and Jackson were accused of being racist, of ignoring a fundamental aspect of children's well-being—their sense of ethnic or racial identity. What had happened is that the paradigm had shifted—whereas the project and its evaluation had been created in the era of 'melting pot' thinking. By the time the evalua-tion was published opinion had moved on to support for anti-racism and anti-oppressive practice. The orthodox view of well-being had been chal-lenged and the evaluation as well as the project itself were now seen as severely lacking—at best naive and at worst racist. Although this is a rather dramatic episode in the history of evaluation, it illustrates the changing nature of the institutions and forces involved in the delivery of services to children and families.

In relation to family support itself, the timing of changes in different levels of the ecology is also important. It is easier to provide direct services to a child and carer at the appropriate developmental point than to ensure that the ongoing environment is appropriate to maintain the child's functioning. Much of the resilience literature shows that there are specific points in a child's development where she is more likely to benefit from positive inputs (and conversely be damaged by negative inputs) and therefore that the timing of events in a child's life is critical (Gilligan, Chapter 4, and Shochet and Ham, Chapter 14 in this volume; see also Bifulco and Moran, 1998). However, these inputs need to be sustained over time if the child is going to have positive long-term benefits from the intervention.

While services can be put into place relatively quickly so that children can be helped at the appropriate developmental stage, communities generally take longer to change and those changes may take a long time to influence the parenting styles of community members. Of course dramatic events can and do happen in communities, such as the closing down of major employ-ers or the influx of capital from government funding. However, it is difficult to envisage these inputs at the level of the community having immediate predictable effects at the level of the family or on individual outcomes for children. Interventions at different levels of the ecology may well have ben-eficial (or deleterious) effects on children; the timing of those interventions may ensure that the children who benefit are of a later generation and not simultaneous with the intervention itself. This process also may work in the opposite direction. A family support service may improve the level of social interaction in a community and may eventually empower the community to take action to improve the local infrastructure, but again the changes at the level of the community will be within a different timescale to the changes within families who attend the service. This has important implications for the design of family support evaluation. The theory of change adopted by an evaluation must take into account the expected timescales for change at the different levels of the ecology. Having said this, the ecological model is still relatively embryonic in its ability to explain or predict interactions between different levels of the ecology.

## Conflict and Power Relationships

One of the effects of the closed system model, which it shares with the linear and circular models, is that it downplays conflict. These models imply a world view which sees conflict and tension as disruptions to the system which, if functional, operates to resolve that conflict and re-create equilibrium. Society is seen as basically benign, while conflict, tension and compulsion are seen as issues to be avoided or remedied. Much thinking about family support is at least implicitly based on this view of the world. Family support is seen as part of a virtuous circle in which individuals are empowered to take control of their own lives, and use their skills for the benefit of their children and their local community. Family support benefits not only the individual but also the family, the neighbourhood and ultimately society as a whole. The managerialist approach is a variation of this, envisaging problems as primarily technical rather than being real conflicts of interest between different stakeholders. In this view more efficient, effective and economic services are beneficial to all stakeholders, and therefore the main challenge is to put in place systems which can achieve these ends.

In contrast to that functionalist view, conflict and tension can be regarded as essential components of an open system, and although conflict is disruptive it is also creative and dynamic. This view of the world recognises and accepts the need be receptive to recurring tension. In resolving one conflict another may be generated. For example, if a group of parents who are users of a family support programme are empowered to take more responsibility for their own lives, this may not lead them to become helpers for other parents. Empowerment may instead lead to them leaving the area or excluding other parents from the resource to which they have gained access. One community may be empowered in a way that allows them to draw resources from government at the expense of other, possibly more deprived communities. These sorts of conflicts are inescapable in any process which involves social change, at the micro or the macro level. There are very few interventions which are entirely win–win and most social processes create losers as well as winners.

Related to conflict is the exercise of power, and again this has been downplayed in both the practice and evaluation of family support. Because of its basic philosophy of inclusion and consensus, family support tends to underplay power relationships, especially between families within the communities it serves. None of the chapters in this book, for example, has dealt with conflict or difficulties between user groups, or between users and service providers, and yet these issues are often in the background of services. It is surprising, for example, that gender power relationships have only recently emerged as a central issue in family support (Ghate et al., 2000). Even now many people see the problem as one of enticing fathers into using family support facilities, rather than as an issue of power and conflict within gender relations.

Another area of conflict which is often elided is the degree to which family support must be voluntaristic and consensual. Partly this is definitional— some would say that services which are provided by compulsion are not family support. Nevertheless it is clear from case studies in this book that family support services (or something very like them) are provided under the rubric of child protection and juvenile justice. Family support is generally seen as being at the 'soft' or 'care' end of welfare, but it can be located at any point on the continuum. In acknowledging this it is helpful to unpack the different processes involved in different aspects of child welfare and the different philosophies applied.

- *Empowering*—Family support is provided on a universal basis to self-referrers who see a need for the service, and the philosophy is one of voluntary self-improvement or empowerment. Self-help is considered better than professionalised services. The family are seen as lead partners.
- *Supportive*—Family support is provided by either experts or trained volunteers and its role is to support less able/fortunate parents. This can accommodate long-term support for vulnerable families, and basic philosophy is non-judgemental. The family are seen as consumers.
- *Preventive*—Aim is to target vulnerable families and prevent specific problems (child abuse, behaviour difficulties, depression, juvenile crime). Interventions and clientele are more prescribed and families may be referred. Philosophy is more 'communitarian', i.e. the family is not the only stakeholder and therefore some compulsion may be involved. Also implies short-term intervention.
- *Therapeutic*—Problems are already identified and the aim of intervention is to prevent further problems occurring. Implies highly trained staff working one-to-one or with small groups and medium to long-term intervention. Intervention is based on assessment and professionals are experts. The basic stance is that some parents are not 'good enough' and need help to become effective. Family members are seen as clients.
- *Forensic/punitive*—Aim is to identify, investigate and assess. Protection of children and communities is the priority and child behaviour difficulties and other family problems are seen as parenting failures. The focus is on individual families and their failures rather than contextual issues such as poverty and racism. Requires highly trained professionals working to specific protocols. Compulsion is either explicit or implicit in all activities. Outcome—child is protected, removed or punished. Family support is a means to an end. The basic stance is suspicion of parents.

The issues of power and conflict that determine these different positions should be made explicit and dealt with by family support programme staff and by evaluators. All these positions on the continuum have some value for some families, and it would be naive to think that family support can always be empowering and conflict free. Even at the empowerment end of that continuum, family support may have (or be seen to have) 'hidden agendas' of conformity and may be perceived as threatening or prescriptive by at least some of its potential users. However, it is not naive to expect family support to be transparent and explicit in its aims and methods, and evaluation should take into account the degree of compulsion, both explicit and implicit, which is used within the programme and by referrers, in order to truly gauge the degree of autonomy of participants.

The evaluations of family support are also beset by some of these conflicts and tensions. There is more and more pressure being exerted on evaluators to be scientifically rigorous, objective, empowering towards service users and sympathetic to the aims and methods of the practitioners. Many of the contributions to this book demonstrate how evaluators have attempted to negotiate with various stakeholders in developing their methodologies. However, these tensions are not always resolvable, especially when different stakeholders are in genuine conflict. Objectivity is not easy to maintain, particularly if the findings of the evaluation seem to favour one or another stakeholder group.

## Unintended Consequences

Because social systems are complex, it is not possible to foresee all the consequences of interventions, and the consequences may manifest themselves at different levels of the ecology. These processes apply as much to evaluation as they do to family support itself. It is because of this complexity that the orthodox model of evaluation hardly ever operates in real life. In virtually every text book of evaluation, quality assurance or management there is a diagram illustrating a virtuous circle in which planning, evaluation and practice development all add value to each other and services are in a process of continuous improvement (Figure 16.2). It is a step forward from the linear model of evaluation, which sees it as an end in itself in which the evaluation report

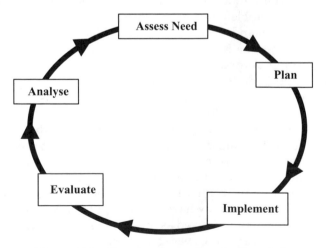

**Figure 16.2**   The planning and evaluation circle

is the final product. It is also a step forward from some of the crude notions of 'evidence-based practice'. It shows an interaction between local planning and needs assessment with service development, rather than seeing that process as merely the local implementation of services which a centralised authority has claimed to be demonstrated as effective.

But why does this model so seldom describe what happens in real life? Why do services often develop quickly without evaluations, or get shut down or reduced despite positive evaluation? The answer to this question is a combination of two factors. Firstly, policy makers and managers do not pay enough heed to evaluation as part of the service development process. Secondly, the virtuous circle is a misrepresentation of the role of evaluation in service development.

The first factor is, at least in part, really about dissemination and public relations. Evaluation results are subject to as much 'spin' as anything else in society, and evaluators are learning to become more sophisticated in disseminating results. Evaluators tread the same tightrope as any other group who spend funder's money and need to justify the expenditure. The evaluation tightrope is well illustrated by the way evaluation results are dealt with. A good example of this is provided by the differential treatment of evaluation results by the same agency.

The Children's Bureau Express, a website devoted to disseminating the results of research on children, announced the results of two evaluative projects in May 2001. The first was the Evaluation of Early Head Start, and the article was headed 'Early Head Start Children and Parents Thriving'. It went on to announce: 'Infants and toddlers from low-income families enrolled in the Early Head Start Program have passed a preliminary evaluation with flying colours. Their parents are also thriving' (Children's Bureau Express, 2001a). The other headline said: 'Study Sheds Light on Family Preservation Programs' and went on to say 'Initial findings from a three-state study suggest that policy makers and practitioners might want to rethink—but not abandon—efforts at family preservation programmes' (Children's Bureau Express, 2001b). The article then discusses the appropriateness of the outcome measures chosen and some of the approaches taken by the practitioners. What is interesting about these announcements is that the successful evaluation was treated without comment on methodology, and the criteria were also treated as self-evident, whereas the more negative evaluation was subject to scrutiny and discussion. This is similar to the well-known debates which followed Bickman's (1995) evaluation of the Fort Bragg experiment (Bickman et al., 1998),[1] where the evaluator had to subject his methodology to intense scrutiny by peers and others.

---

[1] Bickman and colleagues evaluated a programme in Fort Bragg, a military establishment. The aim of the programme was to ensure that child mental health services were delivered in a coherent, multi-agency way. Bickman found that the implementation had been successful, but 'joined up' services had not improved the outcomes for children.

The wider point here is that while evaluators may be aware of and even use more and more sophisticated means of dissemination, they are not able to control the results of their evaluation once these are in the public domain. Commissioners may ignore or shelve reports, policy makers may misrepresent or downplay evaluation results that do not suit their purposes, and evaluators' motives, methods or conclusions may be impugned. This is an inevitable part of the process and is intrinsic to any research that has to hold itself up to public examination.

The second point about the virtuous evaluation circle stems from a similar observation—that evaluation is only one of several factors which intervene at different stages to determine the service development process. Evaluators need to be aware of the other forces which may intervene to sustain programmes despite negative evaluations—stop programmes which have been positively evaluated or change the directions of programmes without evaluative evidence. Some of the more apparent factors are:

- economical forces, such as funding for the programme being exhausted or being curtailed;
- political factors, including the original sponsor being voted out of office or losing interest;
- changing priorities, altering or diverting the programme to meet new demands;
- demographic changes may make the programme irrelevant or no longer cost effective;
- organisational changes may alter the nature of the programme; for example, a different agency may become responsible locally for family support;
- other monitoring influences such as inspection, audit or quality assurance may intervene and contradict an evaluation's findings.

Other, less overt factors may also have significant effect; such as:

- staff may move on and new staff members may have different skills or ideas;
- the particular method or programme may come to be seen as 'old fashioned' and a new model may be more attractive to both service providers and funders;
- users may tire of the programme and move on to some other form of support, or the programme may become associated with a particular section of the community and exclude other members.

In this book, Quiery and her colleagues (Chapter 11) provide a case in point of a fairly common situation in family support. Despite positive evaluation results and commitment to the project by all the stakeholders, the funding for the project was not extended.

Evaluation takes its place as part of an open system and so it is subject to the vagaries of systemic change, conflict and tension. This is not to say that evaluation is a waste of time, or that evaluation results are bound to be ignored, but it does mean that the ideal represented by the evaluation circle is seldom realised. In many cases this is for perfectly good and understandable reasons, and may be the best thing in the context of the wider needs of the community or organisation. Evaluators need to be realistic about the range of political, social and economic forces which provide the context for evaluations.

## IMPLICATIONS OF THE OPEN SYSTEM MODEL FOR EVALUATION OF FAMILY SUPPORT

In positing this open system perspective, the argument being advanced is that the next step in developing family support should be based on applying to programme development and evaluation the ideas behind the ecological approach, the transactional model of development, the resilience perspective and social inclusion. These approaches represent the cutting edge of thinking about how children and families develop and how services are best placed to help them. Many of the contributors in this book have based their theories on this way of thinking (although they do not all use the same terminology or cite the same references). They also acknowledge that this model still has some way to develop and their material demonstrates that it clearly does.

An open system perspective views the relationship between evaluation, service development and outcomes for children and families as intrinsically complex and ever changing. Evaluation is seen as only one of a range of influences which may be brought to bear on service development. Similarly, services interact with other aspects of social ecology when they impact on children and families. On the face of it this is a rather depressing message for evaluators. It implies that there will never be a golden age of 'evidence-based policy and practice' in which evaluation is the main determinant of future service development. Nevertheless, that does seem to be the case if the real world of evaluation as described in the varied chapters of this book is to be taken seriously. Although evaluation does not have the power to determine service development, policy or practice, it can have a great deal of influence over these developments.

Evaluators are in a similar position to all other stakeholders in family support, each of whom, despite real differences in power, is subject to forces beyond his or her control. All stakeholders need to be able recognise both these restrictions and the opportunities within their field of influence. Evaluators need to be able to understand these forces and should aspire to achieving an objective view of the programme, project or policy they are evaluating. While the open system perspective implies that objectivity will never be completely achievable, it would be a mistake for evaluators to conclude from this that the only effective role for them is through political engagement or as advocates for one stakeholder group or another. Evaluators should always be open to the possibility that their previously held views will be challenged by the data. Developing the evidence base requires that current certainties are challenged. Recognising the varied aspects of family support and its evaluation as an international phenomenon has an important role to play in providing the critical perspective to mount that challenge.

# REFERENCES

Ball, M. (2001) *Never Too Early: An Evaluation of Methods of Early Years Intervention.* Aylesbury: Thames Valley Partnership/Crime Concern.

Bateson, G. (1973) *Steps to an Ecology of Mind: Collected Essays in Anthropology, Psychiatry, Evolution and Epistemology.* St Albans: Paladin.

Belsky, J. (1990) Parental and nonparental childcare and children's socioemotional development: A decade in review. *Journal of Marriage and the Family*, **52**(4) 885–903.

Bickman, L. (1995) *Evaluating Managed Mental Health Services: The Fort Bragg Experiment.* New York: Plenum Press.

Bickman, L., Salzer, M.S., Lambert, E.W., Saunders, R., Summerfelt, W.T., Heflinger, C.A. and Hamner, K. (1998) Rejoinder to Mordock's critique of the Ft. Bragg Evaluation: The sample is generalizable and the outcomes are clear. *Child Psychiatry and Human Development*, **29**, 77–91.

Bifulco, A. and Moran, P. (1998) *Wednesday's Child: Research into Women's Experience of Neglect and Abuse in Childhood, and Adult Depression.* London: Routledge.

Buchanan, A. (1999) *What Works for Troubled Children?* Ilford: Barnardo's.

Butt, J. and Box, L. (1998) *Family Centred: A Study of the Use of Family Centres by Black Families.* London: REU.

Cawson, P. (2002) *Child Maltreatment in the Family: The Experience of a National Sample of Young People.* London: NSPCC.

Cawson, P., Wattam, C., Brooker, S. and Kelly, G. (2000) *Child Maltreatment in the United Kingdom: A Study of the Prevalence of Child Abuse and Neglect.* London: NSPCC.

Children's Bureau Express (2001a)
  http://www.calib.com/cbexpress/articles.cfm?issue_id=2001-05&article_id=256

Children's Bureau Express (2001b)
  http://www.calib.com/cbexpress/articles.cfm?issue_id=2001-05&article_id=251

Clarke, J., Cochrane, A. and McLaughlin, E. (Eds) (1994) *Managing Social Policy.* London: Sage.

DoH (2000) *Framework for the Assessment of Children in Need and their Families.* (Dept. of Health/Dept. of Education and Employment/Home Office). London: Stationery Office.

Freude-Lagevardi, A. and Barnes, J. (2002) *Review of Early Interventions to Enhance Young Children's Mental Health, Focussing on Hard to Reach Families.* London: Mental Health Foundation.

Garbarino, J. and Eckenrode, J. (1997) *Understanding Abusive Families: An Ecological Approach to Theory and Practice.* San Francisco, CA: Jossey Bass.

Ghate, D., Shaw, D. and Hazel, N. (2000) *Fathers and Family Centres: Engaging Fathers in Preventive Services.* Policy Research Bureau. York: Joseph Rowntree Foundation.

Gill, O. and Jackson, B. (1983) *Adoption and Race: Black, Asian and Mixed Race Children in White Families*. London: Batsford Academic and Educational in association with British Agencies for Adoption & Fostering.

Gomby, D., Culross, P. and Behrman, R. (1999) Home visiting: Recent programme evaluations—analysis and recommendations. In *The Future of Children (Home Visiting: Recent Programme Evaluations)*, 9 : 1. David and Lucille Packard Foundation. http://www.futureofchildren.org/hv2/index.htm

Hacking, I. (1999) *The Social Construction of What?* Cambridge, Mass.: Harvard University Press.

Henricson, C. and Roker, D. (2000) Support for the parents of adolescents: A review. *Journal of Adolescence*, **23**(6), 763–783.

Jack, G. (2001) Ecological perspectives in assessing children and families. In J. Horwarth (Ed.), *The Child's World: Assessing Children in Need*. London: Jessica Kingsley.

Karoly, L., Greenwood, P., Everingham, S., Houbé, J., Kilburn, M.R., Rydell, C.P., Sanders, M. and Chiesa, J. (1998) *Investing in our Children—What we Know and Don't Know about the Costs and Benefits of Early Childhood Interventions*. Santa Monica: Rand.

Korbin, J.E., Coulton, C.J. and Furin, J.J. (1995) A neighbourhood-based approach to risk assessment. *APSAC Advisor*, **8**(4), 9–11.

Little, M. and Mount, K. (1999) *Prevention and Early Intervention with Children in Need*. Ashgate: Aldershot.

Marsh, P. and Crow, G. (1998) *Family Group Conferences in Child Welfare*. Oxford: Blackwell Publishers.

Olds, D.L., Henderson, C.R., Chamberlin, R. and Tatelbaum, R. (1986) Preventing child abuse and neglect: A randomized trial of nurse home visitation. *Paediatrics*, **78**(1), 65–78.

Olds, D.L., Eckonrode, J., Henderson, C.R., Kitzman, H., Powers, J., Cole, R., Sidora, K., Morris, P., Pettitt, L.M. and Luckey, D. (1997) Long-term effects of home visitation on maternal life course and child abuse and neglect: A fifteen-year follow-up of a randomized trial. *Journal of the American Medical Association*, **278**(8), 637–643.

Seeley, S., Murray, L. and Cooper, P.J. (1996) The outcome for mothers and babies of health visitor intervention. *Health Visitor*, **69**(4), 135–138.

Statham, J. (2000) *Outcomes and Effectiveness of Family Support Services: A Research Review*. London: Institute of Education.

Webster-Stratton, C. (1999) *How to Promote Children's Social and Emotional Competence*. London: Paul Chapman.

Weisz, J.R. and Wiess, B. (1993) *Effects of Psychotherapy with Children and Adolescents*. London: Sage.

Winnicott, D.W. (1965) *The Maturational Processes and the Facilitating Environment: Studies in the Theory of Emotional Development*. London: Hogarth Press.

# INDEX

Note: Abbreviations used in the index are: CPPC = Community Partnerships for Protecting Children; EYP = Early Years Project; NI = Northern Ireland; NSPCC = National Society for the Prevention of Cruelty to Children; NZ = New Zealand; RAP = Resourceful Adolescent Programme; UK = United Kingdom; USA = United States of America.